LYING FOR EMPIRE

How to Commit War Crimes
With A Straight Face

David Model

D0872492

Common Courage Press   Monroe, Maine

Library of Congress Cataloging-in-Publication Data is available from publisher on request.
ISBN 1-56751-320-4 paper
ISBN 1-56751-321-2 hardcover

ISBN 13 paper: 9781567513204
ISBN 13 hardcover: 9781567513212

Common Courage Press
121 Red Barn Road
Monroe, ME 04951

207-525-0900
fax: 207-525-3068

www.commoncouragepress.com
info@commoncouragepress.com

First printing
Printed in Canada

Contents

Acknowledgements   5

Introduction   6

Chapter 1: They Just Can't Stop Themselves   18
Crimes Against Humanity

Chapter 2: Incineration as Diplomacy   40
How Truman Torched Whole Cities With Nukes to Score Points

Chapter 3: The First Banana Republic   79
Eisenhower's Dedication to Destroying Democracy in Guatemala

Chapter 4: Quagmire of Deceit   113
Johnson and the Escalation of the Vietnam War

Chapter 5: Worse Than Hell   140
Nixon Paves the Way to Cambodia With Bad Intentions

Chapter 6: Topple One For the Gipper   164
Reagan and the Destruction of the Nicaraguan Government

Chapter 7: The George H. Bush Formula For War With Iraq   198
Prevent Negotiations at All Costs

Chapter 8: The Empire as Good Guy   246
Clinton Kills Civilians to Save Them

Chapter 9: Finishing the Job   280
George W. Bush and the Bombing of Iraq

Chapter 10: Psychopath Number 43   301

Bibliography   319

Index   325

About the Author   336

Dedication

To all the children who have suffered from war crimes,
may the adults of this world learn to love not hate,
to share not covet, to cooperate not compete, to
seek wisdom not hedonism, and to resolve disputes
through negotiations not war.

Acknowledgements

I am deeply indebted to all those people who helped me with this book. Two people in particular, Michael Rowan and my wife, Nancy Sperling, were invaluable as sounding boards, editors, and critics.

I owe a special thanks to my wife for her patience, understanding and support. She was always there if I needed a sounding board. She has earned sainthood for putting up with me for the past two years.

Michael Rowan's editing skills, knowledge of the issues, and advice were extremely helpful in verifying my data, honing my arguments and polishing my style in the manuscript.

Nancy and her mother Shirley Sperling, sister Susan Sperling and brother-in-law Mark Weitz contributed to the editing of the text. I also owe a special thanks to her brother Allan Sperling.

My colleague, Hugh Dow, not only helped with the editing of the text but was always willing to engage in a discussion of the issues. I also appreciate the patience and attention to detail of Betty Gadoua who copy edited the entire manuscript.

I would also like to thank Greg Bates at Common Courage Press with whom it was a pleasure to work. In his role as editor, he was my severest critic and inspired me to produce my best possible work.

Introduction

The American public's respect, if not love, for all of their presidents since World War II stands in sharp contrast to the fact that a number of presidential lies have paved the way for American crimes against humanity and wars of aggression.

International war crimes or crimes against humanity are defined as violations of international humanitarian law. The International Criminal Court for the Former Yugoslavia describes crimes against humanity as:

> Serious acts of violence that harms human beings by striking what is most essential to them: their life, liberty, physical welfare, health, and dignity. There are inhumane acts that by their very extent and gravity go beyond the tolerable limits of the international community.

Presidential lies have resulted in the death of innocent civilians, the destruction of non-military targets, mistreatment of prisoners, and wars that violate international law. The United States has escaped accountability and culpability for these international crimes because of its military power built up over years of spending significantly more on defence than other major powers.

Throughout history powerful nations with superior military capabilities have built and expanded empires to secure a source of raw materials and cheap labour, to create markets or to enhance their security. For example, the British Empire, one of the greatest empires in history, endured from about 1600 to 1945 and at various times included Canada, the United States, much of Africa, Australia, India, and New Zealand. It reached its peak near the end of World War I, encompassing 25% of the world's population.

Maintaining the American Empire

The American Empire is notorious for its invisibility notwithstanding the fact that sometimes its exercise of power is highly visible such as in Afghanistan and Iraq. The United States has built the modern equivalent of an empire by subversion, surrogates, economic power, and occasionally through direct military intervention. According to Michael Parenti in *Dirty Truths*:

> The history of the United States has been one of territorial and economic expansionism, with the benefits going mostly to the U.S. business class in the form of growing investments and markets, access to rich natural resources and cheap labour, and the accumulation of enormous profits.

The Central Intelligence Agency (CIA) is notorious for its behind-the-scenes subversive tactics used to either maintain a friendly government in power or to overthrow an unfriendly one. Brutal dictators such as the Shah of Iran in 1953, General Suharto in Indonesia in 1967, and Pinochet in Chile in 1973, were all installed in power by the CIA, and relied on American support and weapons to hold on to power. Their dependence on U.S. support all but guaranteed a friendly regime.

Using surrogates is a strategy for overthrowing an "unfriendly government" without the direct use of U.S. military force. In 1954 in Honduras, American military specialists trained anti-government invasion forces to overthrow the democratically elected government of Jacobo Arbenz in Guatemala. After the Sandinista Government in Nicaragua overthrew the corrupt and brutal dictator Somoza, the United States organized, trained, and supplied a guerrilla force known as the Contras in order to restore a friendly government in Nicaragua. In 1979, the Moujahedeen in Afghanistan, an American surrogate army armed and trained by the U.S., overthrew the government of President Noor Mohammed Tureki.

The United States does not always use surrogates. Sometimes the U.S. military acts directly to install a friendly government as in Vietnam from 1956 to 1973, the Dominican Republic in 1966, Grenada in 1983, and Panama in 1989.

Another method of control is through economic power which is exercised in a number of ways to discipline governments and to bring them into the American economic orbit. The United States has a high degree of control in the World Bank and International Monetary Fund because of the extent of its financial contributions and the formula used for weighting votes. The IMF, in particular, imposes strict conditions on debtor nations that force them to concentrate on producing cheap exports in order to increase foreign reserves needed to pay interest on their debt. These structural adjustment programs include currency devaluation, reduced wages, cutbacks to social programs, and reliance on the market system. All of these programs benefit creditor nations such as the United States at the expense of the debtor nations.

Embargoes, sanctions, and tariffs are other economic weapons that punish unfriendly nations and reward favoured nations. Cuba's economy has suffered as a result of the American embargo that has isolated Cuba from the international economic system. When New Zealand refused American nuclear submarines access to its ports, the U.S. retaliated by refusing to buy their butter, one of their major exports.

All these means allow the United States to maintain its empire. American Presidents preside over these empires but unlike some leaders of earlier empires, they are subject to constraints such as the constitution, Congress, the general public, and international agreements.

The constitution prohibits the President from using military force without the consent of Congress. Article 1, Section 8, of the American Constitution states that "The Congress shall have power…to declare war."

In 1964, President Johnson asked both Houses of Congress to expand his powers to protect the peace and security of the United States against any threats posed in Southeast Asia. The Gulf of Tonkin resolution, passed by a Joint Resolution of Congress, authorized the President "…to take all necessary steps, including the use of armed force, to assist any member… of the Southeast Asia Collective Defence Treaty requesting assistance in defence of its freedom. The resolution shall expire when the President shall determine that the peace and security of the area is reasonably assured." The power granted to the President in this resolution was revoked by another joint resolution of Congress when it became apparent that the war in Southeast Asia was a major blunder. On November 7, 1973, Congress passed a "War Powers Resolution" to "insure that the collective judgment of both the Congress and the President will apply to the introduction of United States Armed Forces into hostilities."

Public opinion and elections are an important constraint on the decisions and policies of the president. Presidents are in a continual election campaign. Every action of the President is at least partly based on political calculations such as what effect a decision will have on his traditional base; how the public will react to his decision; and what impact it will have on his chances for reelection.

As well, international agreements such as the Geneva Conventions have the potential to limit the scope of presidential objectives and initiatives. To minimize the backlash from violations of international laws, the American Government likes to find as many partners as possible for its foreign adventures, frequently using bribes and threats to win support. Otherwise, it tries to create the illusion of an international consensus or interprets international law to suit its own purposes. When the U.S. bombed Iraq in 1991, it patched together an ostensibly (because the U.S. frequently uses bribes and threats to win support) international coalition while during its war against Serbia, NATO became the legitimizing organization. For the bombing of Iraq in 2003, the American Government had to settle for the "Coalition of the Willing" to avert accusations of unilateralism.

These constraints become a challenge to the President if they interfere with foreign policy or military initiatives. It became clear after popular disaffection with the Vietnam War that to commit American troops to another war, a president would either need to be sufficiently persuasive in order to win public support or would be forced to take covert actions.

To overcome these obstacles, a president and his top advisors are forced to engineer or "manufacture consent" for policies that might not be acceptable. Edward Bernays, a leading figure of the public relations industry, explains that:

> A leader frequently cannot wait for the people to arrive at even [a] general understanding...Democratic leaders must play their part in...engineering... consent to socially constructive goals and values.

The ideology of political elites, according to Noam Chomsky in *Necessary Illusions,* is that the masses are not the best judges of their own interests and therefore, leaders must resort to deception and propaganda to win public support. Historian Thomas Baily observed that "Deception of the people may in fact become increasingly necessary." Edward S. Herman, a professor of finance, agrees that "...the mass media collaborated with the government to help engineer consent by means of propaganda outbursts that were built in whole or in part on lies." Harold Lasswell, a leading political scientist in the early part of the 20th century, warns American leaders not to succumb to "democratic dogmatism about men being the best judges of their own interests."

Techniques for winning public or congressional approval for foreign and defence policy are frequently based on lies and propaganda. For example, President Nixon deliberately lied about the bombing of Cambodia in the early 1970s and President Reagan lied about Nicaragua's threat to American security in order to persuade the public that the government had to allocate resources to support the overthrow of the Nicaraguan government. President George W. Bush lied about weapons of mass destruction in Iraq in 2003.

Once a President makes a decision to achieve a particular objective, neither national nor international laws seem to be a constraint. The decisions to bomb Hiroshima and Cambodia were not inhibited by the fact that these actions were in violation of international law. When Congress decided not to continue funding the Contras, who were attempting to destroy the government of Nicaragua, President Reagan decided to covertly, and illegally, acquire weapons from Iran. In other words, Presidents will use "any means necessary" to achieve their objectives.

Often lies are invented as a public relations strategy to further American interests. Overthrowing the Sandinista Government in Nicaragua had become a priority in the early 1980s. During the Reagan Presidency, El Salvador was an American client state in Central America and Nicaragua was a threat because, according to the Reagan administration, it had a Communist government that planned to invade the United States. This was completely absurd, as I saw clearly on a visit to Nicaragua in 1989. Nicaragua was a very poor country with neither the will nor the means to attack the U.S. The administration was also desperate to avoid any comparisons between its client state El Salvador and Nicaragua.

The Reagan administration embarked on a campaign of lies to foster fear of Nicaragua's intentions and to destroy the credibility of the Sandinista government. According to the *International Herald Tribune*, January 22, 1984, Henry Kissinger described Nicaragua under the Sandinistas as being as bad as or worse than Nazi Germany. Without any evidence, the State Department told the world that Nicaragua was exporting drugs and was anti-Semitic. To demonstrate the genocidal actions of the Nicaraguan Government, Alexander Haig, Secretary of State, revealed a photograph of blazing corpses, allegedly Miskito Indians killed by the government. It was later discovered that the photo was taken before the Sandinistas came to power. Oliver North, working for the National Security Council, planted stories about Nicaragua acquiring chemical weapons and receiving Soviet MIGs. The Reagan administration also labeled the 1984 election a sham to avoid unfavourable comparisons with elections in its client state El Salvador.

William Blum, in *Killing Hope*, described the elections in Nicaragua as:

> ...open to all parties and candidates, no fraud in the polling booth was reported, or even seriously charged: it was observed by a reported 400 reporters from 40 different countries...

Some presidential lies served to justify direct military intervention.

Panamanian leader Manuel Noriega had been a CIA operative for many years despite the fact that he was a notorious drug dealer. Two factors militated against Noriega remaining a U.S. ally much longer. First, a treaty had been signed in 1978 transferring control of the Canal Zone, a ten mile-wide strip encompassing the Panama Canal, from the United States to Panama. President Reagan wanted to regain control of the Canal Zone and the only justification for revoking the treaty was to demonstrate that the Panamanian Defence Forces (PDF) were incompetent and not capable of defending it. Second, despite the fact that Noriega was working for the American Government, he was also a strong nationalist and did not always take orders from American officials. The American Government needed a strategy for replacing Noriega and for proving that the PDF were incompetent. Therefore, the American administration of George H. W. Bush embarked on a campaign to lure Panama into a war to destroy Noriega and to weaken the PDF.

First Noriega was accused of being a major drug dealer (which was well known for many years while he was an asset for the CIA) who would have to be captured to face drug charges in the U.S. Then to create an incident that would provide the United States with an excuse for invading Panama, they hatched a deceitful scheme to discredit the Panamanian Defence Forces. The Southern Command (headquarters for U.S. forces in Panama) encouraged a group of leaders of the PDF to execute a coup against Noriega with American support. The American forces were to block all routes to Noriega's headquarters so that the mutinous PDF forces would meet with very little resistance. The Americans did not provide the promised support condemning the coup to failure. The next step in the plot was to send a group of American marines known as the Hard Chargers into Panamanian territory to provoke an incident. After extensive harassment, an exchange of shots took place killing a U.S. marine. The Bush administration could now claim that American lives were in danger in Panama and the PDF were incompetent to protect them. Shortly thereafter, the United States invaded Panama ostensibly to capture the "narco-terrorist" Noriega. Between 2000 and 4000 innocent Panamanians lost their lives and entire neighborhoods were leveled to the ground. American forces eventually captured Noriega and installed American-friendly leaders as President and Vice President.

The Pattern of Lies

Several criteria must be met to establish that a presidential lie paved the way for a crime against humanity. The first issue is to prove that the president actually lied. The purported crime against humanity must be shown to have violated humanitarian law. Specific clauses in international conventions, charters, or treaties must be looked at to test whether or not there has, in fact, been a violation of international law that constitutes a crime against humanity or a war of aggression.

The purpose of this book is not only to expose presidents as war criminals. We need to consider a number of factors which, together, show a very distinct pattern evident in all of the cases examined in this book. The campaign against Iraq in 2003 is a typical example of this pattern.

To convince the American public and Congress to approve a foreign or defence policy, the government frequently invents a crisis to instill fear in Americans, and generate support for the chosen policy. First, George W. Bush's administration warned Americans about the development and accumulation of weapons of mass destruction (WMD) in Iraq with no evidence to support their allegations. Then Bush warned about Iraqi ties to Al Qaeda and possible involvement in the September 11, 2001 terrorist attacks on the U.S. without evidence. Neither of these claims were valid. By calling colour-coded security alerts and asking the American public to buy duct tape to protect themselves from chemical attacks, the administration further exacerbated American's fear of terrorism. The resulting atmosphere was a pervasive fear that Saddam Hussein was an imminent threat to American security.

To maintain popular and Congressional support, the government embarked on a propaganda campaign to persuade the public and congress that the chosen policy was necessary and just. One of the primary techniques for indoctrinating the public is to allow the media access only to safe stories. In the first Persian Gulf bombing, the military utilized something called press pools. One member of the media was designated to cover whatever story the military selected for the day and then that reporter submitted the story to the other members of the media but only after military review and censorship. Reporters who stepped outside this protocol were denied visas to Saudi Arabia at the request of the American government.

In the attack on Iraq in 2003, the military implemented a strategy of "embedding" the press. Embedding the media allowed the military to exercise complete control over embedded coverage. The members of the press sacrificed their autonomy in exchange for access to the action. Their access was contingent on satisfying conditions set by the military as each reporter had to sign a 50-clause contract with the military that limited their coverage. In exchange they were allowed to travel with the military on naval vessels engaged in the conflict. Rather than imposing strict military censorship, the strategy was designed to encourage self-censorship. The reporters would identify with the soldiers with whom they were embedded. For example, Ted Koppel from ABC reported to the *Washington Post* that feelings toward the soldiers were "very, very, warm."

The use of language is another important strategy in the propaganda campaign. Calling the American action a preemptive strike was a clever way of implying that the United States had better strike first before the Iraqis struck at the United States. There was no imminent threat, and no need to strike.

Demonizing the enemy, and in particular their leader, is a common device for demonstrating to the American people that the enemy is a far greater threat than they had imagined in order to build a case for the use of overwhelming military force. In the Persian Gulf bombing in 1991, Saddam Hussein was compared to Hitler to exaggerate the strength of his military capability and his ambitions. This served two purposes, justifying the need for overwhelming American military force, and demonstrating the utter necessity of eradicating a dangerous threat to regional stability and world peace.

In the 2003 American bombing of Iraq, American propagandists, to create an inflated sense of the threat to American security, warned that Saddam was prepared to use his weapons of mass destruction. There was no evidence that he either possessed WMD or that he intended to use them. The only evidence was the word of people such as Bush, Rumsfeld, and other government spokespersons.

Another factor, a very common part of this pattern, is to demonstrate that the people in the country where America has militarily intervened welcomed their liberators with open arms. President Eisenhower claimed that Guatemalans were overjoyed when Jacobo Arbenz was overthrown through covert American action. When George H. W. Bush invaded Panama, images of Panamanians jumping up and down with joy belie the fact that

Panamanians were outraged at the death and destruction caused by American forces. In the bombing of Iraq in 2003, there were attempts to convince Americans that U.S. forces were welcomed as liberators. Images of Iraqis cheering as statue of Saddam Hussein was toppled were orchestrated and manipulative.

To ensure protection from criticism which might undermine their propaganda efforts, American administrations employ a strategy referred to as "marginalizing dissent" (Noam Chomsky and Edward Herman, *Manufacturing Consent, 1988)*. Valid criticism might begin to resonate with the American people and it is imperative to avoid any such criticisms. George W. Bush set the stage for marginalizing dissent during the 2003 assault on Iraq by uttering, "you are either for us or against us." In other words, anyone who dares to criticize the government is unpatriotic. Bill Maher was fired from the program "Politically Incorrect" for challenging the administration's refusal to ask what motivated the terrorists of 9/11. The Dixie Chicks, a country music group who criticized the Iraq bombing in 2003, were booed at the 2003 ACM awards, had their number one song "Travelin' Soldier" dropped by radio stations, and had radio stations across the country ban their music. Robert Fisk is one of the most respected and experienced journalists on Middle East affairs but is despised by the administration for his refusal to be embedded and for an interview he gave on Iraqi television. You rarely see his name on a column in the United States press any longer because he had the temerity to seek the truth.

Another factor in the pattern is the imperative attempt to conceal the real motives for the policy, the knowledge of which would erode its support. The plausible motives for the attack on Iraq were threefold beginning with a diversion from the domestic American economy which was becoming highly problematic, particularly with a rapid descent into red ink.

Second, Congressional and Presidential elections can frequently be a factor in Presidential decisions pertaining to defence and foreign policy. Did George H. Bush attack Iraq to bolster his popularity at home? Did Prime Minister Thatcher declare war on Argentina over the Falklands for political purposes? Is George W. Bush using the War on Terror for domestic political considerations? Karl Rove, campaign manager for the Republicans during the 2002 mid-term elections, was quoted in a ZNET article written by Noam Chomsky suggesting that Republicans have to:

"...go to the country" on the issue of national security, because voters "trust the Republican Party to do a better job of...protecting America." One didn't have to be a political genius to realize that if social and economic issues dominated the election, the Bush administration did not have a chance. Accordingly it was necessary to concoct a huge threat to our survival, which the powerful leader will manage to overcome, miraculously.

Gaining control over the world's second largest oil reserves in Iraq was the third motive which was not openly discussed by the administration. The United States did not need to import the oil immediately but control over oil reserves guaranteed them access in the future when new sources of oil might be necessary. Also, the establishment of American military bases in Iraq would help secure control over the entire region.

Falsifying evidence is an essential part of the pattern in order to demonstrate the validity of the U.S. government's claim that a real threat exists. George W. Bush and his administration talked with great confidence about the presence of weapons of mass destruction and quoted so-called expert sources to confirm their existence. On October 7, 2002, Bush announced that:

Iraq possesses ballistic missiles with a likely range of hundreds of miles—far enough to strike Saudi Arabia, Israel, Turkey, and other nations.

No biological or chemical weapons have been discovered after many inspections and a military occupation and claims about a nuclear threat have been invalidated. The most flagrant use of false evidence occurred during the attack on Iraq in 1991 when the George H. Bush administration invented the story about Iraqi soldiers in Kuwait snatching babies from incubators. This story will be examined in detail later.

Another factor in this pattern of deception is to concentrate media coverage on American deaths only. This strategy was used by the senior Bush during the Panama invasion. Only American casualties were newsworthy and George Bush gave a eulogy on television while 15 caskets containing American soldiers were paraded across the screen creating a powerful image. There was no mention of the two to four thousand Panamanian deaths. He also used the same strategy in the first attack on Iraq when American deaths were mourned by the people of the United States while the 100,000 innocent Iraqis who died did not deserve any mention, as that knowledge might have affected American attitudes towards the bombing of Iraq.

Most American military interventions are motivated by the need to protect American economic and military interests. The objective of the invasion of Panama was to regain control over the Panama Canal Zone, a vital American economic and military asset. In Guatemala the economic motive was to regain the land confiscated from the United Fruit Company by the government of Guatemala. The economic motive in the 2003 bombing of Iraq was to gain control over the world's second largest reserves of oil.

The final factor to consider is the use of covert forces to achieve military and economic objectives. Covert operations are used to conceal American involvement from the American public and Congress. The overthrow of the Guatemalan government in 1954 and the overthrow of President Allende of Chile in 1973 are examples of covert operations. The covert aspect of the attack on Iraq in 2003 was the fact that on September 17, 2001, President Bush signed a top secret document directing the Pentagon to begin planning "military operations" for an invasion of Iraq. There was no provision for inspectors to determine the presence of Weapons of Mass Destruction. As well, the U.S. government was secretly funding opposition groups in Iraq.

At least some of the factors in this pattern can be found in all the eight cases examined in this book. The purpose of this book is to expose these patterns so that future presidential military campaigns can be analyzed in this context to counterbalance the propaganda and the one-sided coverage in the mainstream media.

The Other Three Presidents

Presidents Truman, Eisenhower, Johnson, Nixon, Reagan, George H. Bush, Clinton, and George W. Bush are the eight presidents studied in this book. These eight are the most salient examples of presidents who committed war crimes. The other three presidents since World War II, Kennedy, Ford, and Carter were by no means innocent of possible war crimes but I wanted to focus on the most striking cases. In each of these three cases the president supported coup attempts and dictators, armed countries about to commit war crimes and supplied advisors.

For example, President Kennedy frequently supported dictators in developing countries to protect American economic and strategic interests. When the Belgian Congo gained its independence on June 20, 1960, the new Prime Minister, Patrice Lumumba, was viewed as a threat by the Eisenhower administration because of his call for political and economic liberation. The U.S. government's objective was to maintain access to the Congo's rich resources. Allen Dulles, the Director of the CIA under President Eisenhower, ordered the assassination of Lumumba in August 1960. Before the CIA could act, Mobutu Sese Seko, Lumumba's private secretary, intervened militarily and removed Lumumba from power. The CIA and Mobutu were implicated in his assassination in January 1961. President Kennedy supported Mobutu despite his record of human rights abuses and corruption.

The Kennedy administration supported conspiracies that overthrew six popularly elected governments in Latin America. Military dictators took power in Brazil, Argentina, Bolivia, Chile, Guatemala and El Salvador with the support of President Kennedy. These dictators employed brutal methods to maintain themselves in power including the destruction of their civil opponents.

President Ford supplied the arms and gave the green light to General Suharto of Indonesia for the invasion of East Timor. President Carter rearmed the Indonesian military when their supply of arms ran low.

Although the crimes of the three excluded presidents are worthy of discussion, the other eight cases are far more compelling.

All presidents since World War II used "all means necessary" to achieve American economic and defence objectives without concern for the liberty, security, and welfare of the people in the nations enduring the realities of American Empire-building.

CHAPTER 1

THEY JUST CAN'T STOP THEMSELVES

CRIMES AGAINST HUMANITY

Presidents lie all the time and our task is to ferret out the serious lies, the ones that kill, the ones that cause or cover up unspeakable suffering. International law provides a useful acid test for the consequences of presidents' lies. In this chapter, we examine the acid test in detail, reviewing a framework of law which, if it were applied fairly, would convict every single one of these presidents as war criminals.

Presidents ignore or overlook the point of international law. International laws were created to maintain international peace and security and to define a process for resolving disputes without resorting to force. International law also establishes rules of war to ensure that they are conducted in a civilized and humane manner. By ignoring these laws, presidents have waged wars of aggression either overtly or covertly and caused unconscionable adversity and suffering. By violating the laws that attempt to civilize war many innocent people have been tortured or killed.

Until the introduction of international law, people became the casualties of authoritarian institutions that had to answer only to those with greater power than themselves. These unfortunate victims died in a legal vacuum where the notion of crimes against humanity was an amorphous ideal. But the Nazi atrocities of World War II were so excessive that they could not be dismissed as merely the casualties of another war. World War II and the Nazi atrocities served as a catalyst for jumpstarting international law and institutions to end the scourge of war and to punish war criminals.

The Nuremberg Trials Become a Precedent

During World War II, Allied Forces decided to prosecute the leaders of the Nazi regime as war criminals. On October 7, 1942, the Allied Forces announced that a United Nations War Crimes Commission would be created to investigate Nazi war crimes. The Commission was established on October 20, 1943. The decision was reached in the Moscow Declaration on October 30, 1943, signed by the United Kingdom, United States, and USSR, to prosecute and punish German war criminals at the end of the war.

The Moscow Declaration states that:

> Accordingly, the aforesaid three allied powers, speaking in the interest of the thirty-two United Nations, hereby solemnly declare and give full warning of their declaration as follows: those German officers who have been responsible for or have taken a consenting part in the above atrocities…may be judged and punished…

The London Agreement of August 8, 1945, authorized the establishment of a tribunal for prosecuting and sentencing war criminals. The Charter of the Nuremberg Tribunal was drawn up at a conference in London and delineated the structure, jurisdiction, role of the chief prosecutor, and procedures of the International Military Tribunal.

The International Law Commission of the United Nations was commissioned to formulate the principles of international law which were recognized in the Charter of the Nuremberg Tribunal. All subsequent international laws involving crimes against humanity are based on these principles. The Principles of the Nuremberg Tribunal, drafted in 1950, include the following principles:

Principle I

Any person who commits an act which constitutes a crime under international law is responsible therefore and liable to punishment.

Principle III

The fact that a person who committed an act which constitutes a crime in international law acted as Head of State or responsible government official does not relieve him from responsibility under international law.

Principle IV

The crimes hereinafter set out are punishable as crimes under international law:

(a) Crimes against peace;

(b) Planning, preparation, initiation or waging of a war of aggression in violation of international treaties;

(c) Crimes against humanity: Murder, extermination, enslavement, deportation, and other inhumane acts committed against any civilian population, or persecutions on political, racial, or religious grounds, when such acts are done or such persecutions are carried on in execution of or in connection with any crime against peace or any war crime.

The Nuremberg Trials were a milestone in the development of the international judicial system because they defined the principles of crimes against humanity, specified the treatment of persons charged with such crimes, and established a tribunal to judge and punish war criminals.

International law is well established with both ancient and recent principles giving the U.S. no excuse for violating the concept of international law. In ancient Greece, Socrates stated that "I am not an Athenian, or a Greek, but a citizen of the world." Later, the Catholic Church became a strong advocate for the elimination of private wars when their "Peace of God" campaign in the tenth century attempted to end private warfare and compel parties to a conflict to submit their disputes to a tribunal. Gerohus of Regensburg believed that it would suffice for the Pope to forbid war and that all conflicts could be resolved by referring them to Rome. In the fourteenth century, Pierre Dubois of Normandy, advisor to King Philip of France, called for a federation of Christian states with a Council of Nations to arbitrate disputes. The French king Henry of Navarre and his advisor, the Duc de Sully proposed a plan called the "Great Design" in the seventeenth century, in which Europe was to be redivided into 15 equal states, the purpose of which was to ensure a balance of power. These states were to be represented in a Great Council whose members were to be reelected every three years and whose function would be to resolve all disputes and propose reforms. They also proposed an international army and navy to enforce the decisions of the Great Council.

The concept of a federal partnership among sovereign states with a mechanism for the resolution of international disputes was a blueprint for subsequent attempts to create international governments. Twenty years later, Emeric Crucé developed the "Great Design" further by advocating that membership should be open to non-Christians and that war could be eradicated through a comprehensive system of arbitration. In the seventeenth century, William Penn, in his essay *Toward the Present and Future Peace of Europe,* recommended a Permanent International Tribunal to be set up by the sovereigns of Europe with a membership of 90 representatives who would meet every year to discuss and settle all international differences which were unresolved through diplomacy. Decisions could not be approved without the support of three-quarters of the members. Penn understood the need for an enforcement mechanism and proposed international sanctions and, if necessary, more violent methods. Jeremy Bentham, an eighteenth-century philosopher, devised a plan based on four fundamental principles to avert future wars:

- reduction of armaments;
- a permanent court of judicature with powers of arbitration backed by the use of force;
- codification of international law;
- emancipation of all colonies.

Eighteenth-century philosopher Immanuel Kant's contribution to the principle of international law was to elevate the debate to a higher level transcending politics into the sphere of ethics and social conscience. He thought that it was essential to create a public opinion predisposed to the abolition of war. He offered some suggestions about the organization of perpetual peace which included a federation of free republics that would eventually accept the abolition of standing armies and the need to surrender some sovereignty. In the early nineteenth century, Tsar Alexander I put forward the concept of an international treaty the signatories to which would commit their countries to never begin a war until all possible means to resolve the dispute through a third party had been exhausted. The Tsar also recommended the codification of a set of laws to govern international relations. His ideas led to the "Holy Alliance" consisting of Austria, Prussia, and Russia who agreed to abide by the Christian precepts of Justice, Charity, and Peace. Lord Salisbury, Prime Minister of Britain, predicted in 1897 that the arms race in Christian civilization was hurling it toward destruction. He believed that the only hope was to construct an international institution. In 1899, the smaller States of Europe, some Asian States and Mexico met at the Hague and drafted the first four Hague Conventions defining the rules of war and a mechanism for settling international disputes. Another Hague conference was held in 1907 to build on the Conventions of 1899.

The International Red Cross and International Law

The first codification of international humanitarian law took place in Geneva in 1859 when Henry Dunant, a merchant, traveled in Italy and was horrified by the multitude of wounded soldiers left to die on the battlefield. He was inspired to share his shocking experience with the world in a book published in 1862 called *A Memory of Solferino* in which he appealed to the public for the establishment of relief societies with nurses who could tend to the wounded during wartime. He also called for protection for the people in these relief societies through an international agreement. The International Committee for the Relief of the Wounded was formed in 1862. In 1863 fourteen countries sent delegates to a conference in Geneva, and in 1864 representatives of 16 governments adopted a treaty entitled the "Geneva Convention for the Amelioration of the Condition of the Wounded in Armies in the Field." This was the first international agreement to define international humanitarian law. In time, the movement became known as the Red Cross. The Geneva Convention was subsequently expanded to four conventions and two protocols signed by 115 nations:

1. The First Convention (1864) dealt with wounded and sick members of the armed forces in the field.

2. The Second Convention (1899) added wounded, sick, and shipwrecked members of the armed forces at sea as well as shipwreck victims.

3. The Third Convention (1907) included prisoners of war.

4. The Fourth Convention (1949) was about civilians in time of war.

5. The First Protocol (1977) added protection of the victims of international military conflicts.

6. The Second Protocol (1977) brought in protection for victims of local conflicts.

The essential principles of the Geneva Conventions are:

*   respect for human beings and respect for their dignity;

*   individuals who do not take direct part in hostilities and those who can not take part due to illness, wounds, captivity,

or other reasons, are entitled to respect and protection from the conflicting sides' military operations;

- warring sides and combatants are obliged not to attack civilians and civilian objects.

The Third Convention, pertaining to the protection of prisoners of war, includes the following clauses:

Part 1, Article 3, Clause 1:

Persons taking no active part in the hostilities, including members of the armed forces who have laid down their arms and those who suffer from sickness, wounds, detention, or any other cause, shall in all circumstances be treated humanely, without any adverse distinction founded on race, colour, religion, faith, sex, birth, wealth, or any other similar criteria. To this end the following acts shall remain prohibited at any time and in any place whatsoever with respect to the above-mentioned persons:

- (a) violence to life and person, in particular murder of all kinds, mutilation, cruel treatment and torture;

- (b) taking of hostages;

- (c) outrages upon personal dignity, in particular humiliating and degrading treatment;

- (d) passing of sentences and the carrying out of executions without previous judgment pronounced by a regularly constituted court affording all the judicial guarantees that are recognized as indispensable by civilized peoples.

Part 1, Article 4A:

Prisoners of war, in the sense of the present convention, are persons belonging to one of the following categories who have fallen into the power of the enemy:

- (1) Members of the armed forces of a party to the conflict, as well as members of militias or volunteer corps forming part of such armed forces.

Part 1, Article 5:

The present convention shall apply to the persons referred to in Article

4 from the time they fall into the power of the enemy and until their final release and patriation.

Should any doubt arise as to whether persons, having committed a belligerent act and having fallen into the hands of the enemy, belong to any of the categories enumerated in Article 4, such persons shall enjoy the protection of the present convention until such time as their status has been determined by a competent tribunal.

Part 4, Article 118:
Prisoners of war shall be released and repatriated without delay after the cessation of active hostilities.

American Presidents have regularly violated the clauses prohibiting violence against the life and dignity of civilians and the carrying out of executions. The invasion of Panama is an excellent example of President G. H. Bush violating the third Geneva Convention and the First Protocol. During the Panama invasion in 1989, American troops forced 18 Panamanian prisoners to sit in a circle with their hands tied behind their backs. They were each shot in the back of the head in violation of international humanitarian law which requires captors to treat prisoners humanely. The damage to civilians and to non-military targets in that campaign violated a number of clauses in Convention IV of the Geneva Conventions. A poor district called El Chorrillo was completely destroyed, leaving 15,000 people homeless. From 2000 to 4000 people were killed by American forces. Many other atrocities were perpetrated by the American military against the Panamanian people. For example American soldiers at checkpoints forced ambulances to halt in order to search for Noriega loyalists and American soldiers in tanks ran over wounded bodies lying on the road.

The third Geneva Convention's protection for prisoners of war has been completely ignored by the United States. America violated Convention III of the Geneva Conventions when it incarcerated an estimated 384 suspected terrorists from the conflict in Afghanistan in Guantanamo Bay, Cuba. The Bush administration claimed that the prisoners were not combatants but common criminal suspects ("unlawful combatants") and therefore not entitled to the protection of the Geneva Conventions. If these prisoners were criminal suspects, they would have been entitled to due process which includes leveling specific criminal charges without delay, access to a lawyer, and prosecution in accordance with due process requirements.

If they are treated as POWs, they must be released without delay after the cessation of hostilities. There was no doubt that active hostilities had concluded in Afghanistan. Any questions about the status of the prisoners must be resolved by a competent tribunal, not the United States, and until such time, they are entitled to all the protections of Convention III of the Geneva Conventions. According to Human Rights Watch:

> The detainees' status must still be determined in accordance with the Geneva Conventions. The United States should then prosecute, within a reasonable time and with adequate due process, those detainees accused of committing or plotting criminal acts, including war crimes, crimes against humanity, and terrorism. Such prosecutions would be far better then the unlawful alternatives of holding detainees indefinitely without trial or extraditing them to countries where they risk torture.

Convention IV of the Geneva Conventions pertains to the protection of civilians and includes the clauses below. (The clauses are summarized here).

Part 1, Article 3:

In the case of armed conflict not of an international character occurring in the territory in one of the High Contracting Parties, each Party to the conflict shall be bound to apply, as a minimum, the following provisions:

(1) All persons including armed forces who have surrendered must be treated humanely.

To this end, the following acts are and shall remain prohibited at any time and in any place whatsoever with respect to the above-mentioned persons:

(a) Violence to life and person, in particular murders of all kinds, mutilation, cruel treatment and torture;

(b) Taking of hostages;

(c) Outrages upon personal dignity, in particular humiliating and degrading treatment.

Protocol 1 of the Geneva Conventions pertains to the protection of civilians and non-military targets and includes the following clauses:

Chapter II, Article 51:

(1) The civilian population and individual civilians shall enjoy protection against dangers arising from military operations.

(4) Indiscriminate attacks are prohibited. Indiscriminate attacks are:

    (a) those which are not directed at specific military objectives;

    (b) those which employ a method or means of combat the effects of which cannot be directed at a specific military objective; or

    (c) those that employ a method or means of combat the effects of which cannot be limited as required by this Protocol; and consequently, in each case, are of a nature to strike military objectives and civilian or civilian objects without distinction.

Chapter III, Article 52:

(1) Civilian objects shall not be the object of attack or of reprisals. Civilian objects are all objects that are not military objectives.

(2) Attacks should be limited strictly to military objectives.

Contraventions of Convention IV include the Panama invasion of 1989, the bombing of Iraq in 1990, the bombing of Serbia in 1998, the bombing of Afghanistan in 2002, the bombing of Iraq in 2003, and many others. In all these cases, the United States bombed both civilians and non-military objects and is, therefore, guilty of violating international humanitarian law.

Presidents choose to describe American military aggression as war as part of a propaganda campaign to conceal the atrocities which they are perpetrating. Although technically they are wars, they are more accurately described as pseudo-wars. These countries lacked the sophisticated military equipment required to stop stealth bombers or Tomahawk cruise missiles. Infrastructure, industrial and agricultural facilities suffered irreparable damage during the bombing of Iraq in 1991. Despite the increase in the "surgical" accuracy of American weapons, a large number of non-military targets were destroyed. According to the report of the International Action Committee *Impact of the War on Iraq Society* undertaken by Adeeb Gellman and Gavrielle Gemma in April, 1991:

> In every city we visited, we documented severe damage to homes, electrical plants, fuel storage facilities, civilian factories, hospitals, churches, civilian airports, vehicle transportation facilities, food storage and food testing laboratories, grain silos, animal vaccination centres, schools, communication towers, civilian government office buildings, and stores. Almost all facilities we saw had been bombed two or three times, ensuring that they could not be repaired. Most of the bridges we saw destroyed were bombed from both ends.

One example of weapons that violate international law are cluster bombs. Cluster bombs disperse bomblets over a wide area significantly expanding the radius of the area destroyed. They can be fired from surface artillery or from rockets or airplanes. Those dropped from airplanes explode above the ground and break up into hundreds of little bomblets which saturate the target area. Because it is impossible to isolate any target with pinpoint accuracy, these bombs often destroy non-military targets.

When the United States bombed Iraq in 1991 for invading Kuwait, it dropped 62,000 air-delivered cluster bombs and delivered 110,000 by other means, littering the country with 24 to 30 million unexploded sub munitions literally a disaster waiting to happen. (Human Rights Watch)

NATO bombed Serbia into submission under the pretext of a humanitarian war. During the bombing, the United States, Britain, and Holland dropped 1,765 cluster bombs containing more than 295,000 cluster bomblets. Not only did the cluster bombs result in civilian casualties and destroy non-military targets, but an estimated 20,000 unexploded bombs remained after the war waiting for innocent civilians to set them off. (Human Rights Watch)

After 9/11, the United States launched its War on Terrorism. The first acts were the bombing of Afghanistan to eradicate the Taliban accused of harbouring terrorists, the destruction of terrorist training camps, and the attempted capture of terrorists, including the head of Al Qaeda, Osama Bin Laden. The U.S. dropped 1,228 cluster bombs containing 248,056 bomblets leaving an estimated 12,400 duds with the potential to kill years after the conflict. (Human Rights Watch)

The use of cluster bombs violates the First Protocol, Chapter II, Article 51 of the Geneva Conventions. This falls under the category of protection of civilians, "indiscriminate weapons" and weapons which "are of a nature to strike military objectives and civilian or civilian objects without distinction."

Another example of illegal weapons are depleted uranium (DU) weapons. Depleted uranium weapons have been used in Iraq, Afghanistan, and Serbia. They are also in violation of the First Protocol, Chapter II, Article 51 and Chapter III, Article 51, of the Geneva Conventions. To strengthen the penetration capabilities of weapons, the United States has been hardening the tips of warheads or shells with depleted uranium. The depleted uranium tips have the power to penetrate hardened steel and concrete. The uranium-238 utilized to construct DU warheads poses far-reaching health hazards not only to those who are victims of bombing but also to those who are in proximity to the weapons. Depleted uranium vastly increases the penetrating power of shells because its density is 1.7 times that of lead. Depleted uranium is the waste product from the processing of enriched uranium for nuclear weapons and nuclear power plants and remains radioactive for a very long time with a half-life of over 4.5 billion years. It emits particles of radioactive uranium in aerosol form making it easily ingested or inhaled. (International Action Centre)

In April 1991, the United Kingdom Atomic Energy Authority claimed that U.S. ground forces fired between 5000 and 6000 rounds of depleted radiation ordnance in Iraq. In addition, U.S. and British aircraft launched approximately 50,000 DU rockets and missiles. DU weapons burst into flames creating uranium oxide that spreads and contaminates bodies, equipment, and the ground. The uranium-238 that is used to make the weapons causes cancer and genetic defects. According to the report of the UK Atomic Energy Authority, 40 tonnes of radioactive debris could kill 500,000 people.

Nailing the Bastards

As the above examples illustrate, the Geneva Conventions have provided a framework for understanding the depths of American atrocities. After many centuries of people theorizing and dreaming about international laws and systems for protecting humanity against itself, the Geneva Conventions became the archetype of international law to civilize war. But many elements were still needed to create a comprehensive system of international justice such as a body to serve as the final arbiter with the authority to authorize war. A deterrent is imperative if nations are to seek means other than war to settle their differences. Such a deterrent would need to consist of laws outlining crimes against humanity and a court system to prosecute and sentence those who are guilty.

International law provides a benchmark to judge what constitutes a crime against humanity or war of aggression and international courts provides the mechanism for charging and prosecuting war criminals. The first international court was a product of World War I. Following World War I, the idealism of President Woodrow Wilson and the hope of Europe to avoid another war impelled those attending the Paris Peace Conference in 1919 to create an international organization for promoting disarmament, resolving disputes, and determining other measures to ensure peace and security. Woodrow Wilson, in his Fourteen Points which were developed in anticipation of a new international order, proposed that "A general assembly of nations must be formed under specific covenants for the purpose of affording personal guarantees of political independence and territorial integrity to great and small states alike." Thus was born the League of Nations, to resolve disputes, promote disarmament, protect sovereignty, develop a system of international laws, and create an international court. Article 14 of the Covenant of the League of Nations called for the establishment of the Permanent Court of International Justice that became operational in 1921 and was the forerunner to the International Court of Justice, or World Court.

In 1946, the Permanent Court of International Justice became the International Court of Justice at The Hague, or World Court, which serves as the principal judicial organ of the United Nations. The mandate of the World Court is to settle disputes submitted by member nations. It began to function in 1946 and is governed by a statute that is an integral part of the Charter of the United Nations. The Statute of the International Court of Justice contains the following Articles which define the competence or jurisdiction of the Court:

Chapter 2

Article 34;

1. Only states may be parties in cases before the Court.

Article 36;

1. The jurisdiction of the Court comprises all cases that the parties refer to it and all matters specially provided in the Charter of the United Nations or in treaties and conventions in force.

Article 38:

1.   The Court whose function is to decide in accordance with international law such disputes as are submitted to it, shall apply

  (a) international conventions, whether general or particular…;

  (b) international custom, as evidence of a general practice accepted as law;

  (c) the general principles of law recognized by civilized nations.

One of the key issues within the jurisdiction of the court concerns international laws to protect the territorial integrity and political independence of nations. Nicaragua is a prime example of a nation whose territorial integrity was undermined by the United States. Nicaragua responded to American attacks on its territorial integrity and independence by filing charges at the World Court. Nicaragua claimed that its territorial integrity was threatened by the mining of its harbours and by an American-sponsored guerrilla force called the Contras. The Court ruled that "…the US was under duty to cease and desist immediately from the use of force against Nicaragua, [and] from all violations of the sovereignty and political independence of Nicaragua…" In achieving this ruling Nicaragua accomplished two important victories. First, it proved to the world that it was under attack. Second, it identified the U.S. as a rogue state: the U.S., under President Reagan at the time, ignored the ruling.

When presidents commit war crimes they must be held accountable by an international tribunal. When charges against the United States are filed with the court it offers an opportunity for a careful scrutiny of their behavior. The Nuremburg Trials demonstrated the need for a permanent court to prosecute war criminals and the United Nations responded to the challenge. When the General Assembly adopted the Convention on the Prevention and Punishment of the Crime of Genocide in Resolution 260, December 9, 1948, it included in the resolution an invitation to the International Law Commission (agency of the UN) "to study the desirability and possibility of establishing an international judicial organ for the trial of persons charged with genocide…" Following the committee's conclusion that there was a need for a court to try persons charged with genocide and other crimes of similar gravity, the General Assembly established a committee to prepare proposals for the creation of such a court. The committee prepared a draft statute in 1951 and a revised version in 1953, but the General Assembly postponed any further consideration pending a clear definition of "aggression".

Despite periodic consideration of an international criminal court, the UN took no action until the UN Security Council established an ad hoc International Criminal Court for Rwanda to prosecute Rwandan leaders for atrocities in Rwanda. Shortly thereafter, the International Law Commission concluded in its research that there was a need for an international criminal court and submitted the proposal to the General Assembly in 1994. In 1998, a Preparatory Committee completed the drafting of the charter for the proposed court. The General Assembly convened the United Nations Diplomatic Conference of Plenipotentiaries on the Establishment of an International Criminal Court in Rome in 1998. On July 1, 2002, the United Nations created the International Criminal Court at The Hague.

Presidents aren't just war criminals; they seek to undermine the institutions that create and adjudicate international law. These institutions are an impediment to the ambitions of U.S. presidents. Even when such institutions are delegitimized, underfunded and weakened, it is still extremely clear that presidents are war criminals. Two fundamental weakness of the International Criminal Court are the degree to which it has become politicized through funding arrangements and its dependence on the major powers for enforcement. The U.S. has lost a case at the International Court but decided not to abide by the ruling. Despite the fact that NATO countries did commit war crimes in the bombing of Serbia, NATO funding of the Court was a major reason why the Court took no action when a complaint was filed by an international group of lawyers. On the other hand, the NATO countries have charged Slobodan Milosevic and other Serbian leaders with crimes against humanity in Croatia between 1991 and 1992, Bosnia between 1992 and 1995, and Kosovo. They have been charged with violating the Convention on the Prevention and Punishment of the Crime of Genocide, and the Geneva Conventions. The trial for these accused war criminals is being held at the newly created International Criminal Court at The Hague.

How Presidents Should Settle International Disputes

Considerable progress toward building a comprehensive body of laws defining crimes against humanity was ushered in with the birth of the United Nations. The League of Nations failed to live up to expectations and the nadir of its failure was the onset of World War II. WWII hardened the resolve of nations to build an institution that would be effective in preserving the peace, protecting the independence of nations, and resolving disputes. In 1945, delegates from 50 nations met in San Francisco for the United Nations Conference on International Organization. The United Nations was a product of this conference whose purpose, as stated in Article 1 of its charter, was "To maintain international peace and security and to that end: to take effective collective measures for the prevention and removal of threats to the peace, and for the suppression of acts of aggression or other breaches of the peace." The representatives of 51 countries signed the Charter on June 26, 1945. There are currently 191 members.

The Charter of the United Nations expanded the domain of laws pertaining to crimes against humanity by extending them to acts of aggression and breaches of the peace. While the Geneva Conventions provide protection to individuals, specifically civilians and the wounded, the Charter refers to the actions of states. These actions could include unilateral acts of aggression, failure to seek means other than aggression to resolve disputes, and declaring war without the authorization of the Security Council.

To prevent and remove threats to the peace and to suppress acts of aggression, the Charter carefully elucidates a process for resolving disputes without the need for force. The following clauses (summarized here) describe this process:

CHAPTER I

Article 2

3. All members shall settle their international disputes by peaceful means.

4. All members shall refrain in their international relations from the threat or use of force against the territorial integrity or political independence of any state.

CHAPTER VI

Article 33

1. The parties to any dispute shall first of all seek a solution by negotiation, inquiry, mediation, conciliation, arbitration, judicial settlement.

Article 34

The Security Council may investigate any dispute, or any situation that might lead to international friction.

Article 37

1. Should the parties to a dispute of the nature referred to in Article 33 fail to settle it by the means indicated in that Article, they shall refer it to the Security Council.

2. The Security Council shall decide whether to take action under Article 36 or to recommend terms of settlement.

CHAPTER VII

Article 39

The Security Council shall determine the existence of any threat to the peace, or act of aggression and shall make recommendations, or decide what measures shall be taken in accordance with Articles 41 and 42, to maintain or restore international peace and security.

Article 41

The Security Council may decide what measures not involving the use of armed force are to be employed.

Article 42

Should the Security Council consider that measures provided for in Article 41 would be inadequate, it may take action using force.

Article 51

Nothing in the present charter shall impair the inherent right of individual or collective self-defense if an armed attack occurs against a member of the United Nations, until the Security Council has taken measures necessary to maintain international peace and security.

George W. Bush's decision to attack Iraq in 2003 was a clear violation of both the Geneva Conventions and the UN Charter. According to Chapter 1, Article 2, Paragraph 3, of the UN Charter, there is an obligation for members to settle their disputes without endangering international peace and security. Paragraph 4 protects territorial integrity and political independence of any member. The aforementioned UN Charter obligations were ignored on the grounds of a U.S. claim that Iraqi weapons of mass destruction posed a direct threat to their security. To avert such a danger, the United States devised the rationale of a preemptive strike. The Charter only permits the use of force to defend a member's security "if an armed attack occurs" (Chapter VII, Article 51). There was no "armed attack" against the United States. Furthermore, only the Security Council can "determine the existence of any threat" and "make recommendations, or decide what measures shall be taken" (Chapter VII, Article 39). Since the United States was unable to convince the Security Council that attacking Iraq was necessary, they decided to bypass the United Nations altogether. Only the Security Council has the authority to approve the use of force and there are no other legal grounds in international law to justify the actions of the United States. According to Kofi Annon, United Nations Secretary-General, "I've indicated that it [the War on Iraq] was not in conformity with the U.N. Charter from our point of view, and from the Charter point of view it was illegal." (ABC Online, March 2003) More details on the 2003 War on Iraq will be discussed in chapter nine.

In addition, during the attack on Iraq, the U.S. and the Coalition of the Willing violated the Geneva Conventions by killing innocent civilians which is prohibited by the Geneva Conventions in Convention IV, Chapter II, Article 51 ("Civilians shall enjoy protection"). Iraq Body Count, a website created by professors from Keene, New Hampshire and Cambridge Universities to maintain a record of the actual number of deaths of Iraqis, reports that the minimum number of deaths is 16,381 as of March 14, 2005. This number only includes people whose death has been verified.

Non-military objects are also protected (Protocol I, Chapter III, Article 52—"Civilian objects shall not be the object of attack"). Despite the American claim that their bombs and missiles are surgically accurate, the saturation bombing of Baghdad in particular, the "Shock and Awe" strategy destroyed numerous civilian targets and killed numerous civilians.

Protocol I, Chapter III, Article 51, of the Geneva Conventions bans the use of weapons that are incapable of discriminating between military targets and non-military targets. Britain and the United States used cluster bombs and depleted uranium weapons both of which are unable to make this distinction. Iraq Body Count reports that

> Among these incidents [of civilian deaths] are included reliable reports of at least 200 civilian deaths due to cluster bombs, with up to a further 172 deaths which were probably caused by cluster bombs. Of these 372 deaths, 147 have been caused by detonation of unexploded or "dud" munitions, with about half of this number being children.

The exact amount of depleted uranium used in the bombing of Iraq is not known but it has been estimated to be greater than the 340 tonnes in the 1991 war. The radiation from these weapons does not discriminate between military personnel and civilians. Depleted uranium may be a contributing factor to cases of "Gulf War Syndrome" affecting American veterans of the 1991 bombing of Iraq.

Another example of violations of the UN Charter occurred when Indonesia invaded East Timor in 1975 with the support of the American government and imposed a military occupation for 25 years. East Timorese oil reserves off its southern coast were one of the main objectives of the invasion. American and Australian companies were eager to gain access to these reserves in negotiations with the Indonesians rather than the Timorese.

East Timor was one of the few places on earth where many ancient traditions and customs remained intact for thousands of years and where modern technology was relatively rare. They were no match for the American-armed Indonesian military. During the war and subsequent military occupation over 200,000 Timorese were killed, representing one third of the population.

The actions of Indonesia violated a number of clauses of the UN Charter including:

1.   Chapter I, Article 2, Paragraphs 3 and 4—settle disputes peacefully;

2.   Chapter VI, Article 33, Paragraph 1—seek other methods to resolve disputes;

3.   Chapter VI, Article 34 and 37—disputes must be resolved by Security Council;

4.   Chapter 7, Article 39—Security Council decides on what action to take.

Dealing With Genocide

An intriguing aspect of the Nazi genocide was that the revulsion that it evoked led to a convention that defined it as a crime against humanity. Part of the motivation for the attempt to exterminate the Jews was that the Jews provided a convenient scapegoat because:

> Anti-Semitism was prevalent worldwide, [and] it was in central and Western Europe where it began to fester... After the humiliating defeat of WWI, Germany was racked with social-economic upheaval. Jews received much of the brunt of the German people's frustration resulting from the Treaty of Versailles that was further exacerbated by the world economic depression in the 1930's. (David Graham, *The Holocaust Ring*, January 26, 2000)

Although the Holocaust was not the first attempt to destroy an entire group, it alerted the world to the danger and horrors of genocide. This concern was one of the motivating factors in the creation of the United Nations Convention on the Prevention and Punishment of the Crime of Genocide.

The Genocide Convention was the first UN human rights treaty. It was adopted by the 55 member states of the United Nations in Paris on December 9, 1948, and became operational in 1951. One hundred and thirty two nations have since signed the Convention.

The Convention on the Prevention and Punishment of the Crime of Genocide defines the following principles:

Article 2

In the present Convention, genocide means any of the following acts committed with intent to destroy, in whole or in part, a national, ethnical, racial or religious group such as:

(a)   killing members of the group;

(b)   causing serious bodily or mental harm to members of the group;

(c)   deliberately inflicting on the group conditions of life calculated to bring about its physical destruction in whole or in part;

(d) imposing measures intended to prevent births within the group;

(e) forcibly transferring children of the group to another group.

Article 3

The following acts shall be punishable:

(a) Genocide;

(b) Conspiracy to commit genocide;

(c) Direct and public incitement to commit genocide;

(d) Attempt to commit genocide;

(f) Complicity in genocide.

Article 4

Persons committing genocide or any of the other acts enumerated in Article 3 shall be punished, whether they are constitutionally responsible rulers, public officials or private individuals.

Article 6

Persons charged with genocide or any of the other acts enumerated in Article 3 shall be tried by a competent tribunal.

There have been many cases of genocide in history, although they may not have been regarded as aberrant at the time. A salient example was the treatment of native peoples of the Americas under European colonization. Although the huge population loss after the first contacts with Europeans was mostly due to the unintended spread of diseases to which the natives had no immunity, it was compounded by the deliberate spreading of disease by the colonizers, by the effects of imposed slavery, and by massacres, through most of the Americas, aimed at getting rid of inconvenient Native populations.

Christopher Columbus was best known for his travels to the New World but his impact on the Americas was far greater during his Governorship of Española. In 1492, while Columbus was sailing the ocean blue, the native population of Hispaniola exceeded three million but by 1514 only 100,000 survived the murderous hands of Columbus. For recreation, Columbus would summon his soldiers to the town square where he had assembled a group of natives who were waiting for the "games" to begin. Then the soldiers would hack to death all the natives present with their machetes (Ward Churchill, *Columbus Day Commemorates a Holocaust*).

More International Laws for Presidents to Violate

The Charter of the United Nations, the Geneva Conventions, and the Convention on the Prevention and Punishment of Genocide define most crimes against humanity. There are other international agreements that also define crimes against humanity such as the Convention Against Torture and the Convention on the Prohibition of the Development, Production, Stockpiling and Use of Chemical Weapons. Regional conventions and treaties also define crimes against humanity. The North Atlantic Treaty, which established NATO, and the Charter of the Organization of American States (OAS) are two such treaties. For example, Article I of the North Atlantic Treaty states that:

> The Parties undertake, as set forth in the Charter of the United Nations, to settle any international dispute in which they may be involved by peaceful means in such a matter that international peace and security and justice are not endangered, and to refrain in their international relations from the threat or use of force in any manner inconsistent with the purposes of the United Nations.

The OAS Charter states that:

Chapter I, Article 2

The Organization of American States, in order to put into practice the principles on which it is founded and to fulfill its regional obligations under the Charter of the United Nations, proclaims the following essential purposes:

(a) To strengthen the peace and security of the continent;

(b) To promote and consolidate representative democracy, with due respect for the principle of nonintervention;

The United States breached the OAS charter when it mined the harbours of Nicaragua and when it organized a guerrilla force to undermine the government of Nicaragua. The OAS Charter was violated when the U.S. organized the overthrow of the democratically elected government of Jacobo Arbenz in Guatemala in 1954 and also when it sent the marines into the Dominican Republic in 1963.

When crimes against humanity perpetrated by United States presidents are discussed in following chapters, the acid test will be to show if the consequences of a president's lies violate one of the above-described conventions. The international community has recognized these crimes as crimes against humanity.

Presidents flagrantly violate international law to expand the American Empire. To incorporate countries into the Empire, presidents frequently remove democratically elected heads of state such as Jacobo Arbenz of Guatemala or Allende in Chile and replace them with brutal dictators such as Armas in Guatemala and Pinochet in Chile whom the U.S. could count on for support. They have also used military force to expand the Empire such as in the Dominican Republic, Serbia, and Iraq. In order to expand the Empire, American presidents have violated the basic principles on which the United States was founded. Only outrageous lies could protect them from facing the consequences of their actions.

CHAPTER 2

INCINERATION AS DIPLOMACY

HOW TRUMAN TORCHED WHOLE CITIES WITH NUKES TO SCORE POINTS

On December 7, 1941, Japan bombed Pearl Harbor, the home of the American Pacific fleet. The following day, President Roosevelt referred to December 7 as a "date which shall live in infamy" and declared war against Japan. After ferocious, bloody, and relentless battles for dominance in the Pacific Theatre during World War II, the Americans had destroyed much of the Japanese Empire, gained control of Japanese air space, and mined Japanese coastal waters. Major Japanese industries had been crippled, cities had been fire-bombed, and the people cut off from food supplies and oil. By dropping two atomic weapons, one on Hiroshima and one on Nagasaki, President Truman added two more dates "which shall live in infamy," August 6, 1945 and August 9, 1945. Two Japanese cities had become two nuclear wastelands, both victims of crimes against humanity.

After the firebombing and mining of Japanese harbours, there was no longer any hope that Japan could win the War of the Pacific impelling the emperor to send offers of surrender to various embassies which could act as intermediaries between Japan and the United States. President Truman would have been aware of these offers because American intelligence had been intercepting and decoding Japanese diplomatic messages for years. In addition, American military advisors were opposed to using atomic weapons to end the war. Why did President Truman still find it necessary to drop two atomic bombs on Japan? What motivated him to perpetrate these unconscionable crimes against humanity?

The Road to Pearl Harbor and the Bomb:
Dominance of the Pacific, 1853-1942

Truman's horrendous crimes can best be understood in their historical context. The struggle for dominance of the Pacific began in the 19th century and ended on September 2, 1945, when Japan surrendered to General Douglas MacArthur on the battleship Missouri anchored in Tokyo Bay.

Empire-building by Japan involved wars with China, Russia, Germany, and France on route to gaining sovereignty over most of the countries in the Pacific. Great distances separated its various conquered territories necessitating the building of a large navy and air force. After the United States declared war against Japan in 1941, they became engaged in a long, arduous battle of attrition as American forces captured strategic territories from which to launch the final assault on Japan.

Power shifted several times in Japan over the last 500 years. Between the early 16th century and mid-19th century, the eminent landowning clans ruled Japanese society with the support of mercenary and feudal armies led by the samurai, a military class. The Emperor, who was revered in Japanese society as the descendant of the Sun Goddess, played a minor role in the political system. The shogun, a military regent, was the person with supreme authority who ruled in the name of the emperor. The Tokugawa, one of the clans, gained control over Japan in the mid-16th century until the mid-18th century and assumed the office of shogun, ruling the country as a military dictatorship.

In 1853, Commodore Perry, commanding an American fleet, demanded that the Tokugawa establish commercial relations with the United States and other Western powers. Resenting the intrusion of other powers, a rebellious group of Japanese overthrew the shogun and restored power to the emperor. The emperor recognized the necessity to adopt Western technology and organizational methods to encourage industrial and financial modernization. The new regime transformed the samurai into an officer corps and created a modern army and, somewhat later, a navy.

In 1889, the Japanese drafted a constitution which restored the supremacy of the emperor whose function was mostly symbolic, while the premier and his cabinet exercised real power. Michael J. Lyons in *World War II: a Short History,* states that "By the early twentieth century, Japan had shaken off Western domination and had emerged as an important power." In the 1930s, after the army had persistently campaigned for territorial expansion, civil authorities capitulated and Japan developed the earmarks of a military dictatorship.

The building of Japan's empire began at the end of the 19th century and carried through to the early 1940s at which time Japan had gained sovereignty over much of the Pacific. The Japanese government had modernized the economy transforming Japan into a major world power. A. Russell Buchanan, in *The United States and World War II*, described Japan's aspirations to expand its empire because:

> Its leaders accepted the ideas of Western imperialism and saw opportunities for expansion on the mainland of Asia. In some instances using techniques which Western powers had employed against them, the Japanese launched and enlarged their colonial expansion.

From 1894 to 1895, China and Japan fought a war resulting in Japan's acquisition of Formosa. In the aftermath of this victory, Japan's further penetration into China inaugurated the inevitable clash with powers such as neighboring China that were protecting their interests in that part of the world. Russia, one of these powers, competed both economically and militarily with Japan leading ultimately to the Russo-Japanese War of 1904-1905. The outcome of the Japanese triumph was the entrenchment of Japan as a major influence in Korea and Manchuria. Japan also acquired southern Sakhalin, the Kuril archipelago, and an important strategic base in Port Arthur (Lueshun). According to Ronald H. Spector in *Eagles Against the Sun: The American War Against Japan,*

> The army's success against superior forces in the Sino-Japanese War of 1894-1895 and the Russo-Japanese War of 1904-1905 gave its leaders (Japanese) confidence that their unique Japanese spirit would ensure victory even against nominally stronger enemies.

American discrimination against Japanese immigrants heightened tensions between the two countries and encouraged Japan to develop a war plan against the U.S. in the Pacific. In 1907, Japan developed a blueprint for a war in the Pacific. Their objective was to seize control of the Philippines and Guam forcing the United States fleet to traverse the Pacific to rescue its possessions. The Japanese navy was convinced that this plan would give them a decisive edge because of the proximity to its home bases and their ability to choose the best time to attack the weary American fleet.

American strategists recognized that a conflict with the Japanese was a distinct possibility and that the Philippines were very vulnerable to attack by the Japanese. The U.S. considered the Philippines a valuable possession for the protection of its interests in the Pacific and in particular for its access to China. U.S. military strategists also recognized that they would need to dispatch the navy to defend the Philippines. The estimated time for a battle fleet to reach the Philippines was three to four months. A board consisting of four high-ranking officers was assigned the task of developing a plan for the

Pacific referred to as the Orange Plan. There was little agreement about how to defend the Philippines and the board finally reached the conclusion that the Philippines were indefensible. Logistics was one of the impediments to American forces holding the Philippines. The United States needed bases as launching pads and for supplies but Japan had seized the Caroline Islands, Mariana Islands, and Marshall Islands from Germany during World War I. These islands now provided essential logistical support for the Japanese.

Japan's conquest of Korea was consummated in 1912. Japan captured strategically important German possessions in the Pacific Ocean in 1914, such as Truk in the Caroline Islands and Rabaul in the Bismarck Islands and built naval bases to protect a growing empire. These islands were located in the southern Pacific near New Guinea and the Solomon Islands where Japan established a foothold for further conquests.

In the early nineteen thirties, one of Japan's primary objectives was to gain complete control over Manchuria in order to develop it as a source of food supply and other raw materials. Military operations commenced in 1931 and by 1932 Japan had virtual control of Manchuria. Japan's success was relatively effortless due to the lack of Chinese resistance which was partly a result of their need to reserve their troops in anticipation of a conflict with communist forces. China appealed to the League of Nations but the League only called for an end to hostilities and Japanese withdrawal from Manchuria and avoided any call for sanctions. According to Russell Buchanan, in *The United States and World War II,* when the League refused to take any strong action, Secretary of War, Henry L. Stimson's statement to both China and Japan was an announcement that there would be:

> A policy of nonrecognition of forcible changes of government... [and] that the United States would continue to support the Open Door Policy and China's territorial and administrative integrity.

Tensions between the United States and Japan degenerated even further when Japan embarked on a campaign to seize control of China. Hostilities first broke out in July, 1937 at the Marco Polo Bridge south of the major city of Peiping (now Beijing). Japan gained control over Peiping by the middle of August and soon afterward won control of Shanghai at the mouth of the Yangtze River. In December Japan captured Nanking, the Kuomintang (Chinese nationalist) capital. By the end of 1938, Japan had seized control of much of northern and central China in addition to key ports. Its position was somewhat tenuous because of ongoing hostilities. During Japan's occupation of much of China, except for the vast countryside under control of the Communists, the American gunboat Panay was sunk on the Yangtze River. The United States was reluctant to declare war against Japan and only protested the actions of the Japanese while implementing a "moral embargo" on the exporting of airplanes and parts to Japan.

The defeat of France and the Netherlands by Germany during World War II provided Japan with an opportunity to expand her empire further. These defeats, coupled with the preoccupation of the British with the German onslaught and the vulnerability of French and Dutch colonies of Indochina (Vietnam, Laos, and Cambodia), opened the door for trade concessions from the Dutch in the East Indies and a protectorate over Indochina in 1941.

When war broke out in Europe in 1939, the United States toughened its stand toward Japan. The U.S. cancelled a three-year-old commercial treaty with Japan, extended their embargo to include high grade scrap iron and aviation gasoline, and transferred the Pacific Fleet to Hawaii which was an American colony. On September 27, 1940, Japan reacted by forming an alliance with Germany and Italy and signed the Tripartite Pact. The Pact carved up the world into spheres of influence and potential control allocating Europe to Germany and Italy and recognized "the leadership of Japan in the establishment of a New Order in Greater East Asia." The three countries agreed to come to each others' assistance if any one of them were "attacked by a power at present not involved in the European War." The alliance was clearly targeting the United States, which had not yet entered the war.

When Japan established a protectorate over Indochina in 1941, President Roosevelt responded by freezing Japanese assets in the U.S. and implementing a trade embargo. The embargo deprived Japan of its oil imports, swiftly cutting their supply by 88%, and establishing a chokehold on its economy. This move by the U.S. made war with Japan inevitable.

Each side reviewed its choices. As Ronald H. Spector outlined in *Eagles Against the Sun: The American War with Japan,* Admiral Harold Stark pointed out four alternatives:

1. concentrate mainly on hemispheric defence;

2. prepare for an all-out offensive in the Pacific while remaining on the defensive in the Atlantic;

3. make an equal effort in both areas;

4. prepare for a strong offensive in the Atlantic while remaining defensive in the Pacific.

Defending the British Asian Empire was not a high priority for the Americans so they chose option four after much debate and decided to transfer part of their Pacific fleet to the Atlantic. During this time of debate and deliberations over issues relating to the Japanese empire and the threat it posed to American interests, cryptanalysts broke the Japanese diplomatic code. The Americans knew of Japanese proposals before they were received officially and in particular, they knew that Japan was planning to go to war if diplomacy failed to achieve Japanese objectives. The decoded messages were referred to as "Magic." The intercepted messages created a mood of skepticism in discussions about averting war with Japan.

The Japanese concluded that they had three options:

1. abandon their ambitions in Southeast Asia and perhaps China as well;

2. work out a compromise with the United States that would involve resumption of trade at the price of some Japanese concessions;

3. attack Dutch and British possessions in Southeast Asia and, probably, American bases in East Asia and the Pacific.
   (Michael J. Lyons, *World War II: A Short History*)

A fierce debate raged among Japan's political and military leaders but Premier Fumimaro Konoye convinced the army leaders to seek a diplomatic solution on the condition that Japan would resort to war if negotiations failed. When Konoye's attempt at diplomacy failed, he resigned and was replaced by the War Minister, General Hideki Tojo.

Negotiations continued throughout the fall of 1941 without any success. On November 25, 1941, after a meeting of the War Cabinet, Secretary of War Stimson wrote in his diary that the President:

> Brought up the event that we were likely to be attacked perhaps (as soon as) next Monday, for the Japanese are notorious for making an attack without warning and the question was what we should do. The question was how we should maneuver them into the position of firing the first shot without too much danger to ourselves. (A. Russell Buchanan, *The United States and World War II*)

This reveals that the U.S. was angling for a fight, for an excuse and justification to enter the war. Because the Roosevelt administration understood that it had cut off 88% of the oil supply, they knew it was only a matter of time before Japan, starved for oil, would attack in an attempt to regain access to oil. The subsequent claim that Pearl Harbor was an unprovoked surprise attack that "shall live in infamy" counts as one of the most important presidential lies of all time.

As part of the plan to provoke Japan into firing the first shot, the U.S. offered Japan a deal that they would have to refuse. Secretary of State Cordell Hull demanded that Japan withdraw from both Indochina and China as a prerequisite for an American agreement to unfreeze Japanese assets and resume trade. This was an offer designed to be refused, not an offer designed to resolve the conflict. On November 29, 1941, the Japanese considered the proposal an ultimatum and decided that war was now the only option.

The Fierce Struggle for Empire December 1941–June 1945

Japan's overall war plan in the Pacific was to expand the perimeter of their territories in order to create a defensive shell with strategically located naval and air bases and a sufficient source of supplies. Japan would then withdraw into their shell in order to defend it from attack. But first the Japanese hoped to cripple the American fleet by attacking Pearl Harbor.

The Japanese war planners broke the plan into three phases:

1.   attack Pearl Harbour by surprise and establish a defensive perimeter extending from Wake Island through the Gilbert Islands, Guam, Bismarck Archipelago, New Guinea, Timor, Java, Sumatra, Malaya, Burma, Dutch East Indies, Borneo, and the Philippines;

2.   consolidate and strengthen the perimeter;

3.   repulse any attempts to break the ring until the enemy became tired of fighting.

To ensure a surprise attack, Japanese aircraft carriers and their escorts had to travel to within 200 miles of Pearl Harbor without detection. To minimize the risk of confronting foreign ships, the chief of staff, Admiral Kusaka, and his senior assistant Commander Genda, selected a northern route well north of normal shipping lanes beginning in the Kurile Islands, passing north of Midway, and finally turning south toward Hawaii. The danger that bad weather would make refueling difficult was less a concern than achieving a complete surprise.

The shallow waters of Pearl Harbor posed a risk that torpedoes from the subs on the Japanese mission might sink so low that they could detonate on the bottom before reaching their targets. The use of buoyant wooden fins would prevent the torpedoes from sinking too low.

When the Japanese launched their attack on Pearl Harbor they caught the Americans completely by surprise. Despite repeated messages intercepted through "Magic" that warned of a Japanese attack, there was still uncertainty about where these attacks would occur. Furthermore, American military planners believed that an attack on Pearl Harbour was unlikely because of the risks.

Two enlisted men operating a mobile radar unit on December 7, 1941, reported a large number of approaching aircraft to the reporting centre but an inexperienced lieutenant told them not to be concerned because the planes were American bombers scheduled to arrive from California that morning.

The attack on Pearl Harbor was a qualified disaster. By the end of the attack, much of the Pacific fleet was either disabled or sitting on the bottom. Three American carriers were saved because two of them were heading for other destinations while the third was undergoing repairs on the West Coast. Seven heavy cruisers were also at sea and many of the ships that were sitting on the bottom were salvageable because of the shallow waters. On December 8, 1941, Roosevelt appeared before Congress and referred to December 7, 1941, as a "date which will live in infamy." He then successfully asked Congress to declare a state of war against Japan.

In order for the United States to succeed in destroying the Japanese Empire and securing control of the Pacific for themselves and their allies, they would have to overcome Japan's military strength which was much superior to American forces. Japanese naval strength was formidable and included:

- 10 aircraft carriers
- 11 battleships
- the battleship Yamato with 18.1 inch guns—the world's most powerfully armed ship

- 18 heavy cruisers.

The American Pacific fleet included:

- 4 aircraft carriers

- 6 battleships

- 7 cruisers

The differences in the capabilities of the two navies were clearly examined by Ronald H. Spector in, *Eagle Against the Sun,* when he noted that:

> At the outset of the war, the Japanese carrier forces were probably the finest naval weapon in the world. The Zero fighters were superior to anything in the allied forces, their carrier-based torpedo bombers were effective and deadly, and all were manned by experienced veterans, many of whom had fought in China...The American carriers were somewhat larger than their Japanese counterparts and carried more planes, but American naval aircraft were generally inferior to the Japanese. The standard naval fighter, the Grumman Wildcat, was no match for the Zero in a one-to-one fight.

One of the critical advantages that the United States enjoyed was its industrial capacity which could produce new machinery of war at a far greater pace than the Japanese.

To understand the context in which Truman made the decision to use the atomic bombs requires an understanding of how the United States slowly gained control over the Japanese Empire. Despite repeated disputes over tactics, the American war planners' overall strategy was to penetrate the Japanese perimeter at various points and create a wide swath of American-controlled territories in an advance toward Japan as the U.S. built supply routes, ports, lines of communication, and air bases. When the U.S. was within bomber range of Japan without consternation about nearby Japanese air and naval bases, American bombers could bomb Japan into submission and if necessary, launch a land invasion. But first, American forces had to stop the bleeding as Japan mounted a blitz against important U.S. and British possessions in the Pacific.

On the same day as Pearl Harbor, Japan had struck at Wake Island, the Philippines, Guam, Hong Kong, and Malaya. Guam, an American possession, fell to the Japanese in two days. It was the last island in the Mariana chain that the Japanese did not already control and was an easy target because of Japanese control over Saipan.

To interrupt American communications across the Pacific, Japan was prepared to attack Wake and Midway Islands. Wake Island was valuable as a communication station, for its proximity to the Marshall Islands, a Japanese stronghold only 600 miles away, and as a way station for aircraft on route to the Philippines. For these reasons, the U.S. had begun strengthening their defences on Wake. Wake Island was subjected to three days of aerial bombing followed by naval shelling on December 11, 1941. The 500-man garrison's valiant resistance forced the Japanese to send for reinforcements including two carriers. American reinforcements were delayed as the fleet from Pearl Harbor paused for one day to refuel. The war of attrition was won by the Japanese and the loss of Guam and Wake guaranteed Japanese control of the lines of communications in the Central Pacific.

The British-controlled Gilbert Islands fell with little resistance. The Gilberts were the southeastern most point in the Japanese defensive perimeter which protected the Marshalls from an attack from the south.

The Philippines had little to offer the Japanese other than their importance as a base to protect their vital oil supplies in the Netherlands East Indies. When the Japanese attacked Luzon in the Philippines, American aircraft located at Clark Field near Manila attempted to intercept the enemy. When the planes returned to refuel, the Japanese exploited the opportunity and destroyed most of the American aircraft on the ground. During the next few days, further raids by the Japanese reduced the American airbase to a handful of planes by December 19, 1941. The loss of Clark Field combined with the heavy damage inflicted on other American air bases delivered air supremacy in the Philippines to the Japanese.

Japanese attacks on American naval bases forced most of the fleet to escape to Australia and the Dutch East Indies. General MacArthur, Commander of American forces in the Philippines, realizing the strength of Japanese forces converging on Manila, decided to make a stand on Bataan Peninsula. Disease, starvation, and fatigue plagued both sides but Japanese reinforcements settled the issue as they accomplished a breakthrough on April 9, 1942, and on May 5, 1942 and Japanese troops landed on Corregidor, an island just off Bataan, and forced the final American capitulation.

Hong Kong consisted of a group of islands and a small peninsula on the Chinese mainland and was defended by a garrison of British regulars, Canadian militia, and civilian volunteers. The defence of Hong Kong was hopeless and it too was taken by the Japanese on December 25, 1941.

Since the oil fields in the Dutch East Indies made it a valuable Japanese target, the Japanese commenced an attack on January 11, 1942, when they took Borneo and Celebes. The joint command of Britain, the Netherlands, and the United States reached the conclusion that defence of the Dutch East Indies was hopeless but the Dutch insisted that Java be defended to the bitter end. A combined strike force of British, Dutch, and U.S. ships engaged in battle with the Japanese task force. The Japanese advantage of long-range torpedoes and night training proved to be a decisive factor as Japan gained control of the waters surrounding Java allowing the Japanese to land troops and to gain control by March 8, 1942.

Burma was a strategic Japanese objective because of its mineral and food supplies as well as its proximity to India. It also served as a vital supply route for the Allies (U.S., Britain, and Australia). The British forces were ineffective in Burma and Japan achieved control of the air. Rangoon was captured on March 7, 1942, and Mandalay was leveled in early April forcing British soldiers to retreat into the Burmese jungle where they suffered from malaria, fatigue and starvation. By May 1942, the British had completely withdrawn and the Japanese had control of Burma.

By spring 1942, Japanese victories had significantly extended the perimeter of its empire. Michael J. Lyons, in *World War II: A Short History* explained that:

> ... [as of] May 1942, Japan had reached the zenith of its power. Japanese forces dominated Southeast Asia and the Western Pacific. They threatened the Indian Ocean, Australia, and the Central Pacific.

Japan continued her campaign to secure the South Pacific just north of Australia and to advance her perimeter even further. In early 1942, Japan established a major base on Rabaul in New Britain which is just west of New Guinea, and occupied Lae and Salamaua on New Guinea. The objective of these operations was to prepare for an attack on Port Moresby to attain access to the airfield, not only to protect Rabaul, but also to use it as a base from which to bomb northern Australia. By mid-April, intelligence had warned American military planners that Japan was preparing for an offensive in the South Pacific with Port Moresby as the objective. A major Japanese task force was heading toward Port Moresby while an even more powerful force from Truk in the Caroline Islands converged on the Coral Sea which is located southwest of New Guinea. At the same time, an American task force was also steaming toward the Coral Sea. The Battle of the Coral Sea was fought on May 7-8, 1942. The battle took place entirely in the air while the two naval forces were never in sight of each other, the first such encounter in history. Tactically, the battle was a draw because loses on both sides were roughly equal. Strategically, the Americans had scored a victory because the Japanese were never able to capture Port Moresby.

About the same time as the Battle of the Coral Sea, the battle of Midway maintained American momentum. Midway posed a problem for the Japanese. It was some 1137 miles northwest of Oahu in the Hawaiian chain and would be an important strategic asset as an airbase and as a relay station for the transpacific cable. The Japanese reluctance to attack Midway was based on the fact that it was within striking distance of long-range American bombers from Hawaii and the Japanese forces would be far beyond the support of their own long-range bombers. In the end, Admiral Isoroku Yamamoto, commander of the Pacific fleet, and other Japanese naval leaders believed that the benefits outweighed the risks and in June 1942, most of the Japanese naval forces headed toward Midway.

The Japanese, who wanted to complete the job that they began at Pearl Harbor, were counting on another surprise attack against American forces but American cryptanalysts successfully broke the Japanese naval code. By the end of May the Americans knew the time, date, place, and composition of Japanese forces. The Japanese were sailing into a trap. Despite bombing marine command posts, storehouses, fuel storage facilities and destroying many fighter planes, the damage inflicted by the Japanese was not critical and American torpedoes had inflicted severe damage on Japanese carriers. Therefore, a second strike became necessary. As the battle raged on, the Japanese planes that had wreaked so much damage on Pearl Harbor were virtually wiped out. Losing four carriers, many experienced pilots, and a heavy cruiser at Midway was a major defeat for Japan. Midway was a critical American victory for two reasons: it restored the naval balance in the Pacific; and shifted the momentum in favor of the U.S.

The Solomon Islands, located west of New Guinea, were strategically valuable to the Japanese as a base from which to protect Japanese bases in Rabaul in New Guinea and Truk in the Caroline Islands and from which to block the American flow of supplies to Australia. Gaining control over Tulagi in the Solomon Islands would allow the Japanese to patrol the eastern waters of the Coral Sea and solidify the defence of their perimeter.

Originally, the Americans had planned to take the islands of Tulagi and

Gavatu in the Solomon Islands but when they discovered that the Japanese were constructing an airstrip on nearby Guadalcanal, the Americans targeted it as well. All three islands were poorly defended offering little resistance to U.S. forces. Japanese leaders were shocked at the U.S. offensive and immediately dispatched reinforcements to Guadalcanal in October 1942.

The struggle for Guadalcanal was ferocious and became a war of attrition. The opposing fleets fought six major naval battles and many minor ones between August and November in order to seize control of the sea and supply routes. Between November thirteenth and fifteenth, when Japanese forces were endeavoring to protect a supply convoy, U.S. forces headed toward the Japanese fleet leading to a series of savage battles known as the Battle of Guadalcanal. The final attempt to land supplies precipitated the sixth and final battle during which the American forces suffered heavy loses but the Japanese leaders decided to abandon Guadalcanal. They concluded that they could not afford any more loses and by February 9, 1943, the Americans completely controlled the island.

The battle over the Solomon Islands was the first American offensive in the Pacific. American forces also successfully held Guadalcanal against heavy Japanese attacks dispelling any myths about Japanese invincibility on land and at sea. Guadalcanal also deepened the American people's hatred of the Japanese which had its origins in Pearl Harbor and because of the atrocities that resulted from Japanese victories. In addition to racial prejudice there was the perception of the Japanese as ferocious, subhuman, and sadistic.

In the first two years of the war in the Pacific, Japan gradually shifted from an offensive to a defensive stance as they lost more planes, naval vessels, and men. At the beginning of 1942, Japan controlled a vast region of the Pacific and was still expanding her empire. By 1943, American forces not only held off the Japanese but were beginning to capture key territories. American industrial production greatly exceeded that of Japan and new planes, ships, and weapons were rolling off the production line at a far faster rate.

The overall strategy of U.S. leaders was to gain control of strategically important territories while advancing toward Japan for the final onslaught. In *Eagle Against the Sun: The American War With Japan,* Ronald H. Spector explains that the advantage enjoyed by the Americans in driving the Japanese from their bases was because:

The central Pacific was a region of a thousand tiny islands clustered in small groups extending west over 3,000 miles from the Gilberts, the easternmost chain near the equator, and northwest through the Marshalls, the Carolines, and the Marianas. Against these tiny points on the map, where the Japanese could base only limited numbers of troops and airplanes, the Americans could bring to bear all the power of their rapidly growing naval and amphibious forces

When the Japanese initiated an offensive against Wau, New Guinea, in the first half of 1943 to expand the perimeter of her Empire, Australian forces held out until reinforcements arrived. Japanese efforts to send reinforcements were thwarted by American naval forces resulting in the Battle of the Bismarck Sea during which the Japanese lost all their transports and most of their destroyers.

Acquiring air bases was essential to protecting supply routes, communication lines, and for launching attacks. This made the New Georgian airfield, Munda, in the Solomons an important objective. American forces began the assault on New Georgia in late June 1943, and after fierce battles, they gained control of the airfield by August.

New Guinea was another island of strategic importance because of the Japanese base at Madang and the airstrip 25 miles southeast of Salamaua. American forces attacked Japanese bases at Salamaua and Lae which were both evacuated on September 16, 1943. On April 24, 1944, Allied troops occupied Madang.

To weaken Japanese control in the Central Pacific key airfields had to be neutralized in New Britain and the Solomon Islands from which the Japanese could launch a strike. As a first step, the Americans occupied Cape Gloucester in New Britain near the end of 1943 and after a fierce battle over Bougainville, the Japanese forces were overwhelmed. Finally, a major air battle over Rabaul resulted in sufficient Japanese air loses to eradicate Rabaul as a major offensive threat. Japanese air loses and the crippling of their bases and harbours weakened Japanese control in the Central Pacific.

To loosen the Japanese grip on the central Pacific even further, the United States leaders selected the Gilbert Islands, northwest of the Solomons, as their next target because its occupation would provide a base for photo reconnaissance of the Marshalls. The two primary objectives were two small atolls: Tarawa and Makin. With the aid of flamethrowers to counter Japanese bunkers and pill boxes, American troops choked off resistance by November 23, 1943. American victories in the Gilberts extinguished

Japanese plans to attack Fiji and the Samoan Islands.

To seriously damage the Japanese defensive perimeter American forces had to take the Marshall Islands located northeast of the Gilberts. Winning control of the Marshalls required the neutralization of Truk in the Caroline Islands, one of the strongest Japanese bases in the Pacific and considered almost impregnable. On February 17-18, 1944, carrier planes delivered wave after wave of bombing raids on Truk rendering it useless as a major base for the Japanese fleet. After capturing a number of islands in the Marshalls such as Eniwetok Atoll, Kwajalein, and Roi-Namur, the Marshall Islands were no longer a Japanese stronghold.

The significance of the victory in the Marshall Islands was described by Ronald H. Spector in *Eagle Against the Sun: The American War With Japan* in the following terms:

> The swift and relatively easy capture of the Marshalls enabled the Americans to speed up their entire effort in the Pacific. Bolder plans were conceived; timetables adjusted; troops and resources reshuffled.

United States military planners decided to bypass Truk, which had already been rendered ineffective, and other islands in the Carolines in favour of leaping forward to the Marianas located over 1,000 miles northwest of Eniwetok in the Marshalls. Three large islands Saipan, Tinian, and Guam could serve as advanced naval bases for attacks against the Philippines and the Bonin Islands which were within 700 miles of Japan. The airfields on the Marianas could accommodate the new B-29 long-range bombers which were in range of Japanese cities. The campaign against the Marianas was the most ambitious to date in the Pacific involving 535 ships and almost 130,000 troops. After heavy bombardment of Saipan and Tinian, American forces landed on these islands where they met with fierce resistance.

At the same time as the battle for the Marianas, the Japanese and the Americans fought one of the most important naval battles of the war in the waters between the Philippines and the Marianas called the Battle of the Philippine Sea. The Japanese decided to throw everything they had at the American fleet in the Marianas in one final desperate attempt to destroy the American Pacific Fleet. The battle began on June 19, 1944 and the result has been dubbed the "Marianas Turkey Shoot." Both the air and naval battles were decisive as Japan lost about 476 planes and two carriers. Japan would never recover from the crippling blow to its air power.

When it became evident that Japan would lose Saipan, the Japanese leaders in Saipan committed suicide and hundreds of Japanese soldiers and civilians killed themselves rather than face surrender. U.S. forces had control of the island by July 9, 1944. Guam was defeated on August 10. A. Russell Buchanan, in *The United States and World War II, Volume II*, concluded that:

> The seizure of Guam ended the assault campaigns in the Marianas. They [Marianas] were of great significance in the Pacific war, for the loss of the Marianas made responsible Japanese military officials realize that they had lost the war, although, as in the case of the German commanders, they continued fighting long after hope of victory had gone. A sign of the trend was the fall of the Tojo government and its replacement by one more sympathetic to a negotiated peace.

After securing the Marianas, Washington war strategists were engaged in a vigorous debate about the optimum route to Japan. One was through the Philippines, Formosa and Ryukyus to Japan and the other was through the Bonin Islands and Kyushu. The first involved the capture of large land masses and, therefore, would take longer but had a higher probability of success. As well, gaining a foothold in the Philippines would sever Japanese supplies of oil from the south. The second was faster and depended on the navy to control the air and sea but had a lower probability of success. The military planners chose the Philippines route.

On October 20, 1944, American forces landed at three locations on the coast of Leyte, an island midway in the Philippines, and met little resistance. The most significant battle for Leyte occurred in the surrounding waters where Japan, despite their severe loses in the Battle of the Philippines, hoped to destroy the Pacific fleet. According to Michael J. Lyons in *World War II: A Short History*:

> The Battle of Leyte Gulf had dealt a death blow to Japan's naval power. Four carriers, three battleships, six heavy and four light cruisers, and eleven destroyers littered the ocean floor. The Japanese had also lost 500 planes.

Notwithstanding the blow to Japanese naval power, Japanese convoys could still navigate their way through the treacherous waters of the Philippine archipelago. The success of the convoys was directly related to the inadequate American naval power in the Philippines. At this point, Admiral Onishi, commander of the Japanese 1st air fleet believed that the only effective tactic to inflict serious damage on the American fleet would be to employ kamikaze or suicide pilots. It caught the Americans by surprise but the kamikaze pilots sank only one ship and damaged three others.

By December 10, 1944, the real battle for Leyte had ended although fighting continued for several more weeks. The invasion of Luzon, a large island at the northern end of the Philippines where Manila the capital of the Philippines was located, was scheduled for December 20, 1944. The Island of Mindoro, south of Luzon, was captured first to provide land-based air support for the battle against Luzon. The American forces landed on Mindoro on December 15, 1944; Luzon on January 9, 1945; Palawan on February 28, 1945; and on Zamboanga on March 10, 1945. Bataan was recaptured with little resistance late in February. Corregidor was secured on March 2. In the capital, Manila, fighting raged for a month before the Americans gained control on March 3, 1945. On June 30, 1945, the army had captured the strategic points in Luzon that were needed for the conduct of the war.

The loss of the Philippines was another catastrophe for the Japanese. The War Minister commented, "When you took the Philippines that was the end of our resources."

Although U.S. planes on air bases in the Marianas were within striking distance of Japan, the 1,200-mile flight posed risks that could only be averted if American forces captured some of the Japanese airfields on route and established their own bases where planes could refuel or make emergency landings. Iwo Jima fit the bill because of its location only 600 miles from Japan and its terrain which was suitable for the construction of airfields.

To soften Japanese defences on Iwo Jima, American bombers commenced bombing the island in August 1944 with minimal success. The assault forces were scheduled to launch their attack on February 19, 1945, and the number of marines assembled under one command was the largest in United States naval history.

The battle for Iwo Jima was savage and the U.S. marines sustained immense loses. Several days of heavy bombing from the American fleet had little success in weakening Japanese defences. The underground labyrinth of caves, tunnels, and well-concealed pillboxes were immune to American naval bombardment and a formidable obstacle to the marines who were seeking to establish a beachhead. Flame throwers and TNT proved to be an effective method for solving this problem. On March 16, U.S. leaders declared the island secure. Ironically, Iwo Jima never became an important base for fighter escorts or for U.S. B-29s but served as an emergency landing and refueling base.

Airfields and two excellent anchorages were located on Okinawa, a Japanese island only 350 miles from Japan. As such, it was an important strategic objective as a staging area for an assault on Japan. Securing Okinawa would also eliminate the threat of attacks on American ships and planes during the bombing of Japan.

As with Iwo Jima, American carrier planes began bombarding Okinawa on October 10, 1944, to soften Japanese defences. The actual invasion of Okinawa began on April 1, 1945, and ended on June 21, 1945. The battles on Okinawa were a bloodbath and the victory a very costly one for the Americans. As well as the soldiers killed on the ground, the U.S. fleet was subjected to repeated kamikaze attacks. One unusual surprise was the first occasion of thousands of Japanese soldiers surrendering. Ronald H. Spector in *Eagles Against the Sun: The American War With Japan* summed up the cost of the war to Japan at this point with:

> The battle for Okinawa had ended in another overwhelming American victory. An entire Japanese army had been destroyed, together with hundreds of planes and the greatest battleship of the Imperial navy.

American leaders did not wait until the capture of Okinawa to embark on their campaign against the Japanese home islands. United States submarines were destroying unprotected merchant vessels by the middle of 1943. At the end of 1943, when a large number of new submarines became available, the Japanese were forced to use escort protection for their merchant ships. Submarine attacks continued and by the end of 1944 the U.S. had sunk half of Japan's merchant fleet. The loss of its merchant vessels had severely diminished Japan's supply of natural resources, food, and oil, and by the summer of 1945, American submarines had a choke hold on the traffic of merchant vessels serving Japan. The lack of incoming supplies was causing starvation among the Japanese people.

Submarines encircling Japan had severed Japan from its source of supplies, and new American bomber wreaked havoc on Japanese industries and cities. The B-29 super fortress became available in early 1944, was twice as heavy as its predecessor the B-17, and could carry a 20,000-pound bomb over 7,000 miles. American forces did not secure the Marianas until June 1944, so when the B-29s first became available they had to use China as a base. Once the Marianas were secure, airfields needed to be modified for use by B-29 bombers.

The B-29s were first launched on a bombing mission to the Japanese homeland on June 14, 1944, against the huge steel and iron complex at Yawata on the island of Kyushu. The city was blacked out and the bombers did little damage. On August 10, 1944, a bombing raid was carried out against Nagasaki in Kyushu, but again the damage was minor.

After the B-29s were shifted to the Marianas the Americans conducted a raid against an aircraft plant in Tokyo. During this mission, the planes flew at 32,000 feet and were impervious to Japanese flak and fighters. For the next three months, the bombing raids targeted the aircraft industry. General Curtis LeMay, who was in command of the B-29s, concluded that to inflict greater damage during bombing raids, the aircraft would need to shift to incendiary bombs which contained napalm, a jellied form of petroleum that exploded upon impact engulfing everything in the vicinity in flames.

On February 4, 1945, bombers carrying incendiary bombs struck at Kobe, Japan's sixth largest city. The result was that five of the twelve main factories were damaged as well as one of the two shipyards. A second raid with incendiary bombs struck Tokyo on February 25 and destroyed 28,000 structures (homes, factories etc.). On March 8, 1945, LeMay ordered a large-scale bombing of Tokyo involving 334 bombers. Almost sixteen square miles of the city was incinerated and 267,000 buildings were destroyed. More than 83,000 people were killed and another 41,000 were injured. By early June, Tokyo, Nagoya, Kobe, Osaka, Yokohama, and Kawasaki were subject to further bombings. Ronald H. Spector in *Eagle Against the Sun: The American War With Japan,* described the destruction as:

> Over 40% of the total urban area of these cities had been gutted; millions had been rendered homeless. LeMay next turned to the destruction of Japan's smaller cities. His bomber force, now almost 600 strong, ranged over Japan almost at will, visiting destruction on half a hundred smaller cities and manufacturing centres.

At this point in the war, Japan's cities had been severely damaged, the industrial base virtually destroyed, the navy and air force rendered useless, and the people left suffering from starvation.

Delivering the Final Blow

Despite the massive victories scored against Japan, American leaders were not celebrating because they were dreading the invasion of Japan itself. U.S. military planners were very apprehensive about Japanese soldiers fighting in their homeland because they had already demonstrated their unyielding tenacity and truculence elsewhere. A number of options were discussed including:

- invade Japan and fight until the Japanese surrender;
- demand a surrender with terms other than an unconditional surrender and threaten to use a new highly destructive weapon (atomic bomb);
- demand unconditional surrender with the same threat;
- demand either conditional or unconditional surrender and not warn the Japanese about the new weapon;
- demand either conditional or unconditional surrender and demonstrate the new weapon;
- respond to Japanese attempts (mostly through the Soviet Union) to negotiate the terms of the surrender.

Many high level meetings and committees discussed these and other options at great length for many months. The events leading up to the conclusion of the war as well as the behind-the-scene discussions and diary entries of key figures are instrumental in understanding the motives of President Truman (President Roosevelt died in April) in making the decision about how to end the war.

A number of important events preceded the use of the atomic bombs. On April 1945, the Joint Chiefs of Staff ordered their field commanders to make plans for the invasion of Japan. Discussions about where to begin the invasion were heated but a consensus was finally reached to invade Kyushu. The Joint Chiefs of Staff presented the plan to President Truman with an estimate of the number of American lives that would be lost. The number was mere speculation and was not based on any sound rational process but on an extrapolation based on the number of casualties in Okinawa. Some military officers contemplated the possibility of ending the war without an invasion.

One of the most controversial issues in the Pacific theatre was the debate over the terms of surrender to be offered to Japan. In 1943, Roosevelt, Churchill and their military advisors met in Casablanca to discuss strategy. The British War Cabinet and President Roosevelt's advisors had already discussed the terms of surrender and at a press conference held at the end of the Casablanca Conference, Roosevelt announced that the Allied Powers were striving for an "unconditional surrender." The term was first coined by Ulysses S. Grant in the Civil War.

Unconditional surrender implied that the institution of Emperor would be abolished and this was one of the stumbling blocks to a Japanese surrender. Japanese fears about the Emperor were not groundless. American leaders such as Secretary of State, James F. Byrnes, believed that the Emperor symbolized the military clique that dominated Japan and, therefore, must not survive the war. A June 1945 Gallup poll revealed that 33% of Americans wanted the Emperor to be executed as a war criminal.

In Japanese society, the Emperor was regarded as a deity similar to Jesus or Buddha. Gar Alperovitz in *The Decision to Use the Atomic Bomb* described the tradition of the Emperor:

> The godhood of the Emperor was a tradition which traced back to 660 B.C. and the first Japanese Emperor, Jimmu, who was, according to legend, a descendant of the sun goddess Amaterasu, made him and all of his successors also divine beings.

The status of the Emperor would explain Japanese consternation about an "unconditional surrender." It is not clear that losing the Emperor was a critical issue for the Americans since, in the end, the Emperor was retained anyway.

The terms of surrender and the use of the bomb were on the agenda of a high-level committee appointed by President Truman. As a result of a meeting on April 25, 1945, Secretary of War, Henry L. Stimson and President Truman proposed the creation of the Interim Committee. Its mandate was to operate only between early May and the actual use of the bomb (the decision to use the atomic bomb had not been made yet). One of the recommendations of the committee was the retention of the Emperor. The Interim Committee also recommended that:

> ...the Secretary of War should be advised that, while recognizing that the final selection of the target was essentially a military decision, the present view of the Committee was that the bomb should be used against Japan as soon as possible; that it be used on a war plant surrounded by workers' homes; and that it be used without prior warning.

Notwithstanding the fact that the development of the atom bomb was totally unrelated to the war in the Pacific, its use against Japan became a key issue when Japan was on the brink of defeat. Rapid progress in physics during the 1930s created the potential for assembly of a nuclear weapon. German physicists were very advanced in the field of nuclear physics and some of them had fled to the United States where they advised President Roosevelt of the possible danger that Germany would develop an atomic bomb. President Roosevelt appointed a committee of scientists to study the problem and when the U.S. entered the war it launched the Manhattan Project, the purpose of which was to create an atomic weapon as quickly as possible. The bomb was ready in the summer of 1945.

The political context in Japan during the final months of the war was also an important factor in understanding the predisposition of the Japanese leadership to end the war. After the invasion of the Marianas, the Tojo Government collapsed and was replaced by Koiso and a new cabinet. They favoured an early end to the war and allied themselves with other important elements of Japanese society, such as advisors to the Emperor, in an effort to bring hostilities to an end. Out of necessity, Koiso appeased the military leadership by openly advocating prolonging the war in the hope of achieving one final Japanese victory to strengthen their bargaining position. On the other hand, he covertly urged the Soviet Union to assist him in securing a mediated peace. The Soviet Union had no interest in supporting Japanese efforts to secure a better peace because of their own intentions to enter the war in the hope of attaining possession of some of the Japanese territories for negotiations after the war. The loss of Okinawa forced the resignation of the Koiso Government and the ascendancy of Admiral Suzuki Kantaro. His new foreign minister, Togo Shigenori, was the most outspoken critic of the war. Understanding the power of the military, he also spoke in public about fighting to the bitter end while he continued to implore the Soviets to mediate a peace. Again the Soviets manifested no interest. Marquis Kido Koichi, one of the Emperor's closest advisors, called an imperial conference during which the Emperor encouraged those present to end the war by diplomatic means. The Emperor's intervention convinced even the war minister and the army chief of staff to negotiate an end to the war. They concentrated their efforts on another futile attempt to persuade the Soviets to mediate on their behalf.

Japan's overtures to the Soviet Union to mediate a peace settlement with the other Allied powers were based on a lack of understanding of Soviet intentions. From the beginning of the Pacific War, the United States was hoping that Russia would declare war against Japan and draw Japanese forces into Manchuria thereby sapping their strength in the war against the United States. The Soviets were unable to transfer any of their military resources to the Pacific war because they were needed in the struggle against Germany. Their plan was to enter the Pacific war when it was propitious for their own strategic interests. On the other hand, with the atomic bomb becoming a reality, Soviet participation seemed superfluous to the Americans. The Soviet leaders had already stated the price of their entrance into the Pacific War at the Teheran Conference in November 1943, when they asked for the southern half of Sakhalin, the Kurile chain of islands, and Port Arthur. In April 1945, the Soviets notified the Japanese that they intended to terminate their neutrality pact. On August 8, 1945, two days after the bomb fell on Hiroshima, the Soviet Union declared war on Japan.

Events leading up to and during the "big three meeting" at Potsdam are also crucial to understanding the real rationale for using the atomic bomb. President Truman and the newly appointed Secretary of State, James F. Byrnes, traveled to Potsdam on July 17, 1945, to meet with Churchill and Stalin, the last of the Allied summit meetings.

In the months prior to the Potsdam meeting, the Allied leaders were very concerned about the strength and intentions of the Soviet Union after the war. Acting Secretary of State Joseph C. Grew summed up their concern:

> Already Russia is showing us—in Poland, Rumania, Bulgaria, Hungary, Austria, Czechoslovakia, and Yugoslavia—the future world pattern that she visualizes and will aim to create. With her certain stranglehold on these countries, Russia's power will steadily increase and she will in the not distant future be in a favorable position to expand her control, step by step through Europe. (Gar Alperovitz, *The Decision to Use the Atomic Bomb*)

President Truman was advised that:

> If expectations were to be realized, he [Stimson] told me, the atomic bomb would be certain to have a decisive influence on our relations with other countries. And if it worked, the bomb, in all probability, would shorten the war. Byrnes had already told me that the weapon might be so powerful as to be potentially capable of wiping out entire cities and killing people on an unprecedented scale. And he added that in his belief the bomb might well put us in a position to dictate our terms at the end of the war. (Gar Alperovitz, *The Decision to Use the Atomic Bomb*)

The expression "dictating our terms" is in reference to the Soviet Union whose expansionist ambitions were no secret.

Secretary of War Henry L. Stimson reported that:

> I told him [Assistant Secretary of War-John J. Mcloy] that my own opinion was that the time now and the method now to deal with Russia was to keep our mouths shut and let our actions speak for words. The Russians will understand them better than anything else. It is a case where we have got to retain the lead and perhaps do it in a pretty rough and realistic way. (Gar Alperovitz, *The Decision to Use the Atomic Bomb*)

A War Department staff report recognized that:

> In destroying Germany, the nation that set out to dominate Europe using force, we have made Russia, a nation with an economic system of national monopoly, the unquestionably dominant power in Europe. (Gar Alperovitz, *The Decision to Use the Atomic Bomb*)

P. M. S. Blackett, a British Nobel Prize-winning physicist, concluded that:

> ...the dropping of the atomic bomb was not so much the last military act of the Second World War as the first major operation of the cold diplomatic war with Russia.

But using civilians from a third country as a warning of America's new, highly destructive weapon has to rank as one of the greatest crimes against humanity. To sacrifice two cities and about 150,000 people to inform your post-war adversary that they may be next is unadulterated insanity.

Leo Szilard, an atomic scientist who met with James F. Byrnes noted that:

> Mr. Byrnes did not argue that it was necessary to use the bomb against the cities of Japan in order to win the war. He knew at the time, as the rest of the government knew that Japan was essentially defeated and that we could win the war in another six months. At that time Mr. Byrnes was much concerned about the spreading of Russian influence in Europe...[Mr. Byrnes view was] that our possessing and demonstrating the bomb would make Russia more manageable in Europe. (Gar Alperovitz, *The Decision to Use the Atomic Bomb*)

The Soviet Union's growing power, influence, and ambitions were causing the American leaders a gnawing disquietude about the distribution of power in the post-war world. Their apprehensions were based on Soviet ideology, as understood in the West, on Soviet ambitions for world domination and on their maneuvers to gain control of Eastern Europe and as much of Japanese territory as possible. Both became critical factors in Allied thinking about how to end the war. According to Bill Gordon in *Reflections on Hiroshima*:

...American leaders had concerns that the Soviet Union would occupy Manchuria and would share the occupation of Japan with the U.S.; in addition, American leaders believed that dropping the bomb would strengthen their position with the Soviet Union concerning their sphere of influence in Eastern Europe.

As well, Gar Alperovitz, in *The Decision to Use the Atomic Bomb*, observed that:

> The primary focal point...is the fact that throughout the spring and summer of 1945 American officials developed their thinking on the use of the atomic bomb in close relationship in the planning of U.S. diplomacy towards the Soviet Union.

Truman's strong concern about the post-war Soviet threat was the primary factor in his repeated attempts to postpone the Potsdam conference. He was waiting for a successful test of the atom bomb before meeting with Stalin.

Secretary of War Henry L. Stimson suggested at a meeting with President Truman that:

> ...the greatest complication was what might happen at the meeting of the Big Three. He told me he had postponed that until the 15th of July on purpose to give us more time. (Gar Alperovitz, *The Decision to Use the Atomic Bomb*)

When President Truman responded to Prime Minister Churchill's plea for a big three meeting as early as possible, he stated that "...it will be very difficult for me to be absent from Washington before the fiscal year (June 30)." Churchill responded on May 11 with "I would have suggested the middle of June but for your reference to your fiscal year (June 30) because I feel that every minute counts" and on May 13 "In this case I consider that we should try to bring the meeting off sometime in June, and I hope your fiscal year will not delay it..." Finally, in complete frustration, Churchill sent a cable to President Truman protesting that:

> ...I consider that July 15, repeat July the month after June, is much too late for the urgent questions that demand attention between us...I have proposed June 15, repeat June the month before July, but if that is not possible why not July 1, 2, or 3? (Gar Alperovitz, *The Decision to Use the Atomic Bomb*)

In a meeting with President Truman on May 21, Joseph E. Davies, former Ambassador to Moscow, explained that:

> He did not want to meet until July. He had his budget on his hands. He also told me of another reason, etc. The test [of the bomb] was set for June, but had been postponed for July. (Gar Alperovitz, *The Decision the Use the Atomic Bomb*)

President Truman's posture toward the Soviet Union shifted after he became aware that a test of the atomic bomb was imminent. Originally, he needed the Soviet Union to declare war against Japan to draw some of the Japanese resources away from the war against the U.S. After the successful test of the nuclear weapon, Truman decided that he could terminate the war with Japan without Soviet assistance and he did not want the Russians to have a share in the Pacific pie. Ronald H. Spector, in *Eagles Against the Sun: The American War With Japan,* observed that:

> With the atomic bomb a reality, the participation of the Soviets in the war against Japan now appeared unnecessary, if not actually undesirable. Ever since Yalta some American leaders had had doubts about the value of Soviet participation, and now General Marshall again advised the President that the Soviets were not really needed.

The meeting of the Big Three took place on July 17 to resolve several critical and urgent issues. Was it a coincidence that the first successful test of the atomic bomb occurred on July 16 and the first scheduled meeting was on July 17? The most crucial decision facing the leaders at Potsdam was to decide how to end the war with Japan. The question of the status of the institution of Emperor was crucial to the Japanese attitude toward surrendering. Many people in the administration, the military, and on the Interim Committee believed that surrender terms must guarantee retention of the Emperor. Prior to the Potsdam meetings, the U.S.-British Combined Intelligence Committee (CIC) prepared a report on the "Estimate of the Enemy Situation." They concluded that:

> ...to insure survival of the institution of the Emperor, the Japanese might well be willing to withdraw from all territory they have seized on the Asiatic continent and in the southern Pacific, and even agreed to the independence of Korea and to the practical disarmament of their military forces. (Gar Alperovitz, *The Decision to Use the Atomic Bomb)*

Joseph C. Grew, acting Secretary of State, echoes these sentiments when he remarked that:

> The greatest obstacle to unconditional surrender by the Japanese is their belief that this would entail the destruction or permanent removal of the Emperor and the institution of the throne. If some indication can now be given the Japanese that they themselves...will be able to determine their own future political structure, they will be afforded a method of saving face without which surrender will be highly unlikely.

Many military leaders thought that the surrender terms should have been modified. Gar Alperovitz in *The Decision to Use the Atomic Bomb* remarked that:

> Prior to Potsdam (and even before July's Emperor-related intercepts) Stimson, Forrestal [Secretary of the Navy], Leahy [Admiral], Marshall [Army Chief of Staff], McCloy [Assistant Secretary of War], Bard [Under Secretary of the Navy]—as well as Arnold [commander of the Army Air forces], King [Commander in Chief of the U.S. Fleet], and Nimitz [Commander of the Pacific Fleet]—had all in various ways urged that the surrender terms be clarified. And at Potsdam the Joint Chief of Staffs twice tried to find a way to clarify the surrender formula.

According to the minutes of a meeting at the White House on June 18, 1945:

> Admiral Leary said that he could not agree with those who said to him that unless we obtain the unconditional surrender of the Japanese that we will have lost the war. He feared no menace from Japan in the foreseeable future, even if we were unsuccessful in forcing unconditional surrender. (Truman Presidential Museum and Library)

Two crucial questions must be answered about the terms of surrender. Firstly, were the Japanese prepared to surrender if there was a guarantee to retain the Emperor? Secondly, if the Japanese were prepared to surrender on these terms, was Truman aware of it? According to Gar Alperovitz in *The Decision to Use the Atomic Bomb*:

> Truman had been fully aware of the key intercepts (something he had privately confirmed to State Department interviewers four years earlier [than 1960 when the official Potsdam Papers were published], in January 1956).

Fragments of other intercepts to which President Truman was privy included:

- On May 12, 1942, William Donovan, Director of the OSS reported to Truman that Shunichi Kase (Japanese Minister to Switzerland) stated that he "...believes that one of the few provisions the Japanese would insist upon would be the retention of the Emperor..."

- On August 11, 1944, Magic reports of intercepted messages designated "Eyes Only" for the President, such as "Foreign Minister Shigemitsu has instructed Ambassador Sato [in

Moscow] to find out whether Russia is willing to assist in bringing about a negotiated peace…" It seems highly unlikely that he would have taken such a step without having consulted at least some members of the new Japanese Cabinet.

- On May 7, 1945, a peace feeler from Portugal directly to Truman from the OSS representative reported that "…the Japanese are ready to cease hostilities, provided they are allowed to retain possession of their home islands." Then again on May 19, "On this occasion Inoue declared that actual peace terms were unimportant so long as the term 'unconditional surrender' was not employed."

- On July 16, 1945, William Donovan sent the President a report on P. Jacobson (Swedish economic advisor to the Bank for International Settlements) informing Truman that "Throughout discussions with Jacobson, the Japanese officials stressed only two points: (a) the preservation of the Emperor, and (b) the possibility of returning to the constitution promulgated in 1889." (Gar Alperovitz, *The Decision to Use the Atomic Bomb*)

President Truman along with his Secretary of State made a decision not to clarify the meaning of "unconditional surrender" or provide assurances that the institution of the Emperor would be retained. Although the administration exercised caution with respect to the legitimacy of the diplomatic intercepts, the fact that they all were basically communicating the same message might have suggested that they contained a grain of truth. At the very least, the President could have attempted to establish contact with the Japanese to verify whether these intercepts were accurate and under what terms they would surrender.

The final meeting of the leaders of the three major allied powers began on July 17 and ended on August 2, 1945. At this point, Truman was aware of the successful test of the atomic bomb and the peace feelers dispatched to Japanese embassies. President Truman was also aware of the recommendations of the Interim Committee that the new weapon should be used as soon as possible against a military target without any warning.

During the Interim Committees deliberations, several underlying currents were influencing the direction of their recommendations. These currents include the climate of concern about the influence and power of the Soviet Union and the authority of J. Byrnes, the President's closest advisor.

Many of those who were formulating policy on ending the war with Japan, as previously noted, were very concerned about the Russians. Secretary of War Stimson thought that:

> It may be necessary to have it out with Russia on her relations to Manchuria and Port Arthur and various other parts of North China, and also the relations of China to us. Over any such tangled wave of problems, S-1 (i.e., the atomic bomb) secrecy would be dominant... (Gar Alperovitz, *The Decision to Use the Atomic Bomb)*

Historian Herbert Feis believed that:

> It is quite possible that it was thought the proof of the power of the weapon, as demonstrated in actual warfare, might be an effective source of added authority to the American Government in the settlement of matters at issue with the Soviet Union. (Gar Alperovitz, *The Decision to Use the Atomic Bomb*)

Secretary of State Byrnes was not only a friend of President Truman but became his closest advisor. Byrnes strong support for the use of the atomic bomb without any warning not only influenced the President but also influenced the Interim Committee whose recommendations comprised most of the Potsdam Declaration. According to the *New York Times*:

> ...it was understood that Mr. Byrnes would in effect, replace Harry Hopkins as Presidential confidant, and, it was asserted, receive far more authority than a President has yet yielded to any man.

Byrne's assistant Walter Brown observed that:

> The President and Mr. Byrnes talked for an hour and it was apparent Truman was looking to Byrnes for guidance...Truman said he considered Byrnes one of his best friends and realized that he knew more about government than anyone else around and, therefore, he wanted Byrnes' help. (Gar Alperovitz, *The Decision to Use the Atomic Bomb*)

Secretary Byrnes was single-minded with respect to his views about how to end the war. He was uncompromising about the terms of surrender. According to Gar Alperovitz in *The Decision to Use the Atomic Bomb*:

> ...Byrnes is a prime candidate for the advisor who helped Truman draft his still-unexplained June 1 no-compromise stand on unconditional surrender... So far as we can tell Byrnes was the only advisor whose views were fully compatible with this position at this time.

As well, Gar Alperovitz, in the *Decision to Use the Atomic Bomb,* concluded that:

> In general, it appears that Byrnes not only regarded the atomic bomb as extremely important to his diplomacy towards Russia, but that in advising Truman he took a very narrow view of its role. Minimally, he seems to have seen it from the very beginning as leverage to help American diplomacy, and, more likely, as the critical factor which—if shrewdly handled—would allow the United States to impose its own terms once its power was demonstrated.

Given the context in which President Truman would be making the decision about ending the war, there would seem to be a predisposition toward using the bomb. The Interim Committee had recommended dropping the bomb; Truman's closest advisor strongly favoured the bomb; and the climate of apprehension about Soviet expansionism strengthened the case for using the atomic bomb.

The fear of an expanding Soviet Empire after the war was a major problem for American policy-makers because it would threaten the magnitude and strength of the American Empire. Apprehension of Soviet intentions and the expansion of the American Empire would play a key role in how to end the war with Japan.

Another major issue to be considered was whether an invasion of Japan would cost substantially more lives than dropping the bomb. One of the mythical justifications invoked to support the use of atomic weapons assumed a fraudulent dichotomy between dropping the bomb and invading Japan. The justification was mythical because the President did not have any serious discussions with the military about the potential loss of lives and most military leaders rejected the use of nuclear weapons. As well, there were many other options. American leaders were aware of Japanese peace feelers from diplomatic intercepts and therefore, negotiations offered the potential to end the war without the loss of any more lives. Then, there was always the alternative of inserting a clause in the Potsdam Declaration (the final communiqué of the meeting of the big three) to reassure the Japanese that the institution of emperor would not be dismantled. Two other options included issuing a warning about the destructiveness of the new weapon and offering to demonstrate the atomic bomb in a safe venue.

The argument about minimizing the loss of life ignores the fact that most military leaders were opposed to using the bomb and were not consulted. Gar Alperovitz in *The Decision to Use the Atomic Bomb* pointed out that:

When we turn to the testimony of the top military leaders themselves, the evidence not only confirms that their advice was not seriously sought, but also (with one possible ambiguous exception) strongly suggests that none believed the use of the atomic bomb was dictated by overwhelming military considerations. Several expressed deep revulsion at the idea of targeting a city.

That lack of consultation doesn't represent blundering on the part of civilian leaders including Truman. Rather, it supports the idea that the use of the weapon was not going to be a military but a diplomatic decision. The decision was going to be based largely on considerations of empire and therefore military input was secondary.

In a memorandum by Ralph A. Bard, Undersecretary of the Navy, to Secretary of War Stimson, June 27, 1945, Bard reported that:

During recent weeks I have also had the feeling very definitely that the Japanese Government may be searching for some opportunity which they could use as a medium of surrender...emissaries from this country could contact representatives from Japan...and make representations with regard to Russia's position and at the same time give them some information regarding the proposed use of atomic power, together with whatever assurances the President might care to make with regard to the Emperor... (U.S. National Archives)

Fleet Admiral William D. Leay, Chairman of the Joint Chiefs of Staff, offered the opinion that:

...the use of this barbarous weapon at Hiroshima and Nagasaki was of no material assistance in our war against Japan. The Japanese were almost defeated and ready to surrender...in being the first to use it, we...adopted an ethical standard common to the barbarians of the Dark Ages. (Gar Alperovitz, *Was Hiroshima Necessary to End the War*)

Major General Curtis E. LeMay, during a press conference on September 20, 1945, made it clear that military considerations were not in play when he stated that:

The war would have been over in two weeks without the Russians and without the atomic bomb. The atomic bomb had nothing to do with the end of the war at all. (Gar Alperovitz, *The Decision to Use the Atomic Bomb*)

The tragic irony of the ultimatum delivered to the Japanese demanding an unconditional surrender or face dire consequences was that after the United States dropped two nuclear bombs on Japan, they offered to preserve the throne. Byrnes and Truman traveled to Potsdam with a draft copy of the Potsdam Declaration which defined the surrender terms for Japan. The original wording assured the retention of the Emperor but:

> Byrnes was convinced that a retreat from unconditional surrender could have devastating political consequences for the President, since the vast majority of the public was still opposed to the retention of the Emperor. At Byrne's urging, Truman agreed to a rewording of the surrender demand. (Ronald H. Spector, *Eagle Against the Sun: The American War with Japan*)

Gar Alperovitz, in *The Decision to Use the Atomic Bomb,* also confirmed the role of Byrnes when he stated that "There is little doubt that the advice to eliminate the recommended assurances came from Byrnes." Without offering the Japanese hope that the institution of Emperor was unthreatened, there was almost no hope that they would accept the Potsdam Declaration. Another false dichotomy was well entrenched in the declaration and in the minds of Byrnes and Truman, both of whom presupposed that without the acceptance of an unconditional surrender, the only other option was to use the bomb.

The key clauses in the Potsdam Declaration issued on July 26 are:

- There must be eliminated for all time the authority and influence of those who have deceived and misled the people of Japan into embarking on world conquest—for we insist that a new order of peace, security and justice will be impossible until irresponsible militarism is driven from the world.

- We do not intend that the Japanese shall be enslaved as a race or destroyed as a nation, but stern justice shall be meted out to all war criminals...

- We call upon the government of Japan to proclaim the now unconditional surrender of all the Japanese armed forces... The alternative for Japan is prompt and utter destruction.

The first two clauses were interpreted by the Japanese as a threat to the throne. In the first clause the reference to "the authority and influence of those..." was sufficiently ambiguous to include not only the military but possibly the Emperor as well. Also, the second clause's threat about "stern justice shall be meted out to all war criminals" is unclear as to whether the Emperor was considered a war criminal. The last clause's reference to "unconditional surrender" in conjunction with the omission of any reference to preserving the institution of Emperor had virtually one connotation: the position of Emperor would be abolished. According to Doug Long in *Hiroshima: Was It Necessary?* "...the proclamation made statements that, to the Japanese could appear threatening to the Emperor."

The Japanese response to the Potsdam Declaration is complicated by a number of factors not the least of which was the interpretation of the Japanese word "mokusatsu." It can mean "to be silent," "to withhold comment," or "to ignore" although to "withhold comment" is closest to its real meaning. In Premiere Suzuki's response to the Potsdam Declaration, "mokusatsu" was the operative word. Many confusing signals would certainly have prompted the Japanese to withhold comment in an attempt to sort out all the conflicting messages from the allies.

Part of the confusion could be traced to a navy captain, Ellis Zacharias, a psychological-warfare expert who was working in cooperation with the overseas branch of the Office of War Information (OWI). He transmitted thirteen broadcasts in both English and Japanese the last broadcast being the most significant. In that broadcast, he proclaims that "Japan has already lost the war" but then adds "As you know, the Atlantic Charter and the Cairo Declaration are the sources of our policy." The Atlantic Charter's relevant passage signed by 26 nations affirms "…the right of all peoples to choose the form of government under which they will live." The implication of this statement by Zacharias is that the Japanese would be able to retain the position of Emperor. This particular broadcast was not only simultaneously released to the press but appeared on the same day in the authoritative Army and Navy Journal. There is some debate about the extent of the American leadership's approval but the salient point is that there was no official disavowal from Potsdam. On July 24, Arthur Krock of the *New York Times* reported that "He [Ellis Zacharias] knows the President has been one of his consultants on this propaganda."

On the one hand, the terms of the Potsdam Declaration seem to rule out an Emperor for Japan but on the other hand, the ostensibly authoritative reports from Zacharias would seem to suggest otherwise. The confusion is captured in an intercepted message from Japanese Foreign Minister Togo to Ambassador Sato in Moscow which reported:

> … [that] the Americans alluded to the Atlantic Charter is particularly worthy of attention at this time. It is impossible for us to accept unconditional surrender, no matter in what guise, but it is our idea to inform them by some appropriate means that there is no objection to the restoration of peace on the basis of the Atlantic Charter. (Gar Alperovitz, *The Decision to Use the Atomic Bomb*)

The Americans were aware of the confusion plaguing the Japanese because of the failure of the Potsdam Declaration to clarify the issue of the Emperor. Gar Alperovitz in *The Decision to Use the Atomic Bomb* discovered important information through the recovery of secret documents which show that:

> ...Japanese officials were mystified by the juxtaposition of the Atlantic Charter broadcast (together with the signal of Presidential "approval") and the Potsdam Proclamation. They also demonstrated that here, too, U.S. officials were fully aware of the fact.

Another factor perplexing the Japanese related to the position of the Russians throughout this attempt to understand the surrender terms. Did the Russian refusal to sign the declaration signify that there was some hope of persuading them to remain neutral thus giving the Japanese some additional time? All of these issues would have understandably persuaded the Japanese to "withhold comment."

The final question that must be answered in order to shed light on the decision to use the bomb was whether the Americans were aware of the issues the Japanese were grappling with, causing them to delay issuing an immediate response to the proclamation. After studying all the documentation that had been released as of 1995, Gar Alperovitz concluded that:

> There is no longer much doubt that U.S. policy-makers were aware that what was going on inside the Japanese government was an intense effort to figure out just what the Potsdam Proclamation meant—and what precisely, was being demanded of it

Truman's Choice

On August 6, 1945, at 8:15 a.m., a large mushroom cloud appeared over Hiroshima and approximately 100,000 people perished immediately, some of whom simply evaporated from the intense heat. Thousands more died later from burns, shock, and radiation poisoning. The number who were not killed immediately but who died in later years from high doses of radiation is not known.

On August 7, 1945, the Japanese were still desperately trying to contact the Soviets for a clarification of their position. When Togo Shigenori, Japanese Foreign Minister, was informed of the bombing of Hiroshima, he asked to meet with the Emperor who had resigned himself to the fact that Japan must surrender. A meeting of the highest six officials was called for

August 8 but, since army leaders were unable to attend, the meeting was postponed until August 9.

On August 8, the Soviet Union declared war on Japan and the next day they sent troops across the Manchurian border. On the next day, August 9, another large cloud appeared over Nagasaki and 35,000 more people perished immediately, followed by an unknown number of deaths from the same causes as stated above.

Meetings of the "Big Six" persisted all day on August 9, during which time, news of the bombing of Nagasaki became known. Prime Minister Suzuki asked the Emperor to intervene and lend his support to the proposal to accept the allied proclamation on the condition that "...the declaration does not comprise any demand which prejudices the prerogatives of His Majesty as a sovereign ruler." Truman accepted the offer and hence the irony of granting the one condition that was a major obstacle to Japanese acceptance before the dropping of the two bombs.

Several arguments have been propounded to justify the use of the atomic weapon to end the war. The most common argument to justify using the bomb is based on the theory of minimizing the loss of lives. It was previously noted that almost all the American military leaders did not accept this theory nor had they engaged in any real studies to determine its validity. It can also be argued that it would have cost nothing to modify the surrender terms to preserve the Emperor to ascertain whether the Japanese would have surrendered.

It can also be argued that some kind of demonstration of the bomb for the Japanese leadership would have convinced them of the futility of continuing to fight. The defenders of this argument would have called attention to the fanaticism of the Japanese and their willingness to die rather than surrender. There is no evidence that they would have fought to the death once they recognized the futility of fighting any further and that the throne was safe. Recall that after the battle in Okinawa, Japanese soldiers did surrender. Preserving the throne would have allowed the Japanese to surrender with honour.

Hatred of the Japanese is sometimes cited as an explanation for dropping the bomb. After Pearl Harbor and the fierce and bloody battles in the Pacific where many American lives were lost, it is not surprising that this argument might carry some weight. According to Michael Lyons in *World War II: A Short History*:

Hatred for the Japanese was even more pronounced [than for the Germans]. It no doubt had its basis to some extent in racism. Wartime propaganda portrayed the "Japs" as vicious, bloodthirsty, even subhuman, a theme that every Hollywood film about the Pacific war featured during this period.

President Truman's attitude toward the Japanese is revealed in a letter to Senator Richard Russell on August 9, 1945:

I know that Japan is a terribly cruel and uncivilized nation in warfare but I can't bring myself to believe that, because they are beasts, we ourselves should act in the same manner. (Harry Truman's Diary and Papers)

There are clear indications that apprehension of Soviet power and influence after the war was a major factor in determining whether or not to use the bomb. The apprehension was felt by many but was clearly a grave concern of Secretary of State J. Byrnes as well as President Truman. All other alternatives, such as a demonstration of the new bomb in an uninhabited location or simply a warning were ruled out so that Truman's could clearly demonstrate the new highly destructive weapon for the Soviets. President Truman was well aware of the fact that most of his advisors believed that the war could have been ended without using the bomb.

The documentary evidence demonstrates that Truman and Byrnes removed the assurance about the Emperor in full knowledge that the Japanese would not accept an unconditional surrender. He made no attempt to contact the Japanese about the surrender terms or about their lack of response to the proclamation, which he chose to interpret as a rejection. The fact that Truman preserved the institution of emperor after the Japanese surrendered raises questions about his motives in not offering to preserve the throne before the surrender.

A number of military leaders criticized President Truman for using the atom bomb. For example:

- "The first atomic bomb was an unnecessary experiment…It was a mistake ever to drop it…(the scientists) had this toy and they wanted to try it out, so they dropped it…It killed a lot of Japs, but the Japs had put out a lot of peace feelers through Russia long before." (Admiral William "Bull" Halsey, commander of the Third Fleet)

- "…Both felt Japan would surrender without use of the

bomb, and neither knew why a second bomb was used." (W. Averill Harriman in conversation with General Carl "Tooey" Spaatz)

- "I voiced…my grave misgivings, first on the basis of my belief that Japan was already defeated and that dropping the bomb was completely unnecessary and secondly because …the use of a weapon whose employment was, I thought no longer mandatory as a measure to save American lives." (General Dwight D. Eisenhower)

- "…I felt that it was an unnecessary loss of civilian life…We had them beaten. They hadn't enough food, they couldn't do anything." (Fleet Admiral Chester W. Nimitz, commander in chief of the Pacific Fleet, quoted by his widow)

- "Especially it is good to see the truth told about the last days of the war with Japan…I was with the fleet during that period; and every officer in the fleet knew that Japan would eventually capitulate from…the tight blockade. I too felt strongly that it was a mistake to drop the atom bombs, especially without warning." (Rear Admiral Richard Byrd)

- "[Henry H.] Arnold's [Commanding General of the US Army Air Forces] view was that it (dropping the atomic bomb) was unnecessary. He said that he knew that the Japanese wanted peace. There were political implications in the decision…." (Lieutenant General Ira C. Eaker, Arnolds deputy)

- "…he saw no military justification for the dropping of the bomb. The war might have ended weeks earlier, he said, if the United States had agreed, as it did later anyway, to the retention of the institution of the emperor." (Norman Cousins, from an interview with MacArthur)

- "…we have enormous factors in our favour and any step that can be taken to translate those advantages into a prompt and successful conclusion to the war should be taken. I have already indicated in my memorandum to you of 2 July 1945, the reasons which impel me to urge that warnings be delivered to Japan, designed to bring about her capitulation as quickly as possible." And "I then spoke of the importance which I attributed to the reassurance of the Japanese on the continuance of their dynasty, and I felt that the insertion of that in the formal warning was important and might be just the thing that would make or break their acceptance..." (Secretary of War Henry L. Stimson)

These quotes, and others given previously from such people as Admiral William D. Leahy, President of the Joint Chiefs of Staff, Major General Curtis E. LeMay, US Army Air Forces, and Rear Admiral Lewis L. Strauss, Special Assistant to the Secretary of the Navy serve a purpose beyond revealing the opinions of prominent people involved in the war effort. The opinion of these people is critical in assessing the extent to which Truman lied about his motivation to drop the bomb. Even given Truman's knowledge of Japan's peace feelers and of the reverence with which the Japanese people viewed the Emperor, there is, however, a more compelling reason to condemn his decision. As a leader who was about to make a momentous decision, it was incumbent on him to seek the advice of the most knowledgeable and expert people in his administration. As the above quotes indicate, these top advisors, including the Secretary of War and Chairman of the Joint Chiefs of Staff, opposed his decision. Truman's failure to seek advice on many of the important issues, such as minimizing the loss of life, clearly establishes that President Truman was basing his decision on other criteria. The other criteria were to intimidate a new dangerous enemy in a post-World War II bipolar world. The war clearly could have ended quickly without dropping two atomic weapons. Minimizing the loss of life was not a criterion. It seems clear from the evidence that Truman was determined to drop the bomb. By giving the Japanese the choice between unconditional surrender and dire consequences and by allowing only a short period for a response, dropping the bomb became inevitable. The real choice for the Japanese was either the loss of the throne or more bombing. There were unaware of the atomic weapons and therefore could not appreciate the extent of "dire consequences." They also needed time to correctly interpret the meaning of the declaration and to assess the Soviet's intentions.

There are two ways to assess whether President Truman committed crimes against humanity.

The first is the Charter of the International Military Tribunal for the Nuremberg trials which applies to this case. President Truman violated the following clauses in the Charter of the International Military Tribunal:

Article 6

  b.   War Crimes: namely violations of the laws or customs of war. Such violations shall include...murder, ill-treatment...of civilian population...wanton destruction of cities, towns, or villages, or devastation not justified by military necessity;

  c.   Crimes against Humanity: namely, murder, extermination.... of civilian population...

The other way to evaluate President Truman's culpability is to apply international laws which were created after the end of WW II. He violated the following clauses in the Geneva Conventions:

  1.   Convention IV, Part 1, Article 3, clause 1,—protection of civilians;

  2.   Convention IV, Chapter III, article 52—protection of non-military objects:

  3.   Protocol I, Chapter II, Article 51, clause 4—indiscriminate attacks.

President Truman lied to the American people about his motives for dropping the two atomic bombs. He also misled the public about the nature of the first target. In a radio speech on August 9, 1945, he gave assurances that "The world will note that the first atomic bomb was dropped on Hiroshima, a military base." (Public Papers of the Presidents of the United States) The killing of over 100,000 civilians, the devastation of two cities, the deaths and diseases resulting from radiation poisoning, and the ominous precedent of using nuclear weapons are categorically crimes against humanity.

CHAPTER 3

THE FIRST BANANA REPUBLIC

EISENHOWER'S DEDICATION TO DESTROYING DEMOCRACY IN GUATEMALA

Under the pretext of the Cold War between the U.S. and Soviet Union, both superpowers extended their empires ostensibly to protect the countries they invaded. One example where fighting communism was used as a cover for overthrowing a democratically elected government is Guatemala the cost of which was to set in motion decades of human rights violations that killed over 200,000 civilians to date, not an inconsequential crime that President Eisenhower started.

Presidential lying isn't some lonesome activity of wacko politicians but is deeply interwoven throughout the government, instigated often, though not always, by its corporate connections. In the case of Guatemala, the cooperation of many different agencies and departments of the government were able to overthrow the government of Guatemala by essentially a hoax.

In 1954, the American government successfully orchestrated the overthrow of the freely elected government of Jacobo Arbenz in Guatemala and replaced him with their hand-picked alternative. It is essential to understand the dynamics of the cold war in order to understand the rationale for this particular American foreign policy.

The Beginnings of Democracy Become Victim to the Cold War

At the beginning of World War I, in 1914, Russia was an ally of Britain, France, and the United States. For three years, Russia fought shoulder to shoulder with its allies but ultimately, its inferior military could no longer hold off the Germans. There was growing dissatisfaction with the government's conduct of the war and on March 19, 1917, Tsar Nicholas II abdicated his throne. The result was a transformation from a tsarist autocracy to a government by the Bolsheviks, a small radical wing of the Russian Socialists. To support their ally, the Allied forces dispatched troops to Russia to fend off the Germans with whom the Bolsheviks shortly thereafter struck a peace agreement. Events in Russia so alarmed France, Britain, Japan, the United States, and Canada that they deployed 180,000 troops in Russia and provided money and guns to the major opposition group, the White Russians, in an attempt to overthrow the Bolsheviks. Fear of the Bolshevik revolution was based on the fear that:

> ...beneath the Marxist rhetoric was a highly disciplined, highly centralized party grasping at every lever of power it could secure. Motivated by the distant goal of a perfect world, it did not care what methods it used. (Margaret MacMillan, *Paris 1919: Six Months That Changed The World*)

Fear of the Soviet Union and communism deepened between the two world wars. One manifestation of that fear was the "red scare" of the 1920s. This mistrust did not prevent the Soviet Union from eventually joining the allies to battle their common enemy, Nazi Germany, in World War II. The United States government knew at the conclusion of WW II that the Soviet Union would become a major threat. As the war was winding down, both the Americans and Soviets positioned themselves to gain every advantage possible for the post-war period including the expansion of their spheres of influence. For example, the Soviet Union timed its declaration of war against Japan so as to be in a position to acquire as much Japanese territory as possible.

No sooner had World War II reached its conclusion than the Cold War appeared on the horizon. The world became divided between two superpowers that competed, mostly in the developing world, for territory and friendly governments. Since the beginning of the Cold War the U.S. government engendered fear of communism in the United States and then exploited this fear for imperial expansion. Communist threats magically surfaced everywhere forcing the U.S. to save the world from communism. Guatemala, Nicaragua, the Dominican Republic and Jamaica to name a few became threats to U.S. security. Notwithstanding the fear of a growing Communist Empire, the expansion of the American Empire was frequently unrelated to a real communist threat but was based on a determination to gain control over countries that had something the United States wanted such as resources or something the United States feared such as an alternative social and economic model.

American cold war policy was defined in the "Report by the Secretaries of State and Defense on 'United States Objectives for National Security'" or NSC-68. According to Richard H. Immerman, in *The CIA in Guatemala: The Foreign Policy of Intervention*:

> ...its [NSC-68] basic premise was that the world was divided into two

antithetical camps, led by the United States and the Soviet Union. The principal objective of the Soviet camp was to acquire absolute hegemony; thus conflict between the two systems was endemic. Only when one side emerged as the clear victor would this conflict abate. And the struggle would be fierce.

Cold warriors in Washington believed that:

> ...its [Kremlin] master plan for world domination was nothing so gross as an invasion of Western Europe or dropping bombs on the United States. The ever more subtle-one could say fiendishly clever-plan was for subversion... from the inside...country by country...throughout the Third World...eventually surrounding and strangling the First World...verily an International Communist Conspiracy, "a conspiracy," said Senator McCarthy, "on a scale so immense as to dwarf any previous such venture in the history of man."

The real issue was not so much about subversion from within as it was about developing countries implementing reformist, socialist, nationalist, or non-market policies. For example, nationalist ambitions in a developing country where the government sought to become independent of Washington's influence were usually interpreted on the surface as communist subversion whereas the greater threat was a weakening of the American sphere of influence. As well, redistributing wealth or land was usually a sign that the government was apparently poisoned by communist subversion. Gabriel Kolko, in *Confronting the Third World: United States Foreign Policy 1945–1980,* points out that:

> Both privately and publicly, each [Eisenhower and Truman] attributed to the Russians a transcendent ability to shape events in the most remote countries, and even when they did not initiate them they almost invariably knew how to exploit them...Russia "seeks world rule through the domination of all governments by the International Communist Party" as John Foster Dulles typically put it in 1957. Such conspiracies included "extreme nationalism" as one of its tools. And he found their alleged ability "to get control of mass movements" uncanny.

According to a number of scholars, the hypothesis that international Communism infiltrated developing world political and economic structures for the purpose of establishing a communist government was inaccurate and missed the real motivations for American foreign policy which was to expand the American Empire.

One possible rationale for American anti-communist policies was their notion that a government which implemented a social and economic system fundamentally different from the U.S. system must be infiltrated with communist conspirators. Governments which attempted to construct an economic system which was not based on the market system threatened the sanctity of the United States social and economic system which, in fact, serves the interests of the wealthy. The fear was that an alternative system that was perceived as more fair and equitable might undermine faith in the American system. The fear was well founded since today the United States has one of the highest poverty rates, infant mortality rates, incarceration rates, and murder rates in the industrialized world. It also has some of the poorest educational, health-care, and welfare systems. So when freely elected governments in Nicaragua or Guatemala implemented progressive land reforms, labour laws, and welfare systems that benefited everyone, they evoked fear in American elites that such ideas might become infectious. To discredit governments that posed these threats, the U.S. government condemned them as having been infiltrated by Communists. The United States claim that Nicaragua and Guatemala were threats to the U.S. because of communist infiltration was ludicrous. When President Reagan warned that Nicaragua was only two days from Brownsville Texas, his administration's intention was not to warn of a real threat (a silly notion) to U.S. security, but to evoke fear in order to justify intervention. William Blum, in *Killing Hope: U.S. Military and CIA Intervention Since World War II,* points out that:

> In cases such as the above-mentioned Grenada, El Salvador, and Nicaragua, even if the particular target of intervention does not present an immediate lucrative economic opportunity for American multinationals, the target's socialist-revolutionary program and rhetoric does present a threat and a challenge, which the United States has repeatedly felt obliged to stamp out, to maintain the *principle,* and as a warning to others; for what the US has always feared from the Third World is the emergence of a good example: a flourishing socialist society independent of Washington.

Noam Chomsky, in *Understanding Power: The Indispensable Chomsky,* echoes the same theme when he asks:

> Why do we have to get rid of the Sandinistas in Nicaragua? In reality it's not because anybody really thinks that they're a communist power about to conquer the Hemisphere—it's because they were carrying out social programs that were beginning to succeed, and which would have appealed to other people in Latin America who want the same things.

Gabriel Kolko, in *Confronting the Third War,* argues that:

Such information [social and economic conditions in various Third World nations] will allow one to transcend those mystifying Cold War shibboleths that describe America's difficulties merely as a struggle with Communism. It will also enable one to comprehend far better the real nature of U.S. goals. For out of these social structures and class forms in the Third World came those forces that have challenged U.S. goals and interests...

Another possible analysis of American anti-communist policies interprets the instilling of fear of Communism as a justification for excessive spending on defence. Spending on defence was a method for subsidizing research without inviting criticism of corporate welfare. The government would hand out huge sums of money to defence industries for research and the spin-offs were often transferred to the private sector. Transferring the new technologies developed by defence industries to the private sector was a scheme for indirectly subsidizing private sector research. Another factor in this analysis was the aggressive lobbying by defence industries for the funding of new technologies and the bribing of congressmen by, for example, offering to build factories in their districts. Noam Chomsky, in *Perspectives on Power: Reflections on Human Nature and the Social Order,* explains that:

As long as the fable [that flourishing defence industries were ostensibly operating on a purely competitive basis but were, in fact, recipients of government largesse] could be sustained, the Cold War provided the pretext, often as conscious fraud. The first Secretary of the Air Force, Stuart Symington, put the matter plainly in January 1948: "The word to talk was not 'subsidy'; the word to talk was 'security'.... There as elsewhere, the 'private sector' relies extensively on welfare payments, subsidies often called 'security'.

Also, Edward Herman, in *Beyond Hypocrisy: Decoding the News in the Age of Propaganda,* offers the same analysis that:

A basic feature of the MIC [Military-Industrial Complex] is that it keeps developing weapons that the contractors want to sell. The point is to command resources, maintain and enlarge profits, and produce jobs. Missions are needed to justify weapons acquisition, and they are usually couched in terms of some threat, some niche that has to be filled to protect our national security.

William Blum, in *Killing Hope,* suggests that:

....one must examine the role of the military-industrial-intelligence complex. The members of this network need enemies—the military and the CIA [Central Intelligence Agency]—because enemies are their reason d'etre; industry, specifically the defense contractors, because enemies are to be fought with increasingly sophisticated weaponry and aircraft systems...The executives of these corporations...who continue to use their positions, their wealth, and their influence…to nourish and to perpetuate the fear of communism, the enemy…

This analysis has sometimes been extended further, concluding that anti-communism was an excuse for sustaining a war economy to ensure continuing growth. In *Perspectives on Power*, Noam Chomsky concludes that:

> …what finally worked [to reconstruct the rich societies] was a vast rearmament program, what historian William Borden calls "international military Keynesianism" in his important work on postwar reconstruction (*The Pacific Alliance*). The point was well understood by the business world. Reflecting the general understanding, the *Magazine of Wall Street* saw military spending as a way to "inject new strength into the entire economy"…

This analysis is probably true but it needs to be understood in the larger context of expanding the American Empire. To ensure minimal opposition, the United States needed to maintain, by far, the most advanced military machine in the world.

American anti-communist foreign policy, according to another possible analysis, was used to protect American corporate interests, particularly in developing countries where governments sometimes either nationalized American multinationals or interfered with U.S. multinational's ability to maximize their profits. When Chile nationalized two American copper corporations, Anaconda and Kennecott Copper, the government was overthrown with the help of the CIA. As well, when Guatemala nationalized some idle land belonging to the United Fruit Company, its government was overthrown. In *Waging Unconventional Warfare: Guatemala, the Congo, and the Cubans*, this is described as:

> …a high-pressure diplomatic and propaganda offensive, intended to justify intervention in Guatemala, paralleled prototype covert operation combining psychological warfare, mercenary paramilitary forces, and sanitized airpower. The elected Arbenz government had antagonized the United States through its economic policies notably land reform and labor legislation impinging on American companies…

Noam Chomsky, in *What Uncle Sam Really Wants,* refers to a CIA memorandum which states that:

> The "radical and nationalist policies" of the democratic capitalist government including the "persecution of foreign economic interests, especially the United Fruit Company," had gained "the support or acquiescence of almost all Guatemalans." The government was proceeding to mobilize the hitherto politically inert peasantry while undermining the power of large landowners.

This analysis is consistent with the theory that the motivation was to expand the American Empire. The function of the Empire was to serve American corporate interests.

An alternative analysis of American anti-communist policies was the belief that nationalism, economic reforms, land reforms, and any policies that threaten the interests of American corporations are essentially a symptom of the real threat: communist infiltration of developing countries to advance the cause of International Communism. Richard H. Immerman explains in *The CIA in Guatemala* that:

> Washington viewed government programs such as agrarian reform bills, which damaged United States investments, as symptoms of a much larger problem. They were "secondary problems," Assistant Secretary of State John Moors Cabot explained to Guatemala's ambassador to the United States, Guillermo Toriello Garrido, in 1953. The larger problem was communism... John Foster Dulles put it best: "If the United Fruit matter were settled...the problem would remain just as it is today as far as the presence of communist infiltration in Guatemala is concerned."

Again, this theory is consistent with the theory about expanding the Empire. American corporate interests would be threatened by an alternative system whose main purpose was to serve the people.

Fear of infiltration of Communism in Guatemala and its diffusion to the other countries in the hemisphere was the official justification for American intervention in Guatemala. The analysis of why the U.S. intervened in Guatemala is complicated by the fact that the Guatemalan government confiscated some land belonging to a major American corporation, the United Fruit Company. The United Fruit Company, which had many connections with leading officials in the Eisenhower administration, complained bitterly about the actions of the Guatemalan government.

Struggle Between American Supported Totalitarianism and Democracy

The history of Guatemala is essential to understanding the issues surrounding presidential decision-making and the lying that goes with it. Prior to the Spanish conquest, Guatemala was a major centre of the Maya civilization which was advanced in the arts, science, astronomy, and social organization. Their lack of military sophistication rendered them very vulnerable to Hernán Cortés of the Spanish Empire. It remained a part of the Spanish Empire until a struggle throughout Latin America brought independence to Guatemala in 1821.

The threat of assimilation with Mexico propelled Guatemala to organize a federation of Central American Republics. The federation created a National Constituent Assembly and drafted a constitution. Various conflicts resulted in the disintegration of the federation following which Guatemala was ruled by a series of dictators beginning with Rafael Carrera in 1838. The advent of industrialization introduced a middle class into Guatemala and the autocratic ruler, Justo Rufino Barrios, president from 1873 to 1885, handed them land belonging to the conservative landowners. During the next 72 years, the middle class adopted the values of the conservative landlords and supported them politically and economically.

The new ruling elite, consisting of the landowners and middle class, demonstrated no interest in improving the lives of the Mayans who constituted almost 70% of the population. They were marginalized and exploited and the ongoing expropriation of their land made many of them dependent on the landowners who used them as a cheap source of labour to harvest their crops. Government policies worsened the condition of the Mayans and widened the gap between the rich and the poor.

Seventy percent of the land was owned by only 2.2% of the population. Approximately one-third of the land was considered arable while half of the land owned by large landowners was not in use. Conditions were so poor for the Mayans that only 60% of newborn babies survived. Richard H. Immerman, in *The CIA in Guatemala* notes that:

> The rigidly hierarchical and social structure in Guatemala gave rise to extreme inequality and poverty; extreme even by Latin American standards... Guatemala's economy exhibited many of feudalisms most salient features. The racist oppression and economic suppression of the Maya created a virtual serf class and in Guatemala, class and ethnic origin were virtually synonymous.

Although a large majority of people in Guatemala lived in abject poverty, a small minority of the population flourished. These were the landowners and high-ranking employees of several giant American corporations such as the United Fruit Company whose major crop was bananas. The United Fruit Company was originally the Boston Fruit Company founded by Minor C. Keith whose original project was to build railways in Central America. In order to finance his railway business he began to sell bananas and by 1883 owned three banana companies which became known as the United Fruit

Company in 1899. It had become the largest producers of bananas in the world. Much of the cultivated land was providing food for the United States and not for the hungry people of Guatemala.

United Fruit Company's president persuaded other landowners to support Jorge Ubico for president in the mid-nineteen thirties. The United Fruit Company was then granted more land and a 99-year lease on all its land which now comprised half of the land in Guatemala. The Company was also relieved of virtually any taxation, import duties, and export taxes and was allowed to greatly undervalue the worth of its land for taxation purposes. By 1936, the Company paid virtually no taxes.

Since the United Fruit Company was such a significant force in the Guatemalan economy, these benefits deprived the government of a large source of revenue which prevented it from implementing measures to assist the poor.

The depression and World War II exacerbated the hardship of the poor, most of whom were Mayans. Falling coffee and banana prices and the refusal of Europe to buy Guatemalan exports doomed the economy to stagnation resulting in reduced state spending and higher unemployment.

The policies of Ubico and exploitation by the United Fruit Company, combined with the economic stagnation and conditions of the poor, provoked a backlash. Ubico called those organizing against him communists and ordered guards to stand on each street corner and enhance the security of the presidential palace. He claimed that the radical opponents of his regime were a threat to stability and order and that democracy was an unaffordable luxury. He instilled terror among the people by arbitrarily arresting suspected agitators who were either shot on the spot or tortured in prison to deter an uprising. Many of the victims were prominent citizens, workers, and students. It is important to note that Ubico's suppression of his own people was to some extent possible because of the military equipment supplied by the United States.

Ubico eliminated the small degree of self-control the Mayans enjoyed and installed an absolute dictator in each village. He imposed a head tax on Mayan males and if they failed to pay, he forced them to work without wages on road construction. Most Mayans could not afford the head tax. To strengthen the economy he attempted to balance the budget and as a result unemployment increased. The final straw was Decree 2795, which authorized landowners to shoot any Mayan on their land despite the fact that they were either hunting or fishing for food.

Revolutionary movements in El Salvador and Ecuador alarmed Ubico to the point where he instituted more authoritarian methods and attempted to eliminate dissent. Despite his attempt to suppress dissent within the universities and to terrorize students, they became more determined to fight for their rights and freedoms. When students endeavored to demonstrate, Ubico ordered the army to open fire. When lawyers, merchants, professionals and shopkeepers joined the protesters, the army, recognizing the strength of the opposition, forced Ubico to resign.

The army's general staff put together a triumvirate whose purpose was to convene the national assembly in order to elect a new president. The general staff pressured the elected officials to vote for General Federico Ponce Vaides, a member of the triumvirate. Ponce, a puppet of Ubico, implemented oppressive measures and abandoned any pretense of democracy, provoking resentment of another undemocratic and brutal dictatorship. Opposition groups organized again to overthrow the government. Killing the editor of the leading daily newspaper, who had criticized government forces, provoked the protesters into fierce resistance. Then on October 19, 1944, a contingent of army officers led by Jacobo Arbenz Guzman and Major Francisco Javier Araña along with students and the Honor Guard Battalion [Guatemala National Guard] revolted against Ponce forcing him to seek asylum in the Mexican embassy. The victory was supported by a vast majority of the people of Guatemala who were hopeful that the new government would implement programs which served their interests rather than only the interests of the wealthy landowners.

The revolution lived up to its expectations and called for an election before the end of the year. Neither of the two front-runners represented the military, thus alleviating any fears of another military junta. Juan José Arévalo who was previously in the Ministry of Education and fled the country because of his criticism of Ubico, was the popular movement's favourite candidate partly because he had no associations with the former dictatorship. On December 19, 1944, Arévalo won by a landslide and his inauguration ushered in a period of social and economic reform.

Arévalo wasted no time in creating a set of programs to alleviate poverty, illiteracy, unfair land distribution, poor health-care, and neglect of the Mayans. He also embarked on a set of reforms to democratize the political process.

His political reforms were driven by the need to decentralize power and distribute it in such a way that ensured it would not be concentrated in any one branch of government. One method of achieving this aim was to borrow the principle of separation of powers from the American system and divide authority among the legislative, executive, and judicial branches of government. The new constitution granted universal suffrage and included a bill of rights which guaranteed freedom of expression, press, and assembly.

Agrarian reform was desperately needed to distribute land fairly, to increase the efficiency of farming, and to free a sufficient number of farmers so that they would be available to work as industrialization expanded. To accomplish these goals, he implemented a set of controls for land rents and forced landowners to rent out uncultivated land at no more than five percent of the value of the crops produced.

His labour laws were designed to protect workers from arbitrary treatment by management. Forced labour, which included the vagrancy laws, was abolished and dismissal was limited to acts of violence, drunkenness, and willful injury to property. The new labour code prohibited any kind of discrimination in the workplace, required labour-management contracts, collective bargaining, and guaranteed the right to organize.

Arévalo understood the desperate need for social reform to address the abject poverty of a majority of the population. He created the Commission of Social Security to extend benefits to those in need and set up the Guatemalan Institute for Social Security which was financed by workers, employers, and the state.

To improve health-care in Guatemala, Arévalo augmented the Ministry of Public Health and Assistance, placed nurses in White Cross clinics, initiated vaccination programs, and installed water-filtering systems in rural areas.

One of his top priorities was to improve the educational system. He spent over seven million dollars on educational projects, created the National Literacy Committee, built regular, technical, and adult schools, and increased the pay of teachers.

Washington's reaction to these developments in Guatemala bordered on indifference. The programs of Arévalo seemed fairly benign in terms of United States' interests and none of them seemed particularly threatening although his labour codes, minimum wage laws, and land reforms were of concern to some American firms. According to Richard H. Immerman in *The CIA in Guatemala*:

> They [the writings of Arévalo] did not seem to frighten many in the United States. Even during this early cold war period, analysts tended to overlook Arévalo's socialism, perceiving him as some kind of starry-eyed reformer…Arévalo had mentioned virtually every one of these programs [the ones he implemented after becoming president] in his 1944 campaign; there was no radical shift to the left, as commentators would later write.

Arévalo was not a communist but a reformer who genuinely wanted to help his people. Gabriel Kolko, in *Confronting the Third World*, describes him and his followers as:

> This typical group of middle-class officers was, like many others in the hemisphere, anti-United States and for mild but long overdue reforms. Arévalo was anti-Marxist but also a committed reformer and idealist.

Richard H. Immerman, in *The CIA in Guatemala*, concludes that:

> Arévalo likewise rejected classical Marxism. He rejected class struggle and emphasized the ideal of social harmony, fraternity, and the reconciliation of any antagonistic interests. He found the Marxist concept that human nature is essentially materially predetermined either invalid or, at the very least extremely limited and he believed that a genuinely democratic government must represent the legitimate aspirations of all classes: the capitalists, the professionals, and the workers.

Understanding Arévalo's political outlook, his base of support and his social and economic policies is critical to evaluating accusations that he was a communist lackey whose government was a threat to the entire region.

Arévalo's term as president [there was a one-term limitation for president] was anything but smooth as landowners and business owners were opposed to his policies which they believed were an attack on the upper class and also communist in nature. They were determined to field their own candidate in the next election and chose Francisco Javier Araña, Arévalo's chief of staff. Araña endeavoured to organize a revolt before the next election fearing a loss to Arbenz whose support included organized labour and the agricultural community except for the major landowners. He accused Arbenz of being a communist traitor but his revolt backfired when the assembly charged him with treason and ordered his arrest. Before he could be arrested, Araña was assassinated by twenty men. Later the CIA accused Arbenz of the assassination, although their main witness was

Araña's chauffeur who was unable to connect Arbenz to the assassination plot or explain how he escaped the assassins' bullets.

Arbenz won the next election in 1951 with the support of everyone but the upper class receiving 60 percent of the vote. His intention was to expand the reforms and programs which were introduced by Arévalo. His objectives were to create an independent modern industrial economy in order to raise the living standards of Guatemalans and to reach out to the Mayan population in order to assess what they wanted.

While his programs were egalitarian, they were not communist in nature. He believed in capitalism with a heart. Richard H. Immerman, in *The CIA in Guatemala,* observed that:

> ...his emphasis would be on capitalistic modernization, relying essentially on the recommendations made by the IBRD [International Bank for Reconstruction and Development] study mission. In his inaugural address, he explained that the basic policy of his administration would be to "to convert Guatemala from a country bound by a predominately feudal economy into a modern, capitalist one." He would encourage private initiative, he would encourage the accumulation of private capital, and he would encourage the influx of foreign investments and technology. This was virtually the same program announced by Arévalo at his inauguration.

William Blum, in *Killing Hope,* points out that:

> The Guatemalan president, who took office in March 1951 after being elected by a wide margin, had no special contact or spiritual/ideological ties with the Soviet Union or the rest of the Communist bloc. Although American policymakers and the American press, explicitly and implicitly, often labeled Arbenz a Communist, there were those in Washington who knew better, at least during their more dispassionate moments. Under Arbenz's administration, Guatemala had voted at the United Nations so closely with the United States on issues of "Soviet Imperialism" that a state department group planning Arbenz's overthrow concluded that propaganda concerning Guatemala's UN record "would not be particularly helpful in our case".

The large landowners constituted 2.2% of the population but owned 70% of the land. Given the fact that 50% of farmers occupied small plots of land under four acres, farming in Guatemala faced severe impediments. Despite the fact that over-cultivation exhausted the land resulting in small yields small farmers could not afford to buy fertilizer. Also contributing to the low yields was the lack of mechanization due to inadequate transportation facilities. As well, the renters or farmers on these small plots had to pay 50 to 60% of their crops to their landowners.

All these problems in agriculture relegated small farmers, who constituted the majority of the population, to abject poverty. Land reform was meant to serve a number of purposes. First, it was important to distribute more land to farmers, some of whom had no land. Second, farms needed to be modernized to increase their yield so that farmers could afford fertilizer and feed their families. Third, in order to facilitate industrialization, farmers had to be freed from the land to be available to work in factories.

A reform bill was crafted to redistribute the use of the land so that most of the land was not devoted to coffee and bananas which were export crops. As well, these crops demanded a large number of workers at harvest time depriving the factories of potential workers. The overuse of the land for these crops meant that Guatemalans had to depend on imports for food leading to higher food prices. Finally, the practice of allowing thousands of acres of land to lie fallow each year in order to replenish the soil had to be replaced with diversifying land use and redistributing the land more efficiently.

An example of the frustration of the Arbenz government over idle land was the fact that only 15% of the 550,000 acres of the United Fruit Company's land was under cultivation. According to the United Fruit Company, the land had to remain fallow so that it could be flooded periodically to destroy the fungus-caused Panamanian disease to which bananas were particularly vulnerable. Guatemalan experts argued that since it takes ten years for this fungus to infect healthy land, the Company could double its acreage under cultivation and still have 110 years worth in reserve. Furthermore, the government argued that its land reform policies were not discriminatory against the Company but were addressing the plight of the poor peasants whose plots were inadequate to feed their families. The plan for agricultural reform was based on a study from the previous administration which drew on the advice of experts from all over Latin America who agreed that farming methods in Guatemala had to be replaced with more modern, capitalistic methods.

Part of the plan was to redistribute some of the idle land on large farms. In 1950, the 32 largest farms totaled 1,719,740 acres of which 1,575,181 were idle according to the study completed by Arévalo. (Richard H. Immerman, *The CIA in Guatemala*)

Land reform, according to the plan of Arbenz was not to confiscate land from the wealthy landowners but to redistribute some of the idle land to poor peasants and to compensate the company according to the value of the land based on tax declarations. It was not the fault of the Arbenz government that the large landowners undervalued their land for tax purposes. In the end, as Gabriel Kolko, in *Confronting the Third World,* points out:

> The land was given to some 100,000 peasants, who eventually obtained about 1.5 million acres, 234,000 of which had belonged to the United Fruit Company.

Agrarian reform began immediately after it was passed unanimously by the assembly on June 17, 1952. More land was available for small farmers than in previous years but to assist the farmers even further, the government created the National Agricultural Bank to provide credit to those farmers who needed it. One of the outcomes of agrarian reform was that farmers were producing surpluses and selling it to local markets, thus increasing their purchasing power.

Washington's position toward Guatemala had begun to change after the revolution, particularly with every act of the Guatemalan Government that threatened U.S. corporate interests. It was a classical case of interpreting every attempt by the Guatemalan Government to improve conditions for its people as further proof that the government was infiltrated by communists whose ultimate aim was to take power and then infiltrate other countries in Latin America.

Labour codes were one of the first ostensible threats to American corporate interests. It raised suspicions in Washington about Guatemala succumbing to communist infiltrators. Beginning in 1946, a number of strikes were called against the United Fruit Company over wages, overtime, and vacations. One of the responses of the Company was to fire any workers who were actively involved. After the government threatened to confiscate some of the company's land, the company conceded but did not rehire the workers. Paying time and a half for overtime, granting workers ten days vacation every year, and paying $1.50 per day was not acceptable to the Company. Negotiations broke down and another strike occurred between 1948 and 1949. The United Fruit Company refused to negotiate in good faith and attacked the Labour Code as unfair despite the fact the Government was willing to send the dispute to arbitration. The United Fruit Company threatened to shut down its operations. In 1952, the Guatemalan labour court ordered the company to take back the workers who had been fired.

Washington's first reaction to events in Guatemala was that the government was discriminating against American companies and, therefore, threatening relations between the two countries. The CIA concluded that Guatemala was unfriendly to American corporations.

Even before the new labour codes, President Truman ordered the FBI to send agents to Guatemala to search for radical influences and assess the politics of both major and minor persons in the government. The FBI forwarded a number of reports to Washington in which the agents provided an analysis of the extent of communist infiltration. The objectivity of these reports was completely undermined by the fact that the sources of information were people who worked in the Ubico regime and who considered any activism to improve the lives of Guatemalans as subversive. Dictators in surrounding countries, such as Somoza in Nicaragua, who were clients of the United States and opposed to any progressive measures that might threaten their own positions continually condemned Guatemala as a communist threat. The American House Subcommittee on Communist Aggression was constantly identifying communists in the Guatemalan government. William Blum in *Killing Hope* reported that:

> The party formed by the communists…held four seats in Congress [in Guatemala], the smallest component of Arbenz's ruling coalition which commanded a total of 51 seats in the 1953-54 legislature. Communists held several important sub-cabinet posts but none was ever appointed to the cabinet.

Jim Huck, in *1954: Covert War in Guatemala,* also points out the lack of communist influence in the legislature by explaining that:

> In the 1953-1954 legislatures, Arbenz had a majority [government] and the communists only had 4 of 51 seats. But Secretary of State John Foster Dulles claimed that Guatemala was living under a "communism type of terrorism" and President Eisenhower portrayed the government in Guatemala as a "communist dictatorship."

William Blum noted that:

> The Soviet Union could be excused if it was somewhat bewildered by all the rhetoric for the Russians had scant interest in Guatemala, did not provide the country with any kind of military assistance, did not even maintain diplomatic relations with it, thus did not have the normally indispensable embassy from which to conduct such nefarious schemes.

Carlos Manuel Pellecer had held a number of positions in Guatemala including labour organizer for agricultural workers, secretary of the Guatemalan legation in Moscow, and head of the cultural missions to outlying regions in Guatemala to educate the Mayans. These positions, in addition to a comment about "Yankee imperialism", were sufficient evidence for Milton K. Wells, first secretary of the American Embassy in Guatemala, to report that Pellecer was "a communist in heart if not fact…at the same time these backward Indians get their ABC's, they get a shot of communism."

When the Korean War broke out 1950, Guatemala declared their solidarity with the United States and supported the relevant United Nations resolutions but, as with most Latin American countries, did not send troops to Korea. Assistant Secretary for Inter-American Affairs, Edward Miller, prohibited any Latin American country from sending troops unless they could supply a fully trained brigade. Nevertheless, President Eisenhower and others in his administration drew the conclusion that the lack of Guatemalan participation was strong evidence that Guatemala was under communist influence.

In 1947, the unions in Guatemala celebrated May Day by marching through the capital. May Day or International Labour Day is celebrated in many countries around the world but the United States treated the celebration in Guatemala as a symptom of Communism because International Labour Day is also celebrated in the Soviet Union.

The democratically elected President of Costa Rica, José Figueres, cooperated extensively with the CIA on a number of projects which included collaboration on a plan to eliminate the Dominican Republic's dictator, Trujillo. He also referred to the United States as "the standard-bearer of our cause" and was considered by the United States ambassador to Costa Rica as "the best advertising agency that the United Fruit Company could find in Latin America." On the other hand, Figueres was a nationalist, tried to persuade the U.S. to call off the Bay of Pigs, offered asylum to non-communists and communists alike, and received some support from the Guatemalan government. According to Noam Chomsky in *What Uncle Sam Really Wants,* "In the political rhetoric of the United States, this made him possibly a 'Communist.' So if Guatemala gave him money to help him win an election that showed that Guatemala supported Communists."

By the time that Arbenz implemented his new land reform program, Washington was completely convinced that the Soviet Union had successfully infiltrated the Arbenz administration and was preparing to take over the reigns of government as a stepping-stone to infiltrating other countries in the hemisphere.

As suspicions of Communism escalated, pressure in Washington intensified for some kind of response not only to the threat of Communism but also to the threat to American corporate interests. In 1950, Truman's administration decided that some action was needed but it was important that America's role be completely invisible. From the first action to the eventual overthrow of Arbenz, the American government was tenaciously committed to maintaining secrecy in order to prevent public knowledge of America's role.

The Coup

Truman took the first step by instituting a boycott of American military equipment to Guatemala. As the major supplier of military equipment to Guatemala, Washington hoped to minimize the risk to security in the hemisphere. Stronger measures were contemplated such as withholding assistance and canceling the agricultural research program. Finally, Truman withheld $850,000 that had been allocated for Guatemala. At this point, Truman had chosen to be patient and move slowly.

Another dimension of Washington's plan was to launch a propaganda campaign to create public awareness of events in Guatemala. Truman set up the Psychological Strategy Board. Truman's most effective propaganda weapon was the United Fruit Company's public relations counsel, Edward Bernays. He embarked on a campaign to clearly demonstrate the communist threat in Guatemala to the public. Bernays' greatest asset was the publisher of the *New York Times*, Arthur Hays Sulzberger. His Central American correspondent, Crede Calhoun, hired Will Lissner who wrote a number of stories with a powerful impact for the *New York Times* about the threat in Guatemala. Other major publications followed suit and published similar articles about Guatemala. In general, reporters were indoctrinated with cold war propaganda which shaped their perceptions of events and frequently determined how they framed their stories.

One of Bernays' coups was to invite a number of important publishers and editors on a fact-finding junket to Guatemala at the United Fruit Company's expense. Not only did the company's officials select the sights to be observed, but they were the major source of information for their guests (a forerunner of the press pools used in Iraq, 1991, and Panama, 1989).

Under Eisenhower's administration, the State Department established the United States Information Agency. William Blum, in *Killing Hope,* observed that the operations of the United States Information Agency commenced when it:

> ...began to place unattributed articles in foreign newspapers labeling particular Guatemalan officials as communist and referring to various actions by the Guatemala Government as "communist-inspired." In the few weeks before Arbenz's fall alone, more than 200 articles about Guatemala were written and placed in scores of Latin American newspapers...articles placed in one country were picked up by newspapers in other countries, either as a result of CIA payment or unwittingly because the story was of interest.

The objective of the propaganda campaign was to persuade the American public that Communist infiltration in Guatemala posed a threat to American security. Fear of communism was an easier sell than the real motive which was the U.S. determination to protect American corporate interests in Guatemala. One of the explanations for this determination was the close ties between the government and the corporate sector.

The connections between the Eisenhower government and the United Fruit Company created a dangerous conflict of interest. Following is a list of some of the connections:

- Secretary of State, John Foster Dulles, had been a partner with the Sullivan & Cromwell law firm which represented UFC (United Fruit Company);

- Former UFC president, Thomas Dudley was the brother of Eisenhower's first Assistant Secretary of State for Central America;

- Allen Dulles, brother of John Foster Dulles, Director of the CIA, was a Sullivan & Cromwell attorney doing litigation for UFC in the 1930s;

- John Cabot, Assistant Secretary of State for inter-American affairs and former Ambassador to Guatemala, held a substantial amount of stock in UFC;

- Thomas Cabot, brother of John Cabot had been president and director of UFC;

- John J. McLoy, Eisenhower's close friend, who as president of

the International Bank for Reconstruction and Development
ordered the study of Guatemala's agrarian difficulties, was a
director of UFC;

- Ann Whitman, Eisenhower's personal secretary, was the
  ex-wife of a UFC director and vice-president for public
  relations;

- Walter Bedell Smith, Under-secretary of State and former
  CIA director, was a director of UFC and helped plan the
  coup;

- Spruille Braden, Truman's former assistant secretary, was a
  company representative

- John McClintock worked for the State Department and had
  been a UFC's vice-president.

Despite the numerous connections between the Eisenhower
administration and the UFC, the company hired several prominent
lobbyists to persuade Washington to take action against Arbenz. Both the
lobbyists and representatives of the company had easy access to people
in the administration because of the above connections. Gabriel Kolko, in
Confronting the Third World, observed that:

> ...there was an intricate web of personal and political relations between
> United Fruit Company and many of the Republican and Democratic officials
> dealing with the Guatemala issue, the most direct being the former president
> of United Fruit's brother, John M. Cabot, who was Eisenhower's assistant
> secretary of state for Latin America. That United Fruit Company mobilized a
> highly effective lobby of former New Dealers, liberals, and the establishment
> press is an excellent illustration of how pressure groups have an impact...

The first plan to overthrow Arbenz was hatched in 1952, during the
Truman administration, when Somoza, the Nicaragua dictator, offered
to invade Guatemala if Washington would supply him with sufficient
arms. Truman explored the idea but was persuaded by Dean Acheson,
Secretary of State, to cancel the plan because its failure would have been an
embarrassment to the United States. Although Truman scrapped the plan,
Washington was now convinced that anything short of overthrowing Arbenz
would be ineffective in eradicating the Communist threat.

By the time that President Eisenhower assumed office, the momentum for removing Arbenz from office was virtually unstoppable. According to Gabriel Kolko, in *Confronting the Third World*:

> The principle of overthrowing the Arbenz government received the Eisenhower Administration's blessing immediately upon coming to office, and from this time onward it mounted a vast, sustained public-relations campaign to convince the U.S. public and the world that Guatemala had been taken over by communists. As before, United Fruit was involved in every phase of the administration's efforts...

Within months of assuming office, the Eisenhower administration began plotting the overthrow of the Arbenz government. The highest-ranking members of the White House, CIA, and State Department were involved in the planning and they were obsessed with preventing any of the details of the operation from becoming public knowledge. To maintain the utmost secrecy, documents were classified as top secret, the CIA burnt many of its papers, and anyone brought into the project was sworn to secrecy.

President Eisenhower instructed his brother Milton to travel to South America on a fact-finding mission to sell the importance of Latin America's solidarity to the American people. Despite the fact that he never visited Guatemala, Milton Eisenhower reported that there was communist infiltration there. Around the same time, the CIA arranged to send arms to disgruntled officers in the Guatemalan army and the United Fruit Company donated $64,000 in cash.

The team planning the operation decided to replace the current U.S. ambassador to Guatemala with someone who had the right temperament for such an aggressive intervention and who could coordinate operations in the field. John E. Peurifoy was selected for the post because he was considered dynamic and a man of action. One of his primary functions was to act as a liaison between the State Department and the CIA.

PBSUCCESS became the code name of the plot and its headquarters was set up in Opa Locka, Florida, on the outskirts of Miami. The estimate of the costs of the operation was about $7 million and it utilized 100 CIA agents. About 30 planes were stationed in Nicaragua, Honduras, and the Canal Zone, which were to be flown by American pilots. To reinforce the charges of Soviet infiltration, Soviet-marked weapons were acquired to be planted in Guatemala.

Once Arbenz was overthrown, the planners would need someone from the Guatemalan opposition to become leader who was acceptable to the United States. The CIA finally decided on Carlos Enrique Castillo Armas, who received military training in the U.S. and was the son of a wealthy landowner in Guatemala. He was also a supporter of Arãna when he attempted to overthrow the government.

One of PBSUCCESS's imperatives was to create a legal façade for their plot to overthrow Arbenz. The OAS (Organization of American States) could provide the necessary legitimacy for the operation and also the illusion that the United States was not acting unilaterally. Another imperative, according to President Eisenhower was:

> ...to marshal and crystallize Latin American public opinion on the issue. The opportunity presented itself at the Tenth Inter-American Conference of the Organization of American States (OAS) which met in Caracas, Venezuela, in March of 1954. (Dwight D. Eisenhower, *Mandate for Change*)

One of the obstacles which Washington had to overcome was the difference in the agenda of the United States and the Latin American nations. The Americans wanted to focus on a resolution condemning Communist intervention in the hemisphere while the other attendees were more interested in economic issues. To persuade the balance of the representatives at the conference to adopt the American agenda, John Foster Dulles, Secretary of State, used bribes and threats to coerce the other delegates to accept the U.S. agenda. Dulles not only needed the other Latin American countries' support for the resolution, but he also did not want them to interpret the resolution as a guise for authorizing intervention in Guatemala. To achieve this purpose, the draft proposal had to be carefully worded to conceal its real intent. The draft proposal was a "Declaration of Solidarity for the Preservation of the Political Integrity of the American States against International Communism." Dulles proposed that any threat of Communist domination or control to any signatory of the resolution called for "appropriate action in accordance with existing treaties." He also proposed an amendment stating that "This declaration of foreign policy made by the American Republics in relation to dangers originating outside the hemisphere..." referring to communist infiltration. Although only Guatemala voted against the resolution and Mexico abstained, the other countries voted in favour reluctantly because of their doubts about the communist threat in Guatemala. *Le Monde* in Paris summarized the vote as:

> Those who supported [the declaration] most enthusiastically were just those dictatorial governments whose power rests on a military junta and

on the official representatives of the great United States companies. These governments owe their existence solely to the protection of the United States. (Richard H. Immerman, *The CIA in Guatemala*)

The conference was a success because not only were the other 27 items on the agenda subordinated to the U.S. agenda but the resolution passed giving the Americans propaganda fodder. The State Department prepared a documentary focusing on Dulles's speech which was distributed to movie and television outlets and briefings which were provided for the media and public opinion leaders.

Arbenz was so alarmed at the U.S. shipments of arms to his neighbours and at the unmistakable signs that Washington was planning to overthrow his government that in an attempt to defend his country, he ordered a shipment of arms from Czechoslovakia. The shipment consisted of two thousand tons of small arms and light artillery pieces and was transported on a Swedish freighter which landed at Puerto Barrios. The minor boost to Guatemala's defences was vastly outweighed by the propaganda opportunity it bestowed on the American propaganda machine. Various members of the administration exploited the opportunity to instill fear in the public about the communist threat. Richard Immerman, in *The CIA in Guatemala*, refers to the alarmist rhetoric:

> Allen [Dulles] became a legislative liaison encouraging congressional leaders to speak out against this most recent Communist outrage. In response came charges, like those of Senator Wiley who called the shipment "part of the master plan of world Communism," and of California's Representative Patrick J. Hillings, who claimed that the arms "were to be used to sabotage the Panama Canal."

The offensive began on June 18, 1954. Without the direct use of U.S. forces, operation PBSUCCESS was forced to rely on smoke and mirrors to overthrow Arbenz. Guatemala had the strongest army in Central America and only a massive infusion of money and troops to support Castillo Armas, the person chosen by the United States to lead the new government, could have provided any assurance of a victory. Given the clandestine nature of the operation, such overt assistance was out of the question.

To win the coup without any real military strength meant creating the illusion of a powerful invading force led by Armas with the United States waiting in the wings. Hoping that Arbenz and the army would decide that the war was lost, the Americans were counting on a segment of the army deserting Arbenz forcing him to resign.

To make the illusion plausible, Washington provided Armas with money to hire mercenaries who lacked military training. To add to the illusion, CIA agents established training camps in Nicaragua and Honduras. Richard Immerman, in *The CIA in Guatemala* sums up the strategy as an "Army of Liberation [that] was intended to frighten both the government and the people into accepting a Castillo Armas victory as a *fait accompli.*"

In an effort to convince wealthy urban Guatemalans, many of whom were army officers, that Arbenz was doomed to failure, the CIA broadcast antirevolutionary programs from Honduras and Nicaragua. On the air, the broadcasters claimed that Armas was fully prepared to overthrow Arbenz and would be shortly returning to Guatemala with the legions of exiled Guatemalans whom he had recruited. He was only waiting for the opportune moment. The broadcasts were so effective that Arbenz, in a last ditch effort, offered to refer the dispute with the UFC to an independent arbiter. Peurifoy informed Guatemala's Foreign Minister that Washington's main concern was Communism.

The CIA recruited expert pilots who would used outdated planes, which were not identifiable as CIA planes, to fly sorties over Guatemalan cities. The F-47 bombers were so primitive that they could only carry blocks of dynamite attached to hand grenades. They dropped their so-called bombs on key targets in Guatemala's capital convincing the citizens that a major siege was underway.

CIA communications experts jammed local radio stations in order to prevent accurate information from reaching the capital so that only CIA broadcasts were heard. They reported huge Armas victories in the countryside and the relentless march of Armas's troops toward the capital causing many Guatemalans to flee.

Arbenz could easily have defeated the few CIA bombers in the air and made quick work of the approximately 150 soldiers waiting in the wings. The CIA was nervous that if Arbenz ordered his air force to either intercept the small number of CIA bombers or to conduct aerial surveillance, their chicanery would be exposed. The discovery of Armas's position would reveal that his forces only consisted of about 150 ill-equipped soldiers and that Arbenz's planes could have easily intercepted the obsolete CIA bombers.

To solve the problem, the CIA began broadcasting the exploits of alleged heroic Soviet aviators who had defected to the West in the hope that one or more Guatemalan pilots might defect. The CIA found one such defector whom they plied with alcohol to persuade him to make an imaginary appeal [he refused to make an appeal while sober] to his fellow pilots to also defect. Then with careful editing they produced a convincing appeal which was aired throughout Guatemala. By subsequently grounding his air force for fear of more defections, Arbenz lacked any planes to conduct surveillance or attack CIA planes. (Richard H. Immerman, *The CIA in Guatemala*)

As a final resort, Foreign Minister Toriello implored the United Nations to intervene in order to resolve the crisis. Arbenz's hope that the UN would send a team of investigators to Guatemala to evaluate the problem met with resistance from Henry Cabot Lodge, U.S. Ambassador to the UN, who attempted to delay a meeting of the Security Council until after Arbenz's defeat. UN Secretary-General Dag Hammarskjöld exerted heavy pressure to convene the Council. To win the vote, Washington would have to convince Britain and France, both of whom were in favour of Guatemala's resolution, to at least abstain from the vote. The Americans applied pressure on both countries, as demonstrated by Eisenhower's comment that:

> The British expect us to give them a free ride and side with them on Cyprus. And yet they will not even support us on Guatemala! Let's give them a lesson.

In the end, the Guatemalan resolution was defeated by five votes to four with Britain and France abstaining.

In a final, desperate effort to save his presidency, Arbenz ordered his army officers to hand out weapons to local peasants but the army, recognizing the inevitability of their defeat, asked Arbenz to resign. With the American ambassador Peurifoy pulling strings in the background, Armas was chosen to be the new president. Washington's imperative that the entire operation remain secret was successful.

As part of the propaganda campaign, the CIA had to promulgate the lie that the people of Guatemala revolted against the harsh dictator, Arbenz, and succeeded. Several quotes from President Eisenhower and others contributed to the propaganda about the dissatisfaction of the peasants with Arbenz, such as:

- "The major factor in the successful outcome was the disaffection of the Guatemalan armed forces and the population as a whole with the tyrannical regime of Arbenz." (Eisenhower, from *Mandate for Change, The White House Years, 1953-1956*)

- "...the people of Guatemala, in a magnificent effort, have liberated themselves from the shackles of international Communism." (Eisenhower from *The CIA in Guatemala*)
- "The Guatemalan regime enjoyed the full support of Soviet Russia... [the] situation is being cured by the Guatemalans themselves." (Allen Dulles, Director of the CIA, in *Killing Hope*)
- "In conclusion, Mr. Chairmen, let me state that the menace of communism in Guatemala was courageously fought by the Guatemalan people themselves...Communist power was broken by the Guatemalans alone...They fought the battle which is the common battle of all free nations against Communist oppression." (John E. Peurifoy, Ambassador to Guatemala, Testimony before the Congressional Subcommittee on Latin America).

Since the fall of Arbenz and the installation of an American hand-picked leader, conditions in Guatemala have harshly degenerated in terms of basic freedoms, human rights, poverty, land ownership, health-care, and democracy. Armas was the first in a succession of dictators who, with American support, have inflicted a reign of terror and oppression on the Guatemalan people. The American-supported dictators converted the economy from one that served the interests of the people to one that served the interests of Americans and in particular American corporate interests.

These dictators depended on the United States for financial aid and for training of their army in counterinsurgency techniques. The U.S. set up a school called the School of the Americas, located in Fort Benning, Georgia, for the purpose of training soldiers and officers in Latin America in counter-insurgency and torture techniques. Guatemalan dictatorships were confronted with a number of insurgencies caused by a lack of freedoms and growing poverty. The United States' objective was to ensure that the Guatemalan army was prepared. In January 2001, the name of the school was changed to The Western Hemisphere Institute for Security Cooperation because of reports from human right's groups condemning it as a school for training soldiers to violate human rights.

The economy was transformed into an export-oriented economy to serve the interests of the American multinationals located in Guatemala. Now there was an inverse relationship between the growing beef and agricultural exports and the prosperity of most Guatemalans. As exports grew, the population suffered. Land reform policies were reversed and the same concentration of land ownership, where two percent of the people owned twenty percent of the land, prevailed.

Castillo Armas assumed power after the resignation of Arbenz and set the stage for repression and human rights abuses that plagued Guatemala for many decades. One of his first acts was to arrest 1000 people suspected of communist affiliations, many of whom were tortured or murdered. Following his initial purge to eradicate communists and opponents, he established a committee which was authorized to arbitrarily arrest anyone suspected of being a communist and to hold them without due process. After four months, the committee had collected 72,000 names. Next he reversed all agrarian reforms and expropriation of land as well as banning the banana workers' union, whose leaders were murdered. He then disenfranchised three-quarters of the voters by barring illiterates from voting. Books were burnt and opposition newspapers were closed.

In 1958, General Miguel Ydigoras Fuentes, the next "elected" president, engaged in repressive measures, corruption, and anti-democratic practices. One of his more hated decisions was to allow the United States to use Guatemala as a springboard for their invasion of Cuba. Ydigoras provoked many Guatemalans into protesting against his presidency including students who initiated many of the demonstrations, workers and peasant groups. With the assistance of the U.S., Ydigoras easily crushed the protest with the army, many of whom were trained at the School of the Americas.

In 1963, Ydigoras was overthrown by Colonel Enrique Paralta Azurdin in a military coup. His first act was to murder eight union leaders. Paralta's nationalism was his downfall and the United States assisted Cesar Mendez Montenegro to overthrow him in 1966. In the period 1966 to 1968, Amnesty International estimates that between 3000 and 8000 Guatemalans were killed by the police. Death squads were created to execute opponents. By 1972, there had been an estimated 13,000 victims of the death squads and by 1976, the number rose to 20,000. President Lucas Garcia, dictator between 1978 and 1982, brutally tortured and murdered an estimated 100,000 people.

General Efráin Rios Montt took power by a coup in 1982 and promptly announced a state of siege. In the first six months of power he had not only murdered 1600 Mayans and peasants but he also brutally wiped 400 villages off the map.

By 1993 conditions in Guatemala had degenerated to the point where:

- Guatemala had a higher level of malnutrition than Haiti; (UNICEF)

- One-quarter million children were orphaned;

- 87% of Guatemalans lived below the poverty line;

- 72% could not afford a minimal diet;

- 6 million had no access to health services;

- 3.6 million lacked clean drinking water;

- 2% controlled 70% of the land.

In January 2000, two months after his inauguration, President Alfonso Portillo held a national day to commemorate the deaths of the estimated 200,000 victims of the civil war in Guatemala. Despite giving a commitment to bring those responsible to justice, serious human rights problems still exist in Guatemala. Although political violence had decreased in 1997, certain groups, such as peasants and unions are still at risk. According to Amnesty International, the human rights community was still under siege in 2002.

Richard H. Immerman, in *The CIA in Guatemala,* sums up the history since 1944 as follows:

> Castillo Armas was but first in a line of Guatemalan presidents, all supported by the United States, who in the name of anti-Communism have ruled by terror and repression. Their effort to reverse the movement toward reform that began in 1944 has not produced the stability so eagerly sought in Washington. Rather, by pursuing programs inimical to the majority of Guatemalans...They must live with chronic unemployment, chronic malnutrition, high rate of illiteracy and infant mortality, and, for hundreds of thousands of peasants, little or no land.

Eisenhower's Lies

In determining the extent to which Eisenhower lied, a number of pertinent questions need to be posed and addressed. Examining the history of the overthrow of Arbenz evokes questions such as:

- Why were propaganda techniques needed such as distributing Dulles's Caracas speech to movie and television outlets?

- Why was it necessary to pressure France and Britain at the Caracas Conference if the cause was so urgent and the threat very real?

- Why did the United States plant Soviet weapons in Guatemala to incriminate the Guatemalans if they were so certain about their evidence?

- Why was the entire operation planned and conducted in complete secrecy if the threat was very real?

- What about the connection between the Eisenhower administration and UFC and why did the UFC become involved including a donation of $64,000 in cash?

- How reliable and objective was Washington's evidence in reaching the conclusion that Guatemala was under the control of Communists (e.g. the May Day celebration)?

- Why did the United States select the next leader thereby bypassing the electoral system which was already in existence?

- Why did the U.S. promulgate the propaganda that the people themselves had overthrown Arbenz when people involved in the coup knew that it was not true?

- Why was it necessary to fabricate so many lies about Guatemala to strengthen the U.S. case?

- Why did Washington block the UN from forming a committee to investigate the nature of the threat in Guatemala?

- Why did Washington employ propaganda techniques to convince Guatemalans of the oppressive government of Arbenz? Would they not be experiencing it first hand?

I think that the answer to these questions can only lead to one conclusion, namely that the American government was primarily interested in having a friendlier regime in Guatemala that did not engage in radical economic programs such as land and labour reforms which set an example for other countries in the hemisphere. The United States also wanted to protect its corporate interests.

No analysis of the U.S. intervention is complete without referring to the Cold War ethos which dominated the thinking of policy-makers in Washington. The evidence from which the United States drew the conclusion that Guatemala was infiltrated by communists, who had a grand design for the hemisphere, was very flimsy. For example, Milton Eisenhower's fact-finding mission to South America reported that Guatemala was infiltrated by communists although he never traveled there. When Guatemala celebrated May Day, Washington concluded that Guatemala must be infiltrated by communists. As well, there were only four Communists in the Legislative Assembly; nevertheless, leaders in the U.S. concluded that this level of participation in the Assembly was proof of a communist threat.

Washington concluded that eradicating Communism was worth the price as William Blum, in *Killing Hope*, points out:

> ....the educated, urbane men of the State Department, the CIA, and the United Fruit Company, the pipe-smoking men of Princeton, Harvard, and Wall Street, decided that the illiterate peasants of Guatemala did not deserve the land which had been given to them, that the workers did not need their unions, that hunger and torture were a small price to pay for being rid of the scourge of Communism.

Richard H. Immerman, in *The CIA in Guatemala,* notes that:

> What they [Eisenhower Administration] did not understand, or would not admit, was that the communists were a great asset to the reform program and that, for Guatemala nationalists, the threat to the program came from the right [wealthy landowners] not the left. This does not mean that Arbenz depended on the Communists to the extent that they dominated him or his policies.

Also, a leading Soviet expert, George Kennan, wrote:

> It is true that most of the people who go by the name of "Communist" in Latin America are a somewhat different species than in Europe. Their bond with Moscow is tenuous and indirect.

If the United States was so confident about their Communist-infiltration theory, then why was it necessary to manufacture outright lies about Arbenz imprisoning thousands of his opponents and the Guatemalan people leading the rebellion against Arbenz?

The United Fruit Company's publicity office distributed fake photographs of mass graves filled with victims of the atrocities committed by Arbenz. UFC's motive is easy to understand but why did Washington perpetrate lies to convince the world that there was a Communist threat to the entire hemisphere?

The CIA undertook a propaganda campaign directed at the people of Guatemala in an effort to turn them against Arbenz. According to Jim Huck, in *1954: Covert War in Guatemala*:

> ...CIA planes dropped leaflets demanding Arbenz's resignation, while radio stations broadcast the same message. The CIA distributed over 100,000 pamphlets entitled "Chronology of Communism in Guatemala" and made three films critical of Arbenz. Over 27,000 anti-Arbenz posters and cartoons were distributed in Guatemala.

There is no doubt that Eisenhower lied. The evidence clearly reveals that there was no communist infiltration in Guatemala to establish a base from which to infiltrate other countries in the hemisphere. Arbenz was influenced by the ideals of the revolution of 1944 and set out to implement land, labour, educational, health, and political reforms to ameliorate conditions for the majority of Guatemalans. All the arguments invoked to reach the conclusion that Guatemala was infiltrated by communists are invalid and border on the absurd.

Eisenhower's lies were very costly. For the next 35 years, Guatemala was ruled by brutal dictators who were supported by the United States and who reversed all the progressive reforms of the revolution in addition to murdering approximately 200,000 people.

A Real Communist Threat or Lies?

The extent to which Eisenhower knowingly lied is a complex question. There is no doubt that he and others in his administration were affected by the cold war ethos. There was a high level of mistrust and fear on the part of the two superpowers. It would be remiss to ignore this factor. On the other hand, assume that Eisenhower was correct and there was a Communist conspiracy to infiltrate Latin American countries. Also assume that his conviction that Communist governments were brutal and totalitarian was accurate. If these assumptions were correct, then there actually was a major threat to Latin America and American attempts to stop it would be welcomed by the "free world". Why all the need for secrecy? Eisenhower would have been a hero for saving Latin America from such a fate. The only answer to this question is that Eisenhower did not believe he could prove that such a threat existed and, therefore, he lied.

Consider Eisenhower's stated conviction that Communism was brutal, undemocratic, and oppressive, and that either Arbenz was a communist or his government was infiltrated by communists. Why did Eisenhower so vehemently oppose a United Nations investigation into the crisis in Guatemala? Why did he bypass the electoral process and install a dictator? Why did he install Armas? When Armas began torturing and murdering his political opponents, why did Eisenhower not intervene? When Armas reversed all the progressive legislation of the revolution, why did Washington continue to support him? It would seem that the dictator who replaced Arbenz was no better than the Communists Eisenhower feared and, therefore, why did he support him? All these questions seem to lead to an inevitable conclusion that protecting Guatemala and other Latin American countries (some of these countries also had brutal dictators supported by the U.S.) from Communism was not Eisenhower's primary motive.

It is more likely that the very close bonds between the Eisenhower administration and the UFC were part of the motive as well as the American policy of protecting its corporate interests in other countries. He was probably also motivated by fear of a successful social and economic system which challenged the fundamental philosophy of the American system.

The complexity of this analysis is related to the difficulty of separating the various factors which influenced Eisenhower. There is no doubt that he was at least partially influenced by the cold war ethos but there must have been doubts in his mind about the validity of his claims about Guatemala otherwise he would have been open about his intentions and not have felt the need to lie.

A number of members of his administration also lied to cover up American involvement in the overthrow of Arbenz. Eisenhower denied all knowledge of CIA activities in Guatemala. He also stated after the coup had succeeded that "In Guatemala the people of that region rose up and rejected the Communist Doctrine..." John E. Peurifoy, ambassador to Guatemala, during his appearance in the House of Representatives lied when he claimed that "…the struggle of the Guatemalans was to throw off the Communist control."

Eisenhower's involvement in the coup was in violation of the following clauses in the United Nations Charter:

- Chapter II, Article 2, Clause 3—settling disputes by peaceful means;
- Chapter II, Article 2, Clause 4 —refraining from the threat or use of force;
- Chapter VI, Article 33, Clause 1—seeking a solution by other methods;
- Chapter VI, Article 34,—Security Council investigates disputes;
- Chapter VII, Article 37—Clause 1 and 2—Security Council decides whether to act;
- Chapter VII, Article 39—Security Council decides what measures to take;
- Chapter VII, Article 42—Security Council authorizes the use of force.

Eisenhower's actions also violate the following clauses in the OAS Charter:

Article 1
Members shall respect the territorial integrity and independence of other members.

Article 2

(a) Members shall strive to strengthen the peace and security of the continent.

(b) Members shall ensure the peaceful settlement of disputes.

(c) Every state has the right to choose, without external interference, its political, economic, and social system.

The example of American intervention in Guatemala is very instructive because of the pattern of American justification, motivation, scare tactics, and lies which repeats itself in many other cases of American intervention. The threat of Communism, protection of American corporate interests, and the threat to American security have characterized American foreign policy during the cold war.

"Lying" seems often a small crime—most people do it at some point in their lives if not frequently, and it just doesn't merit mention next to larger crimes of theft, murder, etc. But, as the case of Eisenhower demonstrates, the more powerful the person who does the lying, the more devastating the potential consequences. Eisenhower is famous for admonishing the country to be wary of the power of what he termed "the Military Industrial Complex." Yet, in this case, by unleashing forces that killed some 200,000 Guatemalans over 35 years, Eisenhower's little lies illustrate how they can facilitate war crimes.

CHAPTER 4

QUAGMIRE OF DECEIT

JOHNSON AND THE ESCALATION
OF THE VIETNAM WAR

In 1919, Nguyen Ai Quoc, a young kitchen assistant at the Ritz in France, would play a part during the sixties and early seventies in the moral and political turmoil in the United States and in the loss of 55,000 American lives. It took many years for the United States to recover from this trauma and it had a profound influence on American foreign and defence policy. Nguyen Ai Quoc eventually changed his name to Ho Chi Minh and the period in history was the Vietnam War.

As we have seen, little lies, when told by presidents, can have big, even horrific consequences. President Lyndon Johnson's role in the escalation of the war in Vietnam follows this pattern: by arguing that a North Vietnamese ship fired on an American ship in the Gulf of Tonkin, Johnson was able to justify expanding a war, the subject of this chapter. (Ronnie E. Ford, *Shedding New Light on the Gulf of Tonkin Incident*)

One of the paradoxical characteristics of the Vietnam War is the surreal public understanding of the major issues based on a number of myths which have survived to this day. One of the prevalent myths is that the media were instrumental in stirring up opposition to the war with its stark and gruesome images such as an eight year old girl running down a street in South Vietnam, naked, with burns to most of her body from napalm. It is true these images evoked a strong emotional response but in terms of the major issues and events, the media collaborated with the government (Edward S. Herman, *Beyond Hypocrisy: Decoding the News in an Age of Propaganda)* and did not contribute to ending the war. According to another myth, the war was between the South Vietnamese with the support of the United States, and the North Vietnamese, who stealthily made their way down the Ho Chi Minh trail to fight in the jungles of South Vietnam. In fact, until 1965, the war was between the South Vietnamese Government assisted by the United States, and the people of South Vietnam (Noam Chomsky, *Understanding Power, The Indispensable Chomsky*).

So Many Enemies

It is impossible to fully grasp the crime of an imperial president visiting his military on a people unless we understand the depth of the struggle they went through—in this case for centuries prior to the arrival of American troops.

War was not a new phenomenon to the people who lived in Vietnam. Vietnam was under Chinese rule until A.D. 938. In 939, Vietnamese forces under Ngo Quyen defeated the Chinese and created an independent state. In the 13th century, the Chinese under Kubla Khan attacked Vietnam to reincorporate it back into the Chinese Empire but were driven back across the border. Beginning in the 15th century, Vietnamese forces began a march southward until they confronted the Khmer in the flatlands of the Mekong Delta and by the end of the 17th century, Vietnam occupied the lower Mekong Delta. In the early 18th century, Vietnam was divided by warring factions with the Trinh Lords ruling the north and the Lords of the Nguyen line ruling the south. During the early 19th century the French set their sights on Vietnam and when diplomatic overtures failed, they opted for war. By 1893, the French had conquered much of Southeast Asia including Vietnam, Laos, and Cambodia. When the French began to plunder the wealth of their new colonies, many resistance movements sprang up but were quickly extinguished. In 1925, Nguyen Ai Quoc, later called Ho Chi Minh, created a revolutionary movement to force the French to leave Vietnam. His movement's struggle did not succeed until after World War II.

During World War II, Japan occupied Vietnam but allowed the French to continue their colonial administration. Initially, the United States reassured France that at the end of the war, Vietnam would continue to be under French control. On the other hand, the U.S. was strongly committed to the Atlantic Charter, a statement of principle signed by Roosevelt and Churchill, committing themselves to the principle of self-determination and to the settlement of disputes without the use of force. President Roosevelt's commitment to the Atlantic Charter implied that he believed in decolonizing Vietnam and turning it over to a trusteeship as an intermediate step toward autonomy. The policy of applying the Atlantic Charter suffered a major setback when Britain, fearing for her commonwealth, withdrew support for the national independence of Vietnam. The United States did an about-face and stated that former colonies were to be returned to their owners after World War II.

Shortly after Ho Chi Minh's return to Vietnam on February 28, 1941, he created a broad front of patriots, peasants, workers, merchants and soldiers soon to be called the Viet Minh. Their purpose was to fight the Japanese and the French. In 1945, Ho Chi Minh led the Viet Minh into Hanoi and demanded the abdication of Bao Dai, who had been emperor of Vietnam since 1924. After seizing power, Ho Chi Minh decreed the establishment of the Democratic Republic of Vietnam (DRV). The DRV had only ruled Vietnam for twenty days when French forces overthrew them and reestablished their authority.

In 1946, full-scale war broke out between the French and the Viet Minh in Vietnam. The war was temporarily interrupted by negotiations between the French and Viet Minh in the spring of 1946, which resulted in an Accord. The Viet Minh agreed to negotiate because the French had strengthened their position in Tonkin and were about to land a task force at Haiphong. In the accord, Ho Chi Minh agreed to French reentry into North Vietnam in exchange for recognition of the DRV as a free state within the French Union. The Accord ultimately failed because the Viet Minh struggle against their French colonial masters had whetted the appetite of the people of Vietnam for national independence. As well, the Accord was an admission of defeat by Ho Chi Minh who had hoped to internationalize the problem, in particular through his overtures to the United States. For one year, beginning in the autumn of 1945, Ho Chi Minh had reached out to the United States and, invoking the principles of the Atlantic Charter and the United Nations Charter, beseeched the U.S. to at least to recognize them as a trusteeship under the United Nations Charter. The United States neither acted on Ho Chi Minh's request nor offered any assistance to the French although they did seek advice from the French on the matter of Vietnamese independence.

On December 19, 1946, violence erupted in Hanoi between the French and the Viet Minh and quickly spread throughout all of Vietnam. Ho Chi Minh appealed to the French to negotiate a peace settlement, even offering to personally withdraw from Vietnam. The French were not interested in any further negotiations and demanded unconditional surrender. In 1947, an additional division of French troops was dispatched to Vietnam and the French decided to negotiate with the Emperor Bao Dai rather than the Viet Minh.

At the end of World War II, the United States initiated a policy of only considering territories for trusteeship status if they were either territories taken from the enemy (Japan) or territories that volunteered to be placed under trusteeship. As a result of this policy, Indochina's status became a matter for French determination.

Between 1946 and 1949, the United States was very ambivalent about events in Vietnam. Roosevelt had been firmly committed to the Atlantic Charter and viewed Vietnam as a flagrant example of colonial exploitation but the U.S. had guaranteed the French that its colonies would be returned after the war. The U.S. regarded the conflict in Vietnam as a conflict to be resolved by the French. Although the United States formally respected Vietnam's right to self-determination, they refused to endorse Ho Chi Minh or the Viet Minh because of Ho's communist affiliations.

Two events were critical in transforming the U.S. position from one of neutrality to one of deep involvement. When the nationalist government in China was replaced with the communist government of Mao, the United States became alarmed at the possible spread of communism in Asia. The Korean War between 1950 and 1953 further strengthened the conviction that communism had to be contained in Asia. The United States now claimed that the Viet Minh were part of the worldwide communist expansionary movement and the French struggle against the Viet Minh was an important part of the policy of containment of communism. In fact, first the French and then the Americans wanted to secure Southeast Asia as part of their Empire.

In 1950, the French began the process of transferring the administration of Vietnam to Bao Dai's Government followed by recognition of Vietnamese independence on February 4, 1950. Ho Chi Minh refused to accept the legitimacy of Bao's regime and proclaimed that the Viet Minh was the only legal government in Vietnam.

The Viet Minh seemed to be gaining the military advantage over the French in 1950 when Viet Minh forces scored a number of victories along a string of French border posts. Becoming somewhat desperate, the French requested United States military assistance on February 16, 1950. A memorandum to President Truman from the Secretary of Defense, stated that:

> ...[the choice now] confronting the United States is to support the legal government in Indochina or to face the extension of Communism over the remainder of the continental area of Southeast Asia and possibly westward...

Following a recommendation from the JCS (Joint Chiefs of Staff), President Truman sent American bombers, military advisors, technicians by the hundreds, and direct military assistance which totaled $1.4 billion (the equivalent sum in 2005 would be approximately $6.5 billion). In 1953, the CIA airline, CAT, assisted the French in airlifting 16,000 men to a French base just north of Dien Bien Phu and delivered supplies to the crumbling French forces staving off disaster there. The Americans also built airfields, ports, and highways. The *Pentagon Papers* concluded that the assistance to France directly involved the U.S. in Vietnam and paved the way for future American intervention. As the French were fighting the Viet Minh with American assistance but without much prospect of winning, and as the Bao Dai government was unable to win popular support, the future of Vietnam was in doubt.

While the Americans were providing aid to the French, China was aiding North Vietnam. One of the foreign policy objectives of the U.S. was to contain China in Korea and Southeast Asia. American leaders feared that a negotiated settlement between the French and the Viet Minh would leave the Viet Minh in power in Northern Vietnam with strong ties to Communist China. In 1952, the U.S. applied strong pressure on the French to cancel negotiations in Burma with the Viet Minh resulting in a hasty French retreat. The United States attempted to deter any further negotiations between the French and Viet Minh by threatening to withdraw all support and assistance from France.

As the war raged on and the Viet Minh forces were threatening to defeat the French, the United States, fearing a Communist victory, considered a number of options to avert a catastrophe. The United States was not willing to accept either a French loss or a negotiated settlement with North Vietnam. Either option would have placed a key country in Southeast Asia in jeopardy of communist control. The National Security Council paper stated that:

> It was U.S. policy to accept nothing short of a military victory in Indo-China... [The] U.S. actively opposes any negotiated settlements in Indo-China at Geneva.

The Security Council recommended that the United States continue the war if the French were not capable of defeating the Viet Minh. President Eisenhower contemplated sending American troops to Vietnam but abandoned that option because Congressional approval was problematic. The Chairman of the Joint Chiefs of Staff, Admiral Radford, sent a message to the Secretary of Defense, stating that "The employment of atomic weapons is contemplated in the event that such a course appears militarily advantageous." Two American aircraft carriers equipped with atomic weapons steamed toward the Gulf of Tonkin.

French and Viet Minh forces fought the climatic battle of the war at Dien Bien Phu in a remote valley in the Upper Tonkin. The French commander's decision to occupy Dien Bien Phu in November 1953 had been a costly mistake because it eventually became the final battleground for the war between the French and the Viet Minh. The battle, known as the Battle of Dien Bien Phu, took place between March 17 and May 7, 1954, and resulted in a devastating loss for the French and an end to their occupation of Vietnam.

Chinese support for the Viet Minh and the floundering French caused apprehension about a Viet Minh victory. While the French and the Viet Minh were battling for control of Vietnam, Moscow had proposed a five-power peace conference to reduce international tensions. On February 18, 1954, the United States, Great Britain, the Soviet Union, and France announced that in late April, the above countries and any other parties concerned would meet in Geneva in April to seek a solution to the eight year conflict in Vietnam. Differences among the allies appeared to be irresolvable. The Soviets, preoccupied with domestic issues, were hoping for a reduction in international tensions; the French had accepted American assistance but were reluctant to bring in the Americans; the British resented the Americans for their resistance to united action; and the United States wanted a collective security pact to force China to stop supporting the Viet Minh. The conference ended with some major agreements such as the declaration of the formal end to the war in Vietnam and the declaration of France as a guarantor of Vietnamese sovereignty.

Evading the Peace

During the Geneva Conference, the interested parties to the conflict in Vietnam hammered out a set of accords on July 21, 1954. To resolve the Vietnamese issues, the Accords specified that:

- there would be a ceasefire in Vietnam;
- there would be a temporary division of North and South Vietnam to be drawn at the 17th parallel;

- Ho Chi Minh and his government would rule North Vietnam;

- Ngo Dinh Diem would rule a non-communist state in South Vietnam;

- an election would be called in 1956 to allow the people to vote for the government of their choice in a reunited Vietnam.

Both the United States and South Vietnam refused to sign the Geneva Accords because American intelligence reported that Ho Chi Minh would win an election in a united Vietnam. Neither country was willing to risk a united communist Vietnam. One of the main thrusts of U.S. foreign policy was to expand American-style capitalism even if it meant thwarting the democratic aspirations of the people. Secretary of State John Dulles stated that:

> Neither the United States Government nor the Government of Vietnam, [is] of course, a party to the Geneva armistice agreements...the United States believes, broadly speaking, in the unification of countries which have a historic unity, where the people are akin. We also believe that, if there are conditions of really free elections, there is no serious risk that the Communists would win... (*Pentagon Papers*)

Diem noted that:

> Our policy is a policy of peace. But nothing will lead us astray of our goal, the unity of our country, a union in freedom and not in slavery...Now, with a regimen of oppression as practiced by the Viet Minh, we remain skeptical concerning the possibly of fulfilling the conditions of free elections in the North.

As France divested itself of authority in South Vietnam and the United States began to forward aid directly to Diem, Diem became more dependent on the United States. There is some controversy about how much pressure was exerted on Diem by the U.S. to refuse to sign the Accords, but according to a memorandum sent by Secretary of Defense, Robert McNamara, to President Johnson, in 1964:

> Only the U.S. presence after 1954 held the South together...and enabled Diem to refuse to go through with the 1954 provision calling for nationwide free elections in 1956.

North Vietnam was very disposed to pursuing elections with South Vietnam. President Eisenhower believed that in a vote in a united Vietnam, 80% of the Vietnamese people would vote for Ho Chi Minh as their great liberator. A Ho Chi Minh government in Vietnam would have given control to the international communist conspiracy which would now threaten all of Southeast Asia. According to the *Pentagon Papers*:

> The DRV repeatedly tried to engage the Geneva machinery, forwarding messages to the Government of South Vietnam in July 1955, May and June 1956, March 1958, July 1959, and July 1960, proposing consultations to negotiate "free general elections by secret ballot," and to liberalize North-South relations in general. Each time the GVN (Government of South Vietnam) replied with disdain or with silence.

In October 1955, Diem held a vote in South Vietnam and won against Bao Dai with a rather suspect 98% of the vote. The Diem regime controlled the press tightly and implemented measures such as the "political reeducation centres" which were, in fact, concentration camps for potential enemies of the government. Diem also introduced a scheme for identifying the people of South Vietnam by a system of letters according to their connections with the Viet Minh. The irony was that the claim by the Americans and Diem about the oppression and undemocratic character of the government of North Vietnam was, in fact, true of South Vietnam.

Before the ink was dry on the Geneva Accords, the United States moved a paramilitary group into South Vietnam to conduct military and psychological warfare. The paramilitary group was headed by Edward Lansdale, who over a six month period, executed operations such as:

- encouraging the migration of Vietnamese from the north to the south through an extremely intensive campaign of psychological warfare using leaflets warning Catholics that Christ has gone to the south;

- distributing bogus leaflets presumably printed by the Viet Minh demonstrating the harshness of life under communist rule;

- infiltrating paramilitary groups in the north;

- contaminating the oil supply of the bus company in Hanoi to destroy their buses;

- taking initial steps toward sabotaging the railway;

- sending selected Vietnamese to U.S. Pacific bases for guerrilla training.

One of the myths introduced at the beginning of this chapter was that the war was between American-supported South Vietnam and North Vietnam. Until 1965, the United States and the Diem government were waging war against the people in South Vietnam. The enemy in South Vietnam was anyone suspected of being a communist and all members of the Viet Minh. People were rounded up and placed in reeducation centres and prisons, villages were destroyed, and many suspects were murdered. There was a swelling of hatred toward Diem and the Americans between the years 1954 and 1961. Edward Herman and Noam Chomsky, in *Manufacturing Consent*, document the repression by noting that:

> With peaceful settlement successfully deterred, the United States and its client regime turned to the task of internal repression, killing tens of thousands and imprisoning tens of thousands more. Diem supporter and advisor Joseph Buttinger describes "massive expeditions" in 1956 that destroyed villages, with hundreds of thousands of peasants killed, and tens of thousands arrested by soldiers in regions "controlled by communists"...

William Blum confirms the repression in the south by noting that:

> ...[with] the elections cancelled, the nation still divided, and Diem with his "mandate" free to continue his heavy, tyrannical rule, the turn to violence in South Vietnam became inevitable. As if in knowledge of and preparation for this the United States sent 350 additional military men to Saigon in May 1956, an "example of the U.S. ignoring the Geneva Accords stated the Pentagon study." (*Pentagon Papers*)

Furthermore, Diem destroyed the traditional autonomy enjoyed in the villages by abolishing village council elections for fear that the Viet Minh might win.

Diem endeavored to destroy his enemies in the south by seeking out not only the Viet Minh but also their supporters, arresting them, torturing them, and frequently killing them. The campaign to eliminate his enemies alienated the peasants even further because of the fact that the Viet Minh implemented more progressive agrarian policies. According to Noam Chomsky, in *Manufacturing Consent*, the Viet Minh were "virtually decimated by the late 1950s." The Viet Minh refused to respond with violent means until the late 1950s, at which time the communist leaders in Hanoi granted permission to communists and communist sympathizers to start a guerrilla war against the Saigon Government. (Edwin E. Moïse, *The First Indochina War*)

At the end of 1960, the Viet Minh and their sympathizers created the

National Liberation Front (NLF) to lead the guerrilla warfare against Diem. Despite the fact that the NLF was under communist leadership, many non-communists joined because of their hatred for the government in Saigon. Edwin E. Moïse, in *The First Indochina War,* explains that:

> ...the great advantages of the NLF were that in most areas of South Vietnamese countryside, the peasants regarded the NLF as a more local organization, a more purely South Vietnamese organization, than the Saigon Government.

Dissatisfaction with Diem was not limited to his tyrannical rule, but also extended to his policies, in particular, his ineffective land reform measures.

His agrarian reform consisted of three elements:

- resettle refugees and other land-destitute Vietnamese on uncultivated land;

- expropriate all rice holdings over 247 acres and redistribute these to tenant farmers;

- regulate landlord-tenant relations to fix rents within the range 15-25% of crop yield and to guarantee tenant land tenure for 3-5 years. (*Pentagon Papers*)

In theory, the program appears to be fair but in practice it failed miserably because government officials, in particular, the Minister of Agrarian Reform, were landowners themselves and were not devoted to implementing these reforms. The result was that only 10% of the farmers benefited and, by 1959, the program was inoperative.

The impact of the repressive measures and ineffective policies was that the Diem government lost the support of the people in South Vietnam. Philippe Devillers, in the *Pentagon Papers*, remarked that:

> It was thus by its home policy that the government of the South finally destroyed the confidence of the population, which it had won during the early years, and practically drove them into revolt and desperation. The non-Communist (and even the anti-Communist) opposition had long been aware of the turn events were taking. But at the beginning of 1960 very many elements, both civilian and military, in the Nationalist camp came to a clear realization that things were moving from bad to worse, and if nothing were done to put an end to the absolute power of Diem, then Communism would end up gaining power with the aid, or at least with the consent, of the population

Historian Arthur Schlesinger also reports in the *Pentagon Papers* that:

> Diem's authoritarianism, which increasingly involved manhunts, political reeducation camps, and the "regroupment" of population, caused spreading discontent and then armed resistance in the countryside…few scholars believe that the growing resistance was at the start organized or directed by Hanoi. Indeed, there is some indication that the Communists at first hung back…it was not until September, 1960 that the Communist Party of North Vietnam bestowed its formal blessing and called for the liberation of the south from American Imperialism.

Hatred of the United States was growing as money, arms, and advisors poured into South Vietnam to bolster the power of Diem. The Americans were perceived as just another colonizer following in the boot prints of Japan and France.

At this point, the U.S. was in so deep, and committed to rolling back what it called communism but which was, in fact, a democratic expression of the Vietnamese people, that it would have been virtually impossible for a U.S. president to start telling the truth. The entire government apparatus was built on a lie and for a president to take any position resembling honesty would have been devastating to the general aims of U.S. policy.

Kennedy Joins the Club

When J.F. Kennedy took office in 1961, conditions in Vietnam were beginning to deteriorate. The impact of the war in Laos, the question of assistance to South Vietnam, the increasing Buddhist riots, and the problem of Diem's leadership converged to the point where Washington was forced to make some difficult decisions.

As soon as Kennedy took office, the American Ambassador to Saigon was asked if the United States would have to replace Diem because of his failure to gain the confidence of his people. President Kennedy implemented a strategy to improve conditions in South Vietnam by increasing assistance to Saigon through a Counter-Insurgency Plan (CIP) which offered Diem support for a 20,000 man increase to his army which currently stood at 150,000.

The counter-insurgency war against the guerillas in South Vietnam was doomed to failure unless the rural population was brought under control because they provided a base of support for the National Liberation Front and its military wing, the People's Liberation Armed Forces (PLAF). The GVN (Government of South Vietnam) and the United States referred to the members of these two groups as the Viet Cong. Viet Cong is the contraction of the two Vietnamese words, "Vietnamese" and "Communists." To gain control of the population, the GVN would gather people from areas threatened by guerrillas and concentrate them in centralized locations or fortified hamlets. Once physical security was established, the peasants would then be the subjected to a pacification program that was designed to encourage the peasants to identify with the Diem government. The peasants were provided with materials to build homes for themselves and to build fortifications for the hamlet. This strategy of controlling the rural population was called the Strategic Hamlet Program which could only succeed if the peasants were willing to be transferred to these fortified hamlets. When they resisted, the United States engaged in bombing and defoliation to drive the peasants into the strategic hamlets. (Edward Herman and Noam Chomsky, *Manufacturing Consent*) On August 1962, Diem produced his pacification program which included 2,500 completed hamlets and 2,500 more under construction.

The Strategic Hamlet and Pacification programs failed because of the farmers' resentment of being displaced from their land and forced to resettle in hamlets. They were also frustrated over the inadequate materials they were provided with for building shelters and fortification. Diem's program was similar to earlier population resettlement and control programs under the French. Another major reason for the failure of the pacification program was Diem. He regularly refused to accept the advice of the Americans.

On October 18, 1961, General Maxwell Taylor arrived in South Vietnam to compile a report and make recommendations to President Kennedy to resolve the deteriorating conditions in South Vietnam. On November 3, 1961, General Taylor submitted his report to the president. The thrust of his report was that the United States needed to demonstrate its commitment to Diem but at the same time encourage the GVN to assume the offensive. For the plan to succeed, the Diem Government needed to win the support of the people in South Vietnam through reforms to the Diem government

The report was overly sanguine about Diem's prospects. His most acute problem was not troops from the north but the rebellion of the people in the south. Diem's tyrannical rule and ineffective policies were triggering rebellions all over South Vietnam.

In April 1963, Diem banned the traditional Buddhist flag just prior to a major festival to celebrate Buddha's birthday. There were between three and four million practicing Buddhists in South Vietnam and 80% of the population were nominal Buddhists (population South Vietnam: 10-11 million). Buddhists in Hue, the centre of Buddhist learning, defiantly flew their flag despite the order. The local administration's failure to take action encouraged them to continue to fly their flags and, on May 8, Buddhists in Hue met to celebrate Buddha's birthday with their flags held high. Diem viewed the flags as a challenge to his authority and ordered local authorities to disperse the crowds. When the local officials needed assistance, government troops arrived and killed nine demonstrators and wounded fourteen. Buddhists reacted by launching a nationwide protest. On May 9, 10,000 people demonstrated in protest of the killings. The rioting quickly spread from Hue to Saigon and became a full-blown political crisis. According to Colonel William Wilson in *U.S. Complicity*:

> Rioting Buddhists and students were tearing apart South Vietnamese cities while terror squads murdered South Vietnamese officials...South Vietnamese President Ngo Dinh Diem believed, like the former emperors of China, that he possessed a "mandate from heaven," and he expected the people to follow him as leader by divine right. Diem's leadership was limited by his use of his family to maintain power.

The Buddhist clergy submitted a five-point plan to the government calling for freedom to fly the Buddhist flag, legal equality with the Catholic Church, and the arrest of the perpetrators of the May 8 incident. On May 30, 350 Buddhist monks demonstrated in front of the National Assembly and announced a 48-hour hunger strike. On June 11, a Buddhist monk poured gasoline over himself and set himself on fire, an image that was broadcast worldwide.

Diem's family, in particular his brother and sister-in-law, Madame Nhu, were becoming a political liability. Diem's brother and wife bitterly attacked the Buddhists adding fuel to the raging inferno. Diem's sister-in-law warned that the Buddhists were rife with Communist infiltrators.

After unsuccessful negotiations with Buddhists and pressure from the U.S. to resolve the Buddhist crisis, Diem delivered a radio address that granted only minor concessions to the Buddhists. On August 5, a second Buddhist monk publicly burned himself to death. After midnight, on August 21, forces loyal to Diem's brother attacked pagodas throughout Vietnam injuring 30 Buddhists and arresting 1,400 people.

The United States repeatedly asked Diem to resolve the Buddhist crisis and to try to win back public support. Diem's recalcitrance forced the U.S.

administration to reconsider its level of support to South Vietnam and to contemplate the impact of a coup. The United States had three alternatives:

- continue to support Diem despite his growing unpopularity;

- covertly support the overthrow of Diem risking the possibility that the new regime might collapse and accommodate the Viet Cong;

- withdraw completely from South Vietnam risking its instability and possible loss to the Viet Cong.

Washington found itself in a quandary as to the most effective course of action although a number of generals in Diem's army were already plotting a coup. The administration in Washington was apprehensive about supporting a coup for fear of triggering either a civil war or chaos, giving the Viet Cong an opening to launch an attack in South Vietnam.

By September, the situation in South Vietnam had become so critical that President Kennedy asked Robert McNamara, Secretary of Defense, and General Maxwell Taylor to assess the status of the GVN military effort, to recommend to the GVN a strategy to redress the Buddhist crisis, and to advise Washington on methods for pressuring Diem to institute reforms. One of the recommendations in the report submitted by McNamara and Taylor was the selective suspension of economic aid as a means of persuading Diem to implement reforms. The generals plotting the coup interpreted the suspension of aid as a green light to proceed with the coup and they contacted the Americans to announce their intention to strike against Diem's regime. Doubts about the feasibility of the coup motivated Washington to ask Ambassador Lodge to monitor the plans of the generals and assess their chances of success. Lodge believed that the U.S. could not win with Diem and therefore decided not to take any action to thwart the coup. The American mission's main contact with the generals plotting the coup was Lieutenant Colonel Lucien Conein, an experienced CIA agent. Conein maintained close contact with the generals in the fall of 1963 as they were preparing for the coup. On October 5, 1963, Conein met with General Minh, the most senior and respected general in South Vietnam. General Minh told Conein that unless the coup was executed soon, the war would be lost to the Viet Cong.

Ambassador Lodge sent a cable to President Kennedy to call his attention to the urgency of the situation in South Vietnam. Kennedy gave

Lodge a mandate to manage American policy in Vietnam in other words, to support the coup plotters. On November 1, 1963, General Minh executed a coup against Diem who was murdered along with his brother.

Minh set up a civilian government and appointed himself President and Chairman of the Revolutionary Council. The U.S. recognized the new government after a sufficient delay to avoid any implication in the coup.

Despite the effort to distance itself from the coup, Washington played a critical role. According to Noam Chomsky, in *Year 501: The Conquest Continues*:

> The Kennedy Administration therefore resolved to overthrow its client in favor of a military regime that would be fully committed to military victory. The result was achieved with the military coup of November 1 1963.

Colonel William Wilson, in *U.S. Complicity,* describes how Lodge publicly denied U.S. involvement and then boasted to Kennedy about the positive role of the U.S.

Ambassador Lodge was quoted in the *New York Times* on June 30, 1964, as stating: "We never participated in the planning. We never gave any advice. We had nothing whatever to do with it." On November 6, 1963, however, Lodge cabled Kennedy, "The ground in which the coup seed grew into a robust plant was prepared by us, and the coup would not have happened as it did without our participation."

The *Pentagon Papers* defines the Americans' role very clearly:

> For the military coup d'etat against Ngo Dinh Diem, the U.S. must share its full share of responsibility. Beginning in August 1963, we variously authorized, sanctioned and encouraged the coup efforts of the Vietnamese generals and offered full support for a successor government. In October we cut off aid to Diem in a direct rebuff, giving the green light to the generals. We maintained clandestine contact with them throughout the planning and execution of the coup and sought to review their operational plans and proposed new government. Thus, as the nine-year rule of Diem came to a bloody end, our complicity in his overthrow heightened our responsibilities and our commitment in an essentially leaderless Vietnam.

Twenty-two days after the Diem coup, J.F.K. was assassinated and Vice-President Johnson (L.B.J.) became president. Three days after assuming the presidency, L.B. J. endorsed the policies of his predecessor.

The theory that Kennedy was at least thinking about withdrawing from Vietnam is entirely false. According to Stanley Karnow in *Vietnam: A History*:

In April 1961, Kennedy created a "task force" to prepare economic, social, political and military programs aimed at preventing Communist "domination" of South Vietnam…He agreed to send an additional hundred military advisors to Vietnam…All the rhetoric now emanating from his administration reiterated its resolve to stop Communism in Southeast Asia.

Edward Herman and Noam Chomsky, in *Manufacturing Consent: The Political Economy of the Mass Media*, give a synopsis of Kennedy's polices in South Vietnam claiming that:

The Kennedy administration escalated the war in South Vietnam, engaging U.S. military forces directly in bombing, defoliating, and "advising" combat troops from 1961 to 1962 as part of an effort to drive several million people into concentration camps ("strategic hamlets")…"

Following Diem's downfall, a number of disturbing developments would force the new American President and his advisors to carefully rethink their status and policies in Vietnam. Reports from South Vietnam had been overly optimistic about the progress of the war, the military and political leadership, and the success of the pacification program. The Viet Cong were gaining strength and the Government of South Vietnam was losing popular support due to its policies and the lack of military success against the Viet Cong.

Political instability in South Vietnam, caused by frequent changes in leadership, was undermining the peasants' confidence in the government. In January 1964, General Khanh seized power from the Minh government but was unable to marshal South Vietnam's resources to stem the rising tide of the Viet Cong. His failure to gain military control led to mob violence and in September 1964, students and Buddhists demonstrated against the Khanh government. Khanh's unpopularity extended to members of the government and military and was forced to defeat a number of coup attempts. Khanh was voted out of office in February 1965, and replaced by a National Leadership Council of ten Generals chaired by Thieu. Ky became prime minister.

These frequent upheavals in the government of South Vietnam were not caused by an inherent instability in the government but in part by the American government's objective of establishing an anti-communist regime which would be amenable to its will. Noam Chomsky, in *Manufacturing Consent,* concluded that:

Unable to develop any political base in the south, the U.S. government proceeded to expand the war. It was able to do this by continually manipulating the political scene in South Vietnam to assure the attainment of its objective: continued fighting until an anti-communist regime, susceptible to American will, was established in the south...It should be noted in this connection that after the long-standing U.S. manipulation of governments in its client state had finally succeeded in its aim, and the United States had placed in power two former French collaborators, Ky and Thieu...

Edward Herman, in *Beyond Hypocrisy* agrees that:

...from our first entry in support of the French, then with our imported leader "Diem", and up to the time of the Paris Peace Agreement of 1973, we refused to negotiate a political settlement because we had no political base in Vietnam...South Vietnamese governments were installed and overthrown by the United States until it had gotten into place two former French mercenaries, Ky and Thieu who were willing to fight until the end.

The Johnson administration faced a number of problems in finding an optimum strategy for successfully ending the war. The old strategies had proven to be ineffective given the growing success of the Viet Cong and the continued lack of popular support for the government of South Vietnam. Increased aid and pressure on the government of South Vietnam and increased threats to Hanoi were having a minimal effect. The planners in Washington agreed that at some unspecified point in the future, the U.S. would begin to implement a series of gradually mounting strikes against the north although no formal decision had been made at this time. Increasing the U.S. force level in South Vietnam was considered an essential step to at least allow the South Vietnamese forces to hold their ground. Although a decision was made to withdraw 1,000 men from Vietnam in December 1963, the number of Americans had risen to 16,732 in October 1963, and to 23,000 by December 1964.

Lying to Escalate the War

One of the most critical events in the war occurred in August 1964 just prior to the presidential election in November and was a turning point for the United States. But the chain of events that led to it began after the signing of the Geneva Accords in 1954.

Not long after signing the Geneva Accords, the United States and South Vietnam commenced a series of covert operations headed by CIA agent Lucien Conein who trained squads of anti-communist South Vietnamese. The operation involved assassinating and abducting officials in the north, destruction of military installations, establishing bases, organizing local cadres, and propaganda campaigns. In 1964, the covert intelligence effort was code-named Operation Plan 34A or 34 Alpha.

The CIA and South Vietnamese forces launched a covert marine and airborne operation inserting agents to collect intelligence, recruit support, establish bases and carry out psychological operations behind enemy lines. In June 1962, after losing the navy vessel Nautelas II and four commandos, the U.S. initiated a succession of hit-and-run attacks along the coast of North Vietnam. In addition to the covert operations, the U.S. launched the DeSoto patrols which were U.S. naval intelligence collection patrols used to gather electronic signal intelligence from North Vietnam.

To intimidate the North Vietnamese, Washington ordered Commander in Chief Pacific Admiral Ulysses Grant Sharp, Jr. to station a task group in the Gulf of Tonkin and conduct aerial reconnaissance. The carrier Ticonderoga and the destroyer Maddox initiated the naval operations. General William C. Westmoreland, the military commander in South Vietnam, asked for and received the authority to broaden the scope of the 34 Alpha operations by shelling radar sites, defence posts, and other coastal targets. The new operation commenced July 30-31 against Hon Me and Hon Ngu, two islands in the Gulf of Tonkin.

In retaliation, on August 2, 1964, the North Vietnamese conducted an attack against the Maddox during which two North Vietnamese patrol boats were severely damaged by the Maddox. Both patrol boats came under attacked by planes from the Ticonderoga which sank one and further damaged the other.

On August 4, 1964, the National Security Agency (NSA) warned the Maddox of another possible attack. An hour after NSA's warning, the Maddox claimed that she had radar contact with three or four unidentified vessels in the Gulf of Tonkin. The pivotal incident, which had a critical impact on American involvement in South Vietnam, occurred when, allegedly, the unidentified vessels attacked the Maddox. The Ticonderoga launched aircraft to assist the Maddox and C. Turner Joy but stormy seas, low clouds, and thunderstorms thwarted any attempts by the American pilots to locate any Vietnamese ships. Captain John J. Herrick, captain of the Maddox, recommended a thorough investigation of reports from the crew of radar contact, visual sightings, and weapons fire which could have been attributable to the stormy seas, darkness, and inexperienced, nervous crewmen. There was no damage as a result of these alleged attacks.

Despite the request for an investigation by Captain Herrick who was not convinced that there was a second attack, Secretary of Defence, Robert McNamara reported to Congress that there was "unequivocal proof" of a second "unprovoked attack" on U.S. ships. McNamara's account was backed by the administration including President Johnson. As well as lying about the Gulf of Tonkin incident, McNamara denied any American involvement in South Vietnamese operations including 34 Alpha and the DeSoto operations.

Since then, McNamara has admitted that his statements regarding the Gulf of Tonkin were false. According to Captain Ronnie E. Ford, in *Shedding New Light on the Gulf of Tonkin Incident*:

> Former Secretary of Defence McNamara recently visited Hanoi, where he met with Communist Vietnamese Senior General Vo Nguyen Giap. McNamara also invited the Vietnamese to participate in a conference of top Vietnam War decision-makers to, according to press reports of the visit, "correct the historical record." During his visit, Giap told McNamara that "absolutely nothing" happened on August 4, 1964. McNamara later endorsed this statement by his former adversary.

In his recent book, *In Retrospect: The Tragedy and Lessons of Vietnam,* McNamara admitted that the United States "may have provoked a North Vietnam response in the Gulf of Tonkin," albeit innocently.

According to the American Constitution, only Congress has the authority to declare war. President Johnson exploited the Gulf of Tonkin incident to ask Congress to pass a resolution authorizing him to declare war on North Vietnam and conduct the war as he saw fit without approval from Congress. Congress overwhelmingly approved the Gulf of Tonkin Resolution which allowed the President "to promote the maintenance of international peace and security of Southeast Asia." The Resolution states that:

> WHEREAS naval units of the Communist regime in Vietnam…have deliberately and repeatedly attacked US naval vessels lawfully present in international waters;
>
> WHEREAS these attacks are part of a deliberate campaign of aggression;
>
> WHEREAS the US is assisting the peoples of Southeast Asia to protect their freedom;
>
> Resolved…that the Congress approves and supports the

determination of the President…to take all necessary measures to repel any armed attack against the forces of the US and to prevent further aggression. (The American War Library)

On August 4, 1964, President Johnson delivered a speech to the American people explaining what happened in the Gulf of Tonkin and his proposed response. In his speech, he stated that:

Renewed hostile actions against United States ships on the high seas in the Gulf of Tonkin have today required me to order the military forces of the United States to take action in reply. The initial attack on the destroyer Maddox, on August 2, was repeated today by a number of hostile vessels attacking two U.S. destroyers with torpedoes…repeated acts of violence against the Armed Forces of the United States must be met not only with alert defense, but with positive reply…Aggression by terror against the peaceful villagers of South Vietnam has now been joined by open aggression against the United States of America… (Department of Communication at Texas A & M University)

Based on a lie, Congress had given Johnson the authority to conduct the war as he saw fit, another example of "lying for empire." Following the Gulf of Tonkin Resolution there was a massive build-up of U.S. forces in Vietnam, eventually to 550,000 people, a massive escalation of the war which posed a myriad of risks given the tensions of the Cold War and the conflicts in other countries in Southeast Asia.

William Blum, in *Killing Hope,* states that:

Perhaps the most significant fabrication was that of the alleged attack in August 1964 on two US destroyers in the Tonkin Gulf off the coast of North Vietnam. President Johnson used the incident to induce a resolution from Congress to take "all necessary steps, including the use of armed forces" to prevent further North Vietnamese aggression…Serious enough doubts were raised at the time about the reality of the attack, but over the years other information has come to light which has left the official story in tatters.

According to Edward Herman, in *Beyond Hypocrisy*, the Bay of Tonkin incident was a:

….fabricated attack on U.S. warships by the North Vietnamese on August 4, 1964, manufactured by the Johnson administration to obtain a blank check from congress to move to a full-scale war with Vietnam.

Edward Herman and Noam Chomsky, in *Manufacturing Consent,* point out that:

Captain John Herrick of the Maddox…radioed that reports "appear very doubtful" ...and that there were "No actual sightings by Maddox"...Subsequent evidence indicates that almost certainly no attack took place.

In *Shedding New Light on the Gulf of Tonkin Incident*, Captain Ronnie E. Ford refers to Daniel Ellsberg:

> ...the former Johnson Administration member who leaked the Pentagon Papers to the press. In his presentation, Ellsberg addressed the question of whether the Johnson administration deliberately misled Congress: "Did McNamara lie to Congress in 1964 I can answer that question. Yes, he did lie, and I knew it all the time. I was working for John McNaughton...I was his special assistant. He was Assistant Secretary of Defense for International Security Affairs. He knew McNamara had lied.

The Gulf of Tonkin lie and Congressional authorization for war mirror the day that "lived in infamy." In both cases they were provoked, even if Tonkin was not actually as much of a real attack or an attack at all. Truth isn't just a casualty, but an obstacle to war that must be actively crushed... The point is, presidents need these kinds of incidents, real or imagined scarcely matters; plausible will do, to expand war. The lie by McNamara is later echoed by Colin Powell in his UN speech, who argued that we are being provoked into war against Iraq in self-defense. Powell's case was even weaker...but the point was that the justification was the same: we are just defending ourselves.

The build-up of American troops on the ground in South Vietnam went through a number of phases before U.S. forces were engaged in an all out ground war with the Viet Cong. The first phase, already underway, was assigning American military advisors to assist the South Vietnamese forces. By December 1964, the number of Americans in an "advisory" role had climbed to 23,000.

The next step in escalating the war through greater direct American participation was the security phase. On March 8, 1965, the United States shipped two Marine Corps battalions to Da Nang, the location of an American air base. Their mission was to protect the base and associated installations from attack, but according to the *Pentagon Papers*:

> ...at the time the Marines were landed, it was obvious to them from the outset that they had neither the capability nor the flexibility to adequately secure the airbase at Da Nang...

Responding to Ambassador Taylor's request for more soldiers to protect the base, military leaders transferred another 44 battalions to Da

Nang. Ambassador Taylor's judgment of the assignment of Marine Corps battalions to Da Nang was that decision-makers in Washington were operating on the assumption that a ground war in Vietnam was inevitable.

In 1965, the South Vietnamese army experienced a number of defeats which persuaded policymakers to consider building bases throughout South Vietnam from which U.S. forces could project military force into the countryside. However, the President had apprehensions about the capability of American troops to fight in an Asian insurgency environment. American policymakers developed a strategy that would allow American troops to fight on the ground at relatively low risk. The enclave strategy, the third phase in American troop deployment, proposed that U.S. troops be based in coastal enclaves and to provide security for the enclave up to 50 miles outside. The safety factor was the ability of the U.S. troops to leave the enclaves and assist South Vietnam forces protected by the security of the enclaves. Seventeen battalions were assigned to five enclaves.

It was becoming increasingly obvious that the base security and enclave strategies would not be capable of producing a victory. American leaders had shifted their overall objective from denying the enemy a victory to defeating the enemy. The new objective necessitated a new strategy and more troops leading to the fourth phase which involved "search and destroy" missions. The purpose of this strategy was to seek out the enemy, deny him freedom of movement anywhere in the country, and to exploit superior American firepower to deliver a severe blow. The number of battalions assigned for these missions was originally 44 but was revised upward as further intelligence revealed the extent of enemy infiltration.

American air power was utilized for two distinct purposes. The first was to bomb North Vietnam in the hope that it would discourage and deter the North from supporting the revolutionary war in the South, to inject confidence into the troops of South Vietnam, and as a program of reprisals for acts carried out in South Vietnam. Rolling Thunder was the code name for this operation. The targets for the bombing of the North included transportation routes, supply routes, munitions dumps, oil storage facilities, power plants, factories, and airfields. A CIA study discloses that by 1968, there had been approximately 36,000 casualties, 29,000 of which were civilians. Also, according to Colonel William Wilson, in *Rolling Thunder*, by 1968, the number of bombing missions over the North was 148,000 per year, dropping 128,000 tons of bombs although the impact of the bombing based on:

A "Bomb Damage Assessment in the North" by the institute of Defense Analysis summarized, as of 1966, that the U.S. bombing of North Vietnam had had no measurable direct effect on Hanoi's ability to mount and support military operations in the South at the current level...

The second purpose of the bombing was to defoliate South Vietnam. American troops were not as skilled at fighting guerrilla warfare as the Viet Cong forcing American policymakers to shift the war from jungle warfare to conventional warfare by destroying the jungle. Destroying vegetation also destroyed rice and deprived the enemy of a major source of food. The main herbicide defoliant was called Agent Orange which is highly toxic to humans. Approximately 20 million gallons of herbicides were sprayed in Southeast Asia.

Edward Herman and Noam Chomsky, in *Manufacturing Consent,* describe:

"The combined ecological, economic, and social consequences of the wartime defoliation operations have been vast and will take several generations to reverse"...there is no way to estimate the human effects of the chemical poison dioxin at levels "300 to 400% greater than the average levels obtaining among exposed groups in North America."

The damage caused in the south included 9000 hamlets, 25 million acres of farmland, 12 million acres of forest, one-and-a-half-million dead cattle, the creation of one million widows, and approximately 800,000 orphans.

Agent Orange is a chemical weapon and clearly qualifies as a weapon of mass destruction. It was also aimed primarily at foliage in the jungle which is clearly a civilian target. Many civilians died or were severely burned by Agent Orange and many American soldiers who had handled the defoliant experienced effects many years later. Therefore, the use of Agent Orange, authorized by President Johnson on March 9, 1965, was a war crime. It should also be noted that this weapon of mass destruction was used in South Vietnam against the people whom the United States were supporting in this war.

Napalm, a sticky substance which disperses over a wide area and ignites, was another chemical used to defoliate the jungles in South Vietnam. Edward Herman, in *Beyond Hypocrisy,* refers to the effects as follows:

...it burns at 800 to 1300 degrees centigrade and may continue to burn for fifteen minutes, causing deep, severe burns with a very high death rate—about half of those wounded by napalm die from the burns. Among those suffering phosphorus burns, about three fourths die...

Another method of destroying the base of support for communist forces was to destroy the civilian infrastructure of the National Liberation Front. The CIA embarked on a paramilitary program called the Phoenix Program, to identify and then neutralize civilian members of the NLF. Authorized by President Johnson in May 1967, CIA operatives set up offices throughout South Vietnam and served an intelligence function as well as advising South Vietnamese soldiers who were part of the program. According to former CIA Director William Colby, who was testifying before the 1973 Church Committee of Congress:

> The function of the Phoenix offices was to collate intelligence about the "Vietcong infrastructure, interrogate civilians picked up at random by military units carrying out sweeps through villages, and 'neutralize' targeted members of the NLF."

Once the civilians were rounded up, they were held without due process and frequently tortured and murdered. William Colby claims that 20,587 persons were murdered as a result of the Phoenix Program.

CIA operatives in the Phoenix Program were allocated quotas of 1,800 civilians a month, which was hard to fill. As well, members of the NLF civilian infrastructure were hard to distinguish from the general population, resulting in the death of many people who were not members of the infrastructure.

Johnson's Nose Grew Longer

Although the Vietnam War occurred during the Presidencies of Eisenhower, Kennedy, Johnson, and Nixon, the analysis of culpability for committing war crimes will focus on President Johnson because he was the president who sought special powers to escalate the war on the basis of the Gulf of Tonkin incident.

It is now a certainty that there was no hard evidence that the alleged second attack on the Maddox occurred. While the captain was calling for an investigation of the incident, Defense Secretary McNamara was reporting to Congress that there was "unequivocal proof" of the second attack. The first attack was not suitable because the Maddox had struck first. President Johnson supported McNamara's claim after carefully reviewing the evidence. According to the *Pentagon Papers*:

> In repetition of the 2 August incident, the Maddox and the C. Turner

Joy are attacked. After strenuous efforts to confirm the attacks, the President authorizes reprisal air strikes against the North.

"After strenuous efforts to confirm the attacks" and "asks for details" suggest that the President really sought the truth about the Maddox. A series of cables from U.S. Task Force Commander, John J. Herrick, in the Tonkin Gulf described conditions in the Gulf on August 4, 1964, as "freak weather effects," "almost total darkness" and an "overeager sonar man" who "was hearing his ships own propeller beat." As well, the commander, J.J. Herrick, was calling for investigations to assess the validity of reports about the alleged attack on the Maddox by North Vietnamese vessels. Any cursory investigation by L.B. Johnson would have revealed the uncertainty of the attack.

President Johnson was guilty of lying when he said in his speech to the American people that it was "Aggression by terror against the peaceful villages of South Vietnam." The implication was that the communist guerrillas from North Vietnam were destroying the "peaceful villages" in the South when, in fact, most of the American war effort targeted the South Vietnamese people. The President lied to the American people to win support for escalating the war.

If any doubt lingers about the president's dishonesty in asking for a resolution giving him broad powers to escalate the war on the basis of an imaginary attack of an American vessel, consider a 1965 statement by Lyndon Johnson commenting that "For all I know, our navy was shooting at whales out there" in reference to the August 4 incident in the Gulf of Tonkin (Jeff Cohen and Norman Solomon in *Media Beat,* July 27, 1994).

The United States committed a number of war crimes in the Vietnam War. Their involvement in this war was an act of unprovoked aggression and therefore violates the following clauses of the United Nations Charter:

- Chapter I, Article 2—settling differences by peaceful means;
- Chapter I, Article 33—using force against a politically independent state;
- Chapter VI, Chapter 33—seeking a solution through negotiations;
- Chapter VI, Article 37, Clause 1—submitting dispute to Security Council;

- Chapter VII, Article 39—only the Security Council can decide on what measures to take;
- Chapter VII, Article 42—Only the Security Council can authorize the use of force.

Washington's involvement in the war ran much deeper than engaging in unprovoked acts of aggression. The U.S. provoked the war by ignoring the Geneva Accords (1954) which called for an election and a united Vietnam. The U.S. also demanded that their hand-picked dictator Diem not participate in the process.

The United States also violated the following clauses in the Geneva Conventions:

- Convention III, Part 1, Article 3, Clause 1—protection of non-combatants;
- Protocol I, Chapter III, Article 51—indiscriminate attacks are prohibited;
- Protocol I, Chapter III, Article 52—civilian objects are protected from attack

The bombing of North Vietnam destroyed both civilian objects and non-combatants. In South Vietnam, not only were civilian objects destroyed along with non-combatants, but the use of Agent Orange constituted an indiscriminate attack.

Other international conventions were violated as well such as the convention prohibiting the use of chemical weapons and the articles in the Geneva Convention which define the rights of prisoners. The Phoenix program was an extreme example of a violation of prisoner's rights (Geneva Convention I).

During President Johnson's watch, there were many violations of international humanitarian law. In 1971, Telford Taylor:

> ...the chief United States prosecutor at Nuremberg suggested rather strongly that General William Westmorland and high officials of the Johnson administration such as Robert McNamara and Dean Rusk could be found guilty of war crimes under criteria established at Nuremberg. (William Blum, *Killing Hope*)

The Vietnam War caused massive destruction to the land, factories, and infrastructure of North and South Vietnam. It was also devastating to Cambodia and Laos. The estimated death toll in South Vietnam was over 3 million and in North Vietnam over 30,000. By way of comparison, U.S. casualties, though devastating, were far smaller in number. The number of U.S. troops stationed in Vietnam was 540,000. American deaths numbered 58,152, those seriously wounded, 153,303.

Headquarters for the Viet Cong was suspected of being situated in Cambodia and the Ho Chi Minh trail, which was located in Laos and Cambodia, was used for troop movements and supply routes. The United States, in attempting to destroy these targets, was responsible for the death of another one million people, bringing the total death toll for Indochina to over four million. Tens of millions of people in Indochina were displaced from their homes. People are still suffering the effects of the war as Noam Chomsky points out in *Necessary Illusions*:

> Thousands of Vietnamese still die from the effects of American chemical warfare." He [Amnon Kapeliouk] reports estimates of one-quarter of a million victims in South Vietnam in addition to the thousands killed by unexploded ordinance...Kapeliouk describes the "terrifying" scenes in hospitals in the South with children dying of cancer and hideous birth deformities...

Dr. Le Cao Dai, a Hanoi surgeon, and other doctors observed the effects of Agent Orange and its impact on people and the environment. They concluded that the millions of gallons of Agent Orange that poured down on South Vietnam during the Vietnam War caused liver and other cancers, immune-deficiency diseases, miscarriages, birth defects and persistent malaria. Vietnamese estimates show that 400,000 people have been killed or injured by Agent Orange and it has contributed to the birth defects of 500,000 children. (Robert Dreyfuss, *Mother Jones*)

Many of the 2.6 million U.S. vets who served in Vietnam have complained about a litany of ailments that have been traced to exposure to Agent Orange. The Department of Veterans Affairs agreed to compensate 270,000 vets registered with the Veteran Affairs Agent Orange Program for respiratory cancers, soft tissue sarcoma, prostate cancer and skin diseases. (Robert Dreyfus, *Mother Jones*)

The multiplicity of lies and war crimes of a number of presidents that were needed to defend the American sphere of influence in South-East Asia resulted in widespread and massive destruction in Vietnam, Cambodia and Laos. President Johnson contributed his share.

CHAPTER 5

WORSE THAN HELL

NIXON PAVES THE WAY TO CAMBODIA
WITH BAD INTENTIONS

I n the early 1960s, Cambodia was almost a fairy book royal kingdom carved out of the lush jungle. Its villages, where 90% of the people lived, were mostly located on fertile plains across which two great rivers, the Bassac and Mekong flowed. At the centre of the villages were Buddhist temples overlooking and protecting the serenity of the friendly people who lived there. Fish and rice were sufficiently plentiful to feed everyone. Its capital, Phnom Penh, radiated a French provincial charm. There were bandits and revolutionary groups living in the mountains who were largely invisible to the foreigner. It was referred to as a "gentle land" with its "smiling people."

Cambodia was not a "gentle land" with "smiling people" in the late 1960s but a war-torn nation where the people suffered unspeakable horror. It became caught up not only in Cold War politics but the politics of Southeast Asia. In the pursuit of empire, President Nixon lied to Congress and the American people to cover up a massive bombing campaign against a rural people who had become an obstacle to America's empire-building in Southeast Asia.

The United States, apprehensive about Southeast Asia becoming part of the Soviet sphere of influence, were willing to commit whatever resources were needed to incorporate it into the American Empire. American military leaders believed that Cambodian territory was providing a transportation route from North to South Vietnam and a haven where North Vietnam established its headquarters. Despite the fact that in the 1960s and early 1970s, Cambodia was safely in the American camp, its use by North Vietnam was becoming a problem.

In 1969, President Richard Nixon and his National Security Advisor, Henry A. Kissinger, unleashed B-52 carpet bombing for over fourteen months against a people who still tilled the soil with water buffalo. The 3,500 bombing sorties resulted in 600,000 deaths. The American bombing of Cambodia was a closely guarded secret primarily because the U.S. was not at war with Cambodia.

Not only did Nixon and Kissinger not seek the necessary approval from Congress to bomb Cambodia, they tried to conceal the bombing not only from the American public but Congress as well. Nixon and Kissinger believed that these hideous lies were imperative to hold on to South Vietnam as part of the American Empire.

Following the bombing, many peasants were so outraged at the United States and their puppet leader in Cambodia that they chose to join the Khmer Rouge, a marginal revolutionary communist group whose ranks swelled to a major force. After taking power, the Khmer Rouge unleashed a reign of terror killing over one million people.

United States Attempts to Win Over Cambodian Leadership

To fully understand how the United States first triumphed in winning over Cambodia as part of the Empire and then losing it, the history of the different influences in the development of Cambodia must be brought to light.

Throughout its history, Cambodia has experienced war, colonization by foreign powers, and influence from other cultures. Civilizations thrived where there was a plentiful supply of water for irrigation and Cambodia was fortunate to have a number of lakes and rivers including the Tonle Sap (great lake) and the Mekong River. China was one of the earlier influences on the land they named Funan and it became a major stop on the sea routes to China. In the middle of the sixth century, calamitous floods forced the people of Funan to migrate northward marking the end of this period of prosperity.

From the ninth to thirteenth centuries, a new empire emerged with Angkor as its capital. The military prowess of the Khmer enabled expansion of the empire into modern-day Vietnam, Laos, and Thailand.

The Angkor Empire began to decline in the thirteenth and fourteenth centuries when the waterways fell into disrepair, rice fields reverted to swamps, and food production fell. In the fifteenth and sixteenth centuries, the Thai kingdom of Siam was expanding its empire and in 1594, the Thais sacked Angkor. By the early 1800s, much of Cambodia became part of the Siamese empire while at the same time Vietnam was expanding westward into Cambodia. The one element of Cambodia's former empire unscathed by the Siamese and Vietnamese was the king, although he was forced to pay homage to the Vietnamese. During a number of devastating wars, many Khmers were either killed or uprooted and Cambodia was only saved by the arrival of the French.

The French had intended to colonize Vietnam but it was only a matter of time before they set their sights on Cambodia. In 1864, a French protectorate was established in Cambodia although the monarchy did not survive as a source of real power but as a cultural symbol. King Norodom of Cambodia had signed an agreement with the French in 1864 in which France agreed to protect Cambodia from external attacks and internal strife in exchange for the right to exploit the land, import goods duty-free, and establish a separate court for foreigners. France's main interest in Cambodia was as a base from which to protect its control of the rich coastal areas of the peninsula (Vietnam) against Britain and Siam.

Deprived of their independence one more time, a group of nationalist Cambodians rebelled in the provinces against French control and the rebels in the mountains and forests resumed their war against French rule. On June 17, 1894, a contingent of French troops was dispatched to Cambodia to force King Norodom to sign a convention recognizing Cambodia as a colony of France. Cambodia's chief colonial official was the resident general who was appointed by the Minister of Marine and Colonies in Paris. In 1897, the new resident general complained to Paris that King Norodom was not competent to perform his duties as King and was rewarded with permission to assume the king's authority. When Norodom died in1904, Paris handed the throne over to his brother Sisowath.

When King Sisowath Monivong died in 1941, the French were determined to bypass the Sisowath family who were too interested in independence from the French. France was in no position to fend off an independence movement because they were beset by encroachments by the Japanese and defeat in Europe. They opted for Norodom Sihanouk of the Norodom family who was thought to be inexperienced and compliant. Son Ngoc Thanh, appointed Prime Minister by Prince Sihanouk, attempted to create an independent Cambodia when he declared it a republic but was promptly arrested by the French and exiled to France. The weakness of the French in resisting the advances of the Japanese evoked doubts about colonial rule among Cambodians.

In 1941, Japan invaded Southeast Asia and established a military occupation in Cambodia but allowed Sihanouk to retain his throne. At the end of the war, Japan, recognizing the inevitable loss of Indochina, ordered the kings in their Indochinese colonies to declare independence to thwart any attempts by France to regain control. Son Ngoc Thanh returned from exile in May 1945, and was appointed to the position of Foreign Minister by the Japanese. When the Japanese surrendered, Son and his supporters assumed power in Cambodia and urged Sihanouk to retain the throne. One of Son's rivals persuaded the Allied forces to arrest him on the grounds that he threatened the security of the Allied forces. Instead of execution, Allied forces sent him into exile in France.

The French reestablished control over Cambodia in late 1945 but a new spirit of independence posed a challenge to the French. Cambodia was granted autonomy within the French Union on January 7, 1946. Although a Cambodian army was created as a symbol of independence, the French retained control over public order, foreign relations, and public services. France succeeded in maintaining its control until 1953.

Although Prince Sihanouk owed his crown to the French, he was well aware of the growing demand for independence and decided to pursue the route of negotiation rather than armed conflict. As the opposition became more impatient, Sihanouk dissolved the Assembly and declared martial law in 1952. The next step in his campaign was to travel to France to demand independence for Cambodia but he was ignored by the French. The French were preoccupied with their war in Vietnam, a more valuable colony than Cambodia. To embarrass the French, Sihanouk departed for voluntary exile in Bangkok and then Battambang, proclaiming his refusal to return to his palace until Cambodia was independent. The French conceded and Sihanouk returned home to an independent Cambodia. The Geneva Peace Accords proclaimed that Cambodia would be guaranteed the right to remain neutral and non-aligned. It also committed Cambodia to a constitutional monarchy with elections open to everyone.

Despite the growth of his popularity after achieving independence, Sihanouk was apprehensive about his powers if the republican-minded Democratic Party, who was determined to abolish the monarchy, won the next election. His strategy was to abdicate the throne in favor of his father and to pursue his political aspirations. Sihanouk announced that he would establish a truly democratic party and end the rule of privilege. He formed a political movement called the Sangkum Reastr Niyum (People's Socialist Community) and because of his popularity, he had the support of the mass of the peasantry and several other political parties who feared annihilation at the polls. In 1955, Prince Sihanouk was elected premiere.

Over the next ten years, tension between Sihanouk and the United States intensified as American armed forces in South Vietnam made sorties over the Cambodian border and the U.S. attempted to shift Sihanouk's loyalty from pro-communist neutrality to pro-American.

Sihanouk was not really interested in democracy and therefore he ignored the Geneva accords by closing the opposition newspapers and harassing the opposition leaders. His strong-arm tactics did not backfire because of a strong political base among the peasantry.

The United States pressured Sihanouk to join the Southeast Asia Treaty Organization (SEATO) which included the U.S., Britain, France, Pakistan, Thailand, Australia, and New Zealand. Washington viewed SEATO as an organization capable of containing China and protecting Southeast Asia from Chinese domination. Sihanouk refused to recognize SEATO because of his policy of pro-communist neutrality.

Other actions on the part of Sihanouk were cause for alarm to the Americans such as his establishing relations with the Soviet Union and Poland, accepting aid from China, and making overtures to North Vietnam. Although he seemed to be courting relations with communist countries, he did not hesitate to criticize them when Cambodia's neutrality was threatened.

The United States employed two strategies to pressure Sihanouk to move more into the American camp. One was the use of aid and the other was to step up military activities along the Thai-Cambodian and Vietnamese-Cambodian borders. According to William Shawcross in *Sideshow: Kissinger, Nixon, and the Destruction of Cambodia*:

> Strom [Carl Strom—American ambassador to Cambodia] was called to Washington and was told that Sihanouk would now have to go and that United States aid would be cut off to precipitate his fall. He managed to convince the State Department this was not wise, but Washington's displeasure was evident; relations between Bangkok and Phnom Penh completely broke down. NSC [National Security Council] papers of the period [late 50s] cited in the Pentagon Papers confirm that Washington saw Thai and Vietnamese pressure across the borders as one of the principal weapons to be used in an effort to move Sihanouk toward a more pro-American position.

Sihanouk deeply resented the efforts of the Americans to pressure him into abandoning his neutrality in favour of a pro-American position. He was concerned that too many of his generals and ministers were becoming overly dependent on American assistance. After the assassination of Diem in 1963, as an expression of his determination to be independent and neutral, Sihanouk implemented a program of economic reforms and nationalization. He then repudiated American economic and military aid programs and insisted that the United States shut down their aid missions.

In 1958, Cambodia began to experience a number of border encroachments from both Thailand and Vietnam. Sihanouk's army was confronted with a number of incidents along the Thai border and the South Vietnamese Air Force began entering into Cambodian airspace. Five battalions of South Vietnamese troops, supported by aircraft, penetrated ten miles into Cambodian territory in search of communist forces. William Blum, in *Killing Hope,* reports that:

> After some American bombings of Cambodian villages near the South Vietnam border in pursuit of North Vietnamese and Vietcong, the Cambodian government, in October 1964, announced that "in case of any new violations of Cambodian territory by US ground, air, or naval forces, Cambodia will immediately sever diplomatic relations with the United States". The government did just that the following May when American planes bombarded several villages, killing or wounding dozens of peasants.

Over the next few years there were a number of incursions into Cambodia territory by American and South Vietnamese forces in search of supply lines and sanctuaries along the Ho Chi Minh Trail. These forces used napalm and land mines which resulted in a number of Cambodian casualties.

Sihanouk was caught in a dilemma. He was unwavering in his policy of neutrality but did not want to alienate the North Vietnamese. As a result, he quietly tolerated small Viet Cong camps inside Cambodia. Not only did the communists frequently avail themselves of the Ho Chi Minh Trail but supplies were now shipped to the port of Sihanoukville and trucked up the trail.

These developments set off a debate within the U.S. intelligence establishment about whether to destroy this vital source of supply. The CIA began to recruit mercenaries such as the Khmer Krom, Vietnamese of Cambodian descent, to intercept the flow of shipments along the border. The CIA also recruited the Khmer Serei who were responsible for clandestine reconnaissance and sabotage missions inside the Cambodian border. Without the knowledge of Congress, the Khmer Serrei often penetrated as far as

30 miles into Cambodian territory in search of communist trails, hospitals, and bases planting antipersonnel land mines along the way. During their 1,835 missions, they identified 15 possible areas in which the Communists had bases. Among these 15 possible bases was an area referred to as Base Area 353, just north of Tay Ninh in Cambodia surrounded by Cambodian villages, which was considered to be the most significant.

Sihanouk denied the ongoing charges that Cambodian territory was being used as a sanctuary for Viet Cong insurgents despite the insistence by the United States that there was evidence of Communist activity. In July 1966, the "Vesuvius" team of Americans investigated the charges of Communist sanctuaries inside Cambodia and released evidence throughout the year but Sihanouk took virtually no action. The team was present during an American helicopter attack on the Cambodian village of Thlok Trach. According to Noam Chomsky in *Cambodia: The Widening War in Indochina*:

> ...according to official Cambodian statistics, the United States and its allies were responsible for 1,854 border violations, 165 sea violations, 5,149 air violations, 293 Cambodian deaths, and 690 Cambodians wounded.

Chester Bowles, American ambassador to India, traveled to Cambodia to persuade Sihanouk that there was a communist threat along his border. Sihanouk gave the Americans permission to bomb the sanctuaries, but he had been referring only to isolated, small-scale attacks. The foolhardiness of this choice reflects a poor understanding of recent American history. As has been discussed previously, the U.S. is the only country to bomb massive numbers of civilians with nuclear weapons, had already possessed an unparalleled record of indiscriminate carpet bombing, had amassed a record of lies that set new standards for the word "deception," and had used lies over the Gulf of Tonkin incident to escalate the war. In this context, making an agreement permitting the U.S. to bomb—under any circumstances—could easily be understood from history as a license for massive escalation and murder.

The Downfall of Cambodia

Sihanouk's neutrality and his relationship with the two most powerful groups in Cambodia, the urban elite and the officer corps, proved to be his downfall. It also proved to be the downfall of Cambodia as American bombing intensified under his successor and social order disintegrated. T. D. Allman, in *Anatomy of a Coup,* observed that:

...anti-Sihanouk forces' main complaint—when all the charges boiled down—was that the prince, during almost three decades of one-man rule, had deprived the aristocracy, the bourgeoisie and the army of their traditional slice of the financial action and of their accustomed place in the sun. It was an upper-class coup not a revolution.

Sihanouk's new Prime Minister, General Lon Nol, was not neutral but an enemy of the Vietnamese Communists and therefore, useful to the United States. The political and military elites in Cambodia and officer corps including American-friendly Lon Nol were confident that the overthrow of Sihanouk would meet with American approval.

The American military and CIA considered Sihanouk an enemy and Green Beret teams commanded by Americans conducted forays into Cambodian territory on intelligence-gathering missions which numbered 1,000 in 1969 and 1970 (Seymour M. Hersh, *The Price of Power*). A highly secret Special Forces unit was collecting intelligence on Sihanouk before the coup.

Although there has been controversy about the extent of American involvement in the coup to overthrow Sihanouk, there is documented evidence that the United States not only encouraged the coup but offered to support it. Samuel R. Thorton, an intelligence specialist who had been assigned to the U.S. navy in Saigon, has written that General Lon Nol was seeking a military and political commitment from the United States after the overthrow of Sihanouk. Thorton wrote that the United States offered to actually participate in the coup and that the plan was code named "Dirty Tricks." The operation involved the hiring of mercenaries to infiltrate the Cambodian army if military support was needed and a plan to have Lon Nol declare a national emergency calling for American military intervention in Cambodia to destroy communist sanctuaries.

In late February or early March of 1969, operation "Dirty Tricks" was approved by Washington with the message that there was interest in the plan at "the highest level of government," strongly implying that either President Nixon or one of his top advisors had personally approved the plan.

Lon Nol objected to the plan on the grounds that neither he nor the Americans would be capable of quelling the popular uprising that would ensue. He suggested that the coup be executed when Sihanouk was on one of trips to France. The Americans responded that their support would be forthcoming but that publicly the United States would have to tread carefully to avert international criticism.

In March 1970, while Sihanouk was in Paris, Lon Nol exploited anti-Vietnamese sentiment by organizing demonstrations to protest Sihanouk's tolerance of communist sanctuaries in Cambodia in order to discredit his policies. The cabinet cabled Sihanouk in Paris announcing a radical change in military and foreign policy. Sihanouk's efforts to escape the imminent coup failed and on Wednesday, March 18, 1970, the assembly met to terminate an era in the history of Cambodia by voting Sihanouk out of office while he was in Paris.

Cambodia Becomes a Red Carpet

Planners of the American war in Vietnam realized that as long as North Vietnam was able to supply its forces down the Ho Chi Minh Trail in Laos and Cambodia and at the same time provide sanctuaries for those forces, the war was not winnable. Having identified COSVN (Central Office for South Vietnam—Viet Cong headquarters) HQ facilities in Base Area 353, the Americans deemed it necessary to destroy it even though the area contained 1,640 Cambodians of whom 1,000 were peasants. The decision to bomb Area 353 led to a secret, massive bombing campaign inside Cambodia that has been recorded as one of the major evil deeds of history.

A study by the Joint Chiefs of Staff on quarantining Cambodia from Viet Cong and North Vietnamese forces called for "short term preemptive operations by U.S. forces." An initial strategy called for a blockade of Cambodian ports and airports but this would have had to be sustained over a long period of time inviting criticism from the international community. On the other hand, a surprise and speedy series of bombing raids would have been politically more successful.

Richard M. Nixon assumed office in January of 1969 and appointed Henry A. Kissinger as his National Security Advisor, a position which was restructured to transfer extraordinary power to Kissinger which enabled him to devise national security and foreign policy. Alexander M. Haig, Jr. became military assistant and then chief deputy to Kissinger.

During Kissinger's first week in office, the Pentagon reported to the White House that a defector had pinpointed the exact location of COSVN. The legitimacy of this information was supposedly verified by other intelligence sources. General Earle G. Wheeler, Chairman of the Joint Chiefs of Staff advocated a "short-duration, concentrated B-52 attack" on COSVN in order to counter an imminent North Vietnamese offensive.

Kissinger received conflicting advice from two of his top aides about whether to bomb COSVN. Richard L. Sneider, National Security Council aide for East Asia, was skeptical about the efficacy of bombing COSVN because he believed that all it would accomplish would be to force the Viet Cong further into Cambodia. Alexander M. Haig Jr., a military man who was a strong believer in the effectiveness of military force, tried to persuade Kissinger that bombing COSVN would succeed in destroying the Vietnamese sanctuaries.

Air Force Colonel Ray B. Sitton, an aide to the Joint Chiefs of Staff, and Alexander M. Haig were summoned by Nixon to meet with him and Kissinger in Brussels to discuss the proposed B-52 bombing strikes. Sitton, Haig, and Kissinger, while waiting for President Nixon, began discussing the bombing of Cambodia. Kissinger's overriding concern was secrecy. He did not want Congress, the American public, or the world to know that the United States was planning to bomb a country with which it was not at war and violate their neutrality.

To preserve the secrecy of the bombing, Kissinger was prepared to bypass the Strategic Air Command's normal command and control system. His obsession with secrecy was so strong that he did not want the crews bombing Cambodia to be aware of their targets.

Kissinger reported the outcome of the discussions to President Nixon. Nixon then consulted his Secretary of Defense, Melvin R. Laird, and Secretary of State, William Rogers and was warned that there would be intense criticism from both Congress and the press if word of the missions leaked out. Nixon's and Kissinger's obsession with Congress and the media motivated them to ask Sitton to devise a reporting procedure that would ensure absolute secrecy.

The clandestine operation began with a cable from President Nixon to Ambassador Ellsworth Bunker (American Ambassador to South Vietnam) explaining that there were to be no more discussions about the bombing of Cambodia and with full knowledge that despite its top-secret classification, the cable would be read by dozens of senior officers and military clerks. He also ordered another cable delivered through backchannels to General Creighton W. Abrams, commander of the American forces in Vietnam, advising him to ignore the message to Bunker and to continue planning the secret B-52 bombings of Cambodia. William Shawcross in *Sideshow*, points out that despite the enthusiasm of the Joint Chiefs of Staff, Melvin Laird, Secretary of Defence was:

> ...more skeptical. But he acknowledged that if COSVN had really been discovered it should be destroyed and argued that it could be publicly justified as an essential precondition to troop withdrawal. Nixon and Kissinger were adamant that if it were done, it had to be done in total secrecy. Normal "Top Secret" reporting channels were not enough. Later General Wheeler recalled that the President said—"not just once, but either to me or in my presence at least half a dozen times"—that nothing whatsoever about the proposal must ever be disclosed.

The plan to destroy Area 353 involved sending 60 B-52 aircraft on a regular bombing mission to legitimate targets in South Vietnam. Forty-eight of them would be surreptitiously diverted to targets inside Cambodia if the Joint Chiefs of Staff sent the signal "Execute repeat Execute Operation Breakfast." Without the signal, all 60 planes would bomb targets in South Vietnam.

Critical to the secrecy of the operation was the dual reporting system created by Sitton. Before takeoff, the B-52 crews were given their normal briefing for targets in South Vietnam, most of which were cover targets. After the normal briefing, the pilots and navigators of the planes heading for Cambodia would be pulled aside by their commanding officer and told to expect special instructions from a ground radar station inside South Vietnam. Computers at the radar station would take control of the navigation system in the B-52s, guide them to their real targets in Cambodia, and compute the precise moment when the bombs should be released. After the bombing had been completed, the bomber's radio operator would call his base to report that the mission had been accomplished and the intelligence division at the base would enter the South Vietnamese coordinates in the official report. Major Hal Knight, commander of the radar crews, would collect any paperwork related to the real targets and burn them.

At the completion of the missions, the pilots would return to their home bases for a debriefing on the cover targets in South Vietnam. The evaluation of the bombing mission would then be reported in the Pentagon's secret command and control system as if the mission took place over South Vietnam.

The men who worked on the ground radar sites in South Vietnam were provided with top-secret target instructions a few hours before each mission by a special courier flight from Saigon. The radar operators in South Vietnam knew the real targets but maintained secrecy until the Watergate hearings in 1973.

Sitton's plan outlined a media strategy in the event that the press in either Saigon or Washington started to ask questions about bombing missions in Cambodia. General Earle G. Wheeler, Chairman of the Joint Chiefs of Staff, advised that:

> In the event press inquiries are received following the execution of the Breakfast Plan as to whether or not U.S. B-52s have struck in Cambodia, U.S. spokesman will confirm that B-52s did strike on routine missions adjacent to the Cambodian border but state that he has no details and will look into the question. Should the press persist in its enquiries or in the event of a Cambodian protest concerning U.S. strikes in Cambodia, U.S. spokesman will neither confirm nor deny reports of attacks on Cambodia but state it will be investigated. After delivering a reply to any Cambodian protest, Washington will inform the press that we have apologized and offered compensation. (William Shawcross, *Sideshow: Kissinger, Nixon, and the Destruction of Cambodia*)

Kissinger received a cable reporting that the bombing mission inside Cambodia had been an unqualified success and that during their debriefings, the crew members had reported 73 secondary explosions, signaling a direct hit on Viet Cong headquarters and their stores of munitions.

To verify the destruction of COSVN, the U.S. sent a "Daniel Boone" mission into Area 353 to assess the damage. "Daniel Boone" was the code name for highly classified intelligence missions into Laos and Cambodia in search of Viet Cong bases which were used to evade American search and destroy missions. The mission was carried out by two or three Americans wearing nondescript uniforms to protect their secrecy and up to ten local mercenaries. A "Daniel Boone" team was dropped by helicopter into the COSVN area immediately following the bombing. After the helicopters had departed, communists hiding behind trees began firing at the Daniel Boone team who immediately dispersed and radioed for help. A helicopter landed through automatic weapons fire to rescue the four survivors.

Unbeknownst to the planners of the secret operation in Cambodia to destroy COSVN, there was no stationary headquarters. According to Seymour M. Hersh, in *The Price of Power: Kissinger in the Nixon White House*:

> Such accounts of the size and permanence of COSVN emplacements would have amazed North Vietnam's leaders in Hanoi. They had issued orders

early in the war that COSVN was never to stay in one place for more than ten days. The enemy headquarters moved constantly throughout the war, constantly managing to leave a false trail for American intelligence. COSVN was never destroyed.

In the basement of the White House, Colonel Alexander Haig handed a note to Kissinger who then boasted that they had just bombed a base in Cambodia and that many secondary explosions had been set off as a result. There is a parallel here between Kissinger's reaction over Cambodia and news reports emanating from Iraq in 2004. News reports from Iraq repeatedly pointed out that U.S. attacks on "terrorists" hit munitions sites, destroying the ability of the terrorists to strike back. Even though some dumps were hit, the supposition that this meant a crumbling resistance proved to be similar to the delight felt by Kissinger nearly 40 years previously, namely it was a fleeting victory at best.

Initially, General Creighton Abrams had hoped that a single attack would destroy COSVN and as a result violations of Cambodian territorial integrity and neutrality would be limited. When it became clear that Viet Cong headquarters had eluded American bombers, more bombing missions inside Cambodia seemed to be necessary to achieve the objective of destroying COSVN. Once the ice had been broken and the bombing had not been discovered by the media, subsequent missions would not be as difficult. The lack of protest from Sihanouk also facilitated further missions.

The next target selected, Base Area 609, code-named "Lunch," was also suspected of harbouring COSVN, not to mention the 198 Cambodians who lived there. The next target was Base Area 351, or "Snack," where 383 Cambodians resided. The Joint Chiefs of Staff were now committed to destroying all 15 sanctuaries, code-named Menu, where they suspected COSVN to be situated. To escape the repeated bombardments inside Cambodia, the North Vietnamese and Viet Cong penetrated further into the interior forcing the bombing missions to expand their base of operations. Nixon and Kissinger had approved a total of 3,530 flights over Cambodia between February 1969 and April 1970 (Seymour M. Hersh, *The Price of Power*).

An alarming array of key personnel who would normally be involved in the planning, approval, and execution of an operation such as "Menu" were sheltered from the truth. The list includes the Secretary of the Air Force, Dr. Robert Seamans, the Chief of Staff of the Air Force, General John Ryan, the

Office of Strategic Research and Analysis, all the Congressional Committees responsible for approving the funds and authorizing the mission, the Senate Foreign Relations Committee, and most of the Pentagon. Not only were these key persons in the chain of command uninformed about the bombing, they were lied to by Kissinger and Nixon. William Shawcross, in *Sideshow*, affirmed that:

> ...Nixon, Kissinger, Rogers, Laird, Elliot L. Richardson and other officials continued to assure Congress, press and public, without equivocation, that the United States had scrupulously declined to attack Communist positions in Cambodia before spring 1970.

President Nixon delivered a speech to the nation on April 30, 1970, to announce the use of ground forces in Cambodia. The speech denied any previous American involvement in Cambodia after 3,530 bombing raids. William Shawcross, in *Sideshow,* reported that:

> Ignoring Menu, Nixon began with the lie that the United States had "scrupulously respected" Cambodia's neutrality for the last five years and had not "moved against" the sanctuaries. The falsehood was repeated by Kissinger in his background briefing to the press.

Nixon lied about respecting Cambodia's neutrality in order to grab Southeast Asia for the American Empire. The lie also paid huge dividends when Nixon asked Congress for the authority to send land troops into Cambodia to ferret out the Viet Cong headquarters. While American and South Vietnamese troops marched through Cambodia they committed more war crimes when they destroyed towns and villages. Without the lies there would be no empire. With lies, there are massive war crimes.

Seymour M. Hersh, in *The Price of Power,* confirmed that:

> Nixon wrote much of his April 30 speech himself, but he read his final draft to Kissinger and Haldeman for their approval. Kissinger, as he subsequently told the Kalb brothers [authors, reporters], offered "only small comments." The speech included a number of major lies, notably Nixon's statement that the United States had previously done nothing to violate Cambodia's neutrality.

Nixon's speech also stated that:

> ...I warned that if I concluded that increased enemy activity in any of these areas [Laos, Cambodia, South Vietnam] endangered the lives of Americans remaining in South Vietnam, I would not hesitate to use strong and effective measures to deal with the situation...To protect our men who are in Vietnam and to guarantee the continued success of our withdrawal...I have concluded that the time has come for action...Cambodia, a small country

of 7 million people, has been a neutral nation since the Geneva Agreement of 1954...American policy since then has been to scrupulously respect the neutrality of the Cambodian people. We have maintained a skeleton diplomatic mission of fewer than 15 in Cambodia's capital...And for the past five years, we have provided no military assistance whatever and no economic assistance to Cambodia...In cooperation with the armed forces of South Vietnam, attacks are being launched this week to clean out major enemy sanctuaries on the Cambodian-Vietnam border...A major responsibility for the ground operations is being assumed by South Vietnamese forces. (President Nixon's Address to the Nation on Cambodia, April 30, 1970)

The problem of communist sanctuaries had not been resolved by the secret bombing. Military policy-makers were convinced that the war in South Vietnam was not winnable as long as North Vietnam could transport soldiers and supplies along the Ho Chi Minh Trail and communist forces in South Vietnam could escape into their sanctuaries.

Alexander Haig and others on Kissinger's staff were adamant that an attack on the sanctuaries was absolutely necessary. There were four options:

- heavy artillery attacks;
- the use of South Vietnamese troops with U.S. air and artillery support;
- the use of South Vietnamese troops without U.S. support;
- a combined South Vietnamese-American ground operation.

While Nixon and Kissinger were evaluating their options, they decided to provide assistance to Lon Nol who asked for equipment for 400 battalions, 2,500 military trucks, 1,000 jeeps, 30 helicopters, 30 fighters, and 12 transport aircraft. Nixon lied to the Senate Foreign Relations Committee when he reassured them that the assistance would be minimal.

General Creighton Abrams was convinced that South Vietnamese troops were now capable of successfully launching a ground assault in Cambodia and with the acquiescence of Lon Nol, the South Vietnamese air force struck on March 20, 1970 followed by South Vietnamese armored units crossing the Cambodian border.

Nixon believed that if South Vietnamese forces were attempting to destroy some of the sanctuaries, it seemed strategically sound to use American forces to destroy others. On April 28, 1970, Nixon authorized the use of American troops for an invasion of Cambodia. The two areas selected for targeting were Area 352 and Area 353 where Abrams believed COSVN was still operating despite the fact that 29,000 bombs had already been dropped there. According to Nixon, the mission would be limited in mission, scope, and duration. The scope limited American ground forces to within 21.7 miles of the Cambodian border and the invasion was to be terminated at the end of June 1970. Not only did Abrams invade Cambodia with ground troops but one week before the Cambodian invasion, the U.S. Air Force was ordered to commence striking Cambodian targets as far as 18 miles inside Cambodia and to officially report that their targets were in Laos. "Patio" was the code name for the 156 tactical air strikes flown over Cambodia under the same secret system as "Menu."

The United States dispatched 5,000 U.S. troops into Northeastern Cambodia, 1,500 into the Fishhook area and opened a new front with another 6,000 troops. By May 7, 1970, there were 25,000 American troops in Cambodia. American B-52 bombers continued to pound areas suspected of being sanctuaries or COSVN.

American and South Vietnamese forces destroyed a number of towns and all their citizens simply because they suspected that there might be communist forces there. For example, about two thousand people lived in the town of Snuol where they thrived by tapping trees for rubber. William Shawcross, in *Sideshow,* reported that:

> When the cavalry came under fire, Lieutenant Colonel Grail Brookshire, ordered his tank crews to fire their 90-mm guns straight into the town and called in air strikes to discourage further resistance. After twenty-four hours of bombardment, Brookshire judged Snuol safe for his men, and the tanks moved into the centre. Only seven bodies could be seen, four of them Cambodian civilians…As they drove past shattered shops soldiers leaped off their tanks to kick down the doors that still stood, and they looted the town.

Dozens of towns, villages, and hamlets were destroyed and burnt to ensure that they could no longer serve as a base or sanctuary for communist forces. There was no attempt to discriminate between innocent Cambodians and the enemy during these assaults. American and South Vietnamese forces committed acts of rape, looting, and burning to retaliate for the murder of South Vietnamese. These assaults forced about 50,000 Cambodians to seek safety in overcrowded refugee camps in South Vietnam.

The Secretaries of State and Defense were not immediately informed and none of the relevant Congressional committees had any prior knowledge of the new offensive but the day after the ground invasion, the Senate Foreign Relations Committee charged President Nixon with appropriating Congress's war-making powers and not consulting with them in advance. In response to Nixon's illegal actions, the Committee approved a bill to repeal the Gulf of Tonkin Resolution and passed the Cooper-Church amendment which limited further operations in Cambodia. It also prohibited the use of American ground forces in Cambodia after June 30, 1970.

Nixon and Kissinger's strategy backfired because it only served to drive the Communists closer to Phnom Penh and to align the communist forces with disgruntled peasants in Cambodia who resented the American and South Vietnamese incursions into their territory and the continual bombing of their land. Edward Herman and Noam Chomsky, in *Manufacturing Consent*, claimed that:

> One effect of the invasion was to drive the Vietnamese forces away from the border and deeper into Cambodia, where they began to support the growing peasant resistance against the coup leaders [Lon Nol, et al.]. A second effect, as described by U.S. correspondent Richard Dudman, who witnessed these events at first hand after his capture by the Cambodian resistance, was that "the bombing and shooting was radicalizing the people of rural Cambodia and was turning the countryside into a massive, and dedicated revolutionary base." Cambodia was now plunged into civil war, with increasing savagery on both sides.

Despite these failures, Nixon and Kissinger repeatedly claimed that their Cambodian strategy was a victory. According to William Shawcross, in *Sideshow*:

> ...Nixon marked the withdrawal of American troops from Cambodia with an enthusiastic television report on the brilliant success of the invasion. He cited the considerable quantity of arms, ammunition and rice captured and the 11,000 Vietnamese or Cambodian enemies killed. He praised the quality of the ARVN [South Vietnamese forces], of the U.S. army, and of his own decisions.

Although the Cooper-Church amendment limited American bombing in Cambodia to intercepting men and supplies on route to South Vietnam, by the end of the summer of 1970, the United States and South Vietnamese again embarked on a reckless bombing campaign against Cambodia. Since the reporting system falsified the records of the bombing missions, there was very little knowledge of the real targets. At the same time, South

Vietnamese ground forces repeatedly invaded Cambodia, driving the people from their villages. They then looted motorcycles, bicycles, and radios. In *Manufacturing Consent*, Edward Herman and Noam Chomsky noted that:

> U.S. bombing continued at a high level after the withdrawal of U.S. forces from Cambodia. By late 1971, an investigating team of the General Accounting Office concluded that U.S. and Saigon army bombing is "a very significant cause of refugees and civilian casualties," estimating that almost a third of the seven million population may be refugees. U.S. intelligence reported that "what the villagers feared most was the possibility of indiscriminate artillery and air strikes," and refugee reports and other sources confirm that these were the major cause of civilian casualties and the flight of refugees.

American and South Vietnamese assaults in Cambodia, a country whose neutrality the U.S. claimed to respect, caused massive, unconscionable death and destruction. The Finnish Inquiry Commission referred to the number of deaths as genocidal. According to the Commission, 600,000 Cambodians died out of a population of 7 million and another 2 million people became refugees. Carlyle Thayer, an Australian Indochina specialist, estimated the number of dead at 500,000 of which 50,000 to 60,000 were executions. The CIA estimated that 600,000 had died.

Notwithstanding the Paris Peace Agreements, which were signed on January 27, 1973, and which put an end to the war in Vietnam, the United States actually intensified its bombing in Cambodia in a desperate attempt to impede the Khmer Rouge from gaining control. The Khmer Rouge was a monster which began as a marginal revolutionary movement but whose ranks swelled as more and more peasants became alienated from the Cambodian government which depended on the United States. During March, April, and May, the quantity of bombs dropped on Cambodia was twice as great as in the entire previous year. Edward Herman and Noam Chomsky, in *Manufacturing Consent,* explained that the rise of the Khmer Rouge can be attributed to the fact that:

> ...Cambodia was being systematically demolished, and the Khmer Rouge, hitherto a marginal element, were becoming a significant force with substantial peasant support in inner Cambodia, increasingly victimized by U.S. terror. As for the U.S.-backed Lon Nol regime, Michael Vickery points out that their "client mentality" and subsequent "dependency led them to acquiesce in, or even encourage, the devastation of their own country by one of the worst aggressive onslaughts in modern warfare, and therefore to appear as traitors to a victorious peasant army...

By May 26, 1973, Operation Menu had persevered for 14 months and the bombing continued until Congress forced it to end in 1973. The bombing finally ended on August 15, 1973, after a total discharge of 539,129 tons of bombs on Cambodia.

Despite American efforts to prevent the rise of the Khmer Rouge, the Khmer Rouge were victorious and in April 1975 took control of Cambodia and ruled the country until 1978. The Khmer Rouge created a hell on earth for the people of Cambodia.

Their first course of action was to evacuate Phnom Penh and all other towns forcing all Cambodians to live in rural areas. The Cambodian people were expected to work long hours from 5 a.m. until dark. Slave labour and an abysmal lack of food resulted in massive starvation and disease. In addition, Western medicine was abandoned and there was a severe lack of drugs in the country.

The physical hardships of the Cambodian people were accompanied by a complete breakdown in the social order. Family units were no longer recognized and family names abolished. Family members were encouraged to report any deviations of other family members from the new social doctrine. Murder became a tool for social discipline.

Any suggestion of opposition or lack of loyalty during their reign of terror was punishable by death. Members of the Lon Nol government, those who were educated or who showed any sign of discontent, suffered brutal executions. Babies were torn apart and pregnant women disemboweled.

Brutality, carnage, bloodshed, and terror describe conditions under the rule of the Khmer Rouge. The social, political, and economic structure was destroyed by a group of fanatics whose adherence to their sacrosanct doctrine was merciless. William Shawcross, in *Sideshow* asserted that:

> Father Francois Ponchaud, who by then interviewed over a thousand refugees, himself believed that the higher figure [2 million] was more accurate by spring 1978, and that, as a result of starvation, disease and execution, around a quarter of the population had died...Such a massacre is hard to imagine, and the figure could not be verified. But, in a sense, this was not critical. What was important was to establish whether an atrocity had taken place. Given the burden of evidence, it was impossible not to agree with Hanoi's assertions that "In Cambodia, a former island of peace...no one smiles today. Now the island is soaked with blood and tears...Cambodia is hell on earth."

Seymour M. Hersh, in *The Price of Power,* stated that:

There would be few television reports about the fall of the Lon Nol government in Phnom Penh to the ragtag and crazed troops of the Khmer Rouge, whose leader, Pol Pot, would seal Cambodian borders and begin a program of retribution and genocide whose final death toll reached into the millions.

Edward Herman and Noam Chomsky in *Manufacturing Consent* calls the Pol Pot era the:

"Holocaust" that was widely compared to the worst atrocities of Hitler and Stalin, virtually from the outset, with massive public outrage at the suffering of these "worthy" [sarcasm—because they were killed by communists] victims.

Although the Khmer Rouge are fully responsible for the atrocities which they committed in Cambodia, the United States must at least accept some responsibility for creating the conditions that provided the Khmer Rouge with the opportunity to rise to power. Before the American-South Vietnamese bombing and invasion of Cambodia, the Khmer Rouge were a marginal force of about 3,000. The death and destruction resulting from the actions of the United States and South Vietnam drove hundreds of thousands of peasants into the arms of the Khmer Rouge giving them the strength to eventually take over the government.

Nixon's and Kissinger's Lies

The copious lies of both Kissinger and Nixon to the American people and Congress made possible the clandestine nature of and false justifications for the Cambodian incursions. Some of the lies were:

- Nixon and Kissinger decided to keep secret the bombing of Cambodia whose neutrality the administration professed to respect.

- Records were falsified to conceal the fact that the U.S. was bombing Cambodia.

- Nixon and Kissinger assured Congress that the United States scrupulously declined to attack communist positions in Cambodia before the spring of 1970.

- In 1970, Nixon claimed to respect Cambodian neutrality and that the U.S. would not move against communist sanctuaries.

- In 1970, Nixon lied to Congress when he claimed that military assistance to Lon Nol was minimal.

- After Congressional approval for raids ending in June 1970 Nixon and Kissinger claimed that the Cambodian operation was a success.

- The Cooper-Church amendment limited American bombing and Nixon and Kissinger greatly exceeded those limits.

- Kissinger claimed that the sanctuaries were uninhabited or only lightly populated by Cambodians.

- Kissinger claimed that the decision to bomb the sanctuaries was in response to an "unprovoked offensive" by communist forces in South Vietnam.

- Kissinger's insisted that the protection of American lives was the principal reason for the bombing, but regular American bombing occurred after the "unprovoked offensive" had ended.

- Kissinger's memoranda to the defense department claimed that no Cambodian lives were lost.

- Kissinger claimed on June 11, 1969, that he and President Nixon "fully briefed" Senator Stennis and Russell on the Menu operation.

The enormity of Nixon's lies afforded him the opportunity to commit atrocities in Cambodia bordering on genocide. In the Nixon impeachment hearings, the fourth article of impeachment charged that Nixon:

> ...had violated his constitutional oath of office in that he "on and subsequent to March 17, 1969, authorized, ordered and ratified the concealment from Congress of the facts and the submission to Congress of false and misleading statements concerning the existence, scope, and nature of American bombing operations in Cambodia and derogation of the power of Congress to declare war...and by such conduct warrants impeachment and trial and removal from office." (William Shawcross, *Sideshow*)

Violations of International Law

Not only is there no justification in international law for American actions in Cambodia, President Nixon violated the American constitution and a number of international laws including the United Nations Charter, the Geneva Conventions, and the Convention for the Prevention and Punishment of Genocide.

Article 1, Section VIII, of the American Constitution states that "The Congress shall have power to...declare war..." President Nixon's commitment of American forces to military action in Cambodia constitutes an act of war for which he lacked Congressional approval. Nixon's actions in Cambodia were in violation of the American constitution as confirmed by the fourth article of impeachment.

President Nixon's actions also violated the following clauses in the United Nations Charter:

- Chapter I, Article 2, Paragraph 3—"All members shall settle their international disputes by peaceful means...";

- Chapter I, Article 2, Paragraph 4—"All members shall refrain...from...the use of force against the territorial integrity...of any state...";

- Chapter VI, Article 37, Paragraph 2—"Should the parties to a dispute...fail to settle it...they shall refer it to the Security Council.";

- Chapter VII, Article 39—"The Security Council shall determine...what measures shall be taken...";

- Chapter VII, Article 42—Only the Security Council can authorize the use of force.

Chapter VII, Article 51, does state that "Nothing in the present charter shall impair the inherent right of individual or collective self-defense if an armed attack occurs..." This clause is not applicable for several reasons. First and foremost, the American presence in South Vietnam was illegal under international law and therefore any threat to Americans in South Vietnam cannot possibly justify the application of this clause. As for "collective self-defense", Richard A. Falk, in *Cambodia: The Widening War in Indochina* argued that:

> ...under no circumstances can a state satisfy the requirements of self-defense merely by associating its actions with a state that is acting in valid individual self-defense: alliance relations are not sufficient to vindicate the claim of the non-attacked state to participate in the exercise of rights of collective self-defense.

Professor Derek Bowett concluded that:

> ...the requirements of the right of collective self-defense are two in number; firstly that each participating state has an individual right of self-defense, and secondly that there exists an agreement between the participating states to exercise their rights collectively. (Richard A. Falk, *Cambodia: The Widening war in Indochina*)

Neither of these requirements is satisfied by any possible justification proposed by the United States. The United States cannot claim that it had an individual right of self-defense because the United States had no mutual defense pact with South Vietnam and had no agreement with South Vietnam to exercise their rights collectively.

American actions in Cambodia also violated the following clauses in the Geneva Conventions:

- Convention IV, Part 1, Article 3, Paragraph 1—"Persons taking no active part in the hostilities...shall in all circumstances be treated humanely";

- Protocol (1), Chapter II—"The civilian population...shall enjoy protection against dangers arising from military operations";

- Protocol (1), Chapter III, Article 52, Paragraph 1—"Civilian objects shall not be the object of attack...";

- Protocol (1), Chapter III, Article 51, Paragraph 4— "Indiscriminate attacks are prohibited. Indiscriminate attacks are: those which are not directed at specific military objectives..."

The United States also violated the following clauses in the Convention on the Prevention and Punishment of Genocide:

- Article 2—"In the present Convention genocide means any of the following acts committed with intent to destroy, in whole or in part, a national, ethical, racial or religious group such as: (a) killing members of the group; (b) causing seriously bodily or mental harm to members of the group; (c) deliberately inflicting conditions of life calculated to bring about its physical destruction in whole or in part..."

There was no doubt during the bombing of the sanctuaries, the invasion of Cambodia and the subsequent bombing until 1973, that many innocent Cambodians would be killed and that there would be severe damage to the rural areas of Cambodia. Given the number of bombing missions and the tonnage of bombs dropped and the fact that the missions penetrated further and further into Cambodia, it would be naïve to believe that Nixon and Kissinger were not aware of the death and destruction they were causing.

The bombing of Cambodia ranks as one of the most evil deeds perpetrated by any country since World War II. In addition to the approximately 600,000 killed by the bombing, the United States must accept responsibility for the destruction of the country and the estimated two million people murdered by the Khmer Rouge.

Richard A. Falk, in *Cambodia: The Widening War in Indochina* concluded that:

> In essence, then, the Cambodian Operation represents a step backward in the struggle to impose restraints on the use of force in the conduct of foreign relations...The Cambodian Operation is, perhaps, the most blatant violations of international law by the U.S. government since World War II, but it represents only the most recent instance in a series of the illegal uses of force to intervene in the internal affairs of a sovereign society.

It is interesting to note that that in the fourth article of impeachment, Nixon was charged with not informing Congress and conducting war without their approval. There were no charges based on the "high crimes and misdemeanors" of flagrant and gross violation of international law for bombing a civilian population in a country with which we were not at war. This is not an oversight but a strong comment on the political culture in the United States where you are criticized for not informing congress but not for the heinous crimes you were able to commit because of those lies. It also reveals a political culture in which a president can commit war crimes without any sanction from Congress.

CHAPTER 6

TOPPLE ONE FOR THE GIPPER

REAGAN AND THE DESTRUCTION OF THE NICARAGUAN GOVERNMENT

U.S. governments have always claimed to be committed to principles and ideals, including those of the Organization of American States and Monroe Doctrine. For example, the Monroe Doctrine has served as the legitimizing principle for American imperialism in the hemisphere. Created on December 2, 1823, the Monroe Doctrine was originally defined by President Monroe in his seventh annual message to Congress and states that:

> …We owe it, therefore to candor and to the amicable relations existing between the United States and those powers [European] to declare that we should consider any attempt on their part to extend their system to any portion of this hemisphere as dangerous to our peace and safety.

The duplicity of American foreign policy is exemplified by the inconsistency between these commitments and the policies actually implemented by these same governments. While unequivocally agreeing to respect the sovereignty and territorial integrity of nations in the hemisphere, American governments have repeatedly intervened in South and Central American nations to pursue their own economic, political, and military agenda. American presidential signatures on the OAS Charter and on other international agreements are an expedient to create an illusion of commitment to international law while America is engaging in brutal acts of imperialism.

In essence, the United States was informing the powers of the Old World that the American continent was no longer open to European colonization. But the interpretation of the doctrine was revised by different presidents, beginning with President Grant who interpreted it as an authorization for a possible extension of U.S. hegemony in the area. Theodore Roosevelt believed that the Monroe doctrine justified the use of force if disturbances in Latin America made it vulnerable to European intervention. President Franklin Roosevelt redefined the Doctrine as a multilateral undertaking to apply to all nations in the hemisphere acting cooperatively.

The activities of successive American governments since World War II have reflected President Grant's interpretation of the Monroe Doctrine. Interventions in Guatemala, Costa Rica, Haiti, Ecuador, Brazil, Peru, the Dominican Republic, Chile, Bolivia, Jamaica, Grenada, Nicaragua, and Panama have reflected the doctrine of extending American hegemony.

Nicaragua—a History of Crises

American intervention in Nicaragua is a salient example of both an interventionist interpretation of both the Monroe Doctrine and of the Truman Doctrine offering "...to support free peoples who are resisting attempted subjugation by armed minorities or by outside pressures..." (referring to the Soviet Union). When a populist, reformist movement, the Sandinistas, overthrew the brutal and corrupt dictator, Anastasio Somoza in 1979, President Reagan organized a guerrilla force to embark on a war of attrition against the Nicaraguan people which ultimately ended in the Sandinistas' defeat.

To understand the enormity of the American crimes against Nicaragua, it is important to understand the events leading up to the American intervention. The historical context will shed light on how a country throws off the yoke of one oppressor only to have another oppressor rise up and take his place.

The history of Nicaragua is replete with conquests and interventions, including more than a dozen by the United States to secure the Western Hemisphere as an American sphere of influence. Prior to the 1500s, most of Nicaragua's lowland areas were inhabited by tribes that had migrated north from Columbia while the Pacific coast regions and central highlands were inhabited by peoples similar to the Aztec and Maya. The Spaniards arrived in the early 1500s and found three tribes with different laws and customs who were ruled by independent chieftains. The Pacific coast region was occupied by the Niquirano who were ruled by a wealthy ruler, Nicaragua, and the central region was occupied by the Chorotegano. Both these groups intermingled with the Spanish conquerors resulting in a population which was a racial mix of European and native stock now referred to as the Mestizos.

In 1524, the Governor of Panama ordered Francisco Hernández de Córdoba to lead an expedition to establish the first permanent Spanish settlement in the area. After swiftly conquering the native peoples he named the land Nicaragua and founded the cities of León and Granada. Spain manifested little interest in Nicaragua, preferring the wealthy regions of the Inca Empire and by 1531, many Spanish settlers had left Nicaragua. Most Spanish towns founded in the early years of the conquest disappeared, leaving León and Granada as the two main cities.

During Spanish colonial rule, Nicaragua was part of the Viceroyalty of Guatemala under the rule of a five-man audiencia, headed by a president responsible for administrative, judicial, and military matters. The Viceroyalty was divided into five provinces and León was the capital of the province of Nicaragua. Nicaragua suffered many disasters during the seventeenth century, including three major earthquakes, trade restrictions imposed by Spain, foreign attacks, attacks from pirates, and a decline in agricultural production due to the neglect of local governments.

In the late 1600s, the British provoked a rivalry between themselves and the Spanish over sovereignty of Nicaragua's Caribbean lowlands known as the Mosquito Coast. It was inhabited by the Miskito ethnic group, descendants of the local indigenous people who intermarried with African slaves brought over by the British. The English governor of Jamaica declared the region to be under the protection of the British crown and it remained so until the end of the nineteenth century.

The impact of the War of the Spanish Succession (1701-1714) on Nicaragua was long-lasting. When the Hapsburgs, who had supported strict trade policies, were replaced by the Bourbons, who were liberal free-traders, Nicaragua became polarized between León, the centre of free trade, and Granada, where a conservative elite had prospered under protectionism.

National independence movements in the early 1800s threatened Spain's empire in the Americas but Central America was not as important as some of the wealthier colonies and was all but ignored by Spain. In 1811, El Salvador revolted against Spanish rule. The people of Nicaragua staged a popular uprising against colonization which eventually led to Nicaraguan independence. The first step towards independence occurred when the Viceroyalty of Guatemala declared its independence from Spain. The Viceroyalty of Guatemala had been part of the Mexican Empire. Nicaragua remained part of the Mexican Empire until independence was declared in July 1823. Internal conflicts among Nicaraguan provinces interfered with efforts to create a federation until April 30, 1838, when Nicaragua became an independent confederacy.

Although coffee was grown in Nicaragua in the early 1800s, its impact on the economy was not realized until the 1840s when coffee became very popular in North America and Europe. When Central America experienced a coffee boom in the 1870s, large areas of western Nicaragua were cleared to make way for coffee trees. Coffee production required huge capital investment and high labour costs. The government of Nicaragua introduced the Subsidy Laws of 1879 and 1889 offering U.S. $0.50 a tree to growers. The unfortunate consequence of dependence on one export crop to sustain the economy was the creation of a "banana republic" in which foreign investors and local elites gained control of industry and the economy. The flow of coffee profits abroad to a small number of absentee landowners, low tax revenue from coffee production, and vulnerability to fluctuations in the price of coffee were some of the other adverse effects of the "banana republic" economy.

Both the United States and Britain were becoming increasingly interested in Nicaragua in the mid-1800s because of its strategic importance as a possible transit route from the Atlantic to the Pacific Ocean long before the Panama Canal, which wasn't established until 1914. British settlers captured the port of San Juan del Norte in 1848 and forced Nicaraguan officials to leave. Britain then forced Nicaragua to sign a treaty granting Britain the rights over the Miskito on the Caribbean coast. At the same time, the start of the California Gold Rush in 1849 increased U.S. interest in Nicaragua as a possible site for an interoceanic route across the isthmus in southern Nicaragua where the mouth of the San Juan River on the Caribbean Coast connects to Lake Nicaragua near the Pacific coast. Nicaragua encouraged the Americans as a counterbalance to the British presence on the Caribbean coast.

The fear of British colonization led to discussions with the United States in 1849. The result was a treaty which gave the U.S. exclusive rights to a transit route across Nicaragua in exchange for protection from other foreign interventions. On June 22, 1849, Ephraim George Squier became the first official United States representative to Nicaragua and was welcomed by both liberals and conservatives. In addition, Nicaragua signed an agreement with Commodore Cornelius Vanderbilt, an American businessman, granting Vanderbilt's company, the Accessory Transit Company, exclusive rights to build a canal across the isthmus within 12 years.

There was continued unrest in the 1850s as liberals and conservatives based in León and Granada respectively were at war with each other over control of Nicaragua. When liberal forces began losing they became desperate and invited William Walker, an American soldier of fortune, to support them with military assistance. Walker responded and captured Granada in 1855 with 50 soldiers. Then, betraying the liberals, he declared himself president of Nicaragua. He was officially recognized by the United States. Walker exercised poor judgment when he expropriated the transit company owned by Cornelius Vanderbilt, who in retaliation, financed the conservative forces who fought Walker in the "National War" from 1856 to 1857. The United States sent Commander Charles H. Davis of the United States Navy to Nicaragua in an effort to protect its economic interests and he succeeded in arranging a truce in 1857.

Walker attempted on four other occasions to return to Central America but his campaign ended abruptly in 1860 when he was captured by the British, tried in Honduras, and executed by firing squad. Ironically, Walker's repeated attempts to take control of Nicaragua became the catalyst for cooperation between the liberals and conservatives who moved the capital to Managua and launched an era of cooperation. A Constituent Assembly convened in 1857 and General Tomás Martinez, a conservative, served as a bipartisan president from 1858 to 1867.

From 1857 to 1893, under the rule of the Conservative Party, Nicaragua enjoyed economic growth and prosperity. The construction of new railroads, roads, and telegraph lines, along with an increasing international demand for coffee and bananas, contributed to a growing economy.

The period of relative peace ended in 1891 following the election of Conservative Roberto Sacasa as president in 1889. The presidency of Sacasa divided the party because he was a conservative from León. Liberals and dissident conservatives rebelled against his presidency. The hostilities prompted a constitutional convention in 1893 when a liberal, General José Santos Zelaya, was confirmed as president.

Zelaya's rule was significant because his repressive methods eventually provoked ongoing American involvement in Nicaragua and American support for conservative forces which bred the revolutionary movement of Sandino.

Zelaya's rule was very controversial. He presided during a period of strong economic growth and modernization but he was a ruthless dictator. He strengthened the economy by encouraging foreign investment and expanding coffee production and banana exports. Construction of roads, seaport facilities, railway lines, government buildings and schools produced a stronger infrastructure and greater prosperity. One of the shortcomings of his administration was the proliferation of American companies in Nicaragua, to the point where U.S. firms controlled most of the production of coffee, bananas, gold, and lumber.

Another achievement of Zelaya's administration was to end the dispute with Britain over the sovereignty of the Mosquito Coast. Although control of the region was transferred to Nicaragua in 1894, the Caribbean coast remained culturally separate. Despite his accomplishments, his international reputation suffered because of his imperialistic ambitions in Central America and his vocal criticism of American administrations for their interventions in Central America.

Conservative opposition to his policies, mostly by landowners, triggered a wave of repression. Reaction to Zelaya's repression provoked a major conservative rebellion led by Emiliano Chamorro Vargas in 1903, followed by another uprising led by Juan Estrada in 1909 supported by American and British money. Zelaya's capture and execution of two American mercenaries prodded the United States into dispatching 400 marines to the Caribbean coast. Finally, on December 17, 1909, Zelaya resigned.

In 1910, Juan Estrada, a conservative governor, assumed power based on a conservative-liberal coalition with the United States' support. U.S. support was conditional on the creation of an elected constituent assembly which would then write a constitution. When conflict between the two parties broke out, the Minister of War, General Luís Mena, forced Estrada to resign, replacing him with the conservative Vice President, Adolfo Díaz, whose term would expire in 1913. Mena had persuaded the Constituent Assembly to name him successor to Díaz. When the United States refused to accept this decision, Mena rebelled, resulting in the U.S. sending 2,700 marines to Nicaragua. Mena fled the country.

To serve as a reminder that the United States was prepared to protect its interests in Nicaragua and preserve the conservatives' hold on the presidency, the U.S. left 100 marines behind in Nicaragua until 1933. Nicaragua negotiated the Chamorro-Bryan Agreement with the U.S. Senate, ostensibly to grant exclusive rights to the United States to build an interoceanic canal across Nicaragua. Since the United States had already completed the Panama Canal, the real purpose was to bar other countries from building such a canal in Nicaragua and to transform Nicaragua into a virtual protectorate of the United States.

The conservatives with Emiliano Chamorro as President were in power from 1916 to 1925 because of their total collaboration with the United States. Emiliano Chamorro's uncle, Diego Manuel Chamorro, won the 1920 election with the support of the United States.

When Carlos Solórzano became president on January 1, 1925, he asked the United States not to withdraw their troops from Nicaragua in order to provide a measure of security against another Liberal uprising. Solórzano purged the Liberals from his coalition government on August 26 after the U.S. marines withdrew from Nicaragua. Subsequently, Solórzano was forced from power.

During a brief respite from the Liberals and Conservatives ongoing war, the National Congress elected Adolfo Díaz as president in 1926. Violence erupted again between the Liberals and Conservatives. U.S. President Calvin Coolidge, fearing that the violence might threaten U.S. interests, sent Henry L. Stimson (later Herbert Hoover's Secretary of State) as his special envoy to negotiate a peace between the warring parties. Coolidge, a proponent of the interventionist interpretation of the Monroe Doctrine, stated in an address to Congress in 1927 that:

> I have the most conclusive evidence that arms and munitions in large quantities have been on special occasions…shipped to the revolutionists in Nicaragua…I am sure it is not the desire of the United States to intervene in the internal affairs of Nicaragua or of any other Central American Republic. Nevertheless, it must be said, that we have a very definite and special interest in the maintenance of order and good government in Nicaragua at the present time…. The United States cannot, therefore, fail to view with deep concern any serious threat to stability and constitutional government in Nicaragua tending toward anarchy and jeopardizing American interests, especially if such a state of affairs is contributed or brought about by outside influence or by any foreign power. (William Blum, *Killing Hope*)

The revolutionaries mentioned in the address were the Liberals, one being Augusto Cesar Sandino whose name was taken by a successful revolutionary group in Nicaragua in 1961. Sandino was an illegitimate son of a wealthy landowner and a mestizo servant. In 1926, Sandino worked as a gold miner at an American company. He lectured the mine workers about social inequalities, and eventually organized his own army consisting mostly of peasants, workers, and Liberals, to wage war against the Conservative government.

After negotiating with both the Liberals and Conservatives, Stimson achieved a peaceful settlement resulting in the Pact of Espino Negro. Both sides agreed to disarm and to create a nonpartisan military force, the National Guard, to be established and trained under American supervision. As well, the agreement called for the stationing of American forces in Nicaragua to supervise the 1928 elections.

Sandino refused to sign the pact and denounced the U.S. for making Nicaragua an American protectorate. He organized an independent guerrilla force to wage war against the Nicaraguan government and the United States. American marines embarked on a six-year hunt for Sandino without success.

As American casualties increased in Nicaragua, the United States decided to withdraw the marines in 1933. Command of the National Guard was transferred to the Nicaraguan government, which appointed Anastasio Somoza García as its director.

Somoza had attended school in Philadelphia and was trained by U.S. marines. He was fluent in English and had formed friendships with military, economic, and political leaders in the United States. He maintained his close ties with the United States despite his brutal and corrupt leadership, inspiring President Roosevelt to comment that "Somoza may be a son of a bitch, but he's our son of a bitch."

Three years later, Somoza took over the presidency with the assistance of the National Guard, establishing a family dynasty which would rule Nicaragua for the next 43 years. In 1934, Sandino was captured by the National Guard and executed. The National Guard then launched a brutal campaign against Sandino supporters, most of who were executed. William Blum, in *Killing Hope*, summarized the rule of the Somoza dynasty with the assistance of the National Guard, stating that:

> While the Guardsmen, consistently maintained by the United States, passed their time on martial law, rape, torture, murder of the opposition, and massacres of peasants, as well as less violent pursuits such as robbery, extortion, contraband, running brothels and other government functions, the Somoza clan laid claim to the lion's share of Nicaragua's land and businesses.

Somoza won the 1936 election and consolidated his power base within the National Guard, eliminated any opposition to his rule, and enriched himself and his family at the expense of the people of Nicaragua. Somoza doled out important positions in both the government and military to members of his family and close associates. The National Guard repressed any opposition that threatened his position of power.

During the Somoza dynasty, the Somoza family's tentacles extended into all sectors of the Nicaraguan economy, allowing them to amass a large fortune. The family invested heavily in agricultural exports, cattle and coffee, and owned textile companies, sugar mills, rum distilleries, the merchant marine lines, the national Nicaraguan Airlines, and the country's only pasteurized milk factory. Somoza and his family also owned 10 to 20 percent of the arable land.

The corruption, repression, and lack of freedoms triggered the growth of opposition groups including political parties, labour, student, and business groups. To appease the growing opposition against his dictatorship, Somoza struck an agreement with conservative General Emiliano Chamorro Vargas that assured the Conservative Party one third of the Congressional delegates and limited representation in the cabinet. The agreement also guaranteed commercial liberty.

These measures won back limited support from the traditional elite who benefited from the economic growth in the 1950s and 1960s. In 1955 Somoza García was reelected president.

Somoza's policies and brutality had produced many political enemies including some within the National Guard, one of whom assassinated him in 1956. His eldest son, Luis Somoza Debayle, an American-trained engineer, succeeded him as president while another son, Anastasio Somoza Debayle, a West Point graduate, became leader of the National Guard. A brutal campaign of repression including torture, imprisonment, executions, press censorship, and a suspension of civil liberties followed Somoza García's death.

When Luis Somoza's health deteriorated and he was unable to seek another term as president, his brother, Anastasio Somoza, was elected president amid a repressive campaign against his political opponents. After his brother Luis died of a heart attack, Anastasio also became leader of the National Guard, giving him absolute political and military power.

One of the principal opposition groups was headed by Pedro Joaquín Chamorro Cardenal, owner of the newspaper *La Prensa*. Opposition was gaining momentum in response to degenerating social conditions, malnourishment, poor health services and inadequate housing.

On December 23, 1972, a powerful earthquake dealt a severe blow to

Nicaragua and the Somoza family took advantage of the tragedy to prey on devastated sectors of society. The earthquake left in its wake 10,000 dead, an estimated 50,000 homeless, and 80 percent of Managua's commercial buildings in ruins. Not only did the National Guard join in the looting after the earthquake but when international relief aid poured into Nicaragua, the Somoza family and the National Guard illegally appropriated a massive amount of the funds for their own use.

The Struggle Against Somoza

Several major opposition groups emerged in the 1960s and 1970s to oppose and eventually release the Somoza family's grip on power. In 1961, a small group of student activists at the National Autonomous University of Nicaragua in Managua formed the Sandinista National Liberation Front (FSLN). Although the FSLN's members faced imprisonment and exile in the early years of its existence, by the early 1970s new recruits, including students and peasants, empowered it to the point where it could launch limited military initiatives. The FSLN guerillas held a group of leading Nicaraguan officials hostage in 1974 and negotiated an agreement with the government. When a government declaration appeared in the media and 14 Sandinistas were released from prison, the guerillas' prestige soared and the government was humiliated. Somoza's reaction to the growing opposition to his regime was more censorship, torture, and murder.

Differences in philosophy temporarily fractured the guerilla movement but they united under Daniel José Ortega Saavedra's faction which believed that conditions were primed for immediate action.

When Somoza decided to run for another term in 1974, the political opposition, led by Chamorro and former Minister of Education Ramiro Sacasa, created the Democratic Liberation Union (Udel) which included most anti-Somoza elements such as the traditional elites and labour unions. Udel attempted to promote a dialogue with the government but was greeted with more repression and censorship.

In the late 1970s, while the Somoza government stepped up its repressive measures, opposition groups were gaining strength and confidence. The United States feared a possible populist, reformist, FLSN government and increased its military assistance to the Somoza administration until it was clear that they were on the brink of defeat. In 1978, the U.S. finally decided to funnel military assistance to "moderate" opposition groups in the hope that they would succeed Somoza.

By 1977, the FSLN had become sufficiently strong to pose a threat to the Somoza Regime. The Carter administration then shipped weapons to Somoza covertly to avoid accusations of supporting a government that regularly violated the human rights of its citizens.

During Somoza's struggle to hold on to power, the Nicaraguan economy suffered as capital fled the country, foreign investment dried up, inflation accelerated and employment declined. Coupled with the National Guard's brutal repression of the opposition and suppression of civil liberties, the armed resistance grew and opposition groups increasingly joined forces. A group of prominent Nicaraguan businesspeople and academics, known as Los Doce, formed an anti-Somoza alliance and buttressed the FLSN when they insisted that the Sandinistas (FLSN) be represented in any post-Somoza government.

The turning point for the forces opposing Somoza occurred on January 10, 1978 when the editor of *La Prensa*, Joaquín Chamorro Cardenal, who was critical of the government, was assassinated. According to Gabriel Kolko, in *Confronting the Third World*:

> The death of Joaquín Chamorro brought the urban masses out to the streets to fight the National Guard in what was largely a spontaneous upheaval, one that was savagely suppressed, but it gave the FLSN a largely self-directing mass base everywhere in the nation, including much of the countryside, as the people quite informally became the organization itself.

President Carter, fearing a FLSN victory, attempted to cajole Somoza into adopting a more flexible stance in an effort to win back middle class support but Somoza was in no mood to grant concessions. With military support from Israel and Brazil, he continued his brutal acts of suppression. At this point, the United States withdrew all economic and military support although support for the National Guard continued in anticipation of its role in a post-Somoza government.

Seeking a "moderate" alternative to the FLSN, President Carter authorized the CIA to support non-leftist opponents of Somoza. The American definition of "moderate opponents" was a reflection of the Cold War mindset which considered nationalism, reformism, populism and independence from the United States as a signpost of communism. William Blum, in *Killing Hope*, stated that:

Washington's idea of "moderate", according to a group of prominent Nicaraguans…was the inclusion of Somoza's political party in the future government and "leaving practically intact the corrupt structure of the Somoza apparatus", including the National Guard albeit in some reorganized form.

Gabriel Kolko, in *Confronting the Third World*, confirmed the desperate attempts by the U.S. administration to avert an FLSN victory when he reported that:

Within weeks it was clear that it [FLSN] would win because of its popular support, and the United States, whose policy was now being dictated largely by the hawkish Brzezinski, convened the OAS in Washington on June 21 in a last-ditch effort to forestall its victory. "We must not leave a vacuum," Secretary of State Vance warned the meeting, and he proposed sending an OAS delegation to Managua immediately that would arrange a transitional government excluding Somoza but retaining his party, the National Guard as the principal armed force, and all those anti-Somoza conservative elements not aligned in the broad coalition the FLSN had formed. It was a plan to preserve, in effect, an oppressive regime without its leader.

After the mass uprising on January 10, 1978, the ranks of the FLSN swelled with citizens who were eager to join the anti-Somoza movement. The guerrillas who sustained their war on the Somoza government from 1978 until May 1979 launched their final offensive by capturing a number of cities and attacking Managua in July.

While the FLSN was endeavoring to defeat Somoza's forces in Nicaragua, they were creating a coalition of different groups in Costa Rica to serve as their political wing. On February 1, 1979, these groups formed the National Patriotic Front (FPN) of which Los Doce and the Popular Social Christian Party (PPSC) were members. When defeat of the Somoza regime was only weeks away, a provisional Nicaraguan government was created in Costa Rica consisting of a five person junta including Daniel José Ortega Saavedra of the FLSN, Moisés Hassan Morales of the FPN, Sergio Ramí Mercado of Los Doce, Alfonso Robelo Callejas of the Nicaraguan Democratic Movement, and Violeta Barrios de Chamorro who was the widow of La Prensa's editor. The government-in-waiting agreed on the Puntarena Pact, to establish a mixed economy, political pluralism, a non-aligned foreign policy, a non-partisan army, universal suffrage, and ultimately, free elections.

When it became obvious to the Carter administration in 1979 that the FLSN would overthrow Somoza and form the next government, the U.S.

sent officials to Nicaragua to negotiate an agreement with the Sandinistas. The U.S. officials offered to persuade Somoza to resign if the FLSN would incorporate a reformed National Guard into the new government. When the National Guard began to disintegrate on July 17, 1979, Somoza fled to Florida with an estimated $100 million which he had accumulated during his dictatorship. After the departure of Somoza, many members of the National Guard fled to Honduras and Guatemala. On the same day, the FLSN triumphantly marched into Managua concluding the Sandinista revolution.

The junta arrived in Nicaragua on July 18, 1979, and formed the new government. Somoza and the National Guard bequeathed to the junta 600,000 homeless, a stagnant economy, a huge debt, depleted fuel and food supplies, and a deficiency of medical supplies.

Rebuilding the economy, one of the priorities of the new regime, was given a boost by the influx of $100 million of foreign aid from the United States but the conditions attached undermined the benefits. According to William Blum, in *Killing Hope*:

a)   Almost all the aid had gone to non-governmental agencies and to the private sector, including the American Institute for Free Labor Development, a long-time CIA front.

b)   The primary and expressed motivation for the aid was to strengthen the hands of the so-called moderate opposition and undercut the influence of socialist groups in Nicaragua.

c)   All military aid was withheld despite repeated pleas from the Nicaraguan Government...the defeated National Guardsmen and other supporters of Somoza had not, after all, disappeared...

One of the new government's first economic reforms was to pass the Agrarian Reform Law which called for the redistribution of land owned by the Somoza family, which comprised 20 percent of Nicaragua's cultivated land. Nicaragua, like many other developing countries, had to seek a balance between feeding its own people and earning foreign exchange through export crops to repay its debt. Nevertheless, the Sandinistas aimed for complete self-sufficiency by the year 2000.

When the Sandinistas took power, the educational system in Nicaragua was one of the poorest in Latin America. Limited spending on education and severe poverty forced many children into the labour market before their education was complete. By the time Somoza went into exile only 65 percent of primary school-age children were enrolled in school and only 22 percent of those who attended primary school completed the full six years. In rural areas, most secondary schools had only one or two grades and there was a 75 percent illiteracy rate. To improve the educational system, the Sandinistas doubled the proportion of GNP spent on primary and secondary schools, increased the number of teachers, and built more schools. Using volunteer teachers, the Sandinista government succeeded in reducing the illiteracy rate from 50 percent of the population to 23 percent. Enrollment in colleges skyrocketed from 11,142 students in 1978 to 38,570 in 1985.

Health care was a disaster under the Somoza regime with many Nicaraguans having limited or no access to modern health care. The Sandinistas completely restructured the entire health care system by spending substantially more on health care, increasing the number of students entering medical school from 100 to 500, building five new hospitals, and building 363 primary health care clinics.

The Sandinistas, who had themselves been victims of the brutal dictatorship of Somoza, were determined to construct new political institutions and to introduce a new constitution which guaranteed human rights.

The new Minister of the Interior, Tomás Borge Martínez, was committed to eliminating human rights abuses and as a start he allowed all people imprisoned by Somoza to be given a fair trial. As an urgent priority, the Sandinistas wrote and passed a new provisional constitution called the Fundamental Statute of the Republic of Nicaragua which guaranteed human rights, equal justice under the law, the right to free expression, and the abolition of torture.

To replace the National Guard, the Sandinistas created the Sandinista People's Army and a new police force. The goal of the Sandinistas was to build a well-equipped professional military.

An important step toward democratization was the creation of mass organizations representing most popular interests such the Sandinista Workers' Federation representing labour unions, the Luisa Amanda Espinoza Nicaraguan Women's Association, and the National Union of Farmers and Cattlemen.

All these progressive measures were interpreted by the new American

President, Ronald Reagan, as symptoms of communism requiring immediate action by the United States. David Womble, in *The CIA in Nicaragua* stated that:

> In January 1981 Ronald Reagan took office under a Republican platform which asserted that "...it deplores the Marxist Sandinista take-over of Nicaragua" and he greatly expanded the CIA's guerilla warfare and sabotage campaigns. In November 1981 Reagan authorized a covert plan for $19 million to help the Argentina dictatorship train a guerilla force operating from camps in Honduras to attack Nicaragua.

William Blum, in *Killing Hope* wrote that:

> The President [Ronald Reagan] moved quickly to cut off virtually all forms of assistance to the Sandinistas, the opening salvos of his war against their revolution. The American whale, yet again, felt threatened by a minnow in the Caribbean.

Among the many other measures undertaken: Nicaragua was excluded from U.S. government programs which promote American investment and trade; sugar imports from Nicaragua were slashed by 90 percent; ... Washington pressured the International Monetary Fund (IMF), the Inter-American Development Bank (IDB), the World Bank, and the European Common Market to withhold loans to Nicaragua.

As well, Ryan Telford, in *John Wayne Goes to Managua: U.S. Covert Policy in Nicaragua During the Reagan Administration* noted that:

> With the benefit of recently declassified documents from National Security Advisor (NSA) Robert McFarlane and a Presidential Finding signed by President Reagan, it seems clear that from early 1981 the Reagan administration was determined to implement a National Security Council (NSC) and "Central Intelligence Agency (CIA) proposal for a very broad program of covert actions" to address US national security concerns in Nicaragua.

In order to alarm the American people and gain support for the war against Nicaragua, President Reagan warned that Nicaragua was only two days march from Brownsville, Texas. He also stated that, "El Salvador is nearer to Texas than Texas is to Miami. Nicaragua is just as close to Miami, San Antonio, San Diego, and Tucson as those cities are to Washington where we have gathered tonight." (Holly Sklar, *Washington's War on Nicaragua*)

I traveled through Nicaragua while the American surrogate guerrilla force was attempting to overthrow the Sandinista government. I was horrified by the abject, ubiquitous poverty of the people. People lived in small shacks with no amenities and when I took the bus to the market in Managua, I saw people hanging over the sides because no one could afford a car. The preposterous notion that this poor backward country would even consider for a moment marching toward the United States through Mexico is material for the satire of Saturday Night Live.

Overthrowing the Cancer Right Here on Our Land Mass

To overthrow what George Shultz, former Secretary of State, referred to as a "cancer right here on our land mass," the United States decided to create a surrogate guerilla force, feigning to be Nicaraguans, to rise up against the evil communist government in Managua. The alternative, an invasion by American forces, was ruled out for fear of a backlash from the American public who were not quite over the Vietnam War. The CIA covertly created a paramilitary force known as the Nicaraguan Democratic Force (FDN) or the Contras, many of whom were former members of Somoza's National Guard. By 1983, there were between 16,000 and 20,000 Contra troops who were operating along the Honduran border and from bases in Costa Rica.

The purpose of the Contras was not to defeat the Sandinista army in battle but to use terrorist tactics to destroy infrastructure, health, and educational services. Their intention was not to confront Sandinistas but to blow up bridges, power plants, oil pipelines, ports, schools, health clinics, grain silos, irrigation projects, and farmhouses. The underlying purpose of these acts of terrorism was to destroy the morale of the Nicaraguan people and to force the Nicaraguan government to divert a high proportion of its budget to defence as discussed in detail below. Diverting government resources to the war, forcing the Sandinistas to cut back on their reform programs, had a considerable negative impact on the people of Nicaragua. David Womble, in *The CIA in Nicaragua,* discussing the atrocities of the Contras called attention to:

> Witness For Peace, an American Protestant watchdog body, collected a list of Contra atrocities in one year, which include murder, the rape of two girls in their homes, torture of men, maiming of children, cutting off arms, cutting out tongues, gouging out eyes, castration, bayoneting pregnant women in the stomach, amputating the genitals of people of both sexes, scraping the skin off the face, pouring acid on the face, breaking the toes and fingers of an 18 year old boy, and summary executions. These were the people Ronald Reagan called the "freedom fighters" and the "moral equivalent of our founding fathers."

The Contras were trained by the CIA in terrorist warfare and were provided with a manual of instruction which encouraged the use of violence against civilians. According to William Blum, in *Killing Hope*:

> The CIA manual, entitled Psychological Operations in Guerilla Warfare gave advice on such niceties as political assassination, blackmailing ordinary citizens, mob violence, kidnapping, and blowing up public buildings. Upon entering a town, it said, "establish a public tribunal" where the guerillas can "shame, ridicule and humiliate" Sandinistas and their sympathizers by "shouting jeers and slogans".

In the wake of the American public's uproar over the disclosures in 1984 about their government's support for the Contra guerilla army, the State Department was forced to express its strong disapproval for the Contras' terrorist activities, and the Congressional Intelligence Committee publicly condemned the Contras. This was not the first time that Congress had reacted negatively to the CIA covert actions against Nicaragua. Shortly after the CIA had begun its covert actions against Nicaragua without the Congressional Intelligence Committee's approval, an enraged Senate passed the Boland Amendment on December 8, 1982 to amend the War Powers Act of 1973. It prohibited any funding for the Contras and any military support for the purpose of overthrowing the government of Nicaragua. Despite the Boland Amendment, Vice Admiral John Poindexter and Colonel Oliver North secretly diverted funds to the Contras from another secret operation involving the illegal sale of anti-tank and anti-aircraft weapons to Iran, which had explicit Presidential approval.

Although the Contras consisted of local recruits, they were completely dependent on American support, supplies, and training. Americans built airports, docks, radar stations, and communication centres and trained thousands of Contras in Florida and California. Weapons and military equipment were also provided by the United States but one of the most crucial contributions by the United States came from US intelligence, which monitored the movements of the Sandinista army from satellites and sophisticated surveillance aircraft allowing the Contras to move freely in Nicaragua without any danger of confronting Nicaraguan troops.

American pilots covertly participated in the terrorist campaign against Nicaragua by flying combat missions against Nicaraguan troops and by dropping supplies to Contra forces within Nicaragua. Some were flying in civilian clothes and were warned by the CIA that if they were captured, they would be disavowed.

As a result of these raids, foreign companies decided to abandon any economic relationship with Nicaragua. In 1982, the Standard Fruit Company announced that it was suspending its operations in Nicaragua while foreign oil tankers refused to deliver oil to Nicaragua after Contra threats to blow them up. In October 1983, Nicaragua lost its primary oil supply when Esso (Exxon) announced that it would no longer ship oil from Mexico to Nicaragua. Nicaragua suffered the destruction of oil pipelines and the mining of oil-unloading ports, creating a critical shortage of fuel.

Another result was an acute food shortage stemming from Contra attacks on crops, grain silos, irrigation projects, farm silos, and machinery. In addition, the fish industry suffered from lack of fuel for its boats, spare parts, and the mining of Nicaraguan waters.

In addition to the guerilla warfare against the Sandinistas, the United States embarked on a devastating campaign of economic warfare to starve the people of Nicaragua in the hope that eventually they would "vote with their stomachs." Washington's ultimate objective was to impose a complete economic blockade against Nicaragua by blocking foreign aid, trade, and loans. The United States persuaded the World Bank, the International Monetary Fund, and the International Development Fund to cut Nicaragua off from any form of assistance. A total trade embargo imposed by the U.S. was a serious blow to the Nicaraguan economy. Foreign trade with Nicaragua was almost severed when the CIA mined Nicaraguan harbours in 1984. The placing of 300-pound mines in three harbours not only discouraged foreign trade but destroyed Nicaragua's fishing industry.

To a country already facing serious economic hardships, termination of all aid and trade dealt a lethal blow to the economy. By 1985, the Nicaraguan economy was on life support. According to Ryan Telford, in *John Wayne Goes to Nicaragua*:

> The export economy that was specifically targeted by U.S. covert policy dropped from a pre-Revolution high of $134 million in 1977 to under $11 million in 1986...the U.S. stranglehold on Nicaragua during the 1980s resulted in Nicaraguan direct loses of over a billion dollars and indirect loses through 1987 of over $3.6 billion.

Congress had become very disapproving of the Reagan administration's unilateral decisions on matters that were within their jurisdiction—hence the Boland Amendment. Challenges to the administration's policies included the charge that Reagan's Central American activities such as "toppling governments" were responsible for the current problems there. To win approval not only in Congress but from the American people, the Reagan administration planned to put a stamp of legitimacy on their activities in Central America. The strategy was to set up a commission to study the problems in Central America and report back to the president, knowing in advance that the report would not interfere with the president's plans. President Reagan's Central American plan would be safe given the composition of the commission.

In June 1983, Senator Henry M. Jackson proposed setting up a bipartisan commission on Central America. At a convention in Florida, President Reagan announced the establishment of a commission that would "lay the foundations for a long-term unified national approach to the freedom and independence of the countries of Central America." On July 19, 1983 he created the National Bipartisan Commission on Central America (Kissinger Commission). The commission was headed by Henry Kissinger, and included Jack Kemp, William Rogers, and Jeanne Kirkpatrick.

The Kissinger Commission reported that it endorsed the thrust of President Reagan's policies and urged the president to respond boldly to the "real and acute" crisis in Central America. Among its findings were:

- The roots of the crisis are both indigenous and foreign;

- The true threat is the intrusion of aggressive outside powers exploiting the local grievances to expand their own political influence and political controls;

- The United States has a humanitarian interest in alleviating misery and helping the people of Central America meet their social and economic needs.

Some recommendations were that:

- The campaign waged by the anti-Sandinista guerillas, which is in favor of a negotiated settlement, be continued;

- The United States should consider using force against the leftist Nicaraguan government as a "last resort" if it refused to agree to stop supporting guerilla movements in other countries.

The final recommendation is important because part of the Reagan administration's propaganda campaign was to justify its activities against Nicaragua on the grounds that the Sandinistas were supplying weapons to guerilla forces in El Salvador, an American client state. In a formal address to the nation on August 13, 1983, President Reagan stated that:

> We are on the side of peaceful democratic change in Central America and our actions daily prove it. But we aren't the only ones interested in Central America. The Soviet Union and Cuba are intervening there, because they believe they can exploit the problems so as to install ruthless Communist dictatorships, such as we see in Cuba...
>
> That brings me to Nicaragua. We have dealt decently with Nicaragua, more decently than the Sandinista government there has treated its own citizens and neighbors...They betrayed many who fought beside them in the revolution, and they've set up a Communist dictatorship...
>
> We support the elected Government of El Salvador against Communist-backed guerillas who would take over the country by force. And we oppose the unelected Government of Nicaragua which supports those guerillas with weapons and ammunition. (From www.reagan.utexas.edu)

Noam Chomsky, in *Understanding Power*, pointed out that the Reagan administration believed that:

> ...it was necessary for the propaganda system to pretend that the Contras were like the F.M.L.N. [guerillas] in El Salvador—just a regular indigenous guerilla force opposing the government. And part of the method for claiming that these two forces were equivalent was to say that the F.M.L.N. guerillas also had outside support from a foreign government—in other words, from the government of Nicaragua—and that was the only reason they could survive.

David MacMichael, who served with the CIA from 1981 to 1983 as an analyst of military and political developments in Central America, noted after an inter-agency meeting that:

> "Although the stated objective was to interdict arms going to El Salvador, there was hardly any discussion of the arms traffic...I couldn't understand this failure until months later when I realized, like everyone else, that arms interdiction had never been a serious objective...the Administration and the CIA have systematically misrepresented Nicaraguan involvement in the supply of arms to Salvadorian guerillas to justify [their] efforts to overthrow the Nicaraguan Government." (William Blum, *Killing Hope*)

After retiring, David MacMichael testified at the World Court and demonstrated that the State Department's claim that the main arms flow from Nicaragua to the F.M.L.N. across the Gulf of Fonseca was not credible. The

Gulf of Fonseca, which is 30 kilometers wide, is extensively patrolled by the U.S. Navy and an island in the middle of the Gulf is loaded with super-sophisticated U.S. radar systems which were capable of detecting any ships on the Pacific coast. There were also U.S. Navy SEAL teams everywhere, none of whom detected any ships.

According to the Reagan administration, the Sandinistas were a communist dictatorship with fraudulent elections who were exporting communism to El Salvador through their support of the guerilla movement there. President Reagan needed to demonstrate that El Salvador, an American client state, was democratic while the elections in Nicaragua were fraught with critical flaws. This lie provided the United States with the justification for its campaign to purge the hemisphere of a communist threat not only to other Latin American countries but also to the security of the United States.

Election and Reaction

The 1984 elections in Nicaragua were open to all parties and candidates, no fraud was reported in the polling, the vote was legitimately secret, voters were encouraged to vote, and "the fact that there were no deaths reported in connection with the election, by itself, made it rather unique in Latin America." (William Blum, *Killing Hope*)

There were 450 foreign observers to monitor the 1984 Nicaraguan election in addition to the 15-member delegation from the Latin American Studies Association (LASA) who were in Nicaragua eight days prior to the election with complete freedom to interview whomever they chose.

LASA pointed out that "voter turnout was heavy," with "more enthusiasm among voters in low-income areas than in more affluent neighborhoods," and the rate of participation achieved "compares very favorably with the rates achieved in 11 other recent Latin American elections, as well as the 1984 U.S. presidential election." In addition, LASA emphasized the protection of secrecy which was "meticulously designed to minimize the potential for abuses." (Edward Herman and Noam Chomsky, *Manufacturing Consent*).

One of the groups monitoring the election was the Irish delegation who pointed out that:

Recent elections in other Central American countries such as El Salvador and Guatemala did not introduce such measures [creating a complete and up-to-date voter's list], and there was considerable debate concerning the validity of their registers, which were based on out-of-date census figures, incomplete official registers of population changes, and other sources. (Noam Chomsky and Edward Herman, *Manufacturing Consent*)

The Irish delegation, commenting on the freedom of any party to participate, claimed that "The law guarantees participation of political parties of all ideologies."

With respect to freedom of expression and the press, the *Washington Post* (November 4, 1984 p. A1) reported on Election Day that:

> ...even U.S. diplomats here acknowledge that the Sandinistas have allowed expressions of a wide range of political views, including some that were harshly critical of the government. The Sandinistas eased censorship of the sole opposition newspaper, *La Prensa*...

By contrast, elections in El Salvador, the U.S. client state, were critically flawed by, among other factors, the mass murder of civilians by the army during the elections, extreme repression of the majority by a government that ruled on behalf of the elites and suspension of the right to free speech on March 7, 1980. Although free speech was restored ten days before the 1982 election, the voters were not informed. As well, the only newspapers critical of the government, La Crónica del Pueblo and El Independiente, were closed in the early 1980s.

The propaganda apparatus in Washington was determined to demonstrate that El Salvador was a paragon of democracy and Nicaragua a dangerous dictatorship with plans to inject its poison into El Salvador. In fact, El Salvador was run by a brutal dictator who was forced to implement very repressive measures to contend with a negative nationalist reaction to American domination. President Reagan made a statement on May 18, 1984, in which he noted that:

> On Wednesday, May 16, the Central Elections Commission of El Salvador certified Jose Napoleon Duarte as the winner of the May 6 presidential election in that country. By this act, the people of El Salvador have made clear their choice of Mr. Duarte as the first popularly elected President of that country in recent history.
>
> The voters have chosen as president a man who has dedicated his life to achieving democracy for his homeland. (From www.reagan.utexas.edu)

In a radio address to the people of the United States on March 24, 1984, the President stated that:

> Unlike El Salvador, the Nicaraguans don't want international oversight of their campaign and their elections… Nicaragua is a communist dictatorship armed to the teeth, tied to Cuba and the Soviet Union, which oppresses its people and threatens its neighbors.

The Reagan administration referred to the Nicaraguan election as a sham and to ensure that media coverage in the United States on the day of the election would be negative, the State Department leaked a fraudulent story to the media on November 4, 1984, the day of the election, about a Soviet freighter shipping Soviet MIGs to Nicaragua. According to the State Department, U.S. satellites had picked up evidence that a Soviet freighter heading towards Nicaragua contained crates of the type used to hold MIG fighters. The story was prominently played on U.S. news with special bulletins interrupting regular programming to announce the new threat to American security. Edward Herman and Noam Chomsky, in *Manufacturing Consent,* observed that:

> The MIG ploy was, nevertheless, entirely successful. A tone of crisis was manufactured, and "options" against the hypothetical Sandinista "threat" were placed at the centre of public attention. The Nicaragua election was not discussed. LASA points out that "The final results of Nicaragua's election were not even reported by most of the international media. They were literally buried under an avalanche of alarmist news reports." LASA concludes that Nicaraguan electoral process was manipulated, as the U.S. government claims, but by the U.S. government itself in its efforts to discredit an election that it did not want to take place.

The MIG and election stories were only some of the lies propagated by the United States as part of a propaganda campaign to characterize Nicaragua as a Communist dictatorship whose objective was to spread communism to the entire hemisphere. The other lies include:

- Members of the Kissinger Commission concluded that Nicaragua was worse off under the Sandinistas than under Somoza;
- Henry Kissinger believed that Nicaragua was worse than Nazi Germany;
- The State Department reported to the world that Nicaragua was exporting drugs without any evidence;
- Secretary of State Alexander Haig displayed a photograph of

burning corpses and declared that it was an example of the Sandinista atrocities perpetrated against the Miskito Indians. The photo was actually taken before 1978 and therefore was before the Sandinistas came to power;

- George Shultz called the Sandinistas "a cancer in our backyard."

Nicaragua was under attack from the United States on many fronts including the propaganda campaign, the Contra attacks, the economic embargoes and the mining of Nicaraguan harbours. This small country with limited resources was no match for the giant superpower seeking to remove the Sandinistas from power. President Reagan was not some lone psycho at work here but the point man for an apparatus of propaganda and empire building.

Nicaragua responded to these acts of aggression by the only means available to them and that was to institute proceedings at the World Court in 1984. Nicaragua requested the court to adjudge and declare that:

- The U.S. was under a duty to cease and desist immediately from the use of force against Nicaragua, from all violations of sovereignty and political independence of Nicaragua, and from the effort to restrict access to and from Nicaraguan ports;

- The United States has an obligation to pay reparations for damages caused by these violations.

In the judgment of the World Court "the Court finds it established that… the President of the United States authorized a U.S. government agency to lay mines in Nicaraguan ports." The ruling is based on the following violations of International Law:

- The UN Charter, article 2, paragraph 4—"All members shall refrain in their international relations from the threat or use of force against the territorial integrity or political independence of any state…;"

- Geneva Conventions, Protocol 1, chapter 2, clause 3—"Those who employ a method or means of combat, the effects of which cannot be limited as required by this Protocol, and in each such case, are of a nature to strike military objectives and civilians or civilian objects without distinction.";

• Hague Convention viii, Article 2—It is forbidden to lay automatic contact mines off the coast and ports of the enemy, with the sole purpose of intercepting commercial fishing.

With respect to the Contra guerillas, the Court found "It clearly established that the United States intended by its support of the Contras to overthrow the present government of Nicaragua. It [the Court] finds that the support given by the United States to the Contras by financial support, supply of weapons, intelligence and logistical support, constitutes a clear breach of the principle of non-intervention."

On the issue of reparations, the Court determined that "...the court considers appropriate the request of Nicaragua for the nature and amount of the reparations to be determined at a subsequent phase of the proceedings."

In response to the ruling, the State Department commented that the World Court was "...not equipped for complex cases." State Department legal advisor Abraham Sofaer justified the United State's rejection of the World Court decision by explaining that America must "...reserve to ourselves the power to determine whether the Court has jurisdiction over us in this particular case" and that "The United States does not accept compulsory jurisdiction over any dispute involving matters essentially within the domestic jurisdiction of the United States as determined by the United States." In their response, the United States invented a new principle of jurisprudence, namely that the convicted party, and not the court itself, has the right, after the trial, to determine the jurisdiction of the court.

To continue its support for the Contras, the Reagan administration descended to the level of common outlaws and drug dealers. In addition to violating the Boland Amendment, the Arms Export Control Act, and the Neutrality Act, the Reaganites engaged in narcotics trafficking and gunrunning, and ignored the oversight controls of Congress in order to maintain a steady flow of weapons to the Contras.

During the Iran-Iraq war, despite a trade embargo on Iran, President Reagan approved a plan to sell weapons to Iran in order to secure the release of seven American hostages being held by Iranian-controlled terrorists in Lebanon. National Security Advisor Robert McFarlane, who sought President Reagan's approval for the plan, was also motivated by the hope of establishing better relations with Iran and increasing U.S. influence in the Middle East.

The secret funds raised from the arms sale were used to buy arms for the Contras in violation of the Boland Amendment and the second Boland Amendment, which won Congressional approval in 1984. Boland Amendment II prohibited the use of funds "available to the Central Intelligence Agency...or any other agency or entity of the United States involved in intelligence activities" to be used on behalf of the Contras.

When Nicaraguan soldiers shot down an American cargo plane loaded with military supplies for Contra forces, the one surviving crew member, American Eugene Hasenfus, confessed that he worked for the CIA. A Senate Committee also uncovered a scheme to use the sale of cocaine from Colombia to finance the Contras. The same planes that carried weapons to the Contras also carried drugs.

Congress established the Senate Committee on Drugs, Law Enforcement and Foreign Policy in 1986 which was chaired by Senator John F. Kerry. The report of the Committee stated that:

> While the Contra/drug question was not the primary focus of the investigation, the Subcommittee uncovered considerable evidence relating to the Contra network which substantiated many of the initial allegations laid out before the Committee in the spring of 1986. On the basis of this evidence, it is clear that individuals who provided support for the Contras were involved in drug trafficking, the supply network of the Contras was used by drug trafficking organizations, and elements of the Contras themselves knowingly received financial and material assistance from drug traffickers.

When knowledge of these illegal activities became public, Attorney General Edwin Meese III appointed an Independent Counsel (Lawrence Walsh) to investigate and possibly prosecute illegal activities related to the Iran-Contra affair. The conclusions of the investigation include:

- high-ranking administration officials violated laws and executive orders in the Iran/Contra matter;

- the sale of arms to Iran contravened United States government policy and may have violated the Arms Export Control Act;

- the provision and coordination of support to the Contras

violated the Boland Amendment ban on aid to military activities in Nicaragua;

- The policies behind both the Iran and Contra operations were fully reviewed and developed at the highest levels of the Reagan administration;

- Iran operations were carried out with the knowledge of, among others, President Ronald Reagan, Vice President George Bush...;

- Following the revelation of these operations in October and November 1986, Reagan administration officials deliberately deceived the Congress and the public about the level and extent of official knowledge of and support for these operations.

The Independent Counsel charged 14 persons with criminal violations and all but two of them were convicted. President Reagan escaped without any charges but according to a summary of the Independent Counsel:

> Independent Counsel has concluded that the President's most senior advisors and the Cabinet members on the National Security Council participated in the strategy to make National Security staff members McFarlane, Poindexter, and North the scapegoats whose sacrifice would protect the Reagan Administration in its final two years. In an important sense, this strategy succeeded. Independent Counsel discovered much of the best evidence of the cover-up in the final year of active investigation, too late for most prosecutions. (From www.webcom.com)

President Reagan gave a speech to the American people on March 4, 1987 and stated that:

> A few months ago I told the American people I did not trade in arms for hostages. My heart and my best intentions still tell me that's true, but the facts and the evidence tell me it is not as the Tower Board [President Reagan appointed a special commission headed by John Tower to investigate the Iran/Contra affair] reported, which began as a strategic opening to Iran but deteriorated, in its implementation, into trading arms for hostages...
>
> Now, another major aspect of the Board's findings regards the transfer of funds to the Nicaragua Contras. The Tower Board wasn't able to find out what happened to this money, so the facts here will be left to the continuing investigations of the court-appointed Independent Counsel and the two Congressional Committees...

One thing still upsetting me, however, is that no one kept proper records of meetings and decisions. This led to my failure to recollect whether I approved an arms shipment before or after the fact. (www.pbs.org)

The remarkable hypocrisy in Reagan's plan to sell arms to Iran lies in the fact that he was, at the same time, arming Iraq to destroy Iran. Frank Gaffney, under-Secretary of Defense in the Reagan administration admitted on the Canadian CBC television network's program Counterspin that Iraq was armed to "blood-let Iran."

The ongoing American military and financial support of the Contras was only one aspect of a four-sided attack against the Sandinista Government. Economic strangulation, support for opposition groups within Nicaragua, and intervention in the 1990 Nicaraguan election also contributed to the eventual downfall of the Sandinistas.

In 1988-89 the Reagan administration intensified its efforts to ensure the defeat of the Sandinistas in the 1990 election with continued support for the Contras. According to William Blum in *Killing Hope*:

> ...the Reagan administration's obsession with the Sandinistas had inspired both the official and the unofficial squads to embrace tactics such as the following in order to maintain a steady flow of financing, weaponry and other aid to the Contras: dealings with other middle-eastern and Latin American terrorists, frequent drug smuggling in a variety of imaginative ways, money laundering, embezzlement of U.S. government funds, perjury, obstruction of justice, burglary of the offices of American dissidents...all of it to support the band of rapists, torturers and killers known as the Contras.

Economic strangulation was the result of a number of factors beginning with the economic and social conditions inherited from 43 years of Somoza rule. The Sandinistas inherited a country suffering from crushing poverty, a $1.6 billion debt, and a lack of progress under Somoza. The United States tightened the noose with a trade embargo and severed sources of credit. U.S. support for the Contras was also devastating to the Nicaraguan economy as more and more resources had to be diverted to defence. In 1980, the Nicaraguan government spent only 18 percent of its budget on defence and 50 percent on health and education compared to 1987 when the government spent 50 percent on defence and only 20 percent on health and education.

Economic deprivation was fuelling growing opposition in Nicaragua as middle-class professionals fled the country and businessmen and landowners attempted to sabotage the country from within. Shortages of food, buses, taxis, spare parts for machinery, and jobs overshadowed the advances in agrarian reform, healthcare, and education.

As a result of the economic hardships, the Sandinistas began to curtail the rights of opponents although they never resorted to torture or executions. The United States supported opposition groups in Nicaragua to weaken further the Sandinista government. The CIA recruited agents in Nicaragua to promote anti-government rallies and protests in the hope of provoking a brutal Nicaraguan response to tarnish their reputation. One of the responses of the Sandinistas to the growing opposition was to shut down the opposition newspaper, La Prensa on several occasions. *La Prensa* was financed covertly by the CIA, the National Endowment for Democracy (NED) in Washington who received money from Congress, and private American groups. One of the chief editors, Pedro Joaquin Chamorro, Jr., had connections to the Contras and traveled around the United States on speaking tours to raise money for them.

When I was in Nicaragua in 1989, I recall picking up a copy of *La Prensa* which was readily available and was astonished that it was allowed to operate given that it was known to be sponsored by the CIA.

At a time when the reputation of the CIA was tainted from its covert activities, Congress created the NED to overtly perform many of the same political functions such as funding political parties, labour unions, newspapers and other opposition groups. Although Congress enacted a law in 1984 prohibiting the NED from financing candidates for public office, the loopholes in the legislation provided an opportunity for NED to contribute to the building of the National Opposition Union (UNO), the main opposition party in Nicaragua. UNO was formed in 1982 by opponents of the Sandinista government. As the 1990 election approached, UNO became a coalition of 14 political parties, all of whom set aside their differences in order to defeat the Sandinistas, to reach a consensus on a leader, and to support Violeta Barrios de Chamorro for that position. According to S. Brian Wilson in *How the U.S. Purchased the 1990 Nicaraguan Elections*:

> ...the level of funding for creating and sustaining the opposition parties in Nicaragua in preparation for its February 1990 elections perhaps exceeded all prior experiences of electoral intervention...

If the truth were known, the total might approach $50,000,000. Fifty million dollars in Nicaragua, a country of 3.5 million people in the mid 1980s, is equivalent to $3,550,000,000 in the United States, a country in

1990 of nearly 250 million inhabitants.

Examples of funds flowing from the United States to Nicaragua include:

- $13 million (CIA) in 1984-1987 for covert political spending inside Nicaragua;

- $10-12 million (CIA) in 1987-88 for a covert political account designated for Nicaraguan opposition activity;

- $20 million (NED) in 1988-89 for the opposition in Nicaragua;

- $5 million (CIA) in 1989 for the opposition's housekeeping costs;

- $3.5 million (NED) in 1989-90 for NED and/or UNO;

- $9 million (NED) in 1989-90 for NED and/or UNO. (S. Brian Wilson, *How the U.S. Purchased the 1990 Nicaraguan Elections*)

People ultimately vote with their stomachs. When I was in Nicaragua in 1989, all the people to whom I spoke lamented the fact that they were forced to vote for Chamorro to put an end to the Contra attacks and economic warfare which had crippled the economy and people's ability to feed themselves.

They were forced to vote with their stomachs rather than with their hearts. Edward Herman, in *Beyond Hypocrisy: Decoding the News in an Age of Propaganda,* observed that:

> ...the U.S. attacks which devastated the Nicaraguan economy were certainly the primary contributor to a fall in per capita income of over 50 percent between 1980 and 1990. It seems obvious, therefore, that the United States had purposefully tilted the playing field in a direction unfavorable to the ruling party.

As well, Mark Weisbrot, in *What Everyone Should Know About Nicaragua,* reports that:

> By 1990 the Nicaraguans had suffered more than they could take from the war and economic embargo, so when President George Bush I made it clear that their misery would continue until the Sandinistas were voted out of office, a majority cried uncle.

In 1990, Violeta Barrios de Chamorro became President of Nicaragua but the Sandinistas won 43 percent of the popular vote in the election despite the threat of continued American warfare against Nicaragua if the Sandinistas had won. While negotiating the transfer of power, UNO and the Sandinistas negotiated an agreement called the Protocol on Procedures for the Transfer of Presidential powers in which UNO guaranteed that any changes implemented by the Sandinistas during their 11 years in power would not be overturned. The tragic and hypocritical irony of this agreement is that despite all the suffering of the Nicaraguan people resulting from American objections to Sandinista "communist" policies, the new U.S.-backed government agreed to preserve them.

By the time Chamorro assumed office, Nicaragua's economy had plummeted precipitously. On top of a myriad of previous economic problems caused by 43 years of Somoza rule, from 1979 to 1990 interest rates had climbed to unheard-of levels, businesses had collapsed, foreign investors disappeared, the GDP had diminished by two-thirds, infant mortality had increased, the volume of exports diminished by half, and there was a ten-fold increase in foreign debt. Nicaragua was now the poorest country in the Western Hemisphere. Forced to divert half its budget to defence, cut off from the World Bank and the IMF, victimized by a trade embargo, and suffering from American-supported sabotage from within, Nicaragua's economy was doomed.

Once Chamorro became president, the World Bank and IMF opened their doors to Nicaragua again, the trade embargo was lifted, the Contra guerilla attacks ceased, foreign trade resumed, and foreign investment gradually returned. Despite the favourable climate for improvement in social and economic conditions, many problems lingered. Despite economic growth since 1990, as of 1996 Nicaragua remained the second poorest nation in the hemisphere with a per capita GDP of $452. This is below the level of 1979, before the Sandinista takeover. Although unemployment dropped by 16 percent, over 36 percent were unemployed and Nicaragua still suffered from trade and budget deficits. According to Mark Weisbrot, in *What Everyone Should Know About Nicaragua*:

> Washington got the government it wanted, but of course it did not end Nicaragua's suffering. A decade of IMF and World Bank tutelage has left Nicaraguans with the most crushing debt burden in the Hemisphere, 70 percent of its people in poverty, and—alone among Latin Americans—less income per person than they had 40 years ago.

Reagan's Lies and War Crimes

American actions against Nicaragua violated a number of international agreements including the OAS Charter and the UN Charter. The violations of the OAS Charter were as follows:

Article 2

The Organization of American States, in order to put into practice the principles on which it is founded and to fulfill its regional obligations under the Charter of the United Nations, proclaims the following essential purposes:

(a) To strengthen the peace and security of the continent;

(b) To promote and consolidate representative democracy, with due respect for the principles of nonintervention;

Article 3

The American States reaffirm the following principles:

a) International law is the standard of conduct of States in their reciprocal relations;

b) International order consists essentially of respect for the personality, sovereignty, and independence of states, and faithful fulfillment of obligations derived from treaties and other sources of international law;

Article 10

States are juridically equal, enjoy equal rights and equal capacity to exercise these rights, and have equal duties. The rights of each State depend not upon its power to ensure the exercise thereof, but upon the mere fact of its existence as a person under international law.

Article 11

Every American state has the duty to respect the rights enjoyed by every other State in accordance with international law.

Article 13

The political existence of the State is independent of recognition by other States...

Article 19

No State or group of States has the right to intervene directly or indirectly, for any reason whatever, in the internal or external affairs of any State. The foregoing principle prohibits not only armed force but also any other form of interference or attempted threat against the personality of the state or against its political, economic, and cultural elements.

Article 22

The American States bind themselves in their international relations not to have recourse to the use of force, except in the case of self-defense in accordance with existing treaties or in fulfillment thereof.

The American actions in Nicaragua also violated the following clause in the United Nations Charter:

1. Chapter I, Article 2, Paragraph 4—All States must "...refrain from the use of force against the territorial integrity or political independence of any other State."

As well, the judgment of the World Court against Nicaragua cited a number of violations of international law by the United States.

President Reagan lied repeatedly to the American people and Congress to conceal the covert activities of his government to support the Contras. Some of these lies include:

- He warned that Nicaragua was only two days from Brownsville, Texas, implying that the Nicaraguan army intended to attack the United States.

- He suggested that the Contras were Nicaraguan peasants rebelling against their own government.

- He violated the Boland Amendment when he continued to fund the Contras.

- He lied about the elections in Nicaragua and El Salvador.

- He lied about Nicaragua's willingness to allow a team of inspectors to oversee the elections in 1984.

- He lied when he claimed that the Sandinista government was oppressing its own people.

- He lied about the sale of arms to Iran to buy weapons for the Contras.

Nicaragua was a victim of the Cold War and also of the American obsession with creating client states in Latin America. According to U.S. policy-makers, whenever Latin American countries experimented with progressive reforms they were communist and a threat to American corporate interests. Then the mighty American military and intelligence machine jumped into action. Human rights and respect for the sovereignty and political independence of other states dropped off the radar screen. All that remained was American self-interest.

CHAPTER 7

THE GEORGE H. BUSH FORMULA FOR WAR WITH IRAQ

PREVENT NEGOTIATIONS AT ALL COSTS

Geon H. W. Bush discovered a way to go back in time. You take a modern, industrialized country with a modern infrastructure and drop 88,500 tons of explosives on it and, presto, you have bombed it back into the pre-industrialized age. That is exactly what happened to Iraq. Bush was acting on the axiom that we have to destroy the country to save it (articulated by an officer during the Vietnam War who stated that "We have to destroy the village to save it").

The United States didn't always consider Iraq an "evil empire." The complex relationship between Iraq and the United States can only be appreciated in the framework of the modern history of Iraq. The simple version is colony, friend, foe.

From about 1968 to 1991, Iraq enjoyed considerable economic progress with electricity and water available to the entire country. Since 1982 the government built 18 new hospitals some of which were renowned in the Middle East. Health care was virtually free and education was universal and free through college. Food was both inexpensive and abundant. People without land were offered low-interest loans on the condition that the land became productive within five years. Malnutrition was non-existent. A strong infrastructure of highways, dams, hydroelectric power, flood control, irrigation systems, and an efficient telephone system contributed to the growing strength of the economy.

Iraq was at the forefront of the Arab world in its treatment of women. In 1969, the government created the General Federation of Iraqi Women to campaign on behalf of women's rights. By 1983, the Federation launched a four-year plan to encourage women to seek employment.

Overshadowing these advances was the rule of Saddam Hussein who assumed the presidency in 1979 and maintained his rule through one of the most oppressive internal security apparatuses in the world.

Added to the hardships imposed by Saddam Hussein, George H. W. Bush bombed the country resulting in a loss of electricity and clean water, factories in ruins and many homes a mass of rubble. The economy was virtually annihilated. Over 100,000 people were killed in a period of several months. Iraq was again in ruins. After several months of primarily U.S. bombing, one of the most advanced nations in the Middle East was virtually reduced to rubble.

The American justification for attacking Iraq was the Iraqi invasion of Kuwait. Although Iraq had legitimate grievances against Kuwait, there was no justification for their invasion of Kuwait. On the other hand, there was no justification in international law for the American bombing of Iraq which resulted in horrible war crimes against the people of Iraq.

The transition from colony, to independent country, to country in ruins can be explained in terms of the huge oil reserves in Iraq. The American bombing was based on lies with the objective of expanding the American Empire.

The History of a Colony

Iraq had suffered through years of turmoil before it began implementing the progressive policies and programs described above. In 1908, a new ruling clique known as the Young Turks succeeded in gaining control of the Ottoman Empire and implemented a "Turkification" policy that alienated a number of Iraqis who organized an Arab nationalist movement. The centre of the nationalist movement was Basra where they began to demand a measure of autonomy. Iraq entered the twentieth century in a state of turbulence characterized by tribal conflicts which the Ottoman Empire was unable to control. Without any significant development, Turkish rule persisted until the end of World War I.

In 1917, Britain invaded Mesopotamia resulting in the collapse of the Ottoman Empire. Despite the hopes of Arab leaders for independence at the end of World War I, the League of Nations made Mesopotamia a mandated territory under British rule provoking the growth of Arab nationalism. Britain was reluctant to relinquish its mandate in Mesopotamia because of newly discovered reserves of oil.

Britain created a kingdom in Iraq under the rule of Emir Faisal ibn Hussain in 1921 and in 1932 Iraq achieved full independence as a sovereign state. Faisal's son, Ghazi, became king when his father died in 1933.

In 1936, General Bakr Sidqi successfully staged a military coup in violation of the constitution and set a precedent for further coups. After one year, he was murdered in a military coup after alienating his supporters. King Ghazi died in an automobile accident in 1939 and was succeeded by his three-year old son, Faisal II, who assumed power on his 18th birthday in 1953.

During World War II, when Rashid Ali Al-Gaylani became Prime Minister, Iraq supported Nazi Germany. By defying British requests for troop landings in 1941, Al-Gaylani provoked the British into invading Iraq. The war between Britain and Iraq lasted less than a month; Al-Galani and his government sought refuge in Iran and eventually Germany.

After his departure, a pro-British government was established in Iraq consisting of Abd al Ilah as regent and Nuri as-Said as Prime Minister while Britain maintained a presence in Iraq to protect the new government.

The monarchy in Iraq came under attack for a series of foreign policy blunders including the announcement that Iraq was joining a mutual defence pact with Pakistan, Turkey and Iran. The monarchy was finally overthrown in 1958 and King Faisal II, Abd al Ilah, and Nuri as-Said were executed. The new Prime Minister, Abdul Karim Qassem, resisted the monopolies of western oil companies and helped found the Organization of Petroleum Exporting Countries (OPEC) in 1960.

Control over Arab oil reserves was a major foreign policy objective of France, Great Britain, and the U.S. Qassem challenged this control and so provoked the United States into embarking on a campaign to weaken Iraq and its control over its oil.

During Qassem's four years in power, he opposed joining the United Arab Republics (UAR) making him the target of a number of assassination attempts by the Baathists who wanted to join. One of the members of the assassination squad was Saddam Hussein.

The CIA was also plotting to assassinate Qassem because he challenged the stranglehold of the Western oil companies over the marketing of Iraqi oil. At the same time, a group of American generals in Turkey were developing plans to invade Iraq and take control of the oil fields there. The CIA supported a coup in 1963 during which Qassem and his supporters were assassinated.

The assassination was followed by a series of military coups until 1968 when Ahmed Hasan al-Bakr of the Baath Party assumed power. The Baath party was a socialist party with strong nationalist convictions. In attempt to gain control over its own oil reserves, the government nationalized the U.S./ British-owned Iraq Petroleum Company. Saddam Hussein played a major role in the nationalization of Iraqi oil.

Saddam Hussein was born in 1937 to a poor peasant family in a small village. After his father's death in 1947 he moved to Baghdad to live with his uncle. In 1957, he joined the Baath party but was forced into exile in 1959 after participating in an unsuccessful coup attempt against Abdul Karim Qassem. After he returned from exile he was imprisoned in 1963 only to escape in 1966. The Baathist regained power in 1968 and Saddam served as deputy chair of the Revolutionary Council and became vice president of Iraq in 1969. After the resignation of al-Bakr in 1979, Saddam Hussein became president.

Due to the nationalist passion of the Baathist party and its nationalization of the U.S./British-owned Iraqi Petroleum Company, the United States entered a campaign to destabilize Iraq in 1972 by encouraging the leaders in northern Iraq to rebel against the Iraqi government. The United States supplied arms to Iran which were then funneled to the Kurds in Northern Iraq. The plan was to drain Iraq's resources through a war with the Kurds. Therefore, when the Soviet Union volunteered to mediate between the two parties, the Kurds were asked by Henry Kissinger to refuse.

In 1979, the Shah of Iran, a brutal dictator, was overthrown by the Iranian people who then welcomed back the Ayatollah Khomeini from exile in Paris. The Ayatollah Khomeini was born in 1902 and as a child underwent rigorous religious training. In 1963, he became actively engaged in challenging the Shah and his pro-American policies and his fierce attacks led to his exile in 1964. Following Khomeini's return to Iran a nationwide referendum was held declaring Iran an Islamic Republic after which he attained the title "Imam" (highest religious rank in Shia) and the Supreme Leader of Iran. The overthrow of the Shah and the installation of an Islamic republic deprived Washington of its main ally in the Gulf region. In need of a new ally, the United States turned to Iraq in 1979.

Hundreds of Thousands Die for a Stalemate

The transformation of Iran into an Islamic republic headed by the anti-American Ayatollah Khomeini was alarming to both Iraq and the United States. The United States now considered Iran as the major threat to peace in the Middle East and also a threat to a steady supply of cheap oil. Saddam was afraid that the new revolutionary leadership in Shiite Iran would pose a threat to the delicate Sunni-Shiite balance in Iraq where the majority of people were Shiite and Hussein was supported by the Sunni sect. Saddam Hussein also feared that Iran would exploit Iraq's limited access to the Persian Gulf and that the frequent skirmishes between Iran and Iraq over the location of their common border posed a threat. In 1980, Iraq declared that the Algiers treaty was no longer operative and that the 200-kilometer channel up to the Iranian shore known as the Shatt-al-Arab waterway belonged exclusively to Iraq. After Saddam abrogated the Algiers treaty, border hostilities escalated and both sides engaged in bombing raids deep into the other's territory.

There is some uncertainty about the extent to which the United States persuaded Iraq to declare war on Iran. According to Ramsey Clark in *The Fire This Time: U.S. War Crimes in the Gulf*:

> National Security Advisor Zbigniew Brzezinski publicly encouraged Iraq to attack Iran and take back the Shatt-al-Arab waterway—control of which the U.S. had forced Iraq to share with Iran only four years ago.

In the fall of 1980, the United States, acting through Kuwait, Saudi Arabia, and other friendly Arab governments, provided Iraq with intelligence reports that Iranian forces would collapse in the face of an Iraqi advance. At the urging of the Emir of Kuwait, Egypt's Anwar Sadat, and other U.S.-backed Arab rulers, Saddam Hussein followed Brzezinski's advice in late 1980 and unleashed a war with Iran in which hundreds of thousands have died.

John R. MacArthur, in *Second Front: Censorship and Propaganda in the Gulf War* argues that:

> While it might overstate the case to suggest that in 1980 the Carter administration encouraged Hussein to attack Khomeini's Shiite legions, one can safely say that no one in the Carter camp seemed to object very loudly... [it] coming on the heels of the Iranian kidnapping of the U.S. embassy staff in Tehran, guaranteed at the very least official neutrality in the Iran-Iraq war...In this case, however, neutrality rapidly metamorphosed into quiet backing for Iraq, which eventually led to military support.

Without the military and economic assistance of the United States and its allies, Iraq would have lacked the capability to sustain its war effort for eight years. U.S. Airborne Warning and Control Aircraft (AWACS) that had been stationed in Saudi Arabia provided Iraq with intelligence information about troop movements in Iran. The United States also sent CIA and Special Forces operatives to train Iraqi commandos. In order to sell "dual use" (both civilian and military) equipment and technology to Iraq, the Reagan administration had to remove Iraq from the official list of states that allegedly support international terrorism. Subsequently, the U.S. shipped six Lockheed L-100 civilian transport aircraft, six small jets, and 45 large Bell helicopters to Iraq.

As well, the United States provided massive amounts of financial aid both directly and indirectly to Iraq to finance the war. Kuwait and Saudi Arabia, both U.S. allies, contributed tens of billions of dollars to Iraq's war effort. Kuwait alone contributed $30 billion. The U.S. Agricultural Department provided Iraq with $5 million in credits that could be used to finance the purchase of American arms.

The dictatorship in Turkey, a major recipient of U.S. military aid, dispatched troops to Iraqi Kurdistan for the purpose of engaging the Kurdish rebels in war to divert them from fighting against Iraq. Iraq could therefore concentrate on its war with Iran.

On September 22, 1980, both Iranian and Iraqi bombers attacked important targets in each other's territory. At the same time, Iraq ordered six divisions to enter Iran and begin a surprise attack on three fronts. These surprise attacks were very successful and the last major territorial gain occurred in early November 1980. At this point, many believed that the war would be won in a matter of weeks. Iran averted defeat by a rapid mobilization of volunteers. By November 1980, 200,000 Iranian troops were sent to the front. Despite Iraq's superior military forces, Iran rejected a settlement and began a series of counteroffensives in January 1981. By May 1982, Iran penetrated Iraqi defences, split Iraqi forces, and forced Iraq to retreat.

Iraq devised the strategy of "human wave" attacks whereby relatively untrained soldiers aged from nine to fifty would hold hands (so that no one would run off) and march through minefields and fortifications to clear a safe path for Iraqi tanks.

In 1984, Iraq was forced to alter its military strategy from gaining control of Iranian territory to defending against Iranian gains inside Iraq. At this point in the war, approximately 300,000 Iranian soldiers and 250,000 Iraqi soldiers had been killed or wounded.

To inflict greater losses on the other side, both Iraq and Iran began to attack major population centres and industrial facilities. UN Secretary-General Javier Perez de Cuellar formally accused Iraq in March 1986 of using chemical weapons against Iran. Basing his conclusion on the evidence of four UN chemical weapons inspectors, Javier Perez de Cuellar demanded that Iraq cease its violations of the 1925 Geneva Protocol on the use of chemical weapons.

Two of the chemical agents identified by the United Nations were mustard gas and tabun. Mustard gas burns any body tissue that it touches and if it penetrates into the body either through inhalation or through the skin, it causes blindness, blistering, and lung damage. Tabun is such a powerful chemical agent that even small concentrations over a short period of time can result in persistent contraction of the pupils and a tightness or constriction of the chest. A lethal dose, inhaled or absorbed through the skin initially causes a running nose and sweating followed by involuntary urination and defecation, vomiting, convulsions, paralysis and ultimately death.

It has been estimated that about 10,000 people died as a result of exposure to chemical weapons. Some of these chemical weapons were imported and some were produced at from three to five chemical-agent production sites in Iraq including Samawa, Ramadi, and Samarra. Mustard gas was produced at a chemical plant in Samarra but Iraq had to import the precursor agent, thiodiglycol, from Western Europe and the United States.

UN condemnation of Iraq for the use of chemical weapons persuaded the United States government to consider instituting foreign policy controls on the export of five chemicals used in the production of chemical weapons. The implementation of these controls was also in response to an extremely high number of recent orders from Iraq for these chemicals.

When the war appeared to be reaching a stalemate in 1987, an Iranian offensive surrounded a garrison at Mawat endangering Iraqi oilfields near Kirkuk and the oil pipeline to Turkey. The Iraqis changed their strategy from a defensive posture to an offensive one by increasing the number of air strikes against Iran and improving the effectiveness of their military.

Both superpowers feared that an Iranian victory might lead to a pro-Iranian Iraq, with the majority Shiites in Iraq allying themselves with Iran. This fear resulted in more superpower involvement in the war. At first, the Soviet Union became the major supplier of weapons to Iraq with the U.S. increasing its support to Iraq after 1984. The United States, after Congress had cut off funding for the Contras in Nicaragua, surreptitiously supplied arms to Iran to acquire funds in order to purchase weapons for the contras. By supplying both sides, the United States was able to play both countries off against each other to weaken both in order to remove any kind of threat to American aspirations for hegemony in the region.

Between April and August 1988, four major battles were fought in which the Iraqis emerged victorious. After eight years, both sides had been so ravaged by the war of attrition that on August 20, 1988 they agreed to a ceasefire following the passage of United Nations Resolution 598. Resolution 598 was adopted on July 20 1987 and called for an end to hostilities and for both parties to seek a mediated settlement.

When the war finally ended, none of the outstanding issues had been resolved. The casualties on both sides were shocking as Iraq suffered an estimated 375,000 casualties and Iran lost 300,000 people with another 500,000 injured.

One of the outcomes of the war was an apparently powerful Iraqi military machine with over one million men and an arsenal of chemical weapons. Iraq was seen as one of the premier forces in the Middle East.

America Fears the Monster it Created

After the Iran-Iraq war, the United States was apprehensive about the military strength of Iraq because it threatened America's complete control over oil resources in the Middle East and therefore the price of oil. Other oil-producing nations in the Middle East such as Saudi Arabia and the Emirates could be depended on to serve American interests but because of the wealth of oil in Iraq and its military strength the Joint Chiefs of Staff developed a strategy for the Middle East that identified Iraq as the central threat to the region.

Therefore it was no surprise that America's next foreign policy mission would be to weaken Iraq and for that purpose Kuwait was encouraged to conduct "economic warfare" against Iraq. According to Ramsey Clark, in *The Fire This Time*:

> After the Iran-Iraq war ended, Kuwait was used once again by the United States to embark on a campaign of what CSIS director Henry M. Schuler described as "economic warfare" against Iraq.

Brian Becker, in *U.S. Conspiracy to Initiate the War Against Iraq,* maintained that:

The tiny, but oil-rich sheikdom of Kuwait became a tool of a U.S. inspired campaign of economic warfare designed to weaken Iraq as a regional power once the Iran-Iraq war ended... Why would an OPEC country want to drive down the price of oil? In retrospect, it is inconceivable that this tiny, undemocratic little sheikdom [Kuwait], whose ruling family is subject to so much hostility from the Arab masses, would have dared remain so defiant against Iraq (a country ten times larger than Kuwait) unless Kuwait was assured in advance of protection from an even greater power—namely the United States.

One of the least understood issues about the American invasion of Iraq is that it was planned well in advance before Iraq had even considered invading Kuwait. As evidence that the U.S. was preparing for an invasion of Iraq is the fact that in June 1990, two months before Iraq invaded Kuwait, General Norman Schwarzkopf conducted war games in which hundreds of thousands of American troops engaged in a mock battle against (supposed) Iraqi armored divisions. When Iraqi troops were positioning themselves on the Kuwait border, General Schwarzkopf prepared CENTCOM (U.S. Central Command) for war against Iraq.

When Iraq finally did invade Kuwait, President Bush feigned shock and surprise at the boldness of the invasion. It seems that every president professes surprise at attacks such as in the case of Pearl Harbor and the Gulf of Tonkin, and that this is one of the essential lies needed to win support for wars whose aim is to expand the American Empire. For example, Middle East expert Milton Viorst, in an article for the *New York Times*, had interviewed Kuwaiti Foreign Minister Sheikh Salem al-Sabah. The Sheikh reported that Schwarzkopf routinely visited the Crown Prince and the Minister of Defence to discuss military cooperation. These actions of the American military are another indication that the United States was planning to wage war on Iraq long before the invasion of Kuwait. According to Ramsey Clark, in *The Fire This Time*, in 1988 the United States:

...completed new military plans for direct intervention in the Persian Gulf against Iraq. The impotence of the USSR, the isolation and debilitation of Iran, and alliances with Saudi Arabia, Turkey, and Israel reduced the risk of regional government opposition to U.S. intervention. The United States proceeded with a strategy to further isolate, aggravate, and finally provoke Iraq into acts that would justify an assault.

Setting a Trap for the Monster

American leaders were hoping to lure Iraq into a war with Kuwait but needed to maintain a relationship with Saddam Hussein in order to convince him that Iraq had U.S. approval for the invasion of Kuwait. Without U.S. approval, Saddam Hussein would not have risked an invasion of Kuwait for fear of American reprisals.

Iraq had a number of grievances with Kuwait which had to be placed on hold during the war with Iran. During the war, Iraq claimed that Kuwait had stolen $2.4 billion worth of oil from the Rumaila oil fields that ran beneath the vaguely defined border between Iraq and Kuwait. Kuwait had moved its border and claimed an additional 900 square miles of the Rumaila field. Kuwait was also stealing oil that clearly belonged to Iraq by using American-supplied slant-drilling technology. Also, two Gulf islands blocked Iraq's access to the Persian Gulf and Iraq insisted that these islands belonged to them. Iraq also claimed that Kuwait had built military and other structures on Iraqi territory. Kuwait and the United Arab Emirates were exceeding production quotas set by OPEC thereby driving down the price of oil and depriving Iraq of the revenues that were needed to rebuild the country. According to Ramsey Clark in *The Fire This Time*:

> ...Pierre Salinger observed that Kuwait decided to drastically increase oil production on August 8, 1988, one day after Iran agreed to a ceasefire with Iraq. Both Iran and Iraq desperately needed stable oil prices to finance postwar reconstruction. Kuwait's action, which violated OPEC agreements, sent oil prices into a tailspin. Crude oil prices fell from $21 to $11 a barrel, costing Iraq $14 billion a year, according to the *New York Times* [September 3, 1990, A7]... Then, in March 1989, Kuwait demanded a 50 percent increase in the OPEC quotas. This demand was rejected at the June 1989 OPEC meeting, but Kuwait oil minister Sheikh Ali al-Khlifa announced Kuwait would no longer be bound by any quota. Kuwait eventually doubled production to over 2 million barrels per day.

Iraq had incurred a very large debt during the Iran-Iraqi war totaling over $80 billion of which $30 billion was owed to Kuwait. Iraq offered to repay the debt after it rebuilt its economy at which time it could afford to satisfy its creditors. Kuwait demanded its money immediately while at the same time lowering the price of oil again.

The "economic warfare" against Iraq also consisted of a sanction campaign which was not approved by the United Nations until 1990 and involved not only the United States but other Western countries as well. Technology and food sales to Iraq were the main items included in the sanctions. The total impact of the "economic warfare" against Iraq was devastating considering the extent to which the Iraqi economy had suffered from the Iran-Iraq war.

There were a number of efforts to resolve the dispute over oil prices between Kuwait and Iraq. Other Arab nations also suffered economically when Kuwait increased the supply of oil to lower its price. OPEC had set new production quotas in March 1990 but Kuwait refused to comply. In frustration, Iraq dispatched envoys to several Arab states appealing for new quotas that would allow a modest increase in the price of oil. Kuwait again refused to comply. At another meeting on July 10, oil ministers again agreed to gradually raise the price of oil but Kuwait warned fellow members that it intended to increase oil production substantially in October.

It was clear that Kuwait was determined to increase oil supplies without regard for the other oil producing nations in the Middle East. It was also clear that Kuwait was completely unconcerned about an Iraqi invasion because the Emir knew that the United States would defend Kuwait. When Sheikh Sabah of Kuwait was urged by Jordan to take the Iraqi threats more seriously, he responded that:

> We are not going to respond to [Iraq]...If they don't like it, let them occupy our territory...We are going to bring in the Americans. (*The Village Voice*, April 5, 1991, in an interview with King Hussein of Jordan)

The United States used Kuwait as the spark to ignite the Iraqi tinderbox. Capitalizing on all of the disputes between Iraq and Kuwait, U.S. leaders encouraged Kuwait to continue the above policies in order to provoke Iraq into an invasion in which the Americans would claim to be neutral. In fact, as discussed below, they planned to use the invasion as a pretext to declare war on Iraq. The war on Iraq would bring Iraq and its oil into the American Empire.

Saddam Hussein was not prepared to invade Kuwait without either the approval or indifference of the United States. Saddam Hussein met with the American ambassador to Iraq, April Glaspie on July 25, 1990, to seek out the U.S. position on an Iraqi invasion of Kuwait. The following is part of the transcript of the conversation:

U.S. Ambassador Glaspie—I have direct instruction from

President Bush to improve our relations with Iraq. We have considerable sympathy for your quest for higher oil prices, the immediate cause of your confrontation with Kuwait. As you know, I lived here for years and admire your extraordinary efforts to rebuild your country. We can see that you have employed massive numbers of troops in the south. Normally that would be none of our business but when this happens in the context of your threats against Kuwait, then it would be reasonable for us to be concerned. For this reason, I have received instructions to ask you, in the spirit of friendship— not confrontation—regarding your intentions. Why are your troops massed so very close to Kuwait's border?

Saddam Hussein—As you know, for years I have made every effort to reach a settlement in our dispute with Kuwait. There is to be a meeting in two days. I am prepared to give negotiations this one more brief chance. But if we are unable to find a solution, then it would be natural that Iraq will not accept death.

U.S. Ambassador Glaspie—What solutions would be acceptable?

Saddam Hussein—(A list of conditions). What is the United States opinion on this?

U.S. Ambassador Glaspie—We have no opinion on your Arab-Arab conflicts, such as your dispute with Kuwait. Secretary of State James Baker has directed me to emphasize the instruction, first given to Iraq in the 1960s, that the Kuwait issue is not associated with America. (http://www.whatreallyhappened. com/ARTICLES/APRIL.html)

Later, when British journalists confronted Ambassador Glaspie as she was leaving the U.S. embassy in Baghdad, they asked her how she could have conveyed the message that the U.S. was neutral on Arab-Arab conflicts while aware that the U.S. was fully prepared to defend Kuwait. The reporters were greeted with silence.

With Iraqi troops stationed on the Kuwait border and Hussein now convinced that the United States would not interfere if Iraq invaded Kuwait, the invasion of Kuwait was imminent. Other Arab nations fervently hoped that a war between Iraq and Kuwait could be avoided but with Kuwait's intransigence over the price of oil, war seemed inevitable. In one final effort to avert war, King Hussein of Jordan and King Fahd of Saudi Arabia beseeched the Emir to attend a mini-summit on July 31 in Jidda, Saudi Arabia. Although the invitation was addressed to the Emir, he sent the prime minister in his place. On the top of the invitation the Emir wrote:

> We will attend the meeting on the conditions we agreed upon. What is important to us is our national interest. Do not listen to anything you hear from the Saudis and Iraqis on brotherhood and Arab solidarity. Each of them has his own interest…Be unwavering in your discussions. We are stronger than we think. (Ramsey Clark, *The Fire This Time*)

The invasion of Kuwait was now inevitable. Iraq's economy had suffered a severe decline since the decrease in the price of oil, Kuwait demonstrated no interest in negotiating a settlement, and the United States had declared that they had no interest in "Arab-Arab" conflicts. Without fear of American reprisals, Iraq invaded Kuwait on August 2, 1990.

On the same day, the United Nations Security Council passed Resolution 660 which stated that:

> …The Security Council, alarmed by the invasion of Kuwait on August 2, 1990, by the military forces of Iraq
>
> 1. Condemns the Iraqi invasion
>
> 2. Demands that Iraq withdraw immediately and unconditionally…
>
> 3. Calls upon Iraq and Kuwait to begin immediately intensive negotiation…

The propaganda campaign to justify an ultimate attack on Iraq accelerated after the invasion of Kuwait. On August 2, 1990, U.S. Deputy Press Secretary Popadiuk made a statement that:

> The United States is deeply concerned about the blatant act of aggression and demands the immediate and unconditional withdrawal of all Iraqi forces… we are urging the entire international community to condemn this outrageous act of aggression.

Also on August 2, 1990, President Bush exchanged remarks with reporters and said:

Let me make a brief statement here about recent events. The United
States strongly condemns the Iraq military invasion of Kuwait. We call for
the immediate and unconditional withdrawal of all Iraqi forces…We're not
discussing intervention. (President Bush Library, http://bushlibrary.tamu.edu/
index.php)

The American plan to provoke Iraq into an invasion of Kuwait by
creating the perception in the mind of Saddam Hussein that the United States
would not intervene was eminently successful. Condemnations of Saddam
Hussein spewed out of Washington to pave the way for a U.S. invasion
of Iraq. As well, in the interim, the United States had to guarantee that all
attempts by Iraq to settle its dispute with Kuwait were doomed to failure.

Kuwait presented a public relations challenge for the Bush
administration. Kuwait was a small Arab Sheikdom ruled by a family
oligarchy. Since 1961, the emirate had been ruled by the Sabah family who
had dissolved the National Assembly. The Assembly had not been a paragon
of democracy anyway since only 65,000 males and zero women out of a
population of two million were allowed to participate in the political process.
Kuwait depended on foreign workers who were treated as slaves and were
systematically abused often by burning, blinding, and fatal beatings. The
Kuwait government was quite brutal in suppressing any political dissent.
On January 22, 1990 the government brutally attacked a pro-democracy
demonstration with tear gas and batons and beat several politicians.
Following the demonstration, political assemblies were banned.

The buildup of American forces in the Persian Gulf began on the same
day as Iraq invaded Kuwait. On August 2, a group of seven warships led by
the USS Independence headed toward the Persian Gulf followed by another
aircraft carrier and an assault ship on August 5. The United States required a
base of operations in the Persian Gulf and Saudi Arabia was the preeminent
location. To overcome the Saudis' reluctance to serve as a base of U.S.
military operations for an attack on a fellow Arab state, the United States
lied to Saudi Arabia that Iraqi troops were lined up on the Saudi border. On
August 3, Defense Secretary Dick Cheney and Chairman of the Joint Chiefs
of Staff General Colin Powell met with Prince Bandar bin Sultan, the Saudi
ambassador to the United States and showed him satellite photos of Iraqi
troops assembled on the Saudi border. Prince Bandar bin Sultan used the
photos to convince the Saudi government. To apply more pressure to the
Saudi government, a high-level delegation consisting of Dick Cheney, Colin

Powell, National Security Agency Deputy Director Robert Gates, Defense Department aide Paul Wolfowitz, and General Schwarzkopf traveled to Saudi Arabia to meet with King Fahd. Before the high level meeting, King Fahd had sent a team to investigate the presence of Iraqi troops but they returned without a shred of evidence. According to an article in Florida's *St. Petersburg Times,* Soviet commercial satellite photos confirmed that there were no Iraqi troops on the Saudi border. The *Times* hired two defence intelligence experts to study the photos, both of whom refuted Washington's claims about the location of Iraqi troops. Nevertheless, King Fahd finally succumbed to the pressure but asked that it appear as if Saudi Arabia had requested American assistance.

Saudi Arabia consented on August seventh to the deployment of 90,000 American troops, 40,000 of whom were deployed immediately. The buildup escalated rapidly in September long before sanctions, negotiations, or any other attempts to resolve the crisis without using force had any prospect of succeeding. By September fourth, there were 100,000 troops in the Gulf doubling to 200,000 by mid-October. Without any new developments, either positive or negative, Bush had amassed 400,000 troops in the Gulf by the end of October. President Bush was deploying these troops illegally just prior to the congressional elections in an attempt to further guarantee the inevitability of the war. More troops were dispatched to the Gulf and by mid-January, there were now 540,000 troops prepared to pounce on Iraq. Congress had not yet approved of United Nations Resolution 678 authorizing the use of force.

Arab Nations Try to Lead the American Horse to Water

King Hussein of Jordan was determined to fashion an Arab solution to the crisis. He discussed a possible withdrawal with Saddam Hussein who offered to withdraw his troops from Kuwait on the condition that he would not be subjected to condemnation by the Arab League. Following his meeting with Saddam, King Hussein flew to Egypt to secure a promise from President Hosni Mubarak that Egypt would not condemn Iraq. King Hussein was particularly concerned about Egypt because of its close ties to the United States. At the same time, Bush had issued an ultimatum giving Iraq two days to withdraw from Kuwait. King Hussein then met with Saddam Hussein on August 3, 1990, to invite him to a conference set for

August 5 to negotiate a settlement with Kuwait. Saddam promised to begin withdrawing his troops the same day if the conference proved fruitful and issued a communiqué stating that he would begin withdrawing his troops on August 5. Withdrawal was not part of the American strategy so to sabotage any agreement, the U.S. applied immense pressure on Egypt to condemn Iraq for the invasion. On August 3, Assistant Secretary of State for the Near East, sent a message to the Egyptian Foreign Ministry:

> The West has done its duty, but the Arab nations are doing nothing. The United States has sold a lot of arms to Arab countries, especially Egypt. If they do not act, if they do not take a firm stand on the Kuwait affair, they can be sure that in the future they will no longer be able to count on America. (Pierre Salinger and Eric Laurent, *Secret Dossier: The Hidden Agenda Behind the Gulf War*)

The offer made to Iraq to withdraw within two days was meaningless. One day after Iraq's occupation of Kuwait, the United Nation approved the U.S.-drafted Security Council Resolution 661 at 5:48 PM. Security Council Resolution 661 mandated sanctions against Iraq and stated that it was:

> Determined to bring the invasion and occupation of Kuwait to an end and to restore sovereignty, independence and territorial integrity of Kuwait...

Acting under Chapter VII of the Charter of the United Nations [the Security Council]

1. Determines that Iraq so far has failed to comply with Paragraph 2 of Resolution 660 (1990) and has usurped the authority of the legitimate Government of Kuwait...

3. Decides that all states shall prevent

a) The import into their territories of all commodities and products originating in Iraq

4. Decides that all states shall not make available to the Government of Iraq any commercial, industrial or public utility undertaking in Iraq... (UN Resolutions from http://www.un.org/docs/scres/1990/scres90.htm)

A number of offers to resolve the Iraq-Kuwait dispute through negotiations were rejected by the United States. According to Noam Chomsky, in *The Gulf Crisis*:

> Rejection of diplomacy was explicit from the outset...Diplomatic options opened shortly after Saddam Hussein realized the nature of the forces arrayed against him, apparently with some surprise, although we cannot evaluate their prospects because they were barred at once by Washington's rigid rejectionism.

On August 12, Iraq offered to withdraw from Kuwait in exchange for Syrian and Israeli withdrawal from Lebanon and Israeli withdrawal from the occupied territories. The United States immediately rejected any linkage between Iraqi withdrawal and military occupations elsewhere. Another Iraqi offer which was delivered to Brent Scowcroft, President Bush's National Security Advisor, called for Iraq's withdrawal from Kuwait in exchange for the lifting of sanctions, full Iraqi control of the Rumaila oil field, and guaranteed access to the Gulf. The offer was rejected on the grounds that the White House was not interested. President Bush, speaking at a White House press briefing for members of Congress on August 28, stated that:

> ...our intention, and indeed the intention of almost every country in the world, is to persuade Iraq to withdraw, that it cannot benefit from this illegal occupation that it will pay a stiff price by trying to hold on...And of course, we seek to achieve these goals without further violence. (President Bush Library)

When asked if he had done enough on the diplomatic front, President Bush, in an exchange with reporters on October 31, replied that:

> There's no compromise with this aggression...And every time somebody sends an emissary, that gives Saddam Hussein a little bit of hope that there might be some way he can stop short of doing what he must do: get out of Kuwait unconditionally... (President Bush Library)

On January 8, 1991, in a letter to congressional leaders on the Persian Gulf crisis, President Bush stated that:

> The current situation in the Persian Gulf, brought about by Iraq's unprovoked invasion and subsequent brutal occupation of Kuwait, threatens U.S. vital interests. The situation also threatens the peace.
>
> I therefore request that the House of Representatives and the Senate adopt a Resolution stating that Congress supports the use of all means necessary to implement UN Security Council Resolution 678.
>
> Mr. Speaker, I am determined to do whatever is necessary to protect America's security. (President Bush Library)

In a January ninth news conference on the Persian Gulf crisis, President Bush emphasized that:

The record shows that whether the diplomacy is initiated by the United States, the United Nations, the Arab League, or the European Community, the results are the same, unfortunately. The conclusion is clear: Saddam Hussein continues to reject a diplomatic solution...Let me emphasize that I have not given up on a peaceful outcome—it's not too late. (President Bush Library)

In sharp contrast to the words of President Bush, Arab diplomats at the United Nations said that they had received reports from Algeria, Jordan and Yemen, all of whom were on good terms with Iraq, that Saddam Hussein would agree soon after January 15 (the UN deadline) to announce his withdrawal from Kuwait on condition that Iraq would not be attacked, an international peace conference on Palestinian grievances would be convened, and disputes with Kuwait would be settled by negotiations. The U.S. rejected the offer as unacceptable.

President Bush claimed that Saddam Hussein rejected a diplomatic solution, but Bush rejected out of hand every attempt by Iraq to resolve the crisis peacefully. Saddam Hussein's final offer asked only that the United States not attack Iraq if he withdrew his troops from Kuwait and that other disputes be resolved through negotiations. This offer provided the basis for a settlement but did not have any impact on a president committed to war.

Diplomacy was clearly not an option for President Bush. Saddam Hussein's last offer was a very reasonable starting point for negotiations considering that all his demands were based on legitimate grievances against Kuwait. How these disputes might have been resolved in negotiations will never be known because President Bush's goal was not to resolve this crisis peacefully but to declare war on Iraq.

Sanctions became a major weapon to impose extremely harsh economic conditions on Iraq in order to weaken it for the inevitable war. The United Nations established the Sanctions Committee of the Security Council. It was controlled by the United States which now had the power to determine what was included under the sanctions.

Iraq imported 70% of its food and needed oil revenues to pay for imported food. With the passage of Resolution 661 foreign ports rejected Iraqi ships and foreign tankers ceased filling up on Iraqi oil. Iraq asked Turkey, one of its primary sources of food, to provide emergency food assistance for its children. As a major recipient of U.S. aid, Turkey refused the request. Not only did the government's food assistance program to the Iraqi people drop by 60% over a four-month period but there was no feed for livestock forcing farmers to slaughter their animals for food. Resolution 661 exempted food "in humanitarian circumstances" but the U.S. consistently blocked food and medicine from entering Iraq. After several months, Iraqi hospitals were experiencing severe shortages. Infant mortality doubled.

The Invisible Babies Snatched from Incubators

The stage was set for the inevitable war against Iraq. Iraq had invaded Kuwait, Saudi Arabia had agreed to become the staging ground, and Saddam Hussein had been depicted as the Middle Eastern equivalent of Hitler who posed a threat to the region. To win the support of the American people, Washington hired a number of public relations firms to educate the American people about the necessity of declaring war against Iraq. Kuwait funded an estimated 20 public relations firms, lobby groups, and law firms including the Rendon Group (public relations) for a retainer of $100,000, Neill & Co. (lobbyists) for $50,000 per month, and Hill & Knowlton (the world's largest public relations firm at the time) which served as mastermind for the Kuwaiti campaign. Craig Fuller who ran the Washington office of Hill & Knowlton was one of President Bush's closest friends and advisors. Some of their activities included arranging media interviews for visiting Kuwaitis, setting up days of observance such as National Free Kuwait Day, organizing public rallies, releasing hostage letters to the media, distributing news releases and information kits, contacting politicians at all levels, and producing dozens of video news releases which were distributed to the media.

Hill & Knowlton invented a horror story to evoke a strong emotional response to strengthen public support for a war against Iraq. On October 10 the Congressional Human Rights Caucus on Capitol Hill held a hearing on Iraqi human rights violations. Although the hearing bore a resemblance to a congressional proceeding, the ad hoc Human Rights Caucus was, in fact, nothing more than an association of politicians. The caucus was chaired by Democrat Tom Lantos and Republican John Porter who were also co-chairs of the Congressional Human Rights Foundation whose offices were located in Hill & Knowlton's Washington office and were rent-free. John R. MacArthur, in *Second Front,* observed that:

> On October 10, the congressional Human Rights Caucus provided the first formal opportunity for Amnesty [International]-and Hill & Knowlton-to present their evidence against Iraq on Capitol Hill. Conveniently for the Washington war party and its burgeoning Saddam-is-Hitler industry, the

caucus provided the appropriately informal setting in which to spread hysteria. The Human Rights Caucus is not a committee of Congress and therefore it is unencumbered by the legal accoutrements that would make a witness hesitate before he or she lied.

The emotionally-charged horror story came from a 15-year-old Kuwaiti girl named Nayirah who supposedly could not reveal her last name for fear of putting friends and family still in Kuwait at risk. She tearfully recounted that she had witnessed Iraqi soldiers taking babies from incubators and leaving them on the cold floor to die. She also provided written testimony, which was packaged in media kits prepared by Citizens for a Free Kuwait. The story was repeated frequently by President Bush who claimed that 312 babies had suffered the same fate. It was also repeated on television, radio and at the Security Council. According to the Center for Media and Democracy in *How PR Sold the War in the Persian Gulf*:

> Public opinion was deeply divided on Bush's Gulf policy. As late as December 1990, a New York Times/CBS News poll indicated that 48 percent of the American people wanted Bush to wait before taking any action if Iraq failed to withdraw from Kuwait by Bush's January 15 deadline. On January 12, the US Senate voted by a narrow, five-point margin to support the Bush administration in a declaration of war. Given the narrowness of the vote, the babies-thrown-from-incubators story may have turned the tide in Bush's favor.

The real horror story was not about babies and incubators but about how the U.S. government used a lie to sell a war in which over 100,000 people died. Hill & Knowlton had omitted a minor detail about the identity of the 15-year-old Kuwaiti volunteer, namely that she was, in fact, the daughter of Saud Nasir al-Sabah, the Kuwaiti ambassador to the United States. They also failed to mention that she had been coached by Hill & Knowlton before her appearance in front of the Caucus.

After the war, human rights investigators and reporters completely discredited the story. John Martin, an ABC news reporter, traveled to Kuwait and on March, 15 1991, and interviewed Dr. Mohammed Matar, director of Kuwait's health-care system and his wife Dr. Fayeza Youseff, chief of obstetrics at the maternity hospital. They both denied any knowledge of babies being snatched from incubators. Martin also visited al-Addan hospital where Nayirah had claimed that she witnessed the removal of 15 babies from incubators. Dr. Fahima Khafaji, a pediatrician at the hospital, refuted the stories of Nayirah.

Amnesty International, a highly respected international human rights group, had lent support to the story in a report on human rights abuses in Kuwait. In its press release, Amnesty promoted the story as fact. It cited two unidentified doctors and Nayirah's testimony to the Caucus. The Bush administration should have been given credit for duping an organization which prides itself on its scrupulous research. One month later, Amnesty discovered the truth and issued a retraction on April 1991.

In *Second Front*, John R. MacArthur quotes John Chancellor of ABC when he wrote that:

> "The conflict brought with it a baggage train of myth and misconception, exaggeration and hyperbole…Accounts of Iraqi atrocities were accepted without question. There was the tale of premature babies thrown out of incubators in a Kuwait hospital and left to die. It never happened…"

How to Win Friends and Influence People

While the propaganda campaign was preparing the public for the inevitable war against Iraq, Bush was advancing on a number of other fronts. Bush was seeking an international coalition to participate in the war in order to deflect criticism of unilateralism. To achieve international approval, Bush was ramming resolutions through the Security Council to provide UN legitimacy for the war. At the same time, there was a massive buildup of American forces in the Persian Gulf and Saudi Arabia.

Three methods were employed to win support for the war: bribes, coercion, and claiming that the buildup of forces was defensive. William Blum, in *Killing Hope,* explains how:

> …Egypt was forgiven many billions of dollars in debt, China, Turkey, the Soviet Union, and other countries received military and economic aid and World Bank and IMF loans, had sanctions lifted, or were given other perks, not only from the US but, under Washington's pressure, from Germany, Japan, and Saudi Arabia. As an added touch, the Bush administration stopped criticizing the human rights record of any coalition member.

The most crucial test for the United States in terms of manufacturing a UN sanction for war against Iraq was to win sufficient votes to pass Resolution 678 in the Security Council which authorized the use of force. Resolution 678, November 29, 1990, states that:

> The Security Council, noting that despite all efforts by the United Nations, Iraq refuses to comply with its obligation

to implement resolution 660 (1990) and the above mentioned subsequent resolutions, in flagrant contempt of the Security Council... Acting under Chapter VII of the charter

1. Demands that Iraq comply fully with Resolution 660 (1990) and all subsequent relevant resolutions, and decides while maintaining all its decisions, to allow Iraq one final opportunity to do so;

2. Authorizes Member States co-operating with the Government of Kuwait, unless Iraq on or before January 15, 1991, fully implements, as set forth in paragraph 1 above, to use all means necessary to uphold and implement resolution 660 (1990) and all subsequent relevant Resolutions and to restore international peace and security in the area

"All means necessary" bestowed a mandate on the United States to use force against Iraq and secured the international legitimacy which the U.S. was seeking. The legitimacy was specious because the United States used all means necessary to secure the votes it needed in the Security Council while forestalling any vetoes by its permanent members.

New aid packages, World Bank credits, and rearrangements of International Monetary Fund grants and loans were offered to Ethiopia and Zaire. Additional military aid was offered to an Ethiopian government on the brink of defeat by rebel forces. Columbia, already a major recipient of military and economic aid, was offered an increase in assistance. China and Russia's support was crucial because they were both permanent members of the Security Council and had veto power. The U.S.-dominated World Bank offered China $114 million dollars in aid and the day following the vote, Secretary of State James Baker met with Chinese Foreign Minister Qian Qichen to offer diplomatic normalization. The Soviet Union's economy was in a serious state of decline; it was offered $4 billion in loans by Saudi Arabia, Kuwait, and the UAE (United Arab Emirates). Cuba and Malaysia were subject to massive pressure and threats. Yemen, the only Arab country on the Security Council, voted against the resolution after which the United States cancelled a $70 million aid package and persuaded Saudi Arabia to ban 900,000 Yemeni workers from the country. Egypt, whose support was critical, was desperate for economic assistance which arrived in the form of debt forgiveness from the United States, Saudi Arabia, and other Arab States for a total of $14 billion.

Paradoxically, Resolution 678, besides having questionable real support, violated the United Nations Charter, in particular Articles 33, 36, and 42. For example, Article 33 requires disputing parties to:

> ...seek a solution by negotiation, inquiry, mediation, conciliation, arbitration, judicial settlement, referral to regional agencies or arrangements...

The Resolution granted war powers to member states without determining whether or not other specific means would have been effective. Sanctions had already been imposed on the basis of Resolution 661 but their efficacy had not been established because sanctions need more than a few months to work. All Iraq's offers to negotiate were rebuffed by the United States.

President Bush also ignored the Constitution of the United States and usurped the power of Congress to wage war. Article I, Section 8, of the Constitution grants to Congress the power to declare war. He also neglected to report and consult with Congress about waging war against Iraq as required in the War Powers Act of 1973. President Bush sent 200,000 troops to the Gulf without giving proper notification to Congress and only after the November elections did he inform Congress that he had ordered more than 400,000 troops to the Gulf.

War and Collateral Damage

On January 15, New York time or January 16, Iraqi time B-52s were flying towards their targets in Iraq and cruise missiles were fired from ships in the Indian Ocean to unleash a reign of horror on the Iraqi people. The euphemism "collateral damage" refers to the destruction to civilians and civilian targets during a bombing raid. Its sinister purpose is to use a relatively innocuous expression to describe the killing of innocent people. In the bombing of Iraq, the whole country became collateral damage. Iraqi military forces were absolutely incapable of defending Iraq against bombers that drop their bombs from 40,000 feet or cruise missiles which were fired from ships anchored 20 miles out at sea. The result of American (and other coalition members') bombing cannot even be described as a victory but more accurately as the perpetration of unconscionable carnage. Ramsey Clark, former Attorney General of the United States under President Kennedy and

President Johnson produced a documentary based on his findings during a week of traveling through Iraq during the bombing. After viewing this documentary, I can only describe the bombing as one of the more horrid evil deeds of modern history. In *Killing Hope*, William Blum refers to the observations of a UN inspection team that:

> ...declared that the allied bombardment had had a "near apocalyptic impact" on Iraq and had transformed the country into a "pre-industrial age nation," which "had been until January a rather highly urbanized and mechanized society."

To create the illusion that the conflict in Iraq was really a battle, the United States greatly exaggerated the current strength of the Iraqi military. The Pentagon described the Iraqi armed forces as a dangerous threat but according to Major General Matti Peled, a retired Israeli Major General:

> The Iraqi Army was not an unknown quantity. After 8 years of war in Iran it was very clear that it was not a threatening army, it was not a first-class fighting force. But the United States spread throughout the world the legend about the invincibility of the Iraqi Army, knowing full well that it was not true. But this gave the U.S. a justification for conducting what it called "strategic bombardment" of the entire area of Iraq, demolishing their entire civilian infrastructure. (Ramsey Clark, *The Fire This Time*)

During the bombing Iraq did not mount a single attack. Its air force was not capable of defending Iraqi cities and Iraqi commanders considered any attempt to do so as suicidal. Even the anti-aircraft fire lighting the sky over Baghdad created the impression of a real defence but Iraqi ground-to-air defences were incapable of reaching bombers at 40,000 feet. Even the Soviet SA-6 surface-to-air missiles were ineffective. Not one of the B-52 bombers was lost in combat.

The bombing campaign continued for 42 days dropping over 80 million pounds of explosives. In the first days of the campaign, the bombing destroyed the Iraqi ground forces access to military supplies, reinforcements, food, water, and medical supplies. Communications systems were very severely damaged and so were tanks, armored vehicles, artillery, and other mechanized equipment. With these losses the Iraqi forces were effectively defenceless. The United States used weapons such as fuel-air explosives, napalm and cluster bombs that are defined as illegal in international law. Estimates of the number of soldiers killed ranged from 100,000 to 200,000 and the injured were left wherever they were hit because Iraq did not possess field hospitals and American bombers destroyed at least five military hospitals.

Bombing of Iraqi cities served no military purpose but was designed to destroy the civilian infrastructure. War games in July 1990 in South Carolina trained pilots to bomb civilian targets and Pentagon statements about plans to bomb civilian targets in August and September 1990 are evidence that these targets were set well in advance of January 15, 1991.

Critical elements of the civilian infrastructure were destroyed including communication systems, oil refineries, electric generators, water treatment facilities, dams, and transportation centres. Over 90 percent of Iraq's electrical capacity was destroyed in the first days of the bombing.

One of the most diabolical decisions in the campaign was to destroy Iraq's water supply, resulting in the death of hundreds of thousands of Iraqi children long after the war was over. The capacity of Iraq to produce food was severely limited by the attacks on agriculture, food processing, food storage and the food distribution system. Half of Iraq's agricultural output depended on irrigation systems which were also targeted.

The industrial sector suffered heavy damage. Three date processing plants, a baby formula factory, a vegetable oil factory, a sugar refinery, a textile mill, five engineering plants, four car assembly plants, three chlorine plants, 16 petrochemical plants, the country's largest meat storage facility, grain silos, a tractor assembly plant, a fertilizer plant were all bombed. Bombing the chlorine plant was a devastating setback to the country's ability to provide clean water to its citizens. The United States claimed that the baby milk factory was a chemical plant. (In the early 1990s, one of my students who was born in Iraq told me that her grandfather had built it to produce baby formula.) As well, Ramsey Clark, in his documentary, inspected the site after it was bombed and was unable to discover any evidence that the plant was producing chemical weapons but he did discover a large quantity of packages containing milk formula.

Important non-military targets such as 28 civilian hospitals, 52 community health centres, 25 mosques, and 676 schools were bombed. Clearly all these targets were not bombed accidentally particularly given the accuracy of the American bombs and missiles.

Densely populated cities were bombed daily, killing thousands of civilians. Basra, Iraq's second largest city with a population of 800,000, was bombed repeatedly. One of the targets in Basra was a bridge which the Americans attempted to destroy twice, each time bombing surrounding neighborhoods. The people of Basra were so apprehensive about another attempt that they contemplated blowing it up themselves.

One of the worst horror stories of the war was the bombing of the Amariyah bomb shelter in Baghdad where 1500 civilians, mostly women and children, were seeking refuge from the bombing. One bomb penetrated the shelter's roof and opened up a hole through which the second more powerful bomb entered the shelter and exploded, incinerating most of the people in the shelter. After the first bomb struck, a number of people survived screaming for up to four minutes as they tried to escape.

As well, civilian highway traffic was targeted and vehicles such as buses and cars were bombed on a regular basis. Among the victims were truckers transporting humanitarian shipments. Press Secretary Fitzwater reported on February 13, 1991, that:

> The loss of civilian lives in time of war is a truly tragic consequence. It saddens everyone to know that innocent people may have died in the course of military conflict. America treats human life as our most precious value. That is why that even during this military conflict in which the lives of our service men and women are at risk, we will not target civilian facilities. We will continue to hit only military targets. The bunker that was attacked last night was a military target... (President Bush Library)

When there was nothing more to bomb, the American military launched a ground war that was superfluous but, nevertheless, brutal. On February 21-22, 1991, the Soviet Union secured an agreement from Iraq in which they offered to withdraw completely from Kuwait the day after a ceasefire of all military operations went into effect. The agreement included specific timetables and monitoring. George Bush refused to offer a ceasefire although he did promise that retreating Iraqi soldiers would not be attacked.

Iraqi forces began to withdraw from Kuwait on February 25, 1991. Coalition forces ended their campaign on February 27. On March 3, Iraq accepted the terms of the preliminary cease-fire.

One of the more disturbing aspects of the campaign was the slaughter of Iraqi soldiers offering to surrender or retreat back to Iraq. Comments by American pilots such as "turkey shoot," "shooting fish in a barrel," "we toasted them," "we hit the jackpot" and "basically just sitting ducks" were a sad reflection on the state of American culture. Mike Erlich of the Military Counseling Network testified at the European Parliament hearings on the Gulf War that:

...hundreds, possibly thousands, of Iraqi soldiers began walking toward the U.S. position unarmed, with their hands raised in an attempt to surrender. However, the orders for this unit were not to take any prisoners...

The commander of this unit began the firing shooting an anti-tank missile through one of the Iraqi soldiers. This is a missile designed to destroy tanks, but it was used against one man.

At this point, everyone in the unit began shooting. Quite simply, it was a slaughter. (Ramsey Clark, *The Fire This Time*)

Ramsey Clark reported, in *The Fire This Time*, that:

The Pentagon has documentary evidence, including hours of videotape, of this deadly assault on a defenseless unit [the biggest clash in the ground campaign, occurring two days after the ceasefire].

Months later, on September 12, 1991, *Newsday* broke perhaps the most horrifying story of all. Thousands of Iraqi troops had been buried alive in the first two days of the ground offensive. According to *Newsday*:

The U.S Army division that broke through Saddam Hussein's defensive frontline used plows mounted on tanks and combat earth movers to bury thousands of Iraqi soldiers—some still alive and firing their weapons in more than 70 miles of trenches...three brigades of the 1st Mechanized Infantry Division...used the grisly innovation to destroy trenches and bunkers defended by more than 8,000 Iraqi soldiers...

President Bush's reply to charges of atrocities against retreating soldiers was to declare that there were no Iraqi withdrawals.

At the end of the war, Iraq was incapable of feeding itself, purifying water for drinking, healing the sick or rebuilding itself. March 3, 1991 was the end of the bombing and assaults by coalition ground troops but it was not the end of the war against Iraq. The war continued through the imposition of sanctions, no-fly zones, and bombing in the no-fly zones by Britain and the United States. It was an invisible war which did not appear nightly on CNN with expert commentators (the same applies to most of the mainstream media) because it did not meet their criteria of newsworthiness despite the fact that more than 3,000 children were dying every month because of sanctions and depleted uranium shrapnel.

Genocide Disguised as Sanctions

As part of the war strategy, the United Nations, under pressure from the United States, passed Resolution 661 (1990), which imposed a mandatory and complete embargo on all trade with Iraq. It prohibited nations from buying or selling any Iraqi products, medicine being the only exception. Food was permitted "in humanitarian circumstances."

All decisions related to sanctions were made by the Sanctions Committee of the Security Council which was established by UN Resolution 661. The committee had one representative from each nation on the Security Council and any member could veto a contract without cause. Such a veto allowed the United States to prohibit any contract without the inconvenience of an explanation. To enforce the sanctions, the Security Council passed Resolution 665 which authorized the creation of a U.S.-led international naval blockade.

Resolution 666 expanded on Resolution 661 by requiring the Sanctions Committee to "keep the situation regarding foodstuffs...under constant review." On September 13, 1991, the Sanctions Committee was granted the authority to discriminate between "humanitarian circumstances" and non-humanitarian circumstances. According to Ramsey Clark, in *The Fire This Time*:

> The committee, controlled by the United States, was consistently hostile to Iraq. Importation of food and medicines was severely curtailed...From August 6, 1990 to March 22, 1991, efforts to transport food to Iraq through the Persian Gulf were militarily blocked.

United Nations Resolution 687 expanded the scope of exemptions from the sanctions by including "materials and supplies for essential civilian needs...and any further findings of humanitarian needs by the committee."

The prohibition against oil exports, which constituted 90 percent of Iraqi exports, was devastating because it deprived Iraq of the foreign reserves it desperately needed to feed its people. Iraq had been importing approximately 70 percent of its food and now that Iraq lacked foreign reserves it was unable to purchase food from other countries. Although the sanctions were ostensibly intended to be humanitarian, in practice they became a weapon to starve the people of Iraq and deny them access to proper medical treatment in the hope that they would overthrow Saddam Hussein themselves. Starving people until they overthrow their own leader was also the main objective of the Reagan administration in Nicaragua.

The criteria the Sanctions Committee applied to food shipments to assess whether they could be shipped to Iraq under "humanitarian circumstances" were inadequate to avoid a malnutrition crisis. According to Rahul Mahajan, in *Full Spectrum Dominance: U.S. Power in Iraq and Beyond*:

Although in theory, food was exempted from the sanctions, in practice the sanctions were a little more than an attempt to influence Iraqi policy by starving the people. For example, between August 6, 1990, and April 1991, Iraq was able to import roughly 10,000 tons of grain—the equivalent of Iraqi's daily grain requirement before the invasion of Kuwait. At one time, the United States even blocked a contract to import baby food from Bulgaria because, said the U.S. representative on the Sanctions Committee, adults might eat it.

The number of children who died or who were malnourished was unconscionable and reflected a dehumanization of the Iraq people. One of the studies undertaken by the Harvard International Study Group concluded that one million Iraqi children were malnourished and 120,000 suffering from acute malnutrition. A study of 15,000 children conducted by UNICEF concluded that 27.5 percent of children were malnourished and in another study of 24,000 households, UNICEF estimated that 500,000 children had died. Denis Halliday, a former Assistant Secretary General of the United Nations and 2001 Nobel Peace Prize nominee, reports that, "In Iraq, the UN-imposed sanctions probably killed up to one million people. Children are dying of malnutrition and water-borne diseases." Ramsey Clark wrote a letter in 1996 to the Security Council in which he reported that:

The United Nations Food and Agriculture Organization (FAO) reports the UN sanctions on Iraq have been responsible for the deaths of more than 560,000 children in Iraq since 1990. Most children's deaths are from the effects of malnutrition including marasmus [extreme weight loss] and kwashiorkor, wasting or emaciation which has reached 12 percent of all children, stunted growth which affects 28 percent, diarrhea, dehydration from bad water or food which is ordinarily easily controlled and cured, common communicable diseases preventable by vaccinations, and epidemics from deteriorating sanitary conditions. There are no deaths crueler than these. They are suffered slowly, helplessly, without simple remedial medication, without simple sedation to relieve pain, without mercy.

Does torturing so many children through starvation make the world a safer place? Paradoxically, at least one top American official, Madeleine Albright, U.S. Ambassador to the UN, believed it made sense, as demonstrated by her response to a question by Lesley Stahl on the U.N. sanctions, aired on *60 Minutes*, May 12, 1996:

Q.   We have heard that a half million children have died. I mean that's more than died in Hiroshima. And, you know, is the price worth it?

A.   I think this a very hard choice, but the price—we think the price is worth it.

In recognition of the fact that the sanctions were starving the Iraqi people, the UN relented and decided to permit Iraq to sell some of its oil. The money earned from the sale of oil would be used to purchase basic necessities. The program was to be called Oil for Food. Money from Iraqi oil sales was to be placed into a bank account controlled by the United Nations and the Sanctions Committee would have complete control over how the money was spent. On August 15, 1991, UN Resolution 706 was approved which permitted the sale of oil up to $1.6 billion (US) during a six-month period, the spending of which was subject to the approval of the Security Council Committee.

Unfortunately, the United States chose to exploit UN Resolution 706 to create the impression that the Iraqi dictator was responsible for the starvation of his own people. President Clinton told a grand "Lewinsky" when asked about the sanctions killing children as revealed in the following interview with Amy Goodman on *Democracy Now*:

Amy Goodman: President Clinton, UN figures show that up to 5,000 children a month die in Iraq because of the sanctions against Iraq.

President Clinton: That's not true. And that's not what they show…If any child is without food or medicine or a roof over his or her head in Iraq, it's because he [Saddam Hussein] is claiming the sanctions are doing it and sticking it to his own children. We have worked like crazy to make sure that the embargo only applies to his ability to reconstitute his weapon system…

While some of what is described here took place under Clinton, his Iraq policy was largely an extension of the previous Bush administration policy, and largely set in motion by it. Therefore, for the sake of continuity, most of Clinton's Iraq deeds are discussed in this chapter. There is perhaps a sick lesson behind this organizational morass: the presidential lies and deceit are so interwoven in foreign policy and so consistent over the years that, in this instance in any case, it is actually no small task to tease out who instigated what policy.

Before passage of the resolution, Sadruddin Aga Khan was dispatched to Iraq to estimate the cost of restoring basic services to the people of Iraq. He estimated that it would cost $22 billion to achieve that goal and also recommended that a minimum of $6.9 billion would be needed to restore health and agriculture, half of the pre-war electrical capacity, 40 percent of water and sanitation needs, and a subsistence level of food. Khan advised that for a start, Iraq should be allowed to sell $2.65 billion worth of oil over a four-month period, to be renewed if no problems arose.

The United States proposed that the amount be stretched by reducing it to $1.6 billion over a six-month period with a further deduction of 30 percent for a UN compensation fund. When Resolution 706 was passed, the amount of oil revenue available to the Iraqi Government over a six-month period was $930 million. It is not surprising that Iraq turned down such a puny amount which was a very small fraction of what was required to have any impact. Given the small amount offered by the Security Council, it is plausible that the intention of the United States was to present such an unattractive package that the Iraqi government would reject it.

The United States could then claim that Saddam Hussein was responsible for the plight of his own people.

The government was forced to cut food rations by 37 percent after which the people of Iraq were consuming, on average, only 1100 calories a day. Iraq was finally forced into agreeing to Security Council Resolution 986 which allowed the sale of $2 billion of oil every six months subject to the same conditions as Resolution 706. The critical aspect of the time interval is as important as the cash reduction. An amount of $2.65 billion every 4 months, as originally recommended, would have meant $7.8 billion a year; $2 billion reduced by a compensation fund to $1.4 billion every six months is $2.8 billion, well under half what was recommended. Providing less than needed over an extended period of time doesn't mean things improve more slowly, rather, that they steadily disintegrate and worsen over time. Even this was resisted by the U.S. Rahul Mahajan, in *Full Spectrum Dominance* wrote that:

> In the end, the United States accepted the resolution only because international political pressure would have made retaining the sanctions untenable otherwise as Clinton administration official Robert Pelletreau said to a skeptical congressional committee at the time, "Implementation of the resolution is not a precursor to lifting sanctions. It is a humanitarian exception that preserves and even reinforces the sanction regime."

Ramsey Clark, in his letter to the UN Security Council, revealed that the oil for food program was actually a prescription for death and illness:

> If the present agreement pursuant to Resolution 986 is finalized in March, it will be months before this ration can increase and by the most optimistic estimates it still will be far short of basic needs, providing Iraq with only a lower level of malnutrition. If the entire allocation of Resolution 986 oil-sale income available for health was spent on medicine and medical supplies, there would still be severe shortages causing deaths and protracted illness.

The fact that UN Resolution 661 granted the right to any country on the Sanctions Committee to veto a contract without cause presented the United States and Great Britain with the opportunity to exploit the interpretation of "humanitarian circumstances" and "civilian needs." "Dual use" goods are those that can be used for either military or civilian purposes. The U.S. and Great Britain decided to interpret "dual use" goods in the widest possible sense stretching the meaning to absurd extremes. Examples of "dual use" goods that were banned include:

- Vaccines to treat infant hepatitis, tetanus, and diphtheria because vaccines contained live cultures which could be transformed into a fatal strain despite the objections of biological weapons experts who maintained that it was not possible.
- Incubators were banned.
- Cardiac equipment was prohibited.
- Contracts related to electrical power generation were blocked by the U.S.
- The U.S. approved insulin but not syringes
- Blood bags without catheters were approved
- A sewage treatment plant without the generator was approved.
- Pencils for school children were banned.
- Chlorine to treat water was banned.

The shortage of clean water was one of the most widespread and critical humanitarian crises after the 1991 bombing. Bombing and sanctions were responsible for the destruction of the mechanisms for providing purified water by destroying the water-treatment plants and making it impossible to repair them. The destruction of power utilities made it impossible to boil water and the sanctions made it impossible to repair them. Chlorine was prohibited by the sanctions making it impossible to purify water.

Poor sanitation combined with a lack of pure water was a recipe for a whole host of diseases. Most garbage trucks were inoperable because of the bombing and the prohibition of spare parts; as a result garbage was dumped onto the streets. Sewage pipes were also damaged by the bombing, allowing raw sewage to percolate to the surface and flood commercial and residential areas. Poor sanitation and impure water resulted in high levels of cholera, typhoid, dysentery, and diarrhea.

The lack of pure water and an effective sanitation system combined with malnourishment and radiation from depleted uranium ordnance created an extensive medical crisis. Sanctions robbed Iraqi hospitals of the medicine, equipment, and medical supplies needed to cope with the many diseases plaguing the people of Iraq. Medical shortages included ordinary medications, cancer and leukemia drugs, insulin, anesthetics, and antibiotics. The lack of medical equipment included radiology equipment, laboratory equipment, defibrillation and ECG machines, dialysis machines, X-ray equipment, incubators, oxygen tanks, and sterilization equipment. Patients were dying from easily curable diseases and many were dying in extreme pain due to the lack of painkillers such as morphine. Babies suffering from dehydration withered away.

Ramsey Clark, in a letter to the members of the Security Council on March 1, 1996, summed up the tragedy of sanctions as follows:

> One issue between Iraq and the United Nations exceeds all others in importance. That issue is the Security Council sanctions imposed against Iraq at the insistence of the United States. The whole world knows, and history will permanently record, the fact that those savage sanctions have cruelly killed more than one million people in Iraq these last five years, injured millions more, and damaged the population and society for generations to come. Is this the legacy the United Nations wishes to support by failing to completely end the sanctions now?

Every six months the Sanctions Committee reviewed the Oil-for-Food program to evaluate the list of prohibited items and the amount of oil that Iraq could sell. On February 20, 1998, the Security Council doubled the amount of oil Iraq was allowed to export, increasing the value from $2.14 billion to $5.26 billion over six months. Security Council Resolution 1175 granted Iraq permission to purchase $300 billion of spare parts for its oil industry. On January 20, 1999, the Sanctions Committee released more than $81 million to Iraq to purchase parts and equipment needed to increase its supply of electricity. The UN Security Council approved an overhaul of the Oil for Food program on May 14, 2002, that created a new list of "dual use" goods and defined prohibited goods.

In addition to inflicting starvation, disease, and inadequate medical treatment on the Iraqi people, the United States, Britain, and France sustained military operations against Iraq under the guise of a humanitarian campaign in the years immediately following the Gulf War. A no-fly zone was established in northern Iraq, north of the 36th parallel and covering 19,000 square miles, to protect the Kurdish people from attacks by Saddam. The Iraqis were prohibited from flying any aircraft including helicopters in these air exclusion zones. The no-fly zones clearly violated Iraq's territorial integrity but Washington argued that the legal basis for the establishment of the no-fly zones was Security Council Resolution 688. Resolution 688 makes no reference to Chapter VII in the UN Charter which provides the only authorization for the use of force.

On August 26, 1992, the U.S., Britain, and France established a southern no-fly zone south of the 32nd parallel to protect the Shi'ite Muslims who had rebelled against Baghdad. The zone was extended northward in 1996 to include the southern third of Iraq.

There were a number of breaches of the no-fly zones. On December 22, 1992 an Iraqi fighter was shot down. On January 13, 1993 Western forces attacked targets in southern Iraq following Iraqi military activity in the zone. Between December 1998 and June 2000 the RAF alone dropped 78 tons of bombs. The George W. Bush administration used the zones to degrade Iraq's limited capability to defend itself against large-scale U.S. attacks. The CIA began to support efforts by Iraqi opposition groups in the northern zone to stage an attack or possibly a coup against the Iraqi government.

The zones did not coincide with the regions occupied by the two groups in need of protection. General Tommy Franks, commander of U.S. Central Command, testified before Congress in 2001 and defined the real purpose of the no-fly zones as:

- continued and significant troop presence to enhance deterrence and to demonstrate the American commitment to force Iraq to cooperate with the inspection process;

- to maintain access and interaction with other Gulf governments;

- to ensure that Iraq cannot repair or improve its anti-aircraft capabilities in the no-fly zones.

The no-fly zones were established to destroy Iraqi defences against a large-scale bombing attack as well as for training U.S. and British pilots for bombing raids in Iraq. Both of these countries were determined to destroy Iraq's chemical and biological weapons and Iraq's nascent nuclear program, if one existed. These three types of weapons are referred to as weapons of mass destruction (WMD). As well, all facilities and equipment needed to manufacture WMD were to be destroyed.

Looking for Weapons of Mass Destruction

The purpose of the sanctions was to force Saddam Hussein to destroy his WMD. The mechanism for discovering and eliminating any WMD in Iraq was to establish inspection teams under the auspices of the United Nations. Security Council Resolution 687 (April 3, 1991) calls for Iraq to cooperate in the destruction of WMD and for:

> The forming of a special commission which shall carry out immediate on-site inspection of Iraq's biological, chemical, and missile capabilities, based on Iraq's declaration and the designation of any additional locations by the special commission itself;...The provision by the Special Commission to the Director General of the International Atomic Energy Agency [IAEA] of the assistance and cooperation required in paragraphs 12 and 13.

The United Nations Special Committee (UNSCOM) for inspections of biological and chemical weapons and the IAEA inspections for nuclear programs would have to certify that any threat from WMD had been eradicated before sanctions could be lifted (Security Council Resolution 687).

From the very beginning of the inspection process it was clear that the United States had its own agenda for inspections and was not interested in complying with SC Resolution 687. In 1991, Secretary of State James Baker said, "We are not interested in seeing a relaxation of sanctions as long as Saddam Hussein is in power." President Clinton's Secretary of State, Warren

Christopher, wrote in a *New York Times* op-ed piece in 1994 that "The U.S. does not believe that Iraq's compliance with paragraph 22 of Resolution 687 [sanctions end when Iraq meets conditions pertaining to WMD] is enough to justify lifting the embargo." Another Secretary of State under President Clinton, Madeleine Albright, stated on March 26, 1997 that:

> We do not agree with the nations who argue that if Iraq complies with its obligations concerning weapons of mass destruction, sanctions should be lifted. Our view, which is unshakeable, is that Iraq must prove its peaceful intentions...And the evidence is overwhelming that Saddam Hussein's intentions will never be peaceful.

The blatant contradiction between American support for Resolution 687 and public statements from three Secretaries of State exposed the fact that the United States' objective was the removal of Saddam Hussein from power.

It is important to understand the outcome of the inspection process to recognize the extent to which President George W. Bush lied about WMD after his election in 2000. The purpose of his lies was to justify another war against Iraq to further the aims of empire.

Inspections for WMD in Iraq were a very complex technical process. The cooperation of Iraq was essential to gain access to sites scheduled for inspection and to documents describing the location of WMD storage or manufacturing facilities. It was also essential to verify the destruction of weapons. Iraq did not cooperate with the inspectors by concealing documents and weapons and making it difficult for inspectors to gain access to sites. After the passage of Security Council Resolution 687, the Iraq government created an emergency committee chaired by Tariq Aziz, Iraq's Foreign Minister, to save as many of Iraq's WMD as possible. The committee issued instructions to evacuate all weapons-related materials that were to be concealed from UNSCOM. In addition to concealing WMD, Iraqis sometimes held inspectors at gunpoint to prevent them from carrying out their work or simply to block their entrance to facilities.

Despite these obstacles, inspection teams were able to perform their duties because of their broad powers to gain access to sites, their powers to take soil and atmospheric samples, and their access to surveillance photographs. Inspection teams also were aided by the defection to Jordan of Hussein Kamel, Saddam's son-in-law, who was in charge of Iraq's advanced weapons program.

Ultimately the inspection process revealed that Iraq did not possess WMD. It is possible that some biological agents could have been hidden in a freezer somewhere but they would have been ineffective unless they were weaponized. The weaponization facilities and equipment would have been detected by inspection teams if they existed. Chemical and nuclear materials are very difficult to conceal and would have had to be weaponized as well. Biological and chemical agents have limited shelf lives—five years for mustard gas and three years for biological agents. Between 1994 and 1998 the monitoring inspections of UNSCOM never discovered any attempts by Iraq to reconstitute its chemical and biological capability.

Iraq submitted a declaration to the United Nations detailing the location of all its WMD and related documents. The first executive chairman of UNSCOM, Rolf Ekéus, sent a letter to the Iraqi government calling attention to the inaccuracies in the Iraqi declaration and advising the Iraqi government that undeclared sites would be subject to inspection.

An example of a failed attempt to foil the inspection teams occurred in 1991 when an UNSCOM team declared their intentions to inspect a nuclear site at Abu Ghraib, west of Baghdad. Despite the fact that the concealment committee had ordered the nuclear materials to be moved to remote farms, the effort failed because among the materials were electromagnetic isotope separators which are easily identified by surveillance photographs.

Another example occurred in September 1991 when inspectors arrived unannounced at Iraqi nuclear headquarters catching everyone by surprise. The inspectors uncovered millions of pages of documentation pertaining to Iraq's nuclear weapons program.

In the spring of 1992, the work of UNSCOM was assisted by the addition of CIA operatives headed by Moe Dobbs. With Dobbs help, UNSCOM established a functional monitoring system which no longer depended on intrusive confrontational inspections. But when Hussein Kamel defected, he revealed that there was another million pages of documentation of chemical and biological weapons programs which forced UNSCOM to revise its inspection methods. UNSCOM again instituted large-scale intrusive and confrontational inspections supported by a comprehensive information gathering plan that included inspectors on the ground, air craft surveillance, and communication scanners to pick up Iraqi communications related to inspections.

One of the intrusive and confrontational inspections took place in June

1996, when UNSCOM decided to inspect Special Republican Guard (SRG) facilities where there were possibly weapons material and documentation. Iraq refused to allow inspections of the SRG facilities leading to a standoff lasting several days as the inspectors surrounded the building. The incident triggered high-level discussions which centered on whether the Security Council would back up the inspection team. The outcome was an agreement signed by Ekéus and Aziz that respected the sovereignty of Iraq and allowed the inspectors to do their job. The agreement defined those facilities that were sensitive and the number of inspectors allowed to enter a sensitive site. One of Iraq's issues with admitting inspectors into sensitive sites was the presence of CIA agents on inspection teams who were using the opportunity to compile a list of targets.

By the mid-1990s UNSCOM had achieved considerable progress in removing the threat of Iraqi WMD. According to Rahul Mahajan, in *Full Spectrum Dominance*:

> According to the March 1999 Amorim report prepared for the Security Council, the achievements of UNSCOM and IAEA (International Atomic Energy Association) included but were not limited to, removal of all "weapons usable nuclear material" by February 1994; destruction of all or nearly all imported missiles, missile launchers, chemical and biological warheads; destruction of over 88,000 chemical munitions, nearly 5,000 tons of chemical weapons agents and precursor chemicals; and destruction of al-Hakam, the main biological weapons production complex, along with much biological growth media and equipment.

On September 1, 1997, Richard Butler became the new executive chairman of UNSCOM. One of the controversies during his tenure as chairman was whether or not he was an agent for the Americans and as such participated in an attempt to orchestrate the end of UNSCOM.

Shortly after Butler's appointment, an inspection team completed their inspection of the Second Battalion of the Special Republican Guard, which went smoothly. The next site was a housing complex of the 2nd Battalion. Tariq Aziz declared this site to be "sensitive-sensitive" which defined it as a presidential site. Scott Ritter, the chief inspector, and his fellow inspectors were denied access. Two days later the inspection team was stopped at another "sensitive-sensitive" site.

Richard Butler decided that these two cases should be reported to the Security Council as evidence of obstruction by the Iraqis. Following another thwarted inspection attempt when inspectors had been held at gunpoint,

Richard Butler delivered a censorious report to the Security Council prompting the adoption of Resolution 1134 in October 1997 which imposed additional sanctions. Iraq exploited the split in the vote on this resolution by refusing to allow American inspectors to participate in further inspections on the grounds that the U.S. had planted spies on the inspection teams. Butler reacted by asking all inspectors in Iraq to leave. The inspection process was in a state of crisis. Russia then negotiated a deal which would allow inspections to continue if Russia could speak for Iraq on the Security Council. Iraq agreed to the return of the inspectors.

After their return to Iraq, an inspection team headed by Scott Ritter inspected seven sites on January 12, 1998. On another inspection of the Directorate for General Security (DGS), the inspectors discovered that numerous files were missing. The alarmed Iraqis threatened to no longer cooperate because too many inspectors on the inspection teams were either British or American intelligence agents. UN Secretary General Kofi Annan and Tariq Aziz signed a memorandum of understanding that established new rules for inspecting presidential sites that specified the number of inspectors allowed into the building. The test site for the agreement was to be the Ministry of Defense.

Before the inspectors had an opportunity to inspect the Ministry of Defense, Albright informed Butler that Washington had formulated plans to bomb Iraq. The attack would have to end on March 15, 1998, because of the pilgrimages to Mecca in Saudi Arabia. Albright asked Butler to complete the inspections by March 8, 1998. From March fifth to seventh Scott Ritter and his inspection team carried out their inspections on sites in the old Ministry of Defense. In order to inspect the new Ministry of Defense, negotiations were needed to determine the number of inspectors permitted access to the Ministry. Both sides agreed on sixteen. They found no sign of WMD and the attack on Iraq was forestalled.

Deceit about the Inspection Process

There were different expectations of when reductions in sanctions would occur in relation to Iraq's cooperation on arms inspections. The United States was not prepared to reduce sanctions until there was proof that Iraq was completely disarmed while Iraq was expecting a quid pro quo. Section 21 of UN Resolution 687 states that the Security Council:

Decides to review the provisions of paragraph 20 [sanctions] every 60 days in the light of the policies and practices of the Government of Iraq, including the implementation of all relevant resolutions of the Council, for the purpose of determining whether to reduce or lift the prohibitions referred to therein.

In August 1998, Iraq decided to refuse to cooperate with UNSCOM on inspections but to allow monitoring to continue until some of their issues, such as a reduction of sanctions, were addressed. On October 30, Iraq refused to cooperate on monitoring as well, but resumed cooperation on November 14, under the threat of bombing. In the following month, UNSCOM conducted over 300 inspections but Richard Butler had planned a number of confrontational inspections which would provoke obstruction by Iraq. On December 15, he recalled the inspectors without notifying the Security Council. In his report to the Security Council on December 15, he cited only a few relatively minor incidents of obstruction but under pressure from Washington concluded that little progress had been made. According to his report:

It has not been possible to verify Iraq's claims with respect to the nature and magnitude of its proscribed weapons programmes and their current disposition...The commission has not been able to conduct the substantive disarmament work...

While Butler was giving his report to the Security Council a four-day bombing campaign was launched against Iraq called Operation Desert Fox. Only 11 of the 97 targets were related to WMD whereas the others included command and control sites, Republican Guard units, and facilities of the internal security forces. American intelligence agents on the UNSCOM inspection teams had been used to locate these targets.

Several important points must be noted in any analysis of the effectiveness of the UNSCOM and the American response. First, the relationship between Richard Butler and American officials undermined not only the inspection process but the credibility of inspections as well. In theory, he worked for and only took instructions from the Security Council. His relationship with the U.S. was unethical. Second, there was no attempt to reward Iraq by easing the sanctions as a reward for cooperating with the inspectors. Third, there was no debate on Richard Butler's report in the Security Council before the bombing started. The United States acted unilaterally without a confirmation from the Security Council that Iraq was not cooperating with the inspectors or that Iraq did, in fact, possess WMD. Fourth, Iraq was effectively disarmed. Finally, the United States exploited the inspection teams to gather intelligence on Iraq for the purpose of targeting government buildings. According to Scott Ritter, UN Chief Weapons Inspector, in *Frontier Justice: Weapons of Mass Destruction and the Bushwhacking of America*:

> The final straw came in the summer of 1998, when the United States pressured Richard Butler, the executive chairman of UNSCOM from 1997 to 1999, to shut down a sensitive intelligence operation I had been carrying out on behalf of UNSCOM inside Iraq since 1996, turning the capabilities inherent in this project (which included eavesdropping on the private conversations of Saddam Hussein and his inner circle of advisors) over to the United States without any UNSCOM input or control all the while continuing to operate under UNSCOM's operational cover. In short, Richard Butler allowed the United States to use the unique access enjoyed by the UNSCOM inspectors to spy on Saddam Hussein, totally corrupting the integrity of the whole operation.

The inspection process became entangled in a web of deceit, dishonesty, and obstruction. Iraq attempted to conceal documents and weapons and to obstruct access to sites designated for inspection. Washington planted intelligence agents on inspection teams, provoked Iraq into resisting inspections by pressuring Butler to select political sites for inspection, ignored the detailed reports of the inspectors, and bombed Iraq illegally before the final report of UNSCOM was debated by the Security Council. According to Chapter VII, Article 42, of the UN Charter, Security Council authorization would be required for the use of force. The critical question was whether Iraq possessed WMD which were proscribed by United Nations Resolutions. Scott Ritter reported that:

> What Iraq tried for seven years [1991-1998] to conceal from UNSCOM was a weapons of mass destruction program that is little more than the bare bones of the massive projects undertaken prior to Operation Desert Storm. This reduced capability reflects the effectiveness of the UNSCOM and IAEA inspection process, which, despite all of Iraq's efforts to conceal, obfuscate, and distort the truth, managed to dispose of the vast majority of the prohibited weapons programs. (*Endgame: Solving the Iraq Crisis*)

Also, according to Scott Ritter:

> And yet I also knew that, during the course of our difficult work, we inspectors had uncovered the lion's share of Iraq's illegal arsenal. What was left, if anything represented nothing more than documents and scraps of material, seed-stock, perhaps, for any reconstitution effort that might take place in the

future, but by and of themselves, not a viable weapons program….My analysis was shared by no less an authority than Rolf Ekéus, the distinguished Swedish diplomat and UNSCOM's first executive chairman, who had reminded me during a meeting after my 1998 return from Iraq that "by February 1996, we had really managed to get our hands on arms around all the issues: nuclear, chemical, biological, and missiles." (*Endgame: Solving the Iraq Crisis*)

On January 30, 1999, the Security Council established three panels to "consider the parallel objectives of re-establishing an effective presence of the United Nations and the International Atomic Energy Agency in Iraq in the area of disarmament." The panel on disarmament and verification included "the participation and expertise from the United Nations Special Commission, the International Atomic Energy Agency, the United Nations Secretariat, and other relevant expertise." The panel reported to the Security Council on March 27, 1999, that:

> …the Agency [IAEA] is able to state that there is no indication that Iraq possesses nuclear weapons or any meaningful amounts of weapons-usable nuclear material or that Iraq has retained any practical capability (facilities or hardware) for the production of such material…UNSCOM has supervised or been able to certify the destruction, removal, or rendering harmless of large quantities of chemical weapons (CW), their components and major chemical weapons production equipment… the declared facilities of Iraq's BW [biological weapons] programme have been destroyed and rendered harmless.

While UN inspectors searched for Iraqi WMD, American WMD resulted in a severe health problem in Iraq. The deaths caused by sanctions were immediate and obvious. Depleted uranium was more insidious in killing Iraqis and can't be as easily documented. Nevertheless, the use of depleted uranium weapons caused an increase in the levels of cancer in Iraq. In another documentary, *Genocide by Sanctions*, the International Action Centre, headed by Ramsey Clark, visited hospitals in Iraq in 1998 and interviewed doctors, nurses, and patients. A number of patients were suffering from leukemia from depleted uranium weapons but the doctors lacked drugs to treat them due to the sanctions. The doctors reported that there had been an increase in the incidence of cancer since the bombing. Sanctions were killing 300 children a day under the age of five despite the fact that the sanctions were originally imposed to force Iraq to withdraw from Kuwait (Bob Drogin, *On Forgotten Kuwait Road, 60 Miles of Wounds of War*, Los Angeles Times, March 10, 1991). William Blum, in *Killing Hope,* concludes that:

It will never be known how many hundreds of thousands of Iraqis have died from the direct and indirect effects of the war; the count is added to every day. With the United States refusing to end the embargo against Iraq, everything has continued, starvation, lack of medicines and vaccines, contaminated drinking water, human excrement piling up, typhoid, a near-epidemic of measles...By September 1994, with the U.S. government refusing to release its death grip on the embargo...the Iraqi government announced that since the sanctions had begun in August 1990 about 400,000 children had died of malnutrition and disease.

Doubting the Iraqi figures is an irrelevant exercise. The real question is not how many children have died but why did any children have to die because of illegal sanctions on food, medicine, and chlorine.

The continued use of sanctions served several purposes; to weaken Iraq and to convince the Iraqi people to overthrow Saddam Hussein in order to survive. As part of its campaign to weaken Iraq, the United States called on the Iraqi people to force Saddam Hussein to step down. President Bush called for the "Iraqi military and people to take matters into their own hands, and force Saddam Hussein, the dictator, to step aside." The message was specifically aimed at the Kurds who had suffered persecution under Saddam Hussein. Bush appealed directly to the Kurds on a CIA-funded radio station called the Voice of Free Iraq which not only encouraged the Kurds to rebel but implied that U.S. military assistance would be provided.

The Kurds, numbering 25 million, are the fourth largest ethnic group in the Middle East and live mostly in Iraq, Iran, Turkey, and Syria. During the Iraq-Iran war, Iraqi chemical- and conventional-weapons attacks on the Kurds in northern Iraq displaced one million Kurds between the spring of 1987 and fall of 1988. After the ceasefire in 1991, when the United States encouraged the Kurds to rebel against the Hussein regime, the Kurds captured a number of towns in Northern Iraq including Ranya, Arbil, and Aqra. Within one week, Hussein's elite Republican Guard recaptured the towns and forced one million Kurds into exile in Turkey and Iran. Despite assurances of support for a Kurdish uprising, the U.S. did not lift a finger to assist in the overthrow of Saddam. Approximately 750,000 Kurds sought refuge in Iran and about 280,000 fled to Turkey.

Bush Tells Some Big Ones

President Bush lied on many occasions to achieve America's foreign and military objectives in the Middle East. He lied about his real intention in the Persian Gulf which was to lure Iraq into a war for the purpose of crippling a major Middle Eastern power with the second largest oil reserves in the world. The ambiguous comments of April Glaspie, the buildup of troops before any real effort at a peaceful solution was undertaken, the bribes and threats required to obtain UN support, and the dismissal of all Iraqi offers to negotiate were the actions of a President who was determined to declare war. Bush lied when he claimed that Iraq's invasion of Kuwait was unprovoked ignoring all the Iraqi grievances against Kuwait. All Iraq's proposals to settle the crisis peacefully were treated with contempt by President Bush who invented justifications for ignoring the offers. To create the illusion of a real war, he lied about the military strength of Iraq. On many occasions, in public statements to the press or in letters to Congress, he lied when he gave assurances that only military targets would be struck. The war was scripted well in advance with the weakening of Iraq as the final outcome.

In evaluating the extent to which President Bush and other American leaders committed war crimes, it would be useful to examine the results of a War Crimes Tribunal organized by Ramsey Clark and the International Action Center. The Commission of Inquiry for the International War Crimes Tribunal was the outgrowth of the Coalition to Stop U.S. Intervention in the Middle East, formed by a group of American activists during the war. Nineteen criminal charges were laid against President Bush and other members of his administration. The purpose of the commission was to conduct exhaustive research into all the facts related to the charges. It traveled around the world to hold hearings and called on expert witnesses to provide evidence about the war. Tribunal members reviewed the testimony of the hearings, documents from UN agencies, documents of governments, and materials from private organizations and institutions.

The International War Crimes Tribunal first met on February 27, 1992 to consider the evidence and to determine the guilt or innocence of those charged with 19 crimes. The 22 judges on the War Crimes Tribunal represented 18 nations and were from diverse backgrounds. The judges included:

- Lord Tony Gifford, Britain. Human rights lawyer.

- Deborah Jackson, U.S. First vice president of the American Association of Jurists.

- Michael Ratner, U.S. Attorney and former director of the Center for Constitutional rights, past president of the National Lawyers Guild.

- P.S. Poti, India, former Chief Justice of the Gujarat High Court. In 1989 elected president of the All-India Lawyers Union.

- Aisha Nyerere, Tanzania, Resident Magistrate of the High Court in Arusha, Tanzania.

- Dr. Haluk Gerger, Turkey, Founding member of the Turkish Human Rights Association and professor of political science.

Some of the nineteen charges documented against George Bush, James Baker, Colin Powell, Dick Cheney, and others were that:

- The United States engaged in a pattern of conduct beginning in or before 1989 intended to lead Iraq into provocations justifying U.S. military action against Iraq and permanent U.S. military domination of the Gulf.

- President Bush ordered the destruction of facilities essential to civilian life and economic productivity throughout Iraq.

- The United States intentionally bombed and destroyed civilian life, commercial and business districts, schools, hospitals, mosques, churches, shelters, residential areas, historical sites, private vehicles and civilian government offices.

- The United States deliberately bombed indiscriminately throughout Iraq.

- The United States used prohibited weapons capable of mass destruction and inflicted indiscriminate death and unnecessary suffering against both military and civilian targets.

Following are the findings of the War Crimes Tribunal:

The Members of the International War Crimes Tribunal finds each of the named accused guilty on the basis of the evidence against them and that each of the nineteen separate crimes alleged in the Initial attached hereto, has been established to have been committed beyond a reasonable doubt.

Although the War Crimes Tribunal did not have legitimacy as an international court, it did define the crimes committed by President Bush and the aforementioned members of his administration who did violate the UN Charter, Geneva Conventions, and the Convention on the Prevention and Punishment of Genocide.

The Bush administration violated the following clauses in the Geneva Convention:

1. Convention III, Part 1, Article 3, Clause 1—Persons taking no part in the hostilities, including members of the armed forces who have laid down their arms ...To this end the following acts shall remain prohibited:

    a) violence to life and person;

    b) outrages upon personal dignity.

Shooting soldiers from aircraft, shooting soldiers in retreat in the back, or shooting prisoners who surrender all violate the above. As well, Protocol I, Chapter III, Article 51 states that:

4. Indiscriminate attacks are prohibited. Indiscriminate attacks are:

    a) those which are not directed at specific military objectives;

    b) those which employ a method or means of combat the effects of which cannot be directed at specific military objectives.

Bombing the civilian targets mentioned earlier violated 4a. Using napalm, cluster bombs, depleted uranium weapons, and fuel-air explosives violated 4b. These weapons are not designed to hit specific targets and are clearly incapable of discriminating between military and civilian objects.

Bush's war on Iraq violates the United Nations Charter. Chapter I, Chapter VI, Chapter VII, Articles 2, 33, 34, 37, 39, 40, 41, and 42 obligate members not to endanger the maintenance of international peace and security, to seek all possible peaceful means to resolve their disputes, to refer the dispute to the Security Council if a resolution is not reached, and to defer to the Security Council's decision as to what action to take. The United States violated all the above articles. All of Iraq's peace offers were rejected including the final one in which Saddam Hussein agreed to withdraw from Kuwait if the United States agreed to not fire on retreating Iraqi troops. Saddam Hussein also requested that negotiations be held to resolve outstanding Middle Eastern disputes. There was nothing unreasonable in his demands. Attempting to resolve other disputes through negotiations is not a justification for rejecting an offer. Negotiations are the civilized method for settling differences. Furthermore, the United States did not put forward any reasonable offers. Finally, the approval of the Security Council was not a reflection of support for the war but a reflection of the power of the United States to bribe and bully other countries and as explained earlier, Resolution 678 was itself illegal.

The Bush administration also violated the Convention on the Prevention and Punishment of the Crime of Genocide. According to Article 2:

> In the present Convention, genocide means any of the following acts committed with intent to destroy, in whole or in part, a national, ethnical, racial or religious group such as:
>
> (a) killing members of the group;
>
> (b) causing serious bodily or mental harm to members of the group;
>
> (c) deliberately inflicting on the group conditions of life calculated to bring about its physical destruction in whole or in part.

The United States bombing and ground offensive killed up to 125,000 Iraqis. The approximately one million people who died between the two wars on Iraq due to depleted uranium, unsafe water, and lack of medical equipment and medication are also victims of the U.S. war on Iraq. American bombing and refusal to allow the Iraqis to repair infrastructure clearly "inflicted conditions of life calculated to bring about its [the Iraqi people's] physical destruction in whole or in part."

The so-called war against Iraq was, in fact, an act of mass murder and a massive destruction of property. It was a criminal act on an international level and therefore, a crime against humanity. On February 12, 1991, Ramsey Clark wrote a letter to President Bush and UN Secretary General Perez de Cuellar describing the bombing as:

> ...the clearest violation of international law and norms for armed conflict...It is uncivilized, brutal, and racist by any moral standard...The use of highly sophisticated military technology with mass destructive capacity by rich nations against an essentially defenseless civilian population of a poor nation is one of the great tragedies of our time. (Ramsey Clark, *The Fire this Time*)

CHAPTER 8

THE EMPIRE AS GOOD GUY

CLINTON KILLS CIVILIANS TO SAVE THEM

In the name of humanitarian intervention, President Clinton and other NATO leaders bombed Serbia to stop ethnic cleansing. Clinton announced to the American people that "...when ethnic conflict turns into ethnic cleansing where we can make a difference, we must try...Had we faltered...the result would have been a moral and strategic disaster." (*The New Military Humanism*, Noam Chomsky) He also referred to the war as a "Just and necessary war."

Orwellian bastardization of language was never more evident than when the bombing of Serbia was called a humanitarian campaign. In an Orwellian inversion of language where war becomes peace and hate becomes love, Clinton defined the bombing of Serbia as a humanitarian campaign when, in fact, the United States and other NATO leaders were engaged in a campaign to break up the Socialist Federal Republic of Yugoslavia under the pretext of stopping ethnic cleansing. The SFRY was guilty of preserving its socialist approach to social and economic policy after the breakup of the former Soviet Union. Michael Parenti explained, in *To Kill a Nation: The Attack on Yugoslavia,* that:

> ...Yugoslavia (FRY) remained the only nation in the region that would not voluntarily discard what remained of its socialism and install an unalloyed free-market system... It also proudly had no interest in joining NATO. The US goal has been to transform the FRY into a Third World region, a cluster of weak right-wing principalities...

Noam Chomsky in *The New Military Humanism: Lessons from Kosovo* notes that "Serbia is one of those disorderly miscreants that impedes the institution of the U.S.-dominated global system..."

One test of U.S. intentions in the bombing of Serbia is to compare the atrocities in Kosovo to those occurring in Turkey at the same time. Since 1980, Turkey has been committing atrocities against its Kurdish population with $15 billion of arms from the United States. Forty thousand Kurds have been killed and two million rendered homeless. Before the NATO bombing of Serbia began, 2000 people had been killed as a result of the civil war in

Serbia. If the U.S. was pursuing humanitarian goals why was it not only turning a blind eye to the atrocities perpetrated against the Kurds but also arming Turkey?

The History of Six Republics Held Together by a Thread

To understand the bombing of Serbia and what is tells us about presidential lying, it is essential to understand the events leading up to it including the histories of the different peoples who once inhabited Yugoslavia. Modern Yugoslavia was a mosaic of peoples, languages, religions, and cultures. Serbia, Croatia, Slovenia, Bosnia-Herzegovina, Macedonia, and Montenegro were the six republics which joined together to form the Socialist Federated Republic of Yugoslavia (SFRY). Kosovo and Vojvodina were two autonomous regions within Serbia, created to protect their minority groups, the Albanians in Kosovo and the Hungarians in Vojvodina. These six republics had been under the control of different empires at different points in their development, including the Byzantine, the Austrian, and the Ottoman Empires.

When the Turkish Empire began to weaken in the seventeenth century, Bosnia and Herzegovina were caught in the struggles among Austria, Russia, and Turkey. Bosnia and Herzegovina were bounced back and forth between the Austrian and Turkish Empires. In 1850, under Turkish rule, the capital of Bosnia was transferred to Sarajevo. Peasant uprisings in Bosnia and Herzegovina caused by Turkish corruption and taxes intensified into a full-scale revolt. The rebellion in the Balkans broke out into a European war and the defeat of Turkey. The Treaty of Berlin in 1878 led to the occupation of Bosnia and Herzegovina by the Austro-Hungarian Empire. Muslim and Orthodox opposition was suppressed. Both Austria and Hungary endeavored to increase the Christian population of Bosnia where there was already a struggle to maintain harmony among Muslims, Catholic Croats, and Orthodox Serbs. At the turn of the century, nationalist differences were in danger of exploding and Austria-Hungary triggered a major upheaval when it formally annexed the region in 1908. Serbia also wanted to gain control of the region and mobilized for war. The crisis ended when German pressure convinced all of Europe to accept the Serbian annexation.

Although Albania was not one of the six republics in the Yugoslav Federation, its history sheds light on important aspects of the NATO bombing of Serbia. The Illyrians, ancestors of the Albanians, lived in the western Balkans and came into contact with Greek colonies from the seventh century BC. In 167 BC, the Romans extended their rule over Albania and most of the Balkans; they were succeeded by the Byzantine Empire, then by other conquerors. The Ottomans invaded Albania and ruled from 1479 until 1912. A number of uprisings between 1910 and 1912 resulted in a declaration of independence and the formation of a provincial government. Albania's achievement of independence was marred in 1913 when the London Ambassadors' Conference handed one half of Albania, which is now known as Kosovo, to the Serbs.

In 1914, the first year of World War I, only Serbia and Montenegro were independent states while Croatia, Slovenia, Bosnia and Herzegovina were part of the Austro-Hungarian Empire. During World War I, Serbia was invaded by the Central Powers: Austria-Hungary, Germany and Bulgaria. In exile, the representatives of the South Slavic peoples signed the Declaration of Corfu in 1917 which proposed the union of Serbia, Croatia and Slovenia. After the defeat of the Central Powers in 1918, Serbia joined with Montenegro, Macedonia, Slovenia, Bosnia, and Croatia to create the new nation of Yugoslavia. Yugoslavia comprised 13 linguistic groups including Serbo-Croats, Slovenes, Macedonians, Hungarians and Albanians. There were also seven different religious groups including Orthodox, Roman Catholic, Moslem, and Protestant. The Serb/Yugoslav army occupied Kosovo and defeated the Albanian resistance, committed atrocities, banned the teaching of the Albanian language, and encouraged the immigration of Serbians and Montenegrins to Kosovo.

From the time of its inception as a federation to the end of World War II, Yugoslavia was tumultuous. Croatia campaigned for independence and the bitter conflict between Serbia and Kosovo remained unresolved. There was an ongoing struggle between those who wanted a federation of six republics and those who wanted a centralized government.

In the late 1920s, the Serb Nicola Pasic became premier and enacted a centralized constitution, provoking the Croats to set up a separate parliament. King Aleksander dissolved parliament, proclaimed a dictatorship, abolished self-government, and outlawed communism. In 1931, Aleksander abolished his dictatorship and proposed a constitution that provided for limited democracy.

The Communist Party was part of the resistance movement to autocratic rule. The Party only had a few hundred members in the late 1930s due to the fact that Communism was outlawed in Yugoslavia and was subject to police repression. Josip Broz Tito, son of a Croatian-Slovenian peasant family, became secretary general of the party in 1937. Under Tito's leadership the Party expanded to 12,000 full party members and 30,000 members of the youth organization. His call for an uprising against Hitler after Germany attacked the Soviet Union in World War II and his belief in a pan-Yugoslavia won him wide appeal across the country. Tito called for a meeting of the Anti-Fascist Council for the National Liberation of Yugoslavia in 1943 which included various ethnic and political groups and established the basis for a postwar Federal Yugoslavia. In 1945, Tito became premier and the constituent assembly proclaimed a federal republic.

Confronted with six republics, each with their own aspirations, culture, and history, Tito faced a monumental challenge in holding Yugoslavia together. Tito was able to unite the country because he was a charismatic hero who immediately began the process of offering political equality to the six republics. He was the first leader to withdraw from Stalin's Communist bloc and Yugoslavia became a nonaligned nation through its independent foreign policy. Nikita Khrushchev visited Tito in 1955 and in the final communiqué of the meeting known as the Belgrade Declaration, the Soviet Union acknowledged the right of socialist countries to pursuit their own brands of socialism.

In the mid-1960s, liberal reformers used the assembly to implement their own agenda of reducing the role of the state in economic decisions, devaluing the currency, opening the door to market socialism, joining the General Agreement on Trade and Tariffs, and borrowing money from international banks. Yugoslavia borrowed money from the World Bank and International Monetary fund (IMF) to finance the expansion of the country's industrial base, its export production, and its output of domestic consumer goods. When Western economies sank into a recession, they were unable to buy enough of Yugoslavia's exports to provide Yugoslavia with the foreign reserves needed to repay its debt. Unable to meet its payments to Western banks, Yugoslavia fell further and further behind as the unpaid interest on the loans began to accumulate, increasing the debt even further. At this point, the IMF and World Bank demanded that Yugoslavia enter a restructuring program of wage freezes, currency devaluation, abolition of state subsidized prices, and massive cuts in social spending. Restructuring programs are intended to generate funds to repay the country's debt without regard for the resulting unemployment and poverty.

In the late 1960s, Yugoslavia underwent a period of strife. When the Warsaw Pact nations invaded Czechoslovakia in 1968, Tito condemned the invasion and relations between Yugoslavia and the Soviet Union became strained. At the same time, western Macedonia and ethnic Albanians in Kosovo staged violent demonstrations to demand equality and republic status for Kosovo. Political and cultural tensions between Serbia and Croatia strengthened nationalist sentiment in Croatia where university students demonstrated in 1971. Hundreds were arrested by the police and soldiers.

On May 4, 1980, Tito died in office. Tito was a master at preserving the federation of six republics despite their differences in history, language, religion, and culture but the power structure which succeeded him was not as successful.

Yugoslavia Comes Apart

One of the major problems plaguing Yugoslavia in the 1980s was an economic crisis which included rising unemployment, lower living standards, greater regional economic disparities, inflation, and an increasing national debt. Inflation had already begun to spiral out of control between 1975 and 1980 when it reached 50 percent. By 1987, it had reached 150 percent annually. The per capita foreign debt was the highest in all of Europe in 1988. In 1989, 60 percent of workers in Yugoslavia lived at or below the minimum income guaranteed by the state. To add to the crisis, economic disparities widened as Slovenia, Croatia, and Serbia became more developed than Kosovo, Macedonia and Montenegro despite federal programs to redistribute wealth.

In an attempt to pull itself out of this economic quagmire, the Yugoslavian government signed a new agreement with the IMF in which the IMF provided new foreign loans and rescheduled the debt on the condition that the government agreed to lower inflation by limiting bank credit and freezing wages.

Economic hardships and strikes contributed to the downfall of Prime Minister Branko Mikulic in 1988 and threatened the same fate for his successor Ante Markovic in 1989.

By 1991, conditions were ripe for the collapse of Yugoslavia. Ethnic conflicts not only pitted one republic against another but also pitted ethnic minorities against their own republics. International creditors had assumed control of Yugoslav monetary policy and the state-run banks were dismantled. The Serbian government refused to accept the austerity programs of the international banks and about 650,000 Serbian workers staged massive walkouts and protests.

As Yugoslavia edged toward the brink of brutal conflicts, the United States and the western powers actively promoted the breakup of Yugoslavia to serve their own interests. According to Noam Chomsky, in *The New Military Humanism: Lessons From Kosovo*:

> Although the resources of the Balkans are of no great interest, their strategic location is, not only with regard to Europe, West and East, but also the Middle East... As long as Serbia is not incorporated within the U.S.-dominated domains, it makes sense to punish it for failure to conform—very visibly, in a way that will serve as a warning to others that might be similarly inclined. The 1998 crisis in Kosovo offered an opportunity to do just that..."

As well, Evangelos Mahairas, in *The Breakup of Yugoslavia,* states that:

> Beginning in 1990 Germany and the United States sought and achieved the breakup of Yugoslavia...The United States was interested in the more recently established States (Bosnia, Serbia, the former Socialist Republic of Macedonia) which controlled the only route from east to west and north to south through the Balkan mountains. The Balkan area, along with Romania, Bulgaria, Turkey, and the Arab Nations, forms a European-Middle East Bloc, which the United States wants to control...for the complete exploitation of the great oil resources of the Caspian sea.

As Yugoslavia was reeling from its economic crisis and ethnic tensions, the United States and other European nations implemented a number of strategies to advance its breakup. The National Endowment for Democracy and the CIA supported conservative separatist groups in the republics with campaign money and advice. Under pressure from the Bush Administration, Congress passed the 1991 Foreign Operations Appropriations Act which authorized assistance only to the individual republics and not to the Yugoslavian government. Arms shipments and military advisors were dispatched to Slovenia and Croatia which were the first two republics to secede from the federation. Evangelos Mahairas, in *The Breakup of Yugoslavia,* notes that:

> The United States funded the states so as to dissolve the federation. The U.S. also supported parties and movements that would promote the process... In 1993, American officers undertook training of the Croatian army, which was now armed by the United States.

Slovenia and Croatia declared their independence in 1991. The withdrawal of Slovenia from Yugoslavia was relatively painless when only a brief armed conflict ensued, referred to as the "ten-day war." Croatia's attempt to attain independence was a bloody struggle given the large Serbian population living there and the outside support offered to the Croatian forces. In a referendum on May 19, 1991, Croats voted overwhelmingly for independence. The Serbs living in Croatia held their own referendum on May 14, 1991, and chose to remain part of the FRY if Croatia chose to become independent. After the Croatian referendum, the Croats refused to accept the results of the Serbian referendum. War ensued.

Ironically, NATO had been partly responsible for atrocities against the Serbs in Croatia but would later blame the Serbs for atrocities against Albanians in Kosovo. According to Michael Parenti, in *To Kill a Nation*:

> In early August 1995, Croatian forces launched the bloodiest offensive of the war, breaking the Serbian defences in Krajina, killing thousands of Serb citizens, and sending 225,000 fleeing for their lives...US-NATO planes destroyed Serbian radar and anti-aircraft defenses, and jammed Serbian military communications, leaving the skies open for the Western trained and funded Croatian air force to bomb Serbian defenses and strafe refugee columns. Trapped Serbian civilians, pouring into Bosnia, were massacred by Croatian and Muslim artillery.

The atrocities against the Serbs in Croatia were at least as horrifying as anything that occurred in Kosovo later. In *Crimes Without Punishment*, Vojin Dabic and Ksenija Lukic report that:

> During the inter-ethnic war in the republic of Croatia 1991-1996 Croatian armed forces liquidated more than ten thousand Serbs...However, instead of talks scheduled for that day [between Serbs and Croatians] they [Serbs] received bullets, because the Croatian policemen, as soon as they left their vehicles, started to shoot at houses in the centre of the village...The aim is clear—to intimidate local Serb populations for the purpose of ethnic cleansing.

Other atrocities perpetrated against the Serbs include:

- November 1991—27 Serbian villages in Croatia were given 48-hour evacuation notices. Seventeen were burnt to the ground.

- Bosnian Serb women in Novigrad claimed that they were repeatedly gang-raped by local Croatian militia.

- Croatian armed forces took captive a number of Serbs some of whom were wounded. Their bodies were never found and witnesses testified that the Croats burned the bodies of executed POWs or threw them in the Danube.

Muslims and Serbs Commit Atrocities against Each Other in Bosnia

In March 1992, Bosnians voted to secede from Yugoslavia in a plebiscite. The vote was misleading due to the fact that the population of Bosnia consisted of 41 percent Muslim, 32 percent Serbian, and 17 percent Croatian. The European powers called for the vote despite the requirement that all three constituent peoples consented. The Serbs did not consent to the plebiscite for fear that the larger Muslim population would persecute them in an independent Bosnia.

Immediately after Bosnia had proclaimed its independence, the Western powers recognized Bosnia as a sovereign state despite the unresolved ethnic problems which would inevitably degenerate into war. Based on historical experience, the Serbs feared that they would be reduced to second-class citizens in an independent Bosnia. The Serbs in Bosnia and Herzegovina claimed the same right of self-determination in Bosnia as the Bosnians had in Yugoslavia. According to Centre for Peace in the Balkans:

> "What the international community—the Europeans, the Americans, the UN—did, made it sure there was going to be a conflict," states Lord Peter Carrington, the EC [European Union] mediator, who along with UN envoy Cyrus Vance warned against diplomatic recognition of separatist states such as Croatia and Bosnia, before a political settlement could be achieved. "US intelligence agencies were unanimous in saying that if we recognize Bosnia it will blow up," says former State Department official George Kenney.

Predictably, the Bosnian Serbs rose up in rebellion, not to conquer new territory as reported in the Western media but to hold on to territory which already belonged to them. The (now renamed) Federal Republic of Yugoslavia (FRY) supported the Bosnian Serbs with arms and Croatia sent its armed forces into Bosnia-Herzegovina to support the Muslims, escalating what was originally a rebellion to an all-out war. United States and NATO military intervention, with arms and troops on behalf of the Muslims in

Bosnia, was brutal. NATO began air strikes on Bosnian Serb military units in 1994 and in 1995 engaged in carpet-bombing of all Serbian territory in Bosnia. The *New York Times* (December 13, 1995, A16) reported that:

> President Clinton sent a letter tonight to Republican leaders that appears to give them the written assurances they sought that the United States would lead an effort to arm and train the Bosnian Muslims...His letter also said that training the Bosnian Government's forces could begin immediately.

As well, The *Los Angeles Times* (March 1, 1994, pg 1) reported that:

> Although the first reaction of the targeted Bosnian Serb forces was to escalate the bombardment of the northern city of Tuzia, there were signs that Serbian forces may recoil from the punishment rather than retaliate and risk further Western intervention.

One of the most publicized battles in the war was the Serbian siege of Sarajevo, the capital of Bosnia, where, according to western leaders and the media, the great Serbian atrocities against the Muslims reached genocidal proportions. At the outset, Bosnian Serb forces had offered safe passage to all civilians in order to treat Sarajevo as an exclusively military target. Moslem leaders in Sarajevo refused to allow Moslem citizens to leave. Michael Parenti, in *To Kill a Nation,* points out that:

> ...Muslim troops prevented anyone leaving the Muslim-controlled part of Sarajevo, in effect creating a siege within a siege. "This fact does not diminish the guilt of the Serbs, but it undermines the alleged innocence of Muslim authorities regarding the suffering and dying of civilians."

Serbian forces did commit atrocities in Sarajevo but Bosnian Muslims committed atrocities as well. Frequently, Western condemnation of Bosnian Serbs for atrocities against the Muslims in Sarajevo was unwarranted. For example, the three infamous marketplace massacres in Sarajevo in 1992, 1994, and 1995 were blamed on the Serbs when in fact the evidence is either problematic or clearly demonstrates Muslim responsibility. According to Michael Parenti, in *To Kill a Nation*:

> ...the report leaked on French TV, Western intelligence knew that it was Muslim operatives who had bombed civilians in the 1994 incident in order to induce NATO involvement. General Rose (a British General) came to a similar conclusion after the first UN examination of the site. David Owen, who worked with Cyrus Vance, admitted in his memoirs that the NATO powers knew all along that Muslim forces repeatedly hit neutral targets in order to stop relief flights and refocus world attention on Sarajevo. While such fire was usually attributed to the Serbs, "no seasoned observer in Sarajevo doubts for a moment

the Muslim forces have found it in their interest to shell friendly targets."
(Michael Rose)

Steven W. Sowards, in *The Balkans in the Age of Nationalism,* reports that:

> In February 1994, one of the most prominent attacks on civilians during
> the war enraged Western observers, when an explosion killed 68 people in
> Sarajevo's marketplace. Early reports blamed a Serbian mortar attack, and the
> US, the European Union and NATO demanded that the Serbs remove artillery
> from around Sarajevo, or face retaliatory air strikes. Serbian and Russian
> observers, however described the explosion as a Bosnian provocation. Official
> UN investigators were unable to prove either allegation.

According to UN observers, the Muslims frequently began the daily
exchange of fire with artillery barrages aimed at Serb neighborhoods
to incite a response which could then be used for propaganda purposes.
Michael Rose, former UN Commander of the UN protection force in Bosnia,
explained, in *Fighting for Peace,* that:

> More serious were reports we started to receive from the French in the
> city [Sarajevo] that the Bosnian forces were sometimes firing on their own
> citizens…In mid-March, the Bosnian army shelled the Serb town of Ilijas on
> the outskirts of Sarajevo. Ilijas was well within the 20-kilometre exclusion
> zone [agreement between Bosnian and Serbs to establish a 20-kilometre
> exclusion zone around Sarajevo]…and once again Bosnians were in breach
> of the NATO ultimatum [to punish either side if they violate the exclusion
> zone]…By then they [Serbs] were using their own artillery and mortars to fire
> at the Bosnian mortars one of which was established in the grounds of Kosovo
> [Sarajevo] hospital…with the intention of attracting Serb fire, in the hope that
> the resulting carnage would further tilt international support in their favour.

One of the major propaganda coups of the war was a set of photos
which ostensibly corroborated Western claims that Serb forces in Bosnia
were forcing Muslims into concentration camps. Photographers used a small
shed enclosed by a barbed-wire fence in Trnopolje refugee camp to fabricate
one of the most damning images of the war. Journalists and photographers
stood inside the barbed-wire enclosure shooting pictures of Muslim men
who stood outside the fence, thus creating the impression that these Muslims
were behind the barbed-wired fence of a concentration camp. One photo in
particular of an emaciated man, Fikret Alic, which evoked images of Nazi
death camps, appeared on the cover of *Time* magazine. Slobodan Konjevic, a
Serb suffering from tuberculosis who was arrested for looting appeared on the
cover of *Newsweek* as another emaciated prisoner of a concentration camp.

Mention of Bosnia now evokes the horror of genocide perpetrated against Bosnian Croats and Muslims by Bosnian Serbs. Genocide in Bosnia was part of the justification for the bombing of Serbia a few years later and for charging Serbian leaders with genocide in Bosnia. There was no justification for the charges because there was no genocide. Western leaders and media invented the genocide. To strengthen the myth, Bosnia hired Ruder Finn, an American public relations firm which boasted that they had successfully turned world opinion against the Serbs. Marjaleena Repo, in *Demonizing the Serbs* (*CounterPunch*, 1999), states that:

> The PR firm was piling hoax upon hoax…There are…countless stories maligning the Serbs to further the ends of military intervention. These stories and photos of "genocide" and "ethnic cleansing" (à la Hitler) in a civil war, in which Serbs are guilty as sin and others are their innocent victims, are repeated ad nauseam by western reporters without the slightest evidence, and have provided the ground for the public's (hopefully only temporary) acceptance of the illegal and brutal war against the sovereign nation of Yugoslavia.

This was not the first time a U.S. administration had hired a public relations firm to lie on their behalf, in effect privatizing government lies.

The heavy US-led NATO bombing of Serbian targets in Bosnia forced the Serbs to capitulate and to seek an end to the war. The bombing was relentless and was not restricted to military targets. Sixty aircraft flew more than 1000 sorties in the first 50 hours and bombed the towns of Lukavica and Tuzia and Serbian suburbs in Sarajevo. Maurice Williams, in *Bombing Campaign in Bosnia Intensifies* (*The Militant*, September 25, 1995), reported that:

> Washington has stepped up its imperialist assault in Bosnia on positions held by Serbians loyal to Belgrade. After two weeks of intense NATO bombing, dozens of warplanes, mainly from the United States, have flown 3,200 sorties pounding military targets but also inflicting increased civilian casualties.

In November 1995, the Western powers initiated the negotiation of a peace agreement known as the Dayton Accords which were intended to create independent republics for the Bosnian Serbs and the Bosnian Croats. The Bosnian government obstructed the process. Michael Parenti, in *To Kill a Nation,* noted that:

> After a fortnight in Dayton, [Richard] Holbrooke reported to Undersecretary of State Warren Christopher that the most disturbing problem he faced was the "immense difficulty of engaging the Bosnian government in a serious negotiation…Cleary Dayton would never have produced any

agreement at all without the unflagging help of the one participant who really seemed anxious for peace: Slobodan Milosevic..."

In the end, Bosnia-Herzegovina was divided into two new republics: the Muslim-Croat Federation of Bosnia and the Bosnian Serb Republic of Srpska. Although the Dayton Accords were set up to restore autonomy in the new Bosnian republics, they in fact reduced them to colonies of Europe and the United States.

Not only were republics withdrawing from Yugoslavia and declaring their independence, but the province of Kosovo waged a fierce battle for its independence. The conflict was rooted in the fact that Kosovo was inhabited mostly by ethnic Albanians and partly by Serbs and the Serbs were opposed to separation from the republic of Serbia within the Yugoslavian federation.

To understand the clash between ethnic Albanians and Serbs in Kosovo, it is essential to know the historical context in which the Albanians in Kosovo sought more and more independence from the FRY. This history will also illuminate the magnitude of Clinton's lies about the nature of the atrocities in Kosovo.

During World War II, the Albanian fascist militia had expelled 70,000 Serbs from Kosovo and brought in roughly the same number of Albanians from Albania. Albanian nationalist sentiment in Kosovo was strong and to placate the ethnic Albanians, Yugoslav leader Tito declared Kosovo an autonomous region, though still a province of Serbia. This was put into effect by a new constitution which, in 1974, granted additional powers to the provinces. Only Tito's authority held in check further nationalist efforts to become independent.

The ongoing conflict between Albanians and Serbs in Kosovo ultimately provided the necessary justification for the bombing of Serbia under the spurious pretext of humanitarian intervention.

After Tito's death, there was a surge not only of ethnic Albanian nationalist sentiment but also of Serbian nationalist sentiment in Kosovo. Serbs living in Kosovo frequently complained about harassment and discrimination by Albanians in Kosovo. David Binder, in a *New York Times* article (November 1, 1987), reported that:

> Ethnic Albanians in the [provincial] government have manipulated public funds and regulations to take over land belonging to Serbs...Slavic Orthodox churches have been attacked, and flags have been torn down. Wells have been poisoned and crops burned. Slavic boys have been knifed, and some young ethnic

Albanians have been told by their elders to rape Serbian girls…As the Slavs flee the protracted violence, Kosovo is becoming what ethnic Albanian nationalists have been demanding for years…an 'ethnically pure' Albanian region.

Human Rights Watch found that:

> Throughout the late 1970s and 1980s, Kosovo Serbs complained of harassment and discrimination by the ethnic Albanian population and leadership, with the intention, Serbs claim, of driving them from the province. According to a report submitted to the influential Serbian Academy of Sciences and Art in 1988, more than 20,000 ethnic Serbs moved out of Kosovo in the years 1981-1987.

In 1981, ethnic Albanians, led by students, protested in the streets to demand higher wages, greater freedom of expression, the release of political prisoners, and republic status for Kosovo. The demonstrations were forcibly dispersed by the Yugoslav army and federal police with a number of deaths and arrests.

Through the 1980s there were demonstrations by both the ethnic Albanians and the Serbs living in Kosovo. Serbians living in Kosovo continued to complain about discrimination and harassment and the Albanians protested about the growing restrictions imposed on them by the government in Belgrade.

In 1989, Slobodan Milosevic became president of Serbia and immediately implemented a new constitution restoring authority to Belgrade, reversing the powers granted to Kosovo in the 1974 constitution. When Kosovar Albanians ardently protested against the change on March 28, 1989, police opened fire on the crowd killing at least 24 persons.

In July 1989, further restrictions were imposed on the Albanians when the Serbian parliament passed the Law on the Restriction of Property Transactions which prohibited Albanians from buying real estate without the approval of a state commission run by the Serbian Ministry of Finance.

Ethnic Albanian members of the neutered Kosovo assembly declared Kosovo's independence on July 2, 1990. Serbia then dissolved the Kosovo assembly provoking more strikes and protests by ethnic Albanians. Members of the former assembly met secretly, adopted a new constitution for the Republic of Kosovo, and elected a clandestine government. Three weeks later, the Serb assembly formally revoked the autonomous status of Kosovo. In 1992, Ibrahim Rugova was elected president of the new clandestine government.

Rugova was accorded the unconditional support of the United States and Europe because he was a moderate. The West was worried that a war in Kosovo might escalate and engulf the entire region in war. Western countries offered financial and political support to the brutal dictator of Albania, Sali Berisha, because he supported Rugova.

As the conflict became more violent and Albanian demands for the independence of Kosovo became more forceful, the United States was preparing to enter the fray on the side of the Albanians as part of their grand plan to breakup the FRY.

The first organized violence occurred in 1996 against Serbian civilians and police, followed by an attack against Serbian refugee camps with grenades. There was an exchange of violent attacks in 1996 including the assassination of four Serbians on April 22. The responsibility for the deaths was claimed by a previously unknown organization known as the Kosovo Liberation Army (KLA). The KLA's identity was announced in a letter to the press claiming credit for the 1996 massacre.

The apparent lack of progress of the peaceful protest by Albanians in Kosovo had driven more radical ethnic Albanians to form an organization in 1991, the KLA, which would employ violent tactics to achieve independence for Kosovo. The KLA grew to 40,000 members by the mid-1990s and directed a terrorist campaign not only against Serbian targets but also against moderate Albanians. Their targets included police stations, police vehicles, local headquarters of the Socialist party, Serbian villagers, farmers, and officials.

Serbian forces responded more harshly as the acts of terrorism perpetrated by the KLA escalated. Noam Chomsky, in *The New Military Humanism,* explains that:

> By February 1998, guerilla operations reached much greater scale, as the KLA "not only fought Serbian Army and Interior Ministry police but also gunned down civilians, killing Serbian mail carriers and others associated with Belgrade." These events elicited a much harsher Serbian military and police response, with brutal retaliation against civilians regarded as supporters of the KLA.

According to Human Rights Watch:

> The KLA continued its attacks against Serbian policemen and civilians in early 1997, especially in the rural areas, although the group's size, structure, and leadership remained a mystery...The international community condemned the rising state violence in Kosovo while stressing its respect for the territorial

integrity of Yugoslavia. At the same time, most west European governments as well as the US condemned as "terrorist actions" the KLA attacks.

Michael Parenti, in *To Kill a Nation,* reported that:

> The KLA directed its terror campaign against a variety of Serbian targets…in an effort to provoke reprisals, radicalize other Kosovo Albanians, and raise the level of the conflict.

The KLA also targeted Albanians who opposed the violent secessionist movement, or were members of the Socialist Party of Serbia.

Two major factors contributed to the growing strength of the KLA: the drug trade, and support from the U.S. and other NATO countries. The Balkans narcotic trade became a major source of funding for the KLA. According to Michel Chossudovsky, in *Kosovo "Freedom Fighters" Financed by Organized Crime*:

> The multibillion-dollar Balkans narcotics trade has played a crucial role in "financing the conflict" in Kosovo in accordance with Western economic, strategic, and military objectives. Amply documented by European police files and acknowledged by numerous studies, the links of the Kosovo Liberation Army (KLA) to criminal syndicates in Albania, Turkey, and the European Union have been known to Western governments and intelligence agencies since the mid-1990s.

Western governments provided support to the KLA including arms as reported by Michel Chossudovsky, in *Kosovo "Freedom Fighters" Financed by Organized Crime*:

> According to intelligence analyst John Whitley, covert support to the Kosovo rebel army was established as a joint endeavour between the CIA and Germany's Bundes Nachrichten Dienst (BND)…The task to create and finance the KLA was initially given to Germany: "They used German uniforms, East German weapons and were financed, in part, with drug money." According to Whitely, the CIA was, subsequently instrumental in training and equipping the KLA in Albania.

In February 1998, President Clinton sent Robert Gelbard a special envoy to investigate the mounting crisis in Kosovo. During a press conference he declared that:

> The UCK [KLA] is a terrorist group by its actions. I used to be responsible for counter-terrorism policy in the American government. I know them when I see them.

When Gelbard visited Belgrade, he applauded Yugoslavia's cooperation in negotiating the Dayton Accords and affirmed that the United States was "particularly encouraged by the support that we received from President Milosevic." He also said:

> The great majority of this violence we attribute to the police, but we are tremendously disturbed and also condemn very strongly the unacceptable violence done by terrorist groups in Kosovo and particularly the UCK—the Kosovo Liberation Army. This is without any question a terrorist group.

When the U.S. decided to support the KLA, it was done with the complete understanding that they were a terrorist group.

In 1998, the Western perspective on the conflict began to shift from regarding the KLA as a terrorist organization to condemning the actions of Serbian forces in Kosovo as terrorism. The U.S. and other Western Powers had rejected supporting the less extreme Kosovo Democratic League in favour of the KLA, a group they had previously condemned as terrorists. Western Powers wanted to exacerbate the violence to provide the pretext for accusing Serbia of terrorism. For example, in February and March 1998, in response to two KLA ambushes of the police, Serbian forces attacked two villages killing 83 people in the Drenica Valley. The West criticized Serbia for the excessive use of force. On March 31, the Security Council passed Resolution 1160 which criticized both sides for the use of violence, called for a negotiated settlement, and imposed an arms embargo on Yugoslavia.

In fact, the United States was equipping the KLA with very sophisticated weapons and according to Michael Parenti, in *To Kill a Nation*:

> In 2000, CIA intelligence agents admitted to the London *Sunday Times* to having been training, equipping, and supporting KLA fighters as early as 1998.

The Serbian forces continued to scour the countryside for KLA strongholds in order to root them out. About two thousand lives were lost in these conflicts and many of the Kosovar casualties were civilians as the Serbian forces had a difficult time distinguishing between citizens and KLA supporters.

On March 9, 1998, the Contact Group, consisting of the U.S., Germany, France, Italy, and the U.K., met in London and established conditions which the FRY had to meet or otherwise face a number of punitive measures such as a freeze on its foreign-held assets, an investment ban, and sanctions. The conditions included a withdrawal of the special police from Kosovo, ceasing action against the civilian population, allowing access for humanitarian organizations, and beginning a process of dialogue with Kosovo.

The Contact Group ignored the actions of the KLA and focused exclusively on the actions of Serbian police and military. They also ignored the fact that the U.S. and other countries were arming the KLA and that the KLA were brutally attacking Serbians to incite a response which would then be used to confirm their role as victims. Noam Chomsky, in *The New Military Humanism,* reported that:

> By October [1998], as U.S. envoy Richard Holbrooke reached an agreement with Milosevic (formal, and not observed), U.S. intelligence reported "that the Kosovo rebels intended to draw NATO into its fight for independence by provoking Serbian forces into further atrocities." A massacre in Racak on January 15, 1999, with some 45 civilians killed, received extensive coverage and is held to have been the decisive event that impelled Washington and its allies, horrified by the atrocity, to initiate preparations for war.

The conflict in Kosovo was a civil war with outside powers supporting one of the combatants (KLA) and with international attention focused only on the atrocities of one side despite understanding that they were being committed by both sides. Reported KLA atrocities include:

- Human rights groups estimate that 138 Serbs were taken by the KLA.

- On July 19, 1998, the KLA attacked the city of Orahovac and an estimated 85 Serbs were taken into custody although 35 were released later.

- In May 1998, most Serbs in Leocina abandoned their homes after threats from local Albanians.

- Human Rights Watch reported that Serbs were forced to leave the villages of Jelovac, Kijevo, Leocina, Gorni Ratis, Maznik, Dasinovac, Velikii, Mlecane, Dubrava, and Boksic.

- The KLA executed at least 34 people near Glodjane. (Human Rights Watch)

Near the end of 1998, stories about mass expulsions and ethnic cleansing in Kosovo began to surface. These reports were greatly exaggerated but were an important part of the propaganda campaign waged by the West. According to Michael Parenti, in *To Kill A Nation*:

> ...Rollie Keith, who serves as one of 1,380 monitors for an OSCE

(Organization for Security and Cooperation in Europe) Kosovo verification mission [KVM], reports that there were no international refugees during the last five months of peace (November 1998 to March 1999), and the internally displaced persons driven into the hills or other villages by the fighting numbered only a few thousand in the weeks before the bombing commenced. According to Keith, KVM monitors observed that "the ceasefire situation was deteriorating with an increased incidence of Kosovo Liberation Army provocative attacks on the Yugoslavian security forces.

The Racak massacre was also part of the propaganda campaign. The truth about the Racak massacre was well hidden at the time. William Walker, a U.S. diplomat, escorted a group of journalists to the site of the massacre where allegedly 45 civilians were executed by Yugoslav police the previous day. The story made headlines around the world but there was no mention of the Associated Press TV crew who filmed the battle on the previous day. Their footage revealed that the people who were killed by the Serbian police were KLA fighters whose weapons were seized by the police, contrary to Walker's assertions and the assertions of the media that these were civilian deaths. After the departure of the police, the villagers who had fled their village during the battle returned. *Le Figaro* and *Le Monde* reported that the television crew had seen no evidence of a massacre. Independent autopsy reports by Finnish forensic scientists concluded that the shots had been fired from a distance not at close range as Walker had claimed suggesting a battle not an execution. As well, 37 of the corpses had gunpowder on their hands indicating that they had fired guns themselves recently and were KLA combatants killed in action.

The Racak massacre resulted in consultations by Western governments on how to back up diplomacy with force. On one level, these people died horrible deaths, a tragedy whether they were combatants or civilians. Yet the lie that these were civilians, as with so many lies in conflicts we have examined, made a crucial difference in the course of the war. NATO threatened military action if attacks on civilians persisted. Secretary of State Madeleine Albright warned that further atrocities against the civilians of Kosovo would call for a harsh response.

On February 6, 1999, the Kosovar Albanians and Serbs were summoned to a set of meetings with U.S. officials, including Madeleine Albright, in Rambouillet France to negotiate a settlement. Yugoslavia had already drafted a set of proposals which included:

- An agreement to stop hostilities in Kosovo and to pursue a peaceful solution through dialogue;

- Guaranteed human rights for all citizens;

- The facilitated return of all displaced citizens to their homes;

- The widest possible media freedom;

- A legislative assembly elected by proportional representation. (Michael Parenti, *To Kill A Nation*)

The U.S. negotiators completely ignored the Yugoslavian proposals and introduced a set of demands designed to provoke rather than prevent war. Known as the Rambouillet Peace Agreement, it included the following demands:

- Complete autonomy for Kosovo;

- Withdrawal of Yugoslav troops from Kosovo;

- Occupation by NATO forces;

- Kosovo would have representatives in the Serbian parliament but Serbians would be excluded from any input in the Kosovo assembly;

- The Kosovo constitution would override the Serbian constitution;

- Serbia would be required to give aid to Kosovo and an equitable share of Serbian revenues;

- There would be considerable aid to Kosovo but none to the 650,000 Serbian refugees.

- NATO would appoint a Civilian Implementation Mission (CIM) which could issue binding directives to Kosovo and Serbia;

- NATO would maintain sanctions against Yugoslavia.

Yugoslavia was willing to negotiate with the United States and accepted some of the demands of the Rambouillet Treaty while rejecting others. The Yugoslavs were prepared to grant Kosovo almost complete independence including control over religion, education, health care systems and local government but wanted to retain control over economic and foreign policy. As well, they wanted to restrict NATO's role in Kosovo to observation and advice. Predictably, Yugoslavia rejected a military occupation of Kosovo but the U.S. summarily rejected all FRY proposals. Therefore, the negotiations were about whether Yugoslavia would accept all of the U.S. demands or not and face NATO bombing of Serbia.

Accepting such demands would be problematic for any sovereign state. The whole process raises the question of whether the U.S. was really hoping for a settlement or seeking a pretext for bombing Serbia. First, they completely rejected all of Yugoslavia's proposals and imposed their own unreasonable draft that Yugoslavia had to accept in its entirety under the threat of attack. If there were any doubts about U.S. motives they were quickly dispelled when the United States introduced Appendix B to the draft of the treaty. Appendix B stipulates that:

> NATO personnel shall enjoy, together with their vehicles, aircraft, and equipment, free and unrestricted passage and unimpeded access throughout the FRY including associated airspace and territorial waters.
>
> The Parties recognize the need for expeditious departure and entry procedures for NATO personnel. Such personnel shall be exempt from passport and visa regulations and the registration requirements applicable to aliens.
>
> NATO shall be immune from all legal process, whether civil, administrative, or criminal.

No sovereign state would accept these conditions. The Rambouillet draft required Yugoslavia to submit to military occupation and accept the status of a colony. Noam Chomsky, in *The New Military Humanism,* argues that:

> The remainder [of Appendix B] spells out the conditions that permit NATO forces and those they employ to have free access to the territory of the FRY, without obligation or concern for the laws of the country or the jurisdiction of its authorities, who are, however, required to follow NATO orders "on a priority basis and with all appropriate means."…It has been speculated that the wording was designed so as to guarantee rejection. Perhaps so. It is hard to imagine that any country would consider such terms in the form of unconditional surrender.

Lieutenant General Satish Nambiar (Ret.), Force Commander and Head of Mission of the United Nations Forces deployed in the former Yugoslavia, concluded that:

> Ultimatums were issued to Yugoslavia that unless the terms of an agreement drawn up at Rambouillet were signed, NATO would undertake bombing. Ultimatums do not constitute diplomacy. They are acts of war. (The United Service Institution of India (USI), New Delhi, April 6, 1999)

Michael Parenti, in *To Kill A Nation,* points out that:

> The Rambouillet "agreement" was not an agreement at all, not a negotiated settlement but an ultimatum for unconditional surrender, a diktat that spelled death for Yugoslavia and could not be accepted by Belgrade. As John Pilger wrote, "Anyone scrutinizing the Rambouillet document is left with little doubt that the excuses given for the subsequent bombing were fabricated. The peace negotiations were stage managed and the Serbs were told: surrender and be occupied, or don't surrender and be destroyed." ...Secretary of State Madeleine Albright told this [writer] that...a senior State Department official had bragged that the United States 'deliberately set the bar higher than the Serbs could accept.'

As expected, Belgrade refused to sign the ultimatum disguised as the Rambouillet Agreement. President Clinton reinforced the myth that the FRY would not sign a peace agreement when he announced that:

> We and our NATO allies have taken this action after extensive and repeated efforts to obtain a peaceful solution to the crisis in Kosovo. (CNN, *Focus on Kosovo*, March 24, 1999)

The next day, Clinton reported that:

> Our purpose here is to prevent a humanitarian catastrophe or a wider war. Our objective is to make it clear that Serbia must choose peace or we will limit its ability to make war. (CNN, *Focus on Kosovo*, March 25, 1999)

The propaganda campaign was now complete. The Serbs had been accused of holding prisoners in concentration camps, wantonly killing civilians included the widely publicized Racak massacre, and refusing to sign a peace agreement. The ultimatum was delivered on March 24 and took effect on June 10, 1999, when NATO started bombing Serbia to rescue the ethnic Albanians from Serb atrocities.

U.S. leaders repeatedly trumpeted their noble objective to wage a humanitarian war to prevent ethnic cleansing of the Albanians in Kosovo. They painted themselves as the noble saviors of a people greatly endangered by the evil Milosevic who refused to sign a peace agreement and would stop at nothing to wipe out the ethnic Albanians. President Clinton said:

> We cannot respond to such tragedies everywhere, but when ethnic conflict turns into ethnic cleansing where we can make a difference, we must

try, and that is clearly the case in Kosovo. (Noam Chomsky, *The New Military Humanism*)

President Clinton also engaged in a little bit of hyperbole when he stated that:

> When I ordered our armed forces into combat we had three clear goals: to enable the Kosovar people, the victims of some of the most vicious atrocities in Europe since the second World War, to return to their homes with safety and self-government. (Martha Raddatz, PBS Online, Washington Week)

Madeleine Albright, Secretary of State, warned that:

> ...this kind of thing cannot stand, that you cannot in 1999 have this kind of barbaric ethnic cleansing. It is ultimately better that democracies stand up against this kind of evil. (Noam Chomsky, *The New Military Humanism*)

Yugoslavia lacked the sophisticated weapons needed to defend itself from U.S.-led NATO bombing. The only recourse for the Serbians was to hope that American bombs did not land on their homes or villages. American and NATO officials claimed that bombing was restricted to military targets. The stated intent of the NATO bombing campaign was to avoid civilian targets to whatever extent possible. William Cohen, Secretary of Defense, reassured Americans that:

> We are attacking the military infrastructure that President (Slobodan) Milosevic and his forces are using to repress and kill innocent people. (CNN, *Focus on Kosovo*, March 25, 1999)

These claims must be seen as outrageous lies in light of the fact that civilian targets were deliberately bombed including schools, a maternity hospital, and villages all with no possible military significance.

Madeleine Albright stated that "NATO's goal is not to hurt innocent people" (CNN, March 24). The real question is not whether a considerable number of non-military targets were struck but whether NATO deliberately bombed non-military targets. One test is to examine some of the targets and ask whether these targets could have been hit accidentally. A number of villages and towns were struck that completely lacked anything resembling military targets. Here are twelve examples of many:

- Aleksinac—A small mining community without a military presence in the area was struck by five NATO missiles killing 16 people and destroying 400 homes.

- Djakovica—Seventy civilians died and 20 were injured in a refugee camp near Djakovica which housed 500 people. There were 53 bomb craters at the site

- Istok—Two NATO missiles struck a prison in Istok killing one person and seriously injuring another. The attack was repeated killing nine people and injuring ten. NATO bombed the prison several more times, killing a total of 100 people.

- Korisa—Six NATO missiles struck this rural village in Kosovo where 87 Kosovo Albanians died. Journalists who visited the site refuted NATO's claim that there was a Serb military presence there.

- Kraljevo—Four missiles from NATO bombers injured seven people. NATO repeatedly bombed this town destroying the school and a hospital clinic, injuring 20 civilians.

- Kursumlija—A cluster bomb hit a housing complex killing one and wounding two. In two other NATO attacks, 13 citizens were killed and 20 were injured. In one final attack, six citizens were killed and 233 were injured.

- Luzane—NATO planes attacked a bridge hitting a bus with 70 civilian passengers. Half of the bus lay burning on the bridge while the other half plunged into the valley. Another attack occurred 25 minutes later damaging an ambulance and injuring a doctor.

- Sabac—A school and apartment complex in this small town were hit by five cluster bombs killing one person and wounding four.

- Savine—A civilian bus on the Djakovica-Podgorica road was bombed killing at least 20 people and injuring 43.

- Sremska Mitrovica—Four cluster bombs destroyed 1,200 homes killing five people and injuring more than a dozen.

- Surdulica—Five NATO bombs destroyed a sanitarium and retirement home complex killing 20 patients.

- Vajevo—This manufacturing centre was bombed 31 times

killing a dozen people. The City Hospital, an agricultural secondary school, a railway station, and several apartment buildings were destroyed. (*CounterPunch*, *Who NATO Killed*, 1999)

There is overwhelming evidence that NATO planners deliberately targeted non-military targets and civilians. Repeatedly bombing small villages of no possible military value, a maternity hospital, bridges of no military value and industrial sites is clear evidence that the targeting was deliberate. A Spanish pilot who participated in bombing missions confirmed:

> That NATO attacks upon civilian targets were not usually the result of war "errors" was confirmed by Captain de la Hoz, who participated in bombing missions, flying an F-18. Several times his Spanish colonel lodged protests with NATO chiefs regarding their selection of nonmilitary targets, only to be rudely rebuffed. "Once there was a coded order from the North American military that we should drop antipersonnel bombs over the localities of Pristina and Nis," Captain de la Hoz commented. "The colonel refused it altogether and, a couple of days later, [his] transfer order came…All the missions that we flew, all and each one, were planned by US high military authorities…They are destroying the country, bombing it with novel weapons, toxic nerve gas, surface mines dropped with parachutes, bombs containing uranium, black napalm, sterilization chemicals, spraying to poison the crops…" (Michael Parenti, *To Kill A Nation*)

Some atrocities perpetrated by NATO forces transcend conventional war crimes. Rescue workers such as ambulance drivers and paramedics reported that after the initial bombing while they were engaged in their rescue mission, the NATO planes would return and bomb the rescue workers and ambulances. I have witnessed interviews with rescue workers who had suffered a loss of limbs from the bombing and who described with incredulity the reappearance of NATO bombers.

The NATO bombing was responsible for an estimated $100 billion of damage including dozens of bridges, railways and railway stations, major roads, airports, hospitals and health care centres, television transmitters, medieval monasteries and religious shrines, cultural-historical monuments and museums, hundreds of schools, facilities for students and children, thousands of dwellings and civilian industrial and agricultural facilities. An estimated 1,000 civilian men, women and children were killed and 4,400 more injured as a direct result of the NATO bombing (A formal complaint filed with the International Tribunal for the former Yugoslavia against

NATO leaders by a group of international lawyers led by Michael Mandel, Osgoode Hall Law School, March 24, 1999)

The Serbian people and non-military facilities were bombed in the hope that the Serbian population would rebel against Milosevic. According to Lt. Gen. Satish Nambiar, "NATO's massive bombing intended to terrorize Serbia into submission..." As well, Michael Mandel, in the complaint against NATO leaders, concludes that "...there is ample evidence in the public statements of NATO leaders that these attacks on civilian targets are part of a deliberate attempt to terrorize the population to turn it against their leadership." George Kenney, a former State Department official, claimed that "Dropping cluster bombs on highly populated areas doesn't result in accidental fatalities. It is purposeful terror bombing."

The entire NATO rationale for the bombing of Serbia was to end a humanitarian crisis in Kosovo caused by Serbian atrocities against ethnic Albanians. There were fears of mass killings, a mass exodus of Albanians from Kosovo, and other atrocities such as rape. Of the three atrocities, only the exodus of Albanians proved to be true on a large scale. The misconception about the mass exodus was that cause and effect have been deliberately reversed. The argument was that the mass exodus was caused by the Serbs acting without provocation to force the Albanians out of Kosovo. NATO not only bombed Serbia but Serbian forces in Kosovo. The truth was that the NATO bombing in Kosovo frightened people into seeking refuge. Once the bombing of Serbia commenced on March 24, 1999, there was an escalation in Serbian violence in Kosovo that was predicted by many people in authority including U.S.-NATO Commanding General Wesley Clark who announced that following the NATO bombing, the intensification of Serbian violence was "entirely predictable." (*Sunday Times*, London, March 28, 1999) Carnes Lord of the Fletcher School of Law and Diplomacy, formerly a Bush administration National Security advisor claimed that:

> ...enemies often react when shot at...[and] though Western officials continue to deny it, there can be little doubt that the bombing campaign has provided both motive and opportunity for a wider and more savage Serbian operation than was first envisioned. (Noam Chomsky, *The New Military Humanism*)

Lieutenant-General Satish Nambiar stated that:

> I do not believe the Belgrade government had prior intention of driving out all Albanians from Kosovo. It may have decided to implement [mass

deportation] only if NATO bombed, or those expulsions could be spontaneous acts of revenge and retaliation by Serb forces in the field because of the bombing. (Michael Parenti, *To Kill A Nation*)

The effects were in fact foreseen, and worse, that insight was communicated to Clinton who, armed with that understanding could have prevented the tragedy. Italian Prime Minister Massimo D'Alema warned Clinton that if Milosevic did not surrender as soon as the bombing began that "the result…would be 300,000 to 400,000 refuges passing into Albania." (Noam Chomsky, *The New Military Humanism*) The refugee crisis was one of the tragedies of the NATO bombing. A few days after the withdrawal of the international monitors (Kosovo Verification Mission) on March 19, 1999, the number of displaced people had risen to 200,000 most of whom remained in Kosovo. At the end of the bombing and the signing of the peace accord, the United Nations High Commissioner for Refugees (UNHCFR) reported that 671,000 refugees had fled beyond the borders of Yugoslavia as well as 70,000 who fled to Montenegro and 75,000 who fled to other countries. Along with the Albanians who fled Kosovo, 70,000 to 100,000 Serbian residents also took flight from Kosovo. Some of the reasons for the Albanian and Serbian exile from Kosovo include:

- Escape from the NATO bombing;
- Avoiding being caught in the crossfire between the KLA and the Yugoslavia military;
- Attacks by Yugoslav soldiers and Serbian police;
- Escape from pillaging bands of Albanian mafia and the KLA.

Culpability in war crimes—in any crime—depends on one's understanding of what one is doing. Here it is quite clear: Clinton understood the probable consequences of his actions. And, like other presidents, he put the goals of empire ahead of civilian life at every turn, while claiming the opposite.

One myth critical to maintaining the fiction that the West was engaged in a humanitarian action was the extent to which Serbians killed Albanians in Kosovo. Intervention to stop killing can be a noble endeavor. One obvious way to discern whether an intervention was in fact designed to reduce killing is to measure its impact. In this instance, it is all too clear.

Before the bombing, there was a civil war underway between the KLA seeking independence and Yugoslavia attempting to hold on to Kosovo. As described earlier, there were atrocities on both sides before the NATO bombing but not on a large scale. The level of atrocities was higher after the bombing. According to Robert Hayden, director of the Center for Russian and East European Studies of the University of Pittsburgh:

> ...the casualties among Serb civilians in the first three weeks of the war are higher than all of the casualties on both sides in Kosovo in the three months that led up to the war, and yet those three months were supposed to be a humanitarian catastrophe. (Noam Chomsky, *The New Military Humanism*)

As well, the German Foreign Office wrote that:

> Even in Kosovo, an explicit political persecution linked to Albanian ethnicity is not verifiable...The actions of the [Yugoslav] security forces [were] not directed against the Kosovo-Albanians as an ethnically defined group, but against the military opponent and its actual or alleged supporters...There is no sufficient actual proof of a secret program, or an unspoken consensus on the Serbian side, to liquidate the Albanian people, to drive it out or otherwise to persecute it in the extreme manner presently described. (Michael Parenti, *To Kill A Nation*)

Another accusation leveled at the Serbs—and used as a justification for NATO actions—was systematic rape by the Serbian forces in Kosovo. The Organization for Security and Cooperation in Europe reported that incidents of rape did occur, numbering in the dozens. But while any rape is criminal, it is important to understand that it was not on a massive scale. When a spokesperson for the UN High Commissioner for Refugees was questioned about any evidence of mass rapes, he admitted that he had no method to confirm reports of rapes.

These stories were interwoven into a pattern meant to convey the impression of a Nazi-like extermination of ethnic Albanians, an impression that justifies intervention. The mosaic of myths was completed with the fabrication of mass graves. The State Department announced that up to 500,000 Kosovo Albanians were missing and were presumed to have been killed by Serbian forces. Secretary of Defense, William Cohen, reported that 100,000 military-aged men had disappeared and were presumed to be victims of the Serbs. The media, KLA, and the State Department spoke about mass graves without any evidence to support their claims. The FBI sent a team to uncover mass graves. They did in fact discover 200 bodies at thirty sites. But this was not on the scale of mass graves they were looking for. A French team who were searching for a mass grave containing 150 bodies discovered that it was empty. The International Criminal Court for the former Yugoslavia, in preparing its case against Milosevic, sent a team to search for mass graves based on various reports beginning with the largest graves first. Most of these so-called mass graves contained only five bodies. One of the more serious accusations claimed that 1,000 bodies had been thrown down the shaft of the Trepca mine. The International Criminal Court for the former Yugoslavia's investigation was unable to find a single body.

NATO created all these myths, misrepresented the crisis in Kosovo, demonized the Serbs, set up pseudo peace negotiations which they torpedoed with unreasonable demands they knew would not be accepted, intentionally bombed civilian targets and called the bombing of Serbia a humanitarian war. If the Serbs had been engaged in authentic ethnic cleansing, why did NATO and the United States lie? The need for all these lies was to conceal the truth about the crisis in Kosovo. The crisis was a civil war with atrocities on both sides, with one side, the KLA, supported by the U.S. and other Western countries.

Broken Laws

A thorough examination of possible war crimes was undertaken by an international team of lawyers including Professor Michael Mandel, Professor W. Brooks, Professor Judith A. Fudge, Professor H. J. Glasbeek, and Professor Reuben A. Hanson from Osgoode Hall Law School, York University, Toronto, Ontario. The group included Alejandro Teitelbaum from the American Association of Jurists and Permanent Representative to the United Nations; Alvaro Ramirez Gonzalez, President, Del Porton Oriental de la UCA 1 y media cuadra arriba; Vanessa Ramos, Secretary General; Beinusz Szmukler, President of the Consultative Council. The team filed a request with the International Criminal Court for the Former Yugoslavia asking the prosecutor to investigate the named individuals (NATO leaders) for violations of international law.

In the preface to the statement of international laws breached by NATO leaders, the following facts were stated:

AND WHEREAS in addition to these deliberate attacks on civilian infrastructures and objects, there has been a great number of attacks which have caused great direct physical harm and death to civilians;

AND WHEREAS there is ample evidence in the public statements of NATO leaders that these attacks on civilian targets are part of a deliberate attempt to terrorize the population and turn it against its leadership;

AND WHEREAS the NATO bombings have also made use of weapons banned by international convention, including cruise missiles utilizing depleted uranium highly toxic to human beings;

THEREFORE there is abundant evidence that many instances of serious violations of international humanitarian law…;

AND WHEREAS all the above-named persons [NATO leaders]…have admitted publicly to having agreed upon and ordered these actions, being fully aware of their nature and effects;…

According to the Request to the International Court the following international laws had been violated:

United Nations Charter

Article 2

   3.   All members shall resolve their disputes peacefully.

   4.   All members shall refrain from the threat or use of force.

Article 33

   1.   The parties to a dispute shall seek a solution through negotiation, mediation, or arbitration.

Article 37

   1.   Should the parties fail to resolve the dispute as described in Article 33, they shall refer it to the Security Council.

   2.   The Security Council shall decide what action to take.

Article 39

The Security Council shall determine any threat to peace and make recommendations.

Article 42

Should all measures to maintain peace fail, the Security Council shall decide what action to take.

The NATO Treaty

Article 1

The parties undertake to refrain from the use of force in any manner inconsistent with the purposes of the United Nations.

Geneva Conventions Protocol I

Article 51

1. The civilian population and individual civilians shall enjoy protection from military operations.

4. Indiscriminate attacks are prohibited such as:

(a) those which are not directed at a specific military objective;

(b) those which employ a method which cannot be directed at a specific military target;

(c) those which do not discriminate between military and non-military targets.

These violations of international law are documented by volumes of evidence. The appendix names each civilian target destroyed by NATO bombing. The only real attempt by the United States to resolve the dispute between the KLA and Serbia peacefully was the negotiations at Rambouillet. Both the United States and Serbia tabled a set of proposals but the Americans completed ignored the Serbian proposals. Not only did the U.S. issue an ultimatum to Serbia to either accept the American proposals in their entirety or face an attack by NATO forces but U.S. negotiators also attached an appendix that no sovereign state would accept. Following the pseudo-negotiations, NATO decided to bomb Yugoslavia without any effort to comply with the steps which have been outlined by the UN for the peaceful resolution of disputes. As well, NATO contemptuously ignored the imperative that only the Security Council can authorize the use of force.

The bombing itself made a mockery of the Geneva Conventions. NATO bombers killed about 1,000 civilians by deliberately targeting civilians and civilian targets. Small agricultural villages, hospitals, schools and rescue workers are not legitimate military targets. The NATO planners were choosing targets that they would have known were not military targets. The use of cluster bombs almost guarantees that non-military targets will be struck. Dropping a cluster bomb in the middle of a village or town is nothing less than murder. Another illegal weapon, depleted uranium missiles (Geneva Conventions, Protocol 1, article 51, clause 4(g)), was also used and the radiation from these weapons does not discriminate between soldier and civilian.

Unfortunately, we will never have a judgment from the International Criminal Court because it refused to consider the case. Michael Mandel and David Jacobs, both lawyers, delivered three thick volumes of evidence to Carla Del Ponte, a prosecutor of the Tribunal. After two months, Del Ponte advised the team of lawyers that the court would probably not consider their case. In a letter to Louise Arbour, chief prosecutor of the Tribunal, Michael Mandel wrote a stinging critique of why the Court refused to hear the case.

> Unfortunately, as you know, many doubts have already been raised about the impartiality of your tribunal...In early May you appeared at a press conference with the US Secretary of State Madeleine Albright, by that time herself the subject of two formal complaints of war crimes over the targeting of civilians in Yugoslavia. Albright publicly announced at that time that the US was the major provider of funds for the tribunal and that it had pledged even more money to it.

Louise Arbour's own defense of why the case was not brought to trial is damning itself:

> I am obviously not commenting on any allegations of violations of international humanitarian law supposedly perpetrated by nationals of NATO countries. I accept the assurances given by NATO leaders that they intend to conduct their operations in the Federal Republic of Yugoslavia in full compliance with international humanitarian law. I have reminded many of them, when the occasion presented itself, of their obligation to conduct fair and open-minded investigations of any possible deviance from that policy, and of

the obligation of commanders to prevent and punish, if required. (Press release from Chief Prosecutor Louise Arbour, The Hague, May 13, 1999)

The entire purpose of an international court—of any court—is to hear complaints against parties and to assess guilt and punishment, if any. Such a function requires impartiality and an avoidance of prejudgment prior to hearing the evidence and argument. But here we have the chief prosecutor stating she won't press the case simply because she "accepts the assurances given by NATO leaders." By that rationale, no leader should be tried for any war crimes and instead simply be required to issue assurances that they will obey international law.

Meanwhile, Milosevic and other Serbian leaders are currently being tried for war crimes by the International Criminal Court.

Clinton's Lies

As well as committing war crimes, President Clinton lied to the American people about the atrocities against Kosovo Albanians, the existence of mass graves, the number of Kosovar Albanian refugees before the bombing, American pilots risking their lives, the peace negotiations, and the bombing of military targets and those lies proved fundamental to generating support for the prosecution of the war.

To justify the bombing President Clinton had to convince the American people and Congress that Serbia was committing atrocities against ethnic Albanians on a scale that could only be defined as ethnic cleansing. In a question and answer session with the American Society of Newspaper Editors in San Francisco on April 15, 1999, President Clinton claimed that:

> The tragedy in Kosovo is the result of a meticulously planned and long-meditated attack on an entire people simply on the basis of their ethnicity and religion... (National Archives and Records Administration, United States Printing Office)

The conflict in Kosovo was between a group seeking independence from the state and the state itself. It was a civil war. Ethnicity and religion were not the immediate reasons why Serbian forces in Kosovo were battling the KLA. The Serbian attack was not, in fact, directed against an entire people but against members and supporters of the KLA.

The peace negotiations were, in fact, an ultimatum: accept our terms or be bombed. President Clinton hoped the public would believe that the United States had made an effort to negotiate a settlement and that the only alternative was "war." In an address to the nation on March 24, 1999, President Clinton stated that:

> Over the last few months we have done everything we possibly could to solve this problem peacefully. Secretary Albright has worked tirelessly for a negotiated settlement. (National Archives and Records Administration, United States Printing Office)

President Clinton was well aware of the fact that NATO bombers were striking non-military targets. Frequently, the President or other NATO officials were forced to explain the bombing of a non-military target when it came to light. The response was invariably to call it an accident and to explain that when such a large number of sorties are flown it is inevitable that some civilian targets will be hit. The truth is that President Clinton not only knew that NATO was bombing non-military targets, but he was part of the planning process. *Time* magazine reported that:

> Part of the problem for allied planners is that they are under strict orders to avoid "collateral damage"—the famous euphemism that means killing civilians or blowing up things you aren't aiming at. The targets were reviewed with great care at the White House, where Secretary of Defense William Cohen and the Chairman of the Joint Chiefs, General Hugh Shelton, sat down with President Clinton to go over the list. (*Time* magazine, April 5, 1999)

Newsweek reported that:

> When the war began nine weeks ago, Clinton ruled out a ground invasion of Yugoslavia. Last week he budged a little, saying he would not "take any option off the table." But he clearly preferred to stay with the air war, despite its latest mishaps, including accidental hits on a Belgrade hospital and a prison and a rebel base in Kosovo. "I believe the campaign is working," Clinton said. "We ought to stick with the strategy that we have." (*Newsweek*, May 10, 1999)

While President Clinton and his top advisors were planning to bomb non-military targets, the President was telling the American people that NATO forces had a strong commitment to avoid non-military targets. On April 15, 1999, in a question and answer period with the American Society of Newspaper Editors in San Francisco, President Clinton asked the editors:

> ...to think about the hundreds of sorties which have been flown in the last three weeks and the small number of civilian casualties. It should be obvious to everyone in the world that we are bending over backwards to hit military

targets, to hit security targets, even to hit a lot of targets late at night where
the losses in human life will be minimized. These efforts have been made,
and they have been remarkably successful. (National Archives and Records
Administration, United States Printing Office)

Perhaps President Clinton should have been asked to explain why cluster
bombs were being dropped in the centre of towns and villages.

It is very clear that President Clinton lied to justify the bombing of
Serbia. It is also clear that he is guilty of war crimes. He and other NATO
leaders inflicted great suffering and destruction on the Serbian people
because their leaders were attempting to preserve the Federal Republic of
Yugoslavia. The Serbs were by no means innocent of atrocities but neither
were the KLA. The greatest perpetrators of atrocities in Yugoslavia were the
NATO leaders.

The bombing of Serbia and human rights violations are impeachable
offenses. It says something about American political culture that when a
president gets impeached it's for a lie of little consequence compared to the
death he wrought.

President Clinton lied about the atrocities of the Serbs and the targeting
in Serbia to justify an intervention whose real purpose was to dismantle
a country which refused to cooperate with the U.S. and other Western
powers.

CHAPTER 9

FINISHING THE JOB

GEORGE W. AND THE BOMBING OF IRAQ

In the history of warfare there have been many one-sided battles yet this stands out from the rest. Seldom has the conqueror in an overwhelmingly one-sided war defeated the enemy, battered and starved the ravaged people of that nation for 12 years, and bombed them yet again. One example is the two wars against Iraq. The United States and their allies unleashed a reign of terror on a nation with virtually no ability to fight back in order to defend the world from Weapons of Mass Destruction (WMD). The justification of defending the world against WMD was a lie told by President Bush and his administration to conceal their real motive which was to create an American-friendly government, gain control of Iraq's oil reserves and to acquire strategic territory for American bases.

The mighty American war machine destroyed the infrastructure, industry, agriculture and war-making capability of Iraq in 1991. Then, for the next 12 years, the United States and Britain were responsible for denying the Iraqi people access to food, clean water, medicine and for a continual bombing campaign on a smaller scale. Finally, the Herculean American war machine unleashed another round of bombs on Iraq just in case it was still breathing. As Karl von Clausewitz (Prussian General and military strategist) once said, "The conqueror is always a lover of peace; he would prefer to take over our country unopposed."

Myths abounded during America's obsession with the destruction of Iraq and the capture of Saddam Hussein. Millions of dollars were spent on the largest public relations firms and advertising agencies whose objective was to "manufacture consent" in the United States for the atrocities perpetrated against Iraq. Some of the major myths include:

- Iraq had weapons of mass destruction (WMD) in 2003 when George W. Bush bombed Iraq.

- The aim of U.S. military planners was to bomb military targets.

- Sanctions were designed to force Iraq to destroy its WMD.

- Iraq expelled the UNSCOM arms inspectors.

- Iraq posed a threat to the security of the United States.

- Iraq posed a threat to its neighbours.

- Iraq had ties with al Qaeda.

- Iraq was sponsoring terrorist groups.

- The U.S. had the right to bomb Iraq without the support of the United Nations.

- The "Coalition of the Willing" was a legitimate international coalition.

- The world is a safer place without Saddam Hussein.

- The purpose of the United States bombing Iraq was to either destroy WMD or democratize Iraq.

- The Iraqi government diverted revenues from oil to benefit themselves and not the people of Iraq.

- The government of Iraq did not distribute all the food available from humanitarian groups.

The Sanctions

The first bombing of Iraq ended on February 27, 1991. During the bombing, 88,500 tons of explosives were dropped on Iraq but only 6,500 tons were so-called "smart bombs." The country's infrastructure, including power utilities, water treatment plants, and transportation centres was destroyed along with the agricultural and industrial base. By the end of the bombing, Iraq was incapable of producing sufficient food for its citizens and most people lacked access to clean water. Estimates of the number of casualties range from 100,000 to 200,000 people.

After Iraq invaded Kuwait on August 2, 1990, the United States imposed an embargo on oil exports from Iraq and froze Kuwaiti and Iraqi assets. On the same day, the UN Security Council passed Resolution 660 condemning the Iraqi invasion of Kuwait and called for an immediate and unconditional withdrawal.

To force Iraq to withdraw from Kuwait unconditionally and then to destroy their Weapons of Mass Destruction (WMD), the United Nations, led by the United States, imposed sanctions on Iraq which were themselves agents of mass destruction. As reported in chapter 7 they deprived the Iraqi government of the means to repair and restore vital services essential to the sustainability of life. Clean water, food, and medical supplies were in short supply. Sanctions created a crisis in the health-care system, which now lacked basic medicines, parts to repair equipment, and disinfectants to maintain clean hospitals.

George W. Bush handled Iraq WMD issues similarly to his predecessors until 9/11. The 9/11 tragedy provided the Bush administration with the rationale to expand the American Empire under the guise of a "war on terror." The smoking gun for this argument is the decision to abandon Afghanistan, where terrorists had been training and seeking refuge, in favour of a war against Iraq when it was well known that Iraq had no involvement in 9/11.

For this plan to succeed, the inspection process had to be stopped before it was clear that Iraq had no WMD and therefore, could not provide a pretext for declaring war on Iraq.

During the next two years Iraq refused to allow further inspections because of the presence of intelligence agents on inspection teams and because of the UN's refusal to reduce sanctions. On August 29, 2002, U.S. Vice President Cheney declared that a new round of inspections would be futile because they would not be sufficient to guarantee that Iraq had disarmed. At the same time, Iraq declared that future inspections would be a "waste of time" because the United States had already decided upon "changing the regime by force."

President George W. Bush spoke to the General Assembly of the United Nations on September 12, 2002, to warn the world of the "grave and gathering danger" of Iraq's WMD. He also said:

> Right now, Iraq is expanding and improving facilities that are used for the production of biological weapons...Today, Iraq continues to withhold important information about its nuclear program...The conduct of the Iraqi regime is a threat to the authority of the United Nations and a threat to peace.

There are two major flaws apparent in this excerpt from his speech. First his assessment of the status of Iraq's WMD programs was completely inconsistent with the results of the inspection process and the accounts of a number of highly credible sources. Second, the U.S. was in no position to criticize other nations for undermining the authority of the Security Council. Washington's conduct with respect to influencing Richard Butler, planting intelligence agents on inspection teams, taking action against Iraq before any debate on UNSCOM's report, and bombing Iraq without the approval of the UN all undermined the authority of the Security Council.

On September 16, 2002, Iraq's Foreign Minister, Naji Sabri, advised UN Secretary General Kofi Annan that Iraq would accept the return of UN weapon's inspectors "without conditions." Nevertheless, the United States was preparing to declare war against Iraq. President Bush asked Congress to approve a resolution giving him absolute authority to declare war on Iraq. This resolution passed the House of Representatives by a vote of 296-133 and the Senate by a vote of 77-23. The President signed the resolution on October 16, 2003.

While Washington was preparing for war, the United Nations was preparing to preserve the peace by resurrecting the inspection process. The United Nations adopted Resolution 1441 on November 8, 2002, authorizing further inspections, which Iraq had to accept or reject within seven days. Iraq accepted the new inspection process. The Resolution granted UNMOVIC (the United Nations Monitoring, Verification, and Inspection Committee) and the IAEA the right to inspect anywhere in Iraq with unconditional access. As well, Iraq had to provide an "accurate and complete" declaration of its nuclear, chemical, and biological weapons and related materials within 30 days. All violations of the Resolution had to be reported to the Security Council before any further action could be undertaken. Contrary to the U.S. interpretation, there was nothing in the Resolution that authorized the use of force. Paragraphs 4, 11, 12, and 14 specified that any assessment of Iraq's compliance and any consequences that may follow must be debated by the Security Council and could not be acted on by any member state without authorization from the Security Council.

Dr. Hans Blix, executive chairman of UNMOVIC, provided an update to the Security Council on January 27, 2003, 60 days after the resumption of inspections. His report to the Security Council stated that:

> Iraq has on the whole cooperated rather well so far with UNMOVIC in this field [cooperation]. The most important point to make is that access has been provided to all sites we have wanted to inspect and with one exception it has been prompt...These reports do not contend that weapons of mass destruction remain in Iraq, nor do they exclude the possibility. They point to lack of evidence and inconsistencies, which raise question marks, which must be straightened out, if weapons dossiers are to be closed and confidence is to arise...In the past two months, UNMOVIC has built up its capabilities in Iraq

from nothing to 260 staff members...All serve the United Nations and no one else. In the past two months during which we have built up our presence in Iraq, we have conducted over 300 inspections to more than 230 different sites...We have now an inspection apparatus that permits us to send multiple inspection teams every day all over Iraq, by road or by air. Let me end by simply noting that the capability which has been built up in a short time and which is now operating is at the disposal of the Security Council.

On the same day as Hans Blix delivered his report on Iraqi's biological and chemical weapons to the Security Council, the Director General of the IAEA, Mohamed ElBaradei, delivered his report on Iraq's nuclear program. According to his report:

> To verify this information (procurement of high strength aluminum tubes) IAEA inspectors have inspected the relevant rocket production and storage sites, taken tube samples...From our analysis to date it appears that the aluminum tubes would be consistent with the purpose stated by Iraq...I trust that the Council would continue its unified and unequivocal support for the inspection process in Iraq...To conclude: we have to date found no evidence that Iraq has revived its nuclear weapons programme since the elimination of the programme in the 1990s. With our verification system now in place...we should be able [with Iraq's cooperation] within the next few months to provide credible evidence that Iraq has no nuclear weapons programme.

The reports from the two inspection teams concluded that no evidence had been uncovered which demonstrated Iraq's development or storage of WMD. Both reports emphasized that an inspection organization had been established in Iraq to monitor any further developments in Iraq's WMD programs and to uncover any programs or weapons already in existence. Both reports reassured the Security Council that they were prepared to continue their work until they reach the point where the world will have confidence that Iraq no longer poses a threat.

The results of the inspection process were not known to the public other than through presidential and administration pronouncements. These pronouncements contradicted the reports from the various inspection teams and were designed to set the stage for a war on Iraq.

On January 28, 2003, President Bush delivered his State of the Union Address to Congress in which the existence of the UN inspection process and the results of those inspections seemed to be ignored. During his address, he stated that:

> For the next twelve years [1991 to 2003], he [Saddam Hussein] systematically violated that agreement [UN Resolution 687]. He pursued

chemical, biological and nuclear weapons, even while inspectors were in his country. Nothing to date has restrained him from his pursuit of these weapons...With nuclear arms or a full arsenal of chemical and biological weapons, Saddam Hussein could resume his ambitions of conquest in the Middle East. It has not been possible to verify Iraq's claims with respect to the nature and magnitude of its proscribed weapons programmes and their current disposition...The Commission has not been able to conduct the substantive disarmament work...

President Bush also told the American people during his address that "Secretary of State Powell will present information and intelligence about Iraq's illegal weapons" and reassured Americans that if Saddam Hussein does not disarm "we will lead a coalition to disarm him."

Secretary of State Colin Powell contradicted all the data gathered by UNSCOM, UNMOVIC, and the IAEA when he appeared before the Security Council on February 5, 2003. He could not claim that American intelligence had knowledge of WMD which was unknown to the inspection teams. The U.S. would have had an absolute obligation to share that knowledge with the inspection teams. The Security Council is the official body which has the authority to conduct inspections and all nations on the Security Council voted to support this process. Furthermore Clause 10 in Resolution 1441 requires member states to hand over all relevant data to the inspection teams. In fact, Powell claimed that the Bush administration was providing the inspection teams with "all relevant information" on WMD. According to Scott Ritter, in *Frontier Justice*:

> We now know that the U.S. held onto the best sites [for inspection] for exploitation by U.S. Special Operations Forces in the opening moments of Operation Iraqi Freedom, sites that turned out to be empty, but nevertheless had not been shared with the U.N. weapons inspectors.

Powell's remarks to the Security Council include:

> Resolution 1441 gave Iraq one last chance...to come into compliance or face serious consequences....And to assist in its disarmament we called on Iraq to cooperate with returning inspectors from UNMOVIC and IAEA...Indeed the facts and Iraq's behaviour show that Saddam Hussein and his regime are concealing their efforts to produce more weapons of mass destruction.

The most critical flaw in Powell's reasoning was his demand that Iraq prove that it has no WMD. It is almost impossible to prove a negative. Iraq could have produced copious photographs and massive documentation but that would not have proven that WMD did not exist. For example, biological weapons can be stored in a refrigerator. Did the Bush administration want Iraq to produce a photograph of every refrigerator in Iraq? How would you prove that biological weapons were not removed beforehand?

Powell also claimed that although Iraq had declared 8,500 liters of anthrax, "UNSCOM estimated that Saddam Hussein could have produced 25,000 liters." There is no evidence that Iraq had produced that quantity of anthrax. Scott Ritter, in *Frontier Justice* claims that:

> Iraq produced the growth media [for anthrax] in question in the late 1980s, and it had a shelf life of five to seven years. The last known batch of anthrax manufactured in Iraq was in 1991, and the factory used by Iraq to produce anthrax was destroyed, together with its associated production equipment, under U.N. supervision in 1996. Iraq only produced liquid bulk anthrax, which under ideal storage conditions has a shelf life of three years before it germinates and becomes useless...For Iraq to have a viable anthrax stockpile, it would have needed to develop a new manufacturing base since 1999. And the UNMOVIC inspection regime under Hans Blix found no evidence of such a capability. Furthermore, Iraq has never been shown to have perfected the technique needed to produce the dry powder form of anthrax so graphically presented by Colin Powell when he held up his vial of simulated white powder.

In his remarks to the Security Council, Colin Powell presented a surveillance photograph and explained that:

> ...you see fifteen munitions bunkers in yellow and red outlines. The four that are in red squares represent active chemical munitions bunkers...On the left is a close-up of one of the four chemical bunkers. The two arrows indicate the presence of sure signs that the bunkers are storing chemical munitions.

Scott Ritter, in *Frontier Justice* exposes that lie when he reported that:

> ...a German weapons inspector from UNMOVIC had actually visited the site in question. Peter Franck, the inspector in question, told Der Spiegel magazine that he and his fellow inspectors had determined that the vehicles... were in fact nothing but fire trucks.

Colin Powell stated that:

> ...the existence of mobile production facilities used to make biological agents...the description our sources gave us of the technical features required by such facilities are highly detailed and extremely accurate.

Dan Plesch, in a report titled "US Claim Dismissed by Blix", in the *Guardian International* (February 5, 2003) proved that to be a lie when he claimed that:

Hans Blix said there was no evidence of mobile biological weapons laboratories or of Iraq trying to foil inspectors by moving equipment before his teams arrived. Dr. Blix said he has already inspected two alleged mobile labs and found nothing.

Colin Powell claimed in his remarks to the Security Council and President Bush stated in his address to Congress that Iraq was acquiring materials to build nuclear weapons. Powell claimed that:

Saddam Hussein is determined to get his hands on a nuclear bomb.... he has made repeated covert attempts to acquire high-specification aluminum tubes from eleven different countries, even after inspections resumed...they can be used as centrifuges for enriching uranium...Saddam Hussein recently sought significant quantities of uranium from Africa.

The executive director of the IAEA had reported to the Council that "From our analysis to date it appears that the aluminum tubes would be consistent with the purpose stated by Iraq." An IAEA report concluded that the size of the tubes made them unsuitable for Uranium enrichment but were identical to tubes used for conventional artillery rockets. The claim that Saddam Hussein had purchased nuclear material was based on forged documents handed to the U.S. from Britain whose source was the Italian intelligence service. Italian intelligence bought the forged documents from a corrupt Niger embassy official in Rome. Forged documents are not an excuse for being deceived by bad intelligence when a very competent inspection team had already reported that Iraq did not pose a nuclear threat. It is incumbent on the U.S. to carefully verify the credibility of a source before making important decisions based on that intelligence.

In Bush's State of the Union address on January 28, 2003, he claimed that "the British Government has learned that Saddam Hussein recently sought significant quantities of uranium from Africa." In fact, this claim had already been invalidated when Joseph Wilson, former American Ambassador, was assigned by the CIA to investigate this claim. He filed a report with the CIA and State Department repudiating any Niger uranium claims. In a *Washington Post* article, Wilson claims that "it really comes down to the administration misrepresenting the facts on an issue that was a fundamental justification for going to war."

Colin Powell's remarks to the Security Council were crammed with lies. Ignoring all the Blix inspection team's data, he chose to base his report on sources which were highly inferior to the competent on-site work of the inspectors. The tail was clearly wagging the dog. Washington decided to bomb Iraq and to produce information in order to "manufacture consent" for war.

On February 14, 2003, Hans Blix updated the Security Council on the results of UNMOVIC's inspections. His report contradicted President Bush, Colin Powell, and other members of the administration who had been condemning Iraq for continuing to hide and build WMD. According to Hans Blix:

> Since I reported to the Security Council on 27 January, UNMOVIC has had two further weeks of operational and analytical work in New York and active inspection in Iraq...Through the inspections conducted so far, we have obtained a good knowledge of the scientific and industrial landscape of Iraq, as well as of its missile capability but, as before, we do not know every cave and corner. Inspections are helping to bridge the gap in knowledge that arose due to some absence of inspections between December 1998 and November 2002...This impression [cooperation on process] remains, and we do note that access to sites has so far been without problems, including those that have never been declared or inspected, as well as to Presidential sites and private residences...How much, if any, is left of Iraq's weapons of mass destruction and related proscribed items and programmes? So far, UNMOVIC has not found any such weapons, only a small number of empty chemical munitions, which should have been declared and destroyed.

In all their public statements about WMD in Iraq, the Bush administration's evaluation of the progress of the inspection teams in Iraq differed substantially from those of the inspection teams. This raises the question of where the U.S. obtained their information. Since the inspection teams were never criticized for their incompetence, and since the U.S. was required to hand over any information in their possession about WMD, the only possible conclusion is that the Bush administration was exploiting the inspection process to suit their own purposes. On April 9, 2003, after the bombing had started, Hans Blix was very candid about his opinion of American motives. Following are some of Hans Blix's comments:

- "There is evidence that this war was planned well in advance. Sometimes this raises doubts about their attitude to the [weapons] inspections." (Spanish daily *El Pais*)

- "I now believe that finding weapons of mass destruction has been relegated, I would say, to fourth place, which is why the United States and Britain are now waging war on Iraq."

- "Today the main aim is to change the dictatorial regime of Saddam Hussein" (Spanish daily El Pais)

- The war was "a very high price to pay in terms of human lives and the destruction of a country" when the threat of weapons proliferation could have been contained by UN inspections. (Hans Blix: War Planned 'Long in Advance', from News24)

In addition to warning Americans about WMD, the Bush administration linked al Qaeda to Iraq. According to Washington, the attack on Iraq was part of the war on terrorism. The propaganda was so effective that at one point a majority of Americans believed that Iraq was behind 9/11. The linkage was as spurious as was the claim about WMD.

Any claims about a connection between al Qaeda and Iraq ignore the fact that al Qaeda is an extremely rigid religious organization that condemns the "infidel" Ba'ath Party of Saddam Hussein as an aggressively secular organization. One of the arguments for linking the two organizations was based on an alleged meeting in Prague between hijacker ringleader Mohammed Atta and an Iraqi intelligence officer, Ahmed Khalil Ibahim Samir al-Ani, a second consul at the Iraqi embassy, between April 8 and April 11, 2001. Czech intelligence reported that the source, an Arab émigré, only came forward after 9/11 when photos of Atta appeared in the local Prague press. The FBI in the United States conducted an exhaustive investigation into this meeting and discovered that Atta was in Virginia during the times of the alleged meetings. Czech President Vaclav Havel conducted his own investigation and concluded that there was no evidence that such a meeting took place. The lack of evidence did not deter American leaders from using the story.

When Secretary of State Colin Powell made his presentation to the Security Council he referred to a compound in northeastern Iraq as a "terrorist chemicals and poisons factory" run by Abu Musab al-Zarqawi, a Jordanian militant involved with a terrorist group in northern Iraq known as Ansar al-Islam. Luke Harding of the Observer, a British daily, traveled to the site three days later and found no sign of a chemical weapons facility. Abu Musab's only connection to the government of Iraq was that he allegedly received medical care in a Baghdad hospital. Furthermore, Ansaral-Islam was located in northern Iraq where pro-U.S. Kurdish groups sought the overthrow of the Saddam Hussein regime.

The theory of a connection between Iraq and al Qaeda was to a large extent based on a British government public dossier on Iraq. In his February 5 presentation to the Security Council, Powell referred to "the fine paper that the United Kingdom distributed...which describes in exquisite detail deception activities." It was described as a fine example of the analytical work of MI6, the British spy agency. When Cambridge University professor Glen Rangwala read the document, he realized that he had read it before in the Middle East Review of International Affairs. After further investigation, he discovered that the bulk of the British government's public dossier had been plagiarized from a paper in the Middle East Review titled "Iraq's Security and Intelligence Network: A Guide and Analysis." The paper had been written by Dr. Ibrahim al-Marashi, a post-graduate student living in California. The ideas in al-Marashi's dossier were based mostly on Iraqi documents which were more than a decade old. Although most of the information is accurate, some passages had been rewritten or simply concocted to strengthen the allegations against Iraq. The British government's dossier had not even been prepared by MI6 but by junior aides to Alastair Campbell, the chief press secretary for Prime Minister Tony Blair.

The British intelligence agency had, in fact, produced a report, which was ignored by Tony Blair because it contradicted his and President Bush's position. According to the MI6 document there was no evidence of any links between Al Qaeda and Iraq.

The Carnegie Endowment for International Peace, a non-partisan Washington research centre, released a report on January 10, 2004, which destroyed both justifications for the "war" on Iraq, WMD and links to al Qaeda. According to an article in *The Globe and Mail*:

> ...there is no firm evidence that the former Iraqi leader was cooperating with the al-Qaeda network and that Iraq presented an immediate threat to the United States, to the Middle East or to global security...Iraq's nuclear program has been suspended for many years and the country's chemical-weapons production capabilities have been "effectively destroyed"..."It is very likely that intelligence officials were pressured by senior administration officials to conform their threat assessments to pre-existing policies. ..."We had over 1000 people a day search for months, and we found nothing." ("U.S. exaggerated Iraq threat, report says", January 10, 2004, p. A11)

All the evidence supporting the position of the Bush administration in its campaign against Iraq was either grossly distorted or defective. The most reliable sources of information were overlooked because their conclusions interfered with the grand schemes of the Bush administration. According to Sheldon Rampton and John Stauber in *Weapons of Mass Deception: The Uses of Propaganda in Bush's War on Iraq*:

> Graham [Bob Graham, U.S. Senator] who chaired the Senate Intelligence Committee, was so baffled by the contradictory assessments of Iraq coming from different agencies that in July 2002 he asked the CIA to come up with a report on the likelihood that Saddam Hussein would use weapons of mass destruction. When asked this question directly, a senior CIA intelligence witness responded that the likelihood was "low" for the "foreseeable future." Like many of the analyses that conflicted with the drive for war, this statement from the CIA went largely unreported.

Now that the ground had been prepared for a "war" against Iraq, British Foreign Minister Jack Straw announced a Security Council Resolution, supported by the United States, which authorized the use of force against Iraq if it failed to comply with all Security Council Resolutions. The proposed resolution demanded that Iraq hand over all WMD and materials to support their construction, and all documents detailing the destruction of WMD. Both France and Russia threatened to veto any resolution authorizing the use of force.

The threat of a veto persuaded the United States to abandon any attempt to legitimize their war plans with a Security Council Resolution. Instead they attempted to build a coalition to create the illusion of international approval. They had the support of, and military contributions from, Britain and Australia. Overall, Washington was able to create a coalition of 30 nations referred to as the "Coalition of the Willing." "Coalition of the Willing" is a very misleading and deceptive phrase. The majority of the 30 nations provided only token support, such as an endorsement or permission to use their airspace for flyovers by American warplanes. Most of these nations did not provide material support and they demanded substantial aid packages in return for their endorsement. The coalition included Albania, Azerbaijan, the Dominican Republic, El Salvador, Eritrea, Ethiopia, Kazakhstan, the Marshall Islands, Micronesia, Nicaragua, Rwanda, Spain, Uganda, and Uzbekistan. Many people in these countries opposed the war. In Britain a poll in January 2003 showed that 68% were not convinced of the need for war. In Spain 80% opposed the war.

Bombed and Invaded Again

On Thursday March 20, 2003, President Bush announced his intention to use force against Iraq in an address to the nation in which he stated that:

> My fellow citizens. At this hour Americans and coalition forces are in the early stages of military operations to disarm Iraq, to free its people and to defend the world from a grave danger. On my orders, coalition forces have begun striking selected targets of military importance to undermine Saddam Hussein's ability to wage war.

The euphemism "preemptive defence" was created to hide the brutal truth about the atrocities the U.S. was about to perpetrate on the people of Iraq. This phrase is an Orwellian charade to deceive the American people into believing that there was an imminent threat to U.S. security and that the United States had to strike first. In fact, even the phrase "preventive defense" implies that at some future time, the Iraqi war machine would attack the United States. Not only was Iraq broken militarily, it was incapable of even defending itself.

The United States launched the war with its "shock and awe" strategy which meant a massive high-tech, air strike against Baghdad. When originally coined by Harlan K. Ullman, a defence strategist, it meant a strategy "aimed at influencing the will, perception, and understanding of an adversary rather than simply deploying military capability." Ullman told CBS reporter David Martin that:

> You take the city down, you get rid of their power, water. In 2, 3, 4, 5, days they are physically, emotionally, and psychologically exhausted.

A Pentagon official remarked that "there will not be a safe place in Baghdad." It is clear that the real purpose of "shock and awe" was to destroy as much of the Iraqi leadership and army as possible as well as defence installations which would interfere with "coalition" ground troops taking over the country. The strategy was to launch 300 to 400 cruise missiles on the first day of the operation then another 300 to 400 on the second day. That is more than all the cruise missiles launched in the 1991 bombing of Iraq. Former UN Assistant Secretary General Denis Halliday has accused the U.S. "…of proceeding with plans to annihilate Iraqi society."

Following the "shock and awe" operation, a massive force of American, British, and Australian forces marched through Iraq relatively unimpeded and took control of most of the country. On May 1, 2003, President Bush announced that "major combat operations in Iraq have ended." Bush also boasted that the war was "one of the swiftest and most humane military campaigns in history." Well, for once at least, he was half right. The war was anything but humane. Body counts are important in order to understand the extent of the atrocities. An organization called "Iraq Body Count" maintains an up-to-date count of Iraqi deaths based solely on credible news sources and on November 3, 2003, they reported that there had been a minimum of 7,960 deaths and a maximum of 9,792 deaths.

Statistics do not force people out of denial about the brutality and savageness of war. The International Action Center in New York has produced pictures and descriptions of some of the tragedies of real people. For example:

- Down the road, a little girl, no older than five and dressed in a pretty orange and gold dress, lay dead in a ditch next to the body of a man who may have been her father. Half his head was missing. Nearby, in a battered old Volga, peppered with aluminum holes, an Iraqi woman—perhaps the girl's mother—was dead, slumped in the back seat. (*UK Times*, Sunday March 30, 2003)

- Amid the wreckage 12 dead civilians were found lying on the road or in nearby ditches. All had been trying to leave this southern town overnight, probably for fear of being killed by U.S. helicopter attacks and heavy artillery. (*UK Times*, March 30, 2003)

- On March 31, there was a massacre of civilians, mainly women and their children, whose crime was that they were driving on a roadway in their own country. As their van approached a checkpoint, U.S. soldiers destroyed their vehicle with a barrage of 25mm cannon fire from one or more of their M2 Bradley Fighting Vehicles. (*Washington Post*, April 1, 2003)

Numerous non-military objects were deliberately targeted including electrical distribution facilities, three media facilities, civilian telecommunication facilities, government buildings, roads, and bridges.

The most savage executioners of innocent people were two types of "time bombs" dropped on Iraq by American forces. One time bomb was depleted uranium weapons. The effects of these weapons may not surface for up to ten years and will create radioactive hot spots in Baghdad and other cities and towns. Radiation levels in Baghdad have been measured at up to 1,900 times higher than normal background radiation. High radiation levels can cause cancer, chronic fatigue syndrome, joint and muscle pain, neurological damage, mood disturbances, lung and kidney damage, auto-immune deficiencies, miscarriages, maternal mortality, and genetic birth defects. Iraq's National Ministry of Health organized two international conferences and offered detailed epidemiological studies which indicate a six-fold increase in breast cancer, a five-fold increase in lung cancer, and a 16-fold increase in ovarian cancer. According to the *Seattle Post-Intelligencer*, August 4, 2003:

> The Pentagon and the United Nations estimate that the U.S. and Britain used 1,100 to 2,200 tons of armor-piercing shells made of depleted uranium during attacks on Iraq in March and April—far more than the 375 tons used in the 1991 Gulf War.

The second type of "time bomb" was cluster bombs, which has a failure rate of up to 16%. This leaves unexploded small bomblets, which easily explode on contact. British and American forces used cluster bombs frequently, dropping some 13,000 bombs containing nearly two million bomblets, in populated areas. In *Weapons of Mass Deception*, Sheldon Rampton and John Stauber reported that:

> On April 28, the *Chicago Tribune* published a picture of the burial of six-year-old Lamiya Ali, an Iraqi girl who was killed along with her eight-year-old sister when she mistook a bomblet for a toy.

Behind the Scenes—Planning a War

All the evidence leads to the conclusion that neither WMD nor Iraqi support for terrorist groups was the real motive for the American decision to wage "war" against Iraq. The most damning evidence that the above motives were irrelevant is the date when plans to attack Iraq were first formulated. A major initiative to toughen American policies towards Iraq sprang from the Project for the New American Century (PNAC), a private think-tank formed by a group of prominent neoconservatives in 1997 including:

- William Kristol—former Chief of Staff to Vice President Quayle;

- Elliot Abrams—former Reagan Assistant Secretary of State;

- Jeb Bush—Governor of Florida;

- Dick Cheney—Vice President under George Bush;

- Newt Gingrich—former House Speaker;

- Jeanne Kirkpatrick—White House advisor under Reagan and Bush;

- Lewis Libby—Cheney's Chief of Staff;

- Richard Perle—Defense Department in Reagan era;

- Donald Rumsfeld—Secretary of Defense under George Bush;

- Paul Wolfowitz—Rumsfeld's deputy.

PNAC is a non-profit educational organization whose goal is to promote American global leadership. The aims of the organization are to increase defence spending significantly in order to carry out America's global responsibilities and to accept responsibility for America's "unique role for preserving and extending an international order friendly to our security, our prosperity, and our principles." The aims are cleverly crafted to soften the real intent of PNAC which, according to Rahul Mahajan in *Full Spectrum Dominance*, is "maintaining and extending U.S. world dominance." Sheldon Rampton and John Stauber, in *Weapons of Mass Deception,* remark that PNAC's aims were "criticized overseas as a blueprint for U.S. domination." As well, Scott Ritter in *Frontier Justice,* believes that "PNAC resurrected the global domination theme of the Wolfowitz-Libby Defence Policy Document [1992]."

PNAC's focus on Iraq was an important part of their overall plan. The members of the think-tank wrote a letter to President Clinton in which they argue that:

> ...current American policy towards Iraq is not succeeding and that we may soon face a threat in the Middle East more serious...That strategy should aim above all at the removal of Saddam Hussein's regime from power. (*Washington Post*, January 27, 1998, p. 84)

One of PNAC's accomplishments was a successful lobbying campaign to convince Congress to enact the 1998 Iraqi Liberation Act which made regime change in Iraq official American policy. In November 2002, the White House brain trust consisting of many PNAC members formed the Committee for the Liberation of Iraq (CLI) whose mission statement included "replacing the Saddam Hussein regime with a democratic government."

PNAC members hold important positions in the Bush administration and have considerable influence in the shaping of foreign and defence policy. Their determination to overthrow the regime of Saddam Hussein became a priority for Washington. Not only did Bush's brain trust favor regime change but other influential organizations such as the CLI, the American Enterprise Institute, the Center for Strategic and International Studies (CSIS), the Washington Institute for Middle East Policy, the Middle East Forum, the Hudson Institute, and the Hoover Institute were also in favour of the overthrow of Saddam Hussein. Members of these groups frequently appeared on forums on ABC, MSNBC, CNN, and Fox promoting the necessity to wage war against Iraq. They testified before Congressional committees and appeared at gatherings in Washington. It would not be possible for President Bush to be unaware of the agenda of his brain trust and all these other influential organizations. His subsequent statements and actions corroborate the hypothesis that President Bush was determined to change the leadership in Iraq. The issues of WMD and Iraqi ties to Al Qaeda were easier rationales to sell to the American public than regime change and had the added advantage of instilling fear in the American public for the purpose of winning support for military action. Paul Wolfowitz, Rumsfeld's deputy, confessed that "we settled on one issue, weapons of mass destruction, because it was the one reason everyone could agree on." (*Vanity Fair*, May 28, 2003)

Bush's Lies

President Bush lied on numerous occasions in order to sell the decision to attack Iraq. He appeared before the General Assembly of the United Nations and lied when he warned that Iraq was a "threat to peace." He lied in his address to Congress when he made false claims about Iraq's WMD. He also lied in his address to the American people announcing the war, professing the necessity "to defend the world from a grave danger," and claiming that there were links between Iraq and Al Qaeda. At an election campaign rally in October 2002, Bush alleged that Saddam was "a man, who in my judgment, would like to use Al Qaeda as a forward army." (Andrea Mitchell, NBC News, October 31, 2002) There is not the remotest evidence that such a statement has a shred of truth.

President Bush's lies cannot be excused because he was lied to by his advisors or had bad intelligence reports. The President is responsible for the accuracy of his statements. There were other highly credible sources of information. In fact, he already knew that his senior advisors were lying about the rationale for the war. Bush's repeated attempts to alter the rationale for the war were an indication that he was grasping for any justification that the American people would accept. It would stretch credulity to an absurd level to suppose that he was ignorant of the real motive when his brain trust and all the major conservative organizations with ties to his administration had vehemently advocated the overthrow of Saddam Hussein for years.

President Bush was either ignorant of the reports of all the inspection agencies or was aware of them and lied. If he ignored the reports of all the inspection agencies, he was engaging in an act of dishonesty. As president, he had a responsibility to be aware of reports from highly credible agencies which were designated to investigate WMD. George Tenet of the CIA wrote a letter to the Senate Intelligence Committee Chair Bob Graham, stating that "Baghdad for now appears to be drawing a line short of conducting terrorist attacks with conventional or CBW [chemical and biological weapons] against the United States."

The strongest evidence that Bush lied about attempts to avoid war was his decision to sign a top-secret directive on September 17, 2001, ordering the Pentagon to begin planning "military options" for an attack on Iraq. (ZNET, *Lies and More Lies*, September 22, 2003) All his talk about inspections and WMD was completely fraudulent. In fact, serious planning for the "war" against Iraq began in August 2002, with preparations to deploy forces, construct staging areas, and stockpile weapons. According to Michael Klare, a strategic analyst, all "the administration's supposed diplomatic activities regarding Iraq in the fall of 2002 and early 2003 were merely a smokescreen." (Rahul Mahajan, *Full Spectrum Dominance*) To weaken any Iraqi defence capability, Defense Secretary Rumsfeld expanded the area that was covered by the no-fly-zones to include command-and-control centres and defence systems. The attack on Iraq was in the advanced planning stage in the summer of 2002. There is simply no doubt that President Bush was completely aware of these plans and would have approved them before members of his administration could proceed.

Not only did President Bush and many members of his administration commit war crimes, they significantly tarnished the reputation and diminished the credibility of the Security Council. The U.S. attempted to obtain a Security Council resolution authorizing the use of force against Iraq through bribery and threats. When France announced its intention to use its veto powers, President Bush walked away from the United Nations and declared that he did not need UN approval. In other words, the Security Council was irrelevant.

The sanctions imposed on Iraq caused so many deaths and so much suffering that they constituted a crime against humanity despite the apparent authorization by the United Nations. The sanctions were not designed to starve the Iraqi people or deprive them of clean water and medical supplies. United Nations Resolution 687 specifies exemptions from the sanctions which include "materials and supplies for essential civilian needs and any further findings of humanitarian needs by the committee." These exemptions were perverted by the United States through the use of their veto on the Sanctions Committee. Over a million Iraqis died as a result of the sanctions. The only explanation for the use of the U.S. veto to deprive the Iraqis of the necessities of life was that the American administration was hoping to encourage the Iraqi people to rise up and overthrow Saddam Hussein without the need for direct American intervention. The United States wanted a friendly government in a weakened Iraq and control of Iraqi oil.

The sanctions violated the following international laws and protocols:

- Geneva Conventions, Protocol I, Part IV, Section I, Chapter III, Article 54—Starvation of civilians as a method of warfare is prohibited;

- International Conference on Nutrition, World Declaration on Nutrition, FAO/WHO, 1992—We recognize that access to nutritionally adequate and safe food is a right of each individual. We affirm...that food must not be used as a tool for political pressure;

- UN General Assembly Resolution 44/215 (Dec. 22, 1989)—

Calls upon the developed countries to refrain from exercising political coercion through the application of economic instruments with the purpose of inducing changes in the economic or social systems of other countries;

- Constitution of the World Health Organization, 1946—The enjoyment of the highest standard of health is one of the fundamental rights of every human being without distinction of race, religion, political belief, economic, or social condition.

There is no justification in international law for the American declaration of "war" against Iraq. As demonstrated earlier, Security Council resolutions pertaining to Iraq did not authorize the use of force and required that non-compliance with UN Resolutions by Iraq be discussed in the Security Council. In the original drafts of Resolution 1441, the United States proposed a clause that would extend no-fly zones over sites to be inspected and apply the use of force in these zones if necessary but the proposal was defeated. The United Nations Charter's provision in Chapter VII, Article 51, that a nation may use force to defend itself "if an armed attack occurs" clearly does not apply. There was no armed attack against the United States and the Charter does not authorize the use of force for preemptive or preventive strikes. Therefore, the "war" against Iraq was illegal and led to the violations of the following international laws:

United Nations Charter

Article 2

3.   All members shall resolve their disputes peacefully.

4.   All members shall refrain from the threat or use of force.

Article 33

1.   The parties to a dispute shall seek a solution through negotiation, mediation, or arbitration.

Article 37

1.   Should the parties fail to resolve the dispute as described in

Article 33, they shall refer it to the Security Council.

2.   The Security Council shall decide what action to take.

Article 42

Should all measures to maintain peace fail, the Security Council shall decide what action to take.

Geneva Conventions

Article 51

1.   The civilian population and individual civilians shall enjoy protection from military operations.

4.   Indiscriminate attacks are prohibited such as:

    (a)   those which are not directed at a specific military objective;

    (b)   those which do not discriminate between military and non-military targets.

President Bush lied about his agenda in Iraq and his counterfeit interest in the inspection process. In terms of Bush's plans for Iraq, the inspections generated the worst possible outcome: both UNMOVIC and IAEA were satisfied with the inspection process and recommended that inspectors be given the time to complete their work. Since planning for an attack on Iraq had been in the discussion stage since 1998 and in the preparation stage since August 2003, long before the next round of inspections were scheduled to begin, no inspectors' reports could stand in the way of the American military juggernaut. Once the U.S. unleashed its dogs of war, the real victims were not Saddam Hussein and his coterie of thugs, but the people of Iraq, and the United Nations. The future is now fraught with danger as the U.S continues to seek world domination unimpeded by either conscience or international laws and unhindered by the relatively enfeebled military powers of other nations. The consequence of the United States flexing its military muscle whenever it perceives a threat to its interests or security will be a giant step backwards for civilization as power prevails as the ultimate political weapon.

CHAPTER 10

PSYCHOPATH NUMBER 43

Are our Presidents psychotic? Our study of eight presidents since World War II has established that they have committed atrocities in a myriad of ways which include but are not limited to bombing innocent civilians and destroying non-military targets, imposing sanctions that inflict unimaginable hardships on people, conspiring to assassinate democratically elected leaders and replacing them with brutal dictators who are American-friendly and who then commit atrocities against their own people, torturing prisoners, and sending suspected terrorists to Syria, Egypt, etc. to be tortured.

It is difficult not to wonder how people responsible for these atrocities live out their lives without any apparent detrimental impact on their emotional and mental health. It is obvious that they do not have a normal conscience, are skillful at overcoming cognitive dissonance or have a highly cultivated rationalization mechanism. Although unsettling, there had to be a more elaborate explanation. After all, Madeleine Albright very calmly justified the death of 500,000 children in Iraq on "60 Minutes" with a dismissive "We think the price was worth it." After the bombing of towns, villages, a maternity hospital, numerous industries, and schools, President Clinton proudly announced that he had fought the war in Serbia the "right way."

One possible explanation for the behaviour of presidents is that they have psychopathic tendencies. Characteristics that lead to a positive diagnosis include a remarkable disregard for the truth, the inability to accept blame, lack of remorse, shame, or guilt, lack of empathy, lack of conscience, and socially predatory behaviour. Does George W. qualify?

A cursory glance at the traits of a psychopath suggests that George W. Bush probably possesses most of the characteristics. After all, here is a man who bombed Iraq after flagrantly lying about his justification and without missing a beat, changed his justification as reality caught up to him. With arrogant obstinacy, W. ignored the advice of people in his administration and many other respected voices such as James Baker, Brent Scowcroft, Nelson Mandela and former President Jimmy Carter. Obsessively intolerant of even the hint of dissent, he castigated General Colin Powell for "undermining his authority" by informing the public of the "fierce debate within the administration over a possible confrontation with Iraq." During his tenure as Governor of Texas he set a record by signing at least 131 death warrants. He poked fun at killer Karla Faye Tucker who was about to be executed and was asking for clemency on the Larry King Show.

To answer this question we turn to Dr. Robert D. Hare, one of the foremost specialists on psychopaths, who has designed the classic checklist of traits which characterize psychopaths. Not all of the traits need to be present for a positive diagnosis. The test consists of 20 questions to which the answer is either: does not apply (0); applies somewhat, mixed evidence (1); definitely applies, clear evidence (2). Using Dr. Hare's test, we will assess the degree to which President G. W. Bush is a psychopath. A score of 30 or higher is indicative of psychopathic tendencies.

1. Glibness/superficial charm

Superficial charm is a common trait among psychopaths and according to Dr. Hare, "Psychopaths are social predators who charm, manipulate..."

Pol Pot, one of the most brutal, murderous tyrants since World War II, was responsible for the death of over one million Cambodians. Ben Kiernan, associate professor of Southeast Asian history at Yale University, concedes that "Those who know him then insist...that he was charming, self-effacing."

Robert Ressler, the world's leading authority on violence in contemporary society, describes Ted Bundy, notorious serial killer, as charming and popular among women.

President Bush has developed a strategy for winning over friends and opponents alike calling his strategy a "charm offensive" which is something he can turn off and on at will. Wayne Slater, senior political writer for the *Dallas Morning News*, admits that Bush's "charm offensive" was effective in producing positive coverage when he was governor of Texas. As well, ABC online reported that "In a sign that Mr. Bush's charm offensive is bearing fruit, NATO announced..." (February 23, 2005). Gavin Hewitt of the BBC claims that "Although he has his critics, Bush can even charm some of his opponents." (January 28, 2001)

Score (2)

2. Grandiose self-worth

A psychopath has an inflated view of his self-worth and is self-assured, arrogant and a braggart.

Michael Hersh, an Online Journal contributing writer claims that "Bush's sense of unquestionable authority drives him out of control when anyone defies him…" and that "…Bush has embraced this notion of Biblical mission, and now operates with an absolute sense of supreme authority." (September 12, 2002) In addition, an important part of the fundamentalist constituency that supports Bush, Pat Robertson, pointed out on the Paula Zahn show Now, October 21, 2004, that Bush is "the most self-assured man I've ever met in my life." Finally, Walter Cronkite, retired CBS anchor and the "most trusted man in America" reported that Bush's "arrogance" with respect to our allies "has been exceptional." (*The Hanover Eagle*, Anna Weisgerber, March 27, 2003) Delusions of grandeur were very evident when he roared that "I am sick and tired…I have no desire to watch the rerun of an old movie. This is an emperor talking, not the president of a republic." (Bush Watch, March 20) The quintessential manifestation of a megalomaniac is the delusion that he speaks on behalf of God. When Bush was talking to an Amish group in July 2004, he declared that "God speaks through me." The impact of his relationship with God plays out clearly in his political life. As Bob Woodward reveals in his book, *Bush at War*, Bush pontificates in an interview that "I'm the commander…see, I don't need to explain."

Score (2)

3. Need for stimulation/proneness to boredom

An excessive need for novel, thrilling and exciting stimulation is a common trait of psychopaths.

In a *New York Times* article written by Maureen Dowd, the Emperor reveals through the following quotes that he has a serious attention problem and is therefore prone to boredom and in need of constant stimulation:

i) "I find my mind wandering from tasks that are uninteresting or difficult";

ii) "I make quick decisions without thinking enough about their possible bad results";

iii) "I have trouble planning in what order to do a series of tasks or activities";

iv) "In group activities it is hard for me to wait my turn";

v) "I usually work on more than one project at a time, and I fail to finish many of them."

His workday as Governor of Texas, as told by his chief of staff, Clay Johnson, is "two hard half-days" during which "He puts in the hours from 8 to 11:30 A.M., breaking it up with a series of 15-minute meetings, sometimes 10-minute meetings, but rarely is there a 30-minute meeting...At 11:30 he's 'outtahere'....[when he goes] over to the University of Texas track to run a three to five miles...return to the office at 1:30, where he'll play some video golf or computer solitaire until about three, and then it's back to the second 'hard half-day' until 5:30."

Dr. Justin Frank, a prominent Washington psychoanalyst, claims that Bush may have Attention Deficit Hyperactivity Disorder. (Bush Leagues, June 14, 2004)

Score (2)

4. Pathological lying

Psychopaths have no regard for the truth and according to Dr. Hare "Lying, deceiving, and manipulation are natural talents for psychopaths... When caught in a lie or challenged with the truth, they are seldom perplexed or embarrassed...they simply change their stories or attempt to rework the facts so that they appear to be consistent with the lie."

When President Bush declared war against Iraq on March 19, 2003, he claimed that "Intelligence gathered by this and other governments leaves no doubt that the Iraq regime continues to possess and conceal some of the most lethal weapons ever devised." On May 29, 2003, he claimed that weapons of mass destruction had been found. According to Bush "We found the weapons of mass destruction. We found biological laboratories...For those who say that we have not found the banned manufacturing devices or banned weapons, they're wrong, we found them." (CBSNEWS.com) His lies about weapons of mass destruction and ties to al Qaeda have become legendary.

Bush often lied to cover up his reckless behaviour before he became president including the time he appeared on "Meet the Press" with Tim Russert and falsely asserted that, "I got an honorable discharge and I did show up in Alabama." (*Niagara Falls Reporter*, Bill Gallagher) While it is true that he received an honorable discharge, it isn't true that he showed up. The 300 pages of documents recording his service record in the National Guard offer no explanation about why George W. missed months of required drill in Alabama and Houston between May 1972 and May 1973. His superior in Alabama claims that he never saw George W. Bush and another pilot, Bob Mintz, stationed at the same base in Alabama, claims he never saw him either. According to Mintz, "if he did any flying at all, on whatever kind of craft, that would have involved a great number of supportive personnel. It takes a lot of people to get a plane into the air. But nobody I can think of remembers him." (*Niagara Falls Reporter*) One document reads "Verbal orders of the Comdr on 1 Aug 72 suspending 1STLT George Bush...Reason for Suspension: Failure to accomplish annual medical examination."

Another lie occurred after Bush arrived for a photo op at a second-grade classroom in Sarasota , Florida, on September 11, 2001, at the same time that a plane had struck the north tower of the World Trade Center in New York. When President Bush attended a town-hall meeting in Orlando, Florida, he claimed that "I was sitting outside the classroom, waiting to go in, and I saw an airplane hit the tower..." An article by Scott J. Paltrow in the *Wall Street Journal* March 22, 2002, reported that there was no footage of the first plane until much later and the television in the room was unplugged. Bush told the town-hall meeting that "one of the first acts I did was put our military on alert." The *Wall Street Journal* found out that Air Force General Richard Myers, the acting head of the Joint Chiefs of Staff, made that decision himself while Bush was running from the school in Florida to Air Force One.

Score (2)

5. Conning/manipulative

One of the characteristics of a psychopath is the ability to charm and seduce followers or in this case the public. They lie convincingly and are seldom perplexed or embarrassed when caught in their deceit smoothly changing their story. Lies are the main weapon in their arsenal for manipulating others.

One example of manipulation occurred when President Bush distorted the words of former President Jimmy Carter to win support for the invasion of Iraq. President Bush claimed that the former President offered support for the invasion of Iraq when, in fact, Carter concluded that "as has been emphasized vigorously by foreign allies and by responsible leaders of former administrations and incumbent officeholders, there is no current danger to the United States from Baghdad." (*Washington Post*)

While most politicians are guilty of not delivering on all of their promises made during election campaigns, George W. Bush set new lows when he became Governor of Texas. Author Loren Franklin writing in the Portland Independent Media Center maintains that:

> George's record in the State of Texas is one of dismal failure in delivering on his promises for child health care. He, during his Governorship of that state broke nearly every promise he made to help the poor and needy. He drove the state into the ground and lied to the entire nation about it, while he was asking America to make him president. All for the goal of obtaining power…

Misleading the public during election campaigns is a form of manipulation particularly when you break almost all your promises.

Although he lied on the campaign trail as Governor, it can hardly be a sign of a psychopath; it's standard fare to make promises you never intended to keep, to exchange false promises for votes. His record in Texas clearly was destructive, but whether a governor's record is indicative of mental illness is a dicey judgment. But the unrelenting nature of the lies suggests he's really off his rocker. Consider his mischaracterization of Carter's statement on Iraq. And if that weren't enough, how he received and dealt with intelligence that conflicted with his own views on Iraq makes clear that there is no limit to his manipulation.

Seymour M. Hersh, in an article in the *New Yorker* referred to Bush's intention to manipulate the public when he stated that "The former intelligence official went on, 'One of the reasons I left was my sense that they [Bush Administration] were using the intelligence from the CIA and other agencies only when it fit their agenda. They didn't like the intelligence they were getting, and so they brought in people to write the stuff'." Hersh also reports that "A former high-level intelligence official told me that American Special Forces units had been sent into Iraq in mid-March, before the start of the air and ground war, to investigate sites suspected of being missile or chemical-and-biological-weapon storage depots. 'They came up with nothing,' the official said."

Score (2)

6. Lack of remorse or guilt

Dr. Hare explains that "...psychopaths show a stunning lack of concern for the devastating effects their actions have on others. Often they are completely forthright about the matter, calmly stating that they have no sense of guilt, are not sorry for the pain and destruction they have caused, and that there is no reason for them to be concerned."

When George W. Bush was Governor of Texas, he executed at least 131 prisoners, more than any other state, and has denied appeals from all but one of these prisoners. Worse, that number of 131 isn't a fixed number; there's some debate about how many death warrants he signed, and this is simply the lowest reliable number.

Texas is a big state, and the biggest state, California, didn't have the death penalty while Bush was governor of the lone star state. It makes sense then that, because of its large population, Texas would have the largest number of executions. And it is unfair to tag a death penalty proponent with a diagnosis that he is psychotic because he believes in the punishment. But other factors suggest a system—and a governor—had killed people denied a fair trial. James S. Liebman, professor at Columbia University, completed a study of prisoners on death row in the United States which showed that two-thirds of death convictions were upset on appeal for reasons such as incompetent defense lawyers or prosecutors who bent the rules. One-third of all the 131 prisoners in Texas had lawyers who were later disbarred. In 40 cases, the defendants' lawyer produced no evidence except for the occasional witness at the sentencing phase of the trial. In 29 cases a psychiatrist predicted that the defendant was likely to repeat the crime based on a hypothetical question and without having examined the defendant. Prosecution witnesses included a patient from a psychiatric ward and a pathologist who had admitted faking autopsies. When W. was asked about these statistics he replied in his trademark give-no-ground-self-confidence that "We've adequately answered innocent or guilty in each case." Yet it is well known that when cases were appealed to Governor Bush, he either did not read the details of the case or ignored the obvious injustices.

It gets worse: he blocked efforts to make the system more just. In addition to his refusal to recognize the inadequacy of the legal system in Texas to provide a proper defense, he vetoed a bill passed by the legislature that would have permitted counties in Texas to set up a public defender program for the poor.

Finally, he felt neither remorse nor guilt for the people he was sentencing to death. Most politicians, and perhaps most people generally, don't feel remorse or guilt when carrying out duties they believe in, and the absence of such emotions here can't normally be pointed to as evidence of insanity. But in the context in which he was acting, in a system that was unjust, and the manner in which he acted, without regard to the details of the cases, such blundering self confidence becomes an indicator that he lacks remorse and feelings of guilt.

Score (2)

7. Shallow emotional response

Shallow emotional response refers to the psychopath's limited range and depth of emotions. People in general can feel fear, sympathy, sadness because we can place ourselves in their experience and imagine how they would feel. A psychopath does not have this capacity although he can imitate feelings. The emotional poverty, the complete lack of real emotions such as sadness, mourning, fear, guilt, remorse and empathy is replaced by weak and infantile drives displaying themselves theatrically in the absence of ordinary inhibitions.

President Bush lacks the capacity to feel sadness for the loss of lives that are a direct result of his decisions. Author E. L. Doctorow refers to an incident in which "...You see him joking with the press, peering under the table for the weapons of mass destruction he can't seem to find." Despite the fact that over 1500 Americans and tens of thousands of Iraqis have lost their lives so far and countless numbers of Americans and Iraqi would suffer horrible injuries, the president was capable of joking around about the missing weapons of mass destruction. The president also refused at first to greet the body bags as they arrived back from the battlefields of Iraq and did not at first personally honour their sacrifice.

Professor Justin Frank, professor of psychiatry, notes in his book *Bush on the Couch* that:

- "He disregards the pain he inflicts on Iraqi citizens, refusing to comment on civilian casualties."

- "He rejoiced over the footage of Saddam's humiliation in captivity."

- "Bush allowed the media to show off the bodies of Saddam's two sons who were killed in a firefight."

- "Just before the March 20, 2003 speech announcing the commencement of bombing Iraq, Bush was captured on a White House television monitor saying, "Feels good.""

Score (2)

8. Callous/lack of empathy

Psychopaths seem to completely lack the ability to emphasize with others often resulting in very callous behaviour. Unable to empathize with the pain and suffering of others, they are able to exercise power without regard for the anguish of others and then rationalize their behaviour.

One of the most disturbing examples of Bush's lack of empathy revealed itself when the about-to-be-executed killer Karla Faye Tucker appeared on the Larry King Show. President Bush watched the show and, in discussing her appearance on the show, he responded contemptuously to King's question about what would you say to Governor Bush with "'please', Bush whimpers, his lips pursed in mock desperation, 'don't kill me.'" (The *Houston Chronicle*, August 10, 1999) It is one thing to believe in the death penalty but quite another to mock someone on death row, who spent years rehabilitating herself, even earning a plea from the Pope for her life. That behaviour exposes a frightening degree of callousness.

In another death row case, the sister of one African American man went to his office to ask Bush for mercy for her brother. Bush refused to shake her hand and treated her with contempt as she left his office in tears. He later signed the man's death warrant. (Loren Franklin, Portland Independent Media Center) He could have recognized that any relative of a person facing execution is going to feel pain and loss. Even if you are unmoved in your decision, it is surely a natural thing for that relative to plead for the sentence to be commuted, and hardly warrants the reaction of contempt. A truly empathetic person would be able to see that pain and acknowledge it, even if such understanding didn't then change the decision.

As mentioned above, during preparation for his television declaration of war against Iraq on BBC live he pumped his fist and muttered, "Feels good." Declaring a war in which many thousands of people on both sides will be killed or suffer horrible injuries is hardly the time for "feeling good." Once again, President Bush reveals his brutal callousness

Score (2)

9. Parasitic lifestyle

Due to their lack of motivation and low self-discipline, psychopaths frequently develop a financial dependence on others. Manipulation and exploitation are commonly employed to benefit from people who can provide them with financial assistance.

According to George W., in a rare yet accurate self-assessment, "…you know I could run for governor but I am basically a media creation. I've never done anything…I've worked for my dad. I worked in the oil business." In fact, his oil business ventures depended almost entirely on the support of others. It started when Roger Miller of the American Free Press reported that "James R. Bath, a friend and neighbor, used to funnel money from Osama bin Laden's brother, Salem bin Laden, to set up George in the oil business, according to the *Wall Street Journal* and other reputable sources." When the company foundered in the 1980s as oil prices dropped, it merged with Spectrum 7 which was a small oil company owned by two staunch Bush Sr. supporters, William De Witt and Mercer Reynolds. Although George W. did not impress anyone with his business acumen, De Witt and Reynolds installed Bush Jr. as president of the company. These friends were also owners of the Texas Rangers and allowed Bush Jr. to purchase part of the team at a very low price.

He eventually sold his shares in the company for $14 million. Spectrum 7 also began to founder and merged with Harken Energy in 1986. Bush Jr. received $227,000 worth of stock. Either the White House and/or Saudi Arabia smiled upon Harken as this tiny company won a contract from Bahrain to drill for offshore oil. George W. had many benefactors who protected him from failure and provided him with a substantial amount of money.

Score (2)

10. Poor behavioral controls

Psychopaths have very week control over their emotions and in particular annoyance and anger. They are prone to outbursts of irritability, impatience, threats, aggression, anger and verbal abuse.

President Bush's inability to control his feelings is legendary:

- "Within Bush, the tension between his quick temper and his capacity for detachment is not unique." (James Carney, *Time* Online Edition);

- "He is prone, I am told to foul-mouth temper tantrums in the White House." (Andrew Stephen, *The Observer*, London, UK);

- "He's a very angry guy, a hostile guy." (Mark Crispin Miller, Professor of Culture and Communications at New York University);

- "During the interview, given on Thursday in Washington, Bush displayed annoyance and at one point lost his temper when he was contradicted by Irish journalist Carole Coleman." (EU Business);

- "Bush's short-fused fiery temper under daily stress, especially from the news media..." (Jerry Mazza, Online Journal);

- "Bush's sense of unquestionable authority drives him out of control when anyone defies him." (Mike Hersh, Online Journal)

These popular perceptions are confirmed by his own former

speechwriter, David Frum, who admitted that: "He is impatient and quick to anger, sometimes glib, often dogmatic."

When a *Wall Street Journal* editor, Al Hunt, predicted that Bush's father would not be the 1988 Republican nominee, George W. shouted obscenities at him including "You fucking son of a bitch. I won't forget what you said and you're going to pay a price for it." (Real People for Real Change)

Score (2)

11. Promiscuous sexual behaviour

Psychopaths experience many superficial sexual relations, are indiscriminate about their sexual partners, and have a history to sexually coerce others into sexual relations.

There is no substantiated evidence of the above behaviour.

Score (0)

12. Early behavioral problems

Psychopaths usually have a history of behaviour and academic difficulties. As a child, they exhibited aberrant behaviors such as lying, stealing, cruelty to people or animals and vandalism.

There were a number of behavioral mishaps during Bush's childhood that were indicative of a troubled person. When he was at school, he threw a football through a third-grade classroom after being told to stay inside during the rain, sold false IDs to fellow students so that they could purchase alcohol and he was arrested for carrying out Halloween pranks. (*Bush on the Couch*, Justin Frank, professor of psychiatry)

Terry Throckmorton, a childhood friend of Bush, recalled how after a good rain thousands of frogs would come out and "Everyone would get BB guns and shoot them. Or we'd put firecrackers in the frogs and throw them up and blow them up." (Animals in Print, the On-Line Newsletter)

Score (2)

13. Lack of realistic long-term goals

Failure to develop and execute long-term plans and goals is another trait of psychopaths. They are incapable of thinking through their objectives step by step and tend to act impulsively or in terms of immediate emotional needs.

The clearest evidence that President Bush is not able to engage in long-term planning is the invasion and subsequent occupation of Iraq. Mary Shaw, a writer and activist, encapsulates the complete lack of any planning on the war on terrorism by calling to our attention that "...the Bush administration chose to divert troops from their search for the real threat—Osama Bin Laden—and launch a poorly planned war in Iraq, with inadequate supplies and no real exit strategy."

Mike Hersh, in Online Journal reports that "Rather than consider this counsel [top Republicans and foreign leaders] as he claims he's doing, Bush is stepping up his rush to war. This belies Bush's more placid public pronouncements in which he claims he will respect Congressional prerogatives...According to inside sources, this all for show. Bush has already made up his mind to attack Iraq."

Almost two years after the invasion, American forces have not yet gained control over most of Iraq. The so-called elections on the basis of which Bush claims that Iraq is now a democracy were a complete sham. There is no end in sight for peace and stability in Iraq and the withdrawal of American forces.

According to Paul C. Light, director of the Center for Public Services at the Brookings Institute, "George Bush tends to make decisions on the basis of hunch and intuition, and then pulls together groups that confirm his decisions." Ron Hutcheson, a writer for the Knight Ridders Newspapers, claims that "Bush's management style reflects his personality. He's action-oriented, impatient and intolerant of lengthy briefings and long debates."

Score (2)

14. Impulsivity

Often decisions are based on frustrations, temptations, urges or instincts rather than a careful, reflective planning process. There is a failure to consider the consequences of decisions.

President Bush admitted that "I make quick decisions without thinking about their possible results." He also confessed that "I say things and later regret having said them." (Maureen Dowd, *New York Times*) This isn't a particularly disturbing personality trait: lots of fine people make quick decisions they regret. Yet it is both part of a disturbing context outlined here and, worse, not the kind of character defect one wants in the leader of the most powerful nation in the world.

According to Ron Hutcheson, writer for the Knight Ridder Newspapers, "Bush's management style reflects his personality. He's action-oriented, impatient and intolerant of lengthy briefings and long debates. He often cited the importance of instincts in making decisions." Bill Gallagher, of the *Niagara Falls Reporter*, observed that "In dangerous situations requiring subtlety, delicacy and sophistication, George W. relies on his primitivism, sold as boldness, but is really disguised recklessness. That instinctive behaviour has consistently brought great harm to our nation and the world." Bob Woodward, who has written several books about President Bush, claims that "Bush looks at problems, and he told me, he said—'I am a gut player. I play by instincts. I don't play by the book.' And, of course, the book is Policy 101 about how you make these kinds of decisions [on going to war in Iraq]."

Robert Parry, a writer for Consortium News, states that "By overruling the Marine commander [Marine Lt. Gen. James T. Conway was in favour of a measured response as opposed to an all-out assault] in Fallujah in April 2004, Bush managed to make the United States look first reckless and then feckless, as U.S. Marines and Iraqi civilians died in a hasty assault that was then abruptly abandoned."

Score (2)

15. Irresponsibility

Psychopaths repeatedly fail to honour commitments and obligations. They are also frequently absent from or late for work. Another way in which they are irresponsible is to be oblivious or indifferent to the harm that they inflict on others.

The strongest indictment against George Bush for his pervasive irresponsibility comes not from a liberal but from a conservative Republican, Bob Bowman, when he charges that:

George W. Bush, though, while using force to intervene in the internal affairs of other nations, has sought to undermine the United Nations at every opportunity. He denigrated the inspection regime that the U.S. had imposed on Iraq through the UN. He flouted the will of the Security Council, including our closest historical allies. He withdrew from, violated, or ignored treaty after treaty. And he violated international law and the Nuremberg principles which the US instigated by his unprovoked attack on Iraq. He has show utter disdain for world opinion and has alienated both friend and foe with his irresponsible and arrogant go-it-alone cowboy attitude.

George A. Akerlof, American Nobel Prize laureate for Economics, castigates Bush and his administration for irresponsible economic policies. According to Akerlof, "I think this is the worst government the US has ever had in its more than 200 years of history. It [Bush administration] has engaged in extraordinarily irresponsible policies not only in foreign policy and economics but also in social and environmental policy…"

Joseph Wilson, a former American ambassador, was assigned the task of investigating claims that Iraq was buying Uranium yellowcake from Niger. Yellowcake is uranium ore that has been partly processed but not yet enriched for use in nuclear reactors or bombs. After spending a couple of days in Niger in February, 2002 Wilson stated flatly that no evidence existed of such a sale and reported his findings to the CIA and State Department. In January 2003, President George W. Bush used the now debunked Niger uranium claims in his State of the Union Address to bolster his case for declaring war on Iraq. The claim was based on documents that the administration knew were forged. When Wilson reacted to the Bush lie by writing an article in the *New York Times*, the White House exposed his wife Valerie Plame as a CIA agent. Revealing the name of a CIA agent is the pinnacle of irresponsibility. Note that this vindictive act was meant to serve as a deterrent to others who had the temerity to criticize the President.

Score (2)

16. Failure to accept responsibility for their own actions

The psychopath cannot accept responsibility for his self-destructive behaviour or for the harm he inflicts on others. He will usually deny categorically responsibility for his actions and will transfer the blame elsewhere.

On the personal level, George W. has frequently refused to take responsibility for the mistakes he has made before he became president. Bush denied that he was stopped by a state trooper for drunk driving in 1976 and when he finally did admit his actions, he said that he paid a fine on the spot whereas, in fact, he had to attend a court hearing. (*George W. Bush, The Dark Side*)

President Bush has produced a procession of lies to justify the invasion of Iraq. As each justification was exposed as invalid, he introduced a new lie to prove the necessity of the invasion. The first justification was WMD, then it was ties to al-Qaeda, purchasing nuclear material, removing Saddam and finally building a democracy in Iraq with a few more lies thrown in for good measure. When it was abundantly clear that Iraq did not possess weapons of mass destruction he continued to lie about it until he was forced to invent a new lie. When Joseph Wilson reported that Niger was not selling uranium to Iraq, he still mentioned it in his State of the Union Address. He never accepted responsibility for using any of those justifications but instead, he lied more until it was no longer possible.

Score (2)

17. Many short-term relationships

There is no evidence of the above behaviour.

Score (0)

18. Juvenile delinquency

After the age of 13, psychopaths experience behaviour problems involving aggression, manipulation, or exploitation. They also exhibit resentment towards authority.

Three independent sources close to the Bush family have confirmed that in 1972 George Bush was arrested three times for cocaine possession and taken to Harris County Jail but avoided formal charges. (Real People for Real Change)

On September 4, 1976, a state trooper observed George W. swerve onto the shoulder, then back onto the road. He blew .10 alcohol on a sobriety test and was convicted of driving under the influence of alcohol and had his license suspended.

He was also a truant when as a young man he went AWOL from the National Guard.

When he was 26 years old, he crashed a car while drinking under the influence of alcohol. On arriving home, his father asked him to step into the den to which George W. replied, "You wanna go mano a mano right here" demonstrating resentment toward authority. (Robert Parry, Consortium News)

Score (2)

19. Revocation of conditional release

A revocation of probation due to technical violations.
There is no evidence of the above behavior

Score (0)

20. Criminal versatility

A psychopath demonstrates a diversity of types of criminal offenses regardless of whether the person has been arrested or convicted. He takes pride in the crimes that he has committed.

There is no evidence of the above behavior

Score (0)

Total score (32)

* * *

According to Dr. Hare, any score above 30 indicates strong psychopathic tendencies. Based on the above test results, President Bush qualifies as a psychopath. This explains much of George W's behaviour including the killing of thousands of innocent people in Afghanistan and Iraq. It would also explain his ability to tolerate the torturing of prisoners in Afghanistan, Iraq and Guantanamo Bay. His ability to lie point-blank with seeming honesty and candor can also be attributed to his psychopathic tendencies.

As even a cursory look at the evidence from preceding chapters suggests, George W. Bush is not the only president with psychopathic tendencies. Although the test establishes George W. as a psychopath, it is safe to conclude that any president engaged in lying and empire-building must have some of the traits of a psychopath as well. To murder innocent people in order to aggrandize the American Empire would be extremely difficult if not impossible for someone who feels empathy, remorse and guilt and who is incapable of lying. It might even be suggested that having at least some psychopathic traits is a qualification for the job. What this means is that no person in either the Democratic or Republican Party could be a serious contender for their party's nomination if they were not prepared to maintain and expand the American Empire. The imperatives of empire have become larger than any one person, even the President. His job is to lie and serve the empire.

Bibliography

Abrahams, F. and Anderson, E. (2004, October). *Humanitarian Law Violations in Kosovo*. Retrieved from the Human Rights Watch Web Site: http://www.hrw.org/reports98/kosovo/.

Allen, M. (2003 August 3). *Bush Aces Physical, Begins a Month at Ranch*. Washingtonpost.com:http://wwwwashingtonpost.com/ac2/wp-dyn/A15546-2003Aug2?

Alperovitz, G. (1989). *Was Hiroshima Necessary to End the War*. Retrieved from the War Resisters League Web Site: https://www.peacewire.org/photoexibits/hiroshima/articles/hironecessary.html.

Alperovitz, G. (1995). *The Decision to Use the Atomic Bomb*. Toronto: Random House of Canada.

Austin, B. S. (1996). *The Nuremberg War Crime Trials*. Retrieved from Middle Tennessee State University Web Site: http://www.mtsu.edu/~baustin/trials.htm.

Avalon Project. (n.d.). *The Moscow Conference: October 1943*. Retrieved from Yale Law School Web Site: http://www.yale.edu/lawweb/avalon/imt/moscow.htm.

Avalon Project. (1964 August 7). *The Gulf of Tonkin Resolution* (Joint Resolution of Congress: H.J. Res 1145 August 7, 1964). Retrieved from Yale Law School Web Site: http://www.yale.edu/lawweb/avalon/tonking.htm.

Avalon Project. (1996). *President Johnson's Message to Congress Aug. 1964*. Retrieved from Yale Law School Web Site: http://www.yale.edu/lawweb/avalon/tonlein-g.htm.

Beane, L. (Ed.). (2000 July/August). *George W. Bush Blew up Frogs*. Retrieved from the Animals in Print On-Line Newsletter Web Site: http://www.allcreatures.org/aip/nl-3nov2000-frogs.html.

Becker, B. (1992). *Iraq*. Retrieved from the Commission of Inquiry for the International War Crimes Tribunal Web Site: http://www.deoxy.org/WC/WC-consp.htm.

Black, I. (2003 January 21). *Serbian Leaders Surrender to Hague Tribunal*. London: The Guardian. Retrieved from http://www.guardian.co.uk/serbia/article/0,2479,879146,00.html.

Blackburn, R. (1999 May 25). *Kosovo: The Lost Chances and Continuing Dangers*. Petrolia (CA): Counterpunch. Retrieved from http://www.counterpunch.org/wtarchive.html.

Blix, H. (2003 January 27). *An Update on Inspection* (Report to the UN). Retrieved from the UN Web Site: http://www.un.org/Depts/unmovic/Bx27.htm.

Blix, H. (2003 February 14). *Briefings of the Security Council, 14 February 2003: An Update on Inspections*. Retrieved from the UN Web Site: http://www.un.org/Depts/unmovic/new/pages/security_council_briefings.asp.

Blix, H. (2003 April, 9). *War Planned 'Long in Advance'*. News24. Retrieved from http://www.news24.com/News24/World/Iraq/0, 2-10-1460_1345303,00.html.

Blum, W. (1998). *Killing Hope: Military and CIA Intervention Since World War II*. Montreal: Black Rose Books.

Blum, W. (2003). *America: Rogue States* (Extract). Monroe (ME): Common Courage Press. Retrieved from http://www.doublestandards.org/usmurder.html.

Bogdarich, G. and Lettmayers, M. (Producers). (2000 October). *Yugoslavia: The Avoidable War* [videotape]. New York: Frontier Theatre and Film Inc.

Bowman, B. (2003 November). *A Conservative Republican Challenge to George W. Bush*. Retrieved from Space & Security News Web Site: http://www.rmbowman.com/ssn/ConservativeRepublican.htm.

Boyle, A. B. (2002 December 14). *International Crisis and Neutrality: US Foreign Policy Toward the Iran/Iraq war*. Petrolia (CA): CounterPunch. Retrieved from http://www.counterpunch.org/boy/c1214.

Brière, E. (Producer). (1996). *Bitter Paradise: The Sellout of East Timor* [videotape]. Vancouver: Snapshot Productions.

Buchanan, A. R. (1964). *The United States and World War II*. New York: Harper and Row.

Bureau of European Affairs, U.S. Department of State. (1999). *Understanding the Rambouillet Accords* (Fs-990301). Retrieved from http://www.state.gov/www/regions/eur/fs_990301_rambouillet.html.

Burrows, G. (2002). *The Arms Trade*. Toronto: New Internationalist Publications.

Bush Watch. (2001 February 9). *Do We Really Want A Part-Time President*. Retrieved from the Bush Watch Web Site: http://www.bushnews.com/dyslexia.htm.

Byrne, M. (1990 January 25). *The Iran-Contra Scandal in Perspective*. The Nation-al Security Archives. Retrieved from http://nsarchive.chadwych.com/icessay.htm.

Carvin, A. (1999). *Cambodia Colonized: The Fall of Angkor to the Arrival of the French*. Retrieved from http://wwwedwebproject.org/sideshow/history/French.html.

Center for History. (n.d.). *Quotes by U.S. Military Leaders WW II*. Retrieved from http://hnn.us/comments/7362.html.

Chomsky, N. (1989). *Necessary Illusions: Thought Control in a Democratic Society*. Toronto: CBC.

Chomsky, N. (1991 February). *The Gulf Crisis*. Woods Hole (MA): Z Magazine. Retrieved from http://www.zena.

secureforum.com/Znet/zmag/articles/chomulfalb.

Chomsky, N. (1993). *What Uncle Sam Really Wants*. Berkeley (CA): Odonian Press.

Chomsky, N. (1993). *Year 501: The Conquest Continues*. Montreal: Black Rose Books.

Chomsky, N. (1997). *Perspectives on Power: Reflections on Human Nature and the Social Order*. Montreal: Black Rose Books.

Chomsky, N. (1999). *Profits Over People: Neoliberalism and the New World Order*. Montreal: Black Rose Books.

Chomsky, N. (1999). *The New Military Humanism: Lessons From Kosovo*. Vancouver: New Star Books.

Chomsky, N. and Albert, M. (1991 February). *Gulf War Pullout*. Woods Hole (MA): Z Magazine. Retrieved from http://www.zena.secureforum.com/Znet/zmag/articles/chomgulfalb.

Chomsky, N. and Albert, M. (2003 April 13). *Noam Chomsky Interviewed*. Woods Hole (MA): Z Magazine. Retrieved from http://www.zmag.org/CrisesCurEvts/Iraq/noam_chomsky.htm.

Civil Intelligence Association. (1973). *Results of the 1973 Church Committee Hearings on CIA Misdeeds*. Retrieved from http://pwl.net.com/~ncoic/CIA_info.htm.

Clark, R. (Producer). (1991 March 5). *Nowhere to Hide: Ramsey Clark in Iraq* [videotape]. San Francisco: International Action Center.

Clark, R. (1996 January 29). *Letter to the UN Security Council*. Retrieved from http://www.iacenter.org/rcsan.htm.

Clark, R. (2002). *The Fire This Time: War Crimes in the Gulf*. New York: International Action Center.

Cleckley, H. (2004). *THE PSYCHOPATH—The Mask of Sanity*. Retrieved from: http://www.cassiopaea.com/cassiopaea/psychopath.htm.

Cockburn, A. and St. Clair, J. (Eds.). (1999 June). *Who NATO Killed*. Petrolia (CA): Counterpunch. Retrieved from http://www.counterpunch.org/dead.html.

Coleman, C. (2004 June 26). *White House Axes Laura Bush Interview*. EU Business: http://www.eubusiness.com/afp/040626185643+dutspl.

Conover, B. (2001). *Bush isn't a moron, he's a cunning sociopath*. Retrieved from Serendipity Web Site: http://www.serendipity.li/wot/conover01.htm.

Cornell Law School. (2002). *International Court of Justice*. Retrieved from Cornell Law School Web Site: www.lawschool.cornell.edu/librar.

Crime Prevention Group. (n.d.). *Early Efforts to Prevent Genocide, Act Against Mass Killing, and Maintain Peace on an International Basis*. Retrieved from http://medicolegal.tripod.com/earlyintlaw.htm.

Cronin, R. P. (1984). *The Kissinger Commission*. Retrieved from http://www.uscubacommission.org/kisscom.htm.

Damon, D. (2001 January 8). *News from Serbia: Depleted Uranium*. Central Europe Review. Retrieved from http://www.ce-review.org/index_01_3.html.

Doctorow, E. L. (2004 September 9). *The Unfeeling President*. Retrieved from the East Hampton Star Web Site: http://www.easthamptonstar.com/20040909/col5.htm.

Dreyfuss, R. (2000 January/February). *Apocalypse Still*. Retrieved from Mother Jones Web Site: http://www.motherjones.com/news/feature/2000/01/orange.html.

EuropaWorld. (2001 June). *The Convention on the Prevention and Punishment of the Crime of Genocide*. Retrieved from the EuropaWorld Web Site: http://www.europaworld.org/issue40/the conventiontheprev ention22601.htm.

Farrel, J. (n.d.). *To Start a War: The Tonkin Gulf Incident*. Retrieved from the Cold War Web Site: http://www.audfaz.com/coldwar/tonkin.htm.

Ferrel, R. H. (Ed.). (1966). *Truman and the Bomb, a Documentary History*. Boulder: High Plains Publishing Co. Retrieved from the Truman Presidential Museum and Library Web Site: http://www.trumanlibrary.org/whistlestop/study_collections/bomb/large/ferrell.htm.

Flounders, S. (2003 August 18). *Another War Crime? Iraqi Cities "Hot" with Depleted Uranium*. Retrieved from the International Action Center Web Site: http://www.iacenter.org/du-warcrime.htm.

Flounders, S. (2003 August 28). *How U.S. Policies Made the UN a Target*. Retrieved from the International Action Center Web Site: http://iacenter.org?iraq-un3.htm.

Foley, G. (1999 April). *Under Cover of U.S./NATO's Intervention, Serbs Intensify Attack on Kosovo*. Retrieved from the Socialist Action Web Site: http://www.socialistaction.org/news/199904/kosovo.html.

Franklin, L. (2001 October 24). *Socialized Psychopath, George W. Bush, America's Number One Evildoer*. Retrieved from the Independent Media Centers Web Site: http://portland.indymedia.org/en/2001/10/4188.

shtml.

Gill, N. S. (1987 December). *Ancient Iran-Persia, the Medes and the Persians.* Retrieved from www.ancienthistory. about.com/cs/persiaempirl/a/persiaintro.htm.

Goodman, A. (2004 June 22). *Bill Clinton Loses His Cool on Democracy Now!* Retrieved from the Democracy Now Web Site: http://www.democracynow.org/article.pl?sid=4/06/22/1482588mode=thread&fid=25.

Goose, S. (2003 April 1). *U.S. Using Cluster Munitions in Iraq.* Retrieved from Human Rights Watch Web Site: http://www.hrw.org/press/2003/04/us040103.htm.

Gordon, B. (2000 May). *Reflections on Hiroshima.* Retrieved from the Wesleyan University Web Site: http://www.wgordon.web.wesleyan.edu/papers/author.htm.

Graham, D. (2000 January 26). *The Holocaust.* Retrieved from the Holocaust Ring Web Site: www.datasync.com/~davidg59/genocide.html.

Grant, J. S., Moss, L. A. G. and Unger, J. (Eds.). (1971). *Cambodia: The Widening War in Indochina.* New York: Washington Square Press.

Grimm, N. (2003 April 25). *Pressure on US to Remove Depleted Uranium from Iraq.* Retrieved from ABC Radio Australia Web Site: www.abc.net.au/am/content/2003/s840116.htm.

Grobe, W. and Eineit, N. (1999 December). *Rambouillet: NATO Demanded the Right of Military Occupation of the Whole of Yugoslavia.* Berlin: Neue Einheit Magazine. Retrieved from www.neue-einheit.com.

Harry S. Truman Library. (1945). *Hiroshima.* (Harry Truman's Diaries and Papers). Retrieved from https://www.doug-long.con/hst.htm.

Herman, E. (1992). *Beyond Hypocrisy: Decoding the News in an Age of Propaganda.* Montreal: Black Rose Books.

Herman, E. S., and Chomsky, N. (1988). *Manufacturing Consent: The Political Economy of the Mass Media.* New York: Pantheon Books.

Hersh, M. (2002). *White House insiders say Bush is "out of control".* Retrieved from Online Journal Web Site: http://www.onlinejournal.com/Special_Reports/Hersh091202/hersh091202.html.

Hersh, S. M. (1983). *The Price of Power: Kissinger in the Nixon Whitehouse.* New York: Simon & Shuster, Inc.

History of the U.N. (2000). *Basic Facts About the United Nations.* Retrieved from http://www.un.org/aboutun/history.htm.

Holm, E. (2005 February 15). *Iraq Vets Say Services, Compassion Lacking.* Retrieved from Common Dreams Web Site: http://www.commondreams.org/cgibin/print.cgi?file=/headlines05/0215-07.htm.

Huck, J. (2003 January, issue #50). *Covert War in Guatemala.* Press for Conversion, pp. 14-15. Retrieved from www.coat.ncf.ca/our_magazine/links/issue50/files/50_14- 15.pdf.

Human Rights Watch. (1998). *Violations of the Rules of War by Insurgents.* Retrieved from http://www.hrw.org/reports98/kosovo98-10.htm.

Human Rights Watch. (2001). *Human Rights Developments in Guatemala.* Retrieved from https://www.hrw.org/wr2k1/americas/guatemala.html.

Human Rights Watch. (2001). *Under Orders: War Crimes in Kosovo.* Retrieved from https://www.hrw.org/reports/2001/kosovo/undworld-01.htm.

Human Rights Watch. (2001 October). *Cluster Bombs in Afghanistan.* Retrieved from http://www.hrw.org/backgrounder/arms/cluster-bck1031.htm.

Human Rights Watch. (2002 January). *Background Paper on Geneva Conventions and Persons Held by U.S. Forces.* Retrieved from http://www.hrw.org/backgrounder/usa/pow-bck.htm.

Human Rights Watch. (2002 December). *U.S. Cluster Bombs Killed Civilians in Afghanistan.* Retrieved from http://www.hrw.org/press/2002/12/arms1218.htm.

Human Rights Watch. (2003). *U.S. Using Cluster Munitions in Iraq.* Retrieved from http://www.hrw.org/press/04/us040103.htm.

Hutcheson, R. (2004 March 25). *Insiders offer unflattering accounts of Bush's decision-making style Knight Ridder Newspapers Web Site:* http://www.realcities.com/mld/krwashington/news/nation/8277263.htm.

Immerman, R. H. (1982). *The CIA in Guatemala: The Foreign Policy of Intervention.* Austin: University of Texas Press.

International Action Center. (n.d.). *Sanctions Violate International Law.* Retrieved from http://www.iacenter.org/sanction.htm.

International Action Center. (2003 April 2). *The World Stands Together Against War.* Retrieved from http://www.iacenter.org/iraq_watch.htm.

International Atomic Energy Agency: Iraq Nuclear Verification Office. (2002 November 27). *IAEA's Mandate in*

Iraq. Retrieved from http://www.iaea.org/worldatom/Programmes/ActionTeam/.

International Court of Justice. (1986 June 27). *Military and Paramilitary Activities in and Against Nicaragua (Nicaragua v. United States of America)*. Retrieved from http://212.153.43.18/icj/www/icases/inus/inusframe.htm.

International Criminal Tribunal for the Former Yugoslavia. (1999 May 6). *Notice of the Existence of Information Concerning Serious Violations of International Human-itarian Law Within the Jurisdiction of the Tribunal*. Retrieved from http://jurist.law.pitt.edu/icty.htm.

International Law Commission. (1950). *Principles of the Nuremberg Tribunal*. Retrieved from http://deoxy.org/wc/wc-nurem.htm.

International Red Cross. (n.d.). *International Humanitarian Law*. Retrieved from http://www.redcross.lv/en/conventions.htm.

Iraq Body Count Project. (2003 November). *How Many Civilians were Killed by Cluster Bombs*. Retrieved from http://www.iraqbodycount.net/bodycount.htm.

Iraq Body Count Project. (2003 December). *Iraq Body Count*. Retrieved from http://www.iraqbodycount.net/bodycount.htm.

Joint Resolution of Both Houses of Congress. (1973 November 7). *War Powers Resolution* (Public Law 93-148). Retrieved from http://www.usconstitution.com/WarPowersResolution.htm.

Karnow, S. (1999). *Vietnam: A History*. New York: Penguin Books.

Kolko, G. (1988). *Confronting the Third World: United States Foreign Policy 1945-1980*. Toronto: Random House of Canada Limited.

La Riva, G. (Producer). (1999 June). *NATO Targets* [videotape]. San Francisco: International Action Center.

Lee, R. A. (2000). *Warfare and Conflict Between Kosovar Albanians and Serbs since 1912*. Retrieved from the History Guy's Web Site: www.historyguy.com/kosovar_serb_warfare.html.

Lewis, A. (2000 June 17). *Texas Executions: GW Bush Has Defined Himself Unforgettably, As Shallow and Callous*. Retrieved from the Common Dreams Web Site: http://www.commondreams.org/views/061700-102.htm.

Linder, D. (n.d.). *Charter of the International Military Tribunal*. Retrieved from the University of Missouri-Kansas City Law School Web Site: http://www.law.umkc.edu/faculty/projects/ftrials/nuremberg/nuremberg.htm.

Linder, D. (n.d.). *The Nuremberg Trials: A Chronology*. Retrieved from the University of Missouri-Kansas City Law School Web Site: http://www.law.umkc.edu/faculty/projects/ftrials/nuremberg/nuremberg.htm.

Long, D. (1995). *Hiroshima: Was it Necessary?* Retrieved from http://www.douglong/hiroshima.htm.

Lyons, M. J. (1999). *World War II: A Short History*. Upper Saddle River (NJ). Prentice-Hall Inc.

Macarthur, J. R. (1992). *Second Front: Censorship and Propaganda in the Gulf War*. New York: Hill and Wang.

Mackay, N. (2004 September 12). *Unmasked: The George W. Bush the President Doesn't Want the World To See*. Sunday Herald Online: http://wwwsundayherald.com.44773.

Macmillan, M. (2001). *Paris 1919: Six Months that Changed the World*. New York: Random House.

Mahajan, R. (2003). *Full Spectrum Dominance: U.S. Power in Iraq and Beyond*. Toronto: Hudson House.

Marjaleena, R. (1999 May 20). *Demonizing the Serbs*. Petrolia (CA): CounterPunch. Retrieved from http://www.counterpunch.org/disinfo.htm.

Masri, R. (1998). Sanctions are Criminal. In B. Becker and Sara Flounders (Eds.), *Challenge to Genocide: Let Iraq Live*. (pp. 33-37). New York: International Action Center.

Mazza, J. (2004 October 14). *The Big Picture Shows Bush in Big Mental Trouble*. Online Journal: http://www.onlinejournal.com/Special_reports/101404mazza.htm.

Mennonite Central Committee. (2003). *Cluster Bombs in Afghanistan*. Retrieved from http://www.mcc.org/clusterbomb/afghanistan/index.html.

Miller, R. (2001). *Bush & Bin Laden – George W. Had Ties to Billionaire bin Laden Brood*. Retrieved from American Free Press Web Site: http://www.americanfreepress.net/10_07_01/Bush_Bin_Laden-George_W_B/bush_bin_laden.

Mitchel, P. R. and Schoeffel, J. (Eds.). (2002). *Understanding Power: The Indispensable Chomsky*. New York: The New Press.

Möise, E. E. (1998 November 4). *The First Indochina War*. Retrieved from Clemson University Law School Web Site: http://hubcap.clemson.edu/~eemoise/viet3.htm.

Nambiar, S. (1998). The Fatal Flaws Underlying NATO's Intervention in Yugoslavia. In Michael Parenti, *To Kill A Nation: The Attack on Yugoslavia* (p. 32). New York: Verso.

Office of the United Nations High Commissioner for Human Rights. (2002). *Geneva Conventions Relative to the Protection of Civilian Persons in the Time of War.* Retrieved from the United Nations Web Site: http://www.unhchr.ch/htm/menu3/b/92.htm.

Organization of American States. (1997). *Charter of the Organization of American States.* Retrieved from http://www.unhchr.ch/htm/menu3/b/92.htm.

Oziewicz, E. (2004 January 9). *U.S. Exaggerated Iraqi Threat.* Toronto: The Globe and Mail.

Parenti, M. (1996). *Dirty Truths: Reflections on Politics, Media, Ideology, Conspiracy, Ethnic Life and Class Power.* San Francisco: City Light Books.

Parenti, M. (2000). *To Kill a Nation: The Attack on Yugoslavia.* New York: Verso.

PBS Television Network. (1987 March 4). *President Reagan's Speech About Iran Contra.* Retrieved from http://pbs.org/wgbh/amex/reagan/filmmore/reference/primary/irancontra.html.

Peurifoy, J. E. (1954). *Communist Aggression in Guatemala, 1954.* Report to the Subcommittee on Latin America of the Select Committee on Communist Aggression (U.S. House of Representatives). Retrieved from http://www.wadsworth.com/history_features/ext/ap/chapter28/chapter28.3.html.

Pilger, J. (2003 September 23). *Lies and More Lies.* Znet Commentaries. Retrieved from http://www.zmag.org/sustainers/content/2003-23/01pilger.cfm.

Plesch, D. (2003 February 5). *U.S. Claims Dismissed by Blix.* London: The Guardian. Retrieved from http://www.guardian.co.uk/Iraq/story/0,2763,889135,00.html.

Politex, J. (2003). *Bush And Busher: What Is His Problem.* Retrieved from the Bush Watch Web Site: http://bushwatch.org/ego.htm.

Public Papers of the Presidents. (August 9, 1945). *Radio Report to the American People on the Potsdam Conference—August 9, 1945.* Retrieved from http://www.presidency.ucsb.edu/site/docs/index_ppus.php.

Public Papers of the Presidents. (1999 March 24). *President Clinton's Address to the Nation on Airstrikes Against Serbian Targets in the Federal Republic of Yugoslavia* (DOCID: pap_text-247). Washington (DC): Government Printing Office. Retrieved from http://www.frwebgate4.access.gpo.gov/cgi-bin/waisgate.cgi.

Public Papers of the Presidents. (1999 April 15). *President Clinton's Question and Answer Session with the American Society of Newspaper Editors* (DOCID: pap_text- 308). Washington (DC): U.S. Government Printing Office. Retrieved from http://frwebgate.access.gpo.gov/cgi-bin/multidb.cgi.

Raddatz, M. (1999 June 11). *Washington Week: Interview with President Clinton.* Retrieved from PBS Online's Web Site: http://www.pbs.org/weta/washingtonweek/transcripts/transcripts990611.html.

Rampton, S. and Stauber, J. (2003). *Weapons of Mass Deception: The Use of Propaganda in Bush's War on Iraq.* New York: Penguin.

Reagan, R. (1985 April 14). *Letter to the Presidents of Columbia, Mexico, Panama and Venezuela on the Central American Peace Process.* Washington: Office of the Press Secretary. Retrieved from http://www.reagan.utexas.edu/resource/speeches/1985/40485h.htm.

Ritter, S. (1999). *Endgame: Solving the Iraq Crisis.* Toronto: Simon & Shuster.

Ritter, S. (2003). *Frontier Justice: Weapons of Mass Destruction and the Bushwacking of America.* New York: Context Books.

Robinson, J. P. and Goldblat, J. (1984 May). *Chemical Warfare in the Iran-Iraq War.* Retrieved from Stockholm International Peace Research Web Site: http://projects.sipri.se/cbw/research/factsheet-1984.html.

Salinger, P. and Laurent, E. (1991). *Secret Dossier: The Hidden Agenda Behind the Gulf War.* New York: Penguin Books.

Saltveit, M. (Ed.). (2003). *George W. Bush Jr.—The Dark Side.* Retrieved from Real People for Real Change Web Site: http://www.realchange.org/bushjr.htm.

Scahill, J. (2001 January 31). *Depleted Uranium, Just the Tip of the Iceberg in Serbia.* Common Dreams Newscentre. Retrieved from http://www.commondreams.org/views01/0131-05.htm.

Senate Committee on Drugs, Law Enforcement and Foreign Policy. (1988 December). *Narcotic Traffickers and the Contras.* Retrieved from http://www.webcom.com/pinknoiz/covert/contracoke/html.

Shaw, M. (2005 January 1). *The Sociopathic Bush Administration.* Retrieved from Philadelphia Independent Media Centers Web Site: http://wwwphillyimc.org/article.pl?op=Print&sid=05/01/011925259&mode=thread.

Shawcross, W. (2002). *Sideshow: Kissinger, Nixon, and the Destruction of Cambodia* (2nd ed.). New York: First Cooper Square Press.

Simic, A. (1993). *The First and Last Yugoslav State: Some Thoughts on the Dissolution of the State.* In David A.

Kideckel (Ed.), Anthropology of East Europe Review (ch.1). Chicago: DePaul University. Retrieved from http://depaul.edu/~rrotenbe/aeer/aeer11_1/simic.html.

Sklar, H. (1988). *Washington's War on Nicaragua*. Toronto: Between the Lines.

Sowards, S. W. (2003). *The Yugoslav Civil War*. In Twenty-five Lectures on Modern Balkan History, Humanities and Social Sciences Online. Retrieved from http://www.lib.msu.edu/sowards/balkan/lect25.htm.

Spector, R. H. (1984). *Eagles Against the Sun: The American War with Japan*. Toronto: Random House.

Streeter, S. M. (2000 November). *Interpreting the 1954 U.S. Intervention in Guatemala: Realist, Revisionist, and Postrevisionist Perspectives*. Retrieved from McMaster University History Cooperative Web Site: http://www.historycooperative.org/journals/ht/34.1/streeter.htm.

Streitz, M. (2003 July 29). *US Nobel Laureate Slams Bush Gov't as "Worst" in American History*. Retrieved from Common Dreams News Center Web Site: http://www.commondreams.org/cgi-bin/print.cgi?file=/he.

Telford, R. (2001). *John Wayne Goes to Managua: US covert Policy in Nicaragua During the Reagan Administration*. Paper presented at the 2001 Symposium of the Conference of Defence Associations Institute. Paper retrieved from: http://www.cdacdai.ca/pdf/telfordpaper.pdf.

The American War Library. (1988). *Gulf of Tonkin Notebook*. Retrieved from http://members.aol.com/warlibrary/vwton3.htm.

The American War Library. (1988). *Notes on the Gulf of Tonkin Incident*. Retrieved from http://members.aol.com/warlibrary/vwton2.htm.

The Odyssey: World Trek for Service and Education. (1999 February 27). *U.S. Responsibility for Guatemalan Genocide*. Retrieved from http://www.worldtrek.org/odyssey/latin america/022799/022799dumbnina.html.

The Pentagon. (1971). *The Pentagon Papers*. Boston: Beacon Press. Retrieved from http://www.mthdyoke.edu/acad/intrel.htm.

Thompson, D. (2004 June 4). *Bush's Erratic Behavior Worries White House Aides*. Retrieved from Capitol Hill Blue Web Site: http://www.capitolhillblue.com/artman/publish/printer_article_4636.shtml.

Trent, B. (Producer), Kasper, D. (Director). (1992). *The Panama Deception: Exposing the Cover Up* [videotape]. Los Angeles: Rhino Home Video.

Trent, M., McCormick, J. (n.d.). *Psycho or Not*. Retrieved from the Stewart Productions Web Site: http://wwwibduk.org/psycho_or_not.htm.

Truman Presidential Library. (1945 June 18). *Minutes of Meeting Held at the White House on Monday, 18 June 1945*. Retrieved from http://www.trumanlibrary.org/whistlestop/study_collections/bomb/large/meeting-minutes/bmil13-5.htm.

Truman Presidential Library. (1945 August 9). *Truman's Diary Entries August 1945*. Retrieved from http://www.trumanlibrary.org/whistlestop/study_collections/bomb/large/trumandiaries/bma3-5.htm.

United Nations Human Rights Website. (2002). *Charter of the United Nations*. Retrieved from http://193.194.138.190/html/menu3/b/ch-chpl.htm.

United Nations Security Council. (n.d.). *Security Council Resolutions*. Retrieved April 29, 2003, from http://www.un.org/documents/scres.htm.

Walsh, L. E. (1993 August 4). *Final Report to the Independent Council for Iran/Contra Matters*. Retrieved from http://www.fas.org/irp/offdocs/walsh/.

Weisbrot, M. (2001 November 9). *What Everyone Should Know About Nicaragua*. Znet Commentaries. Retrieved from http://www.zmag.org/Sustainers/content/200111/09weisbrot.cfm.

Williams, M. (1995 September 25). *Bombing Campaign in Bosnia Intensifies*. The Militant (pp. 1). Retrieved from http://www.themilitant.com/1995/5935/5935_12.html.

Willson, B. (1990). *How the U.S. Purchased the 1990 Nicaraguan Elections*. Retrieved from http://www.brianwillson.com/awolniceelection.html.

Wolf, J. (2000). *The Iran-Contra Affair*. Retrieved from PBS Television Web Site: http://www.pbs.org/wgbh/amex/reagan/peopleevents/pande08.html.

Womble, D. D. (n.d.). *The CIA in Nicaragua*. Wake Up Magazine. Retrieved from http://www.wakeup.co.uk/articles/cias.htm.

Woodward, B. (2004, October 12). *Bush Looks at Problems*. PBS Frontline: http://www.pbs.org/wgbh/pages/frontline/shows/choice2004/interviews/woodward.

Zobecki, D. T. (Ed.). (2002). *Vietnam: A Reader*. New York: I Books Inc.

Index

A

Abrams, Creighton W., 149, 152, 154–55
Abrams, Elliot, 295
Accessory Transit Company, 167
Acheson, Dean, 98
Agent Orange, 135, 139
Akerlof, George A., 315
al-Ani, Ahmed Khalil Ibahim Samir, 289
al-Bakr, Ahmed Hasan, 200
al-Gaylani, Rashid Ali, 200
al-Ilah, Abd, 200
al-Islam, Ansar, 289
al-Khlifa, Ali, 207
al-Marashi, Ibrahim, 290
al-Sabah, Salem, 206
al-Zarqawi, Abu Musab, 289
Albania, 247–48
Albright, Madeleine, 226–27, 233, 236, 263, 266–67, 276, 278, 301
Aleksander, King, 248
Alexander I, 21
Alic, Fikret, 255
Allman, T.D., 146–47
Alperovitz, Gar, 60–73
American House Subcommittee on Communist Aggression, 94
American Society of Newspaper Editors, 277–78
Amnesty International, 105, 106, 217–18
Anatomy of a Coup (Allman), 146–47
Annon, Kofi, 34, 236, 283
Araña, Francisco Javier, 88, 90–91
Arbenz, Jacobo, 7, 88, 90–96, 98–104, 108–109
Arbour, Louise, 276–77
Arévalo, Juan José, 88–90
Armas, Carlos Enrique Castillo, 100–106
Arms Export Control Act, 189
as-Said, Nuri, 200
Atlantic Charter, 72–73, 114–15
Atta, Mohammed, 289
Aziz, Tariq, 233, 235–36
Azurdin, Enrique Paralta, 105

B

Baily, Thomas, 9
Baker, James, 209, 219, 232, 242, 301
Balkans in the Age of Nationalism, The (Sowards), 255
Bao Dai, 115, 120

Bard, Ralph A., 70
Barrios, Justo Rufino, 86
Bath, James R., 310
Battle of Guadalcanal, 52
Battle of the Bismarck Sea, 53
Battle of the Coral Sea, 50–51
Battle of the Philippine Sea, 54
Battle of the Philippines, 55–56
Becker, Brian, 205–206
Belgrade Declaration, 249
Bentham, Jeremy, 21
Berisha, Sali, 259
Bernays, Edward, 9, 96
Beyond Hypocrisy (Herman), 83, 113, 129, 132, 135, 193
Bin Laden, Osama, 27
Bin Laden, Salem, 310
Binder, David, 257
Blackett, P.M.S., 63
Blair, Tony, 290
Blix, Hans, 283–84, 286–89
Blum, William, 10, 82–84, 91, 94, 97, 104, 108, 121, 132, 138, 145, 170, 171, 174–75, 176, 178, 180, 183, 184, 191, 218, 239–40
BND, 260
Boland Amendment, 180, 189–90, 196
Bolsheviks, 79
Borden, William, 84
Bosnia
    "genocide" in, 256
    and secession from Yugoslavia, 253–57
Boston Fruit Company, 86. See also United Fruit Company
Bowett, Derek, 162
Bowles, Chester, 146
Bowman, Bob, 314–15
Braden, Spruille, 98
Breakup of Yugoslavia, The (Mahairas), 251–52
Brooks, W., 273
Brookshire, Grail, 155
Brown, Walter, 68
Brynes, James F., 60, 62–63, 68–71, 75
Brzezinski, Zbigniew, 202
Buchanan, A. Russell, 41–43, 55
Bunker, Ellsworth, 149
Bush at War (Woodward), 303
Bush, George H.W.
    and "coalition building," 218–20
    and incubator story, 217
    and invasion of Panama, 11, 24
    and Iraq War (1991), 198–99, 206, 212, 214–16, 220, 223–24

on Iraqi invasion of Kuwait, 210–11
and Nicaragua, 190
use of deceit by, 241–45
Bush, George W.
and executions in Texas, 307–308
and Iraqi-Al Qaeda link, 289–91
and Iraq War (2003), 16, 287–91
and Iraqi WMD, 9, 12, 15, 233, 282–91
mental health of, 301–302
psychopathic characteristics of, 302–18
and UN, 315
war crimes of, 296–300
and WMD inspections, 284–85
Bush, Jeb, 295
Bush on the Couch (Frank), 309, 312
Butler, Richard, 235–36, 237–38, 282
Buttinger, Joseph, 121
Byrd, Richard, 76

C

Cabot, John Moors, 85, 97–98
Cabot, Thomas, 97
Calhoun, Crede, 96
Callejas, Alfonso Robelo, 175
Cambodia
and Base Area 351, 152
and Base Area 353, 148–55
and Base Area 609, 152
COSVN in, 148–55
history of, 140–46
U.S. attack on, 146–63
Cambodia (Chomsky), 146
Cambodia (Falk), 161–62, 163
Carnegie Endowment for International Peace, 290
Carney, James, 311
Carrera, Rafael, 86
Carrington, Peter, 253
Carter, Jimmy, 17, 174–75, 301, 306
Center for Media and Democracy, 217
Central Intelligence Agency (CIA)
in Cambodia, 145
in Chile, 7
in Congo, 16–17
in Guatemala, 99, 102–103, 109
in Indonesia, 7
in Iran, 7
in Iraq, 231, 234–35
in Kosovo, 260

in Nicaragua, 174, 176, 179–81, 183, 192–93
and plot to assassinate Qassem, 200
in Vietnam, 129–30, 136
in Yugoslavia, 251
Chamorro-Bryan Agreement, 169
Chamorro, Diego Manuel, 170
Chamorro, Emiliano, 169–70, 172
Chamorro, Pedro Joaquín, 172, 174, 192
Chamorro, Violeta Barrios, 175, 192, 193–94
Charter of the Organization of American States (OAS), 38
Cheney, Dick, 211–12, 242, 295
Chile, 84
Chomsky, Noam, 9, 14–15, 82–84, 95, 113, 121, 124, 127, 128–29, 132–33, 135, 139, 146, 156–57, 159, 183, 184–86, 213–14, 246, 251, 259, 262, 265–67, 270–72
Chossudovsky, Michel, 260
Christopher, Warren, 232–33, 256
Church Committee, 136
Churchill, Ward, 38
Churchill, Winston, 62, 64
CIA in Guatemala, The (Immerman), 80–81, 85, 86, 90–92, 100–104, 106, 108
CIA in Nicaragua, The (Womble), 178, 179
Citizens for a Free Kuwait, 217
Clark, Ramsey, 202, 205–206, 207, 210, 220–24, 225, 226, 229, 230, 241, 245
Clark, Wesley, 270
Clausewitz, Karl von, 280
Clinton, Bill
and attack on Serbia, 246, 266–67, 301
and Bosnia, 254
on Iraq, 227
and Kosovo, 260, 271
war crimes committed by, 277–79
cluster bombs, 27
CNN, 224, 267
Cohen, Jeff, 137
Colby, William, 136, 267, 272, 278
Cold War, 80
Coleman, Carole, 311
Columbus, Christopher, 37–38
Columbus Day Commemorates a Holocaust (Churchill), 38
Committee for the Liberation of Iraq (CLI), 296
Conein, Lucien, 126, 129
Confronting the Third World (Kolko), 81, 82–83,

90, 93, 98–99, 174–75
Congressional Intelligence Committee, 180
Contras, 179–84, 188–89
Convention Against Torture, 38
Convention on the Prohibition of the Development, Production, Stockpiling and Use of Chemical Weapons, 38
Conway, James T., 314
Coolidge, Calvin, 170
Cooper-Church Amendment, 156, 160
Córdoba, Francisco Hernández, 165
Cortés, Hernán, 85
Counter-Insurgency Plan (CIP), 123
CounterPunch, 256
Cousins, Norman, 76
covert operations, 16
Crimes Without Punishment (Dabic and Lukic), 252
Croatia, 251–53
Cronkite, Walter, 303
Crucé, Emeric, 20
Cuba, U.S. embargo against, 7

D

Dabic, Vojin, 252
D'Alema, Massimo, 271
Dallas Morning News, 302
Davies, Joseph E., 64
Davis, Charles H., 168
Dayton Accords, 256–57
de Cuellar, Javier Perez, 204, 245
De Witt, William, 310
Decision to Use the Atomic Bomb, The (Alperovitz), 60–73
Declaration of Corfu (1917), 248
Democracy Now!, 227
Democratic Liberation Union (Udel), 173
Department of Veterans Affairs, 139
depleted uranium, 27–28, 239, 276, 294
Devillers, Philippe, 122
Díaz, Adolfo, 169–70
"Dirty Tricks," 147
Dirty Truths (Parenti), 6
Dixie Chicks, 14
Dobbs, Moe, 234
Doctorow, E.L., 308
Dominican Republic, U.S. attack on, 38
Donovan, William, 66–67
Dowd, Maureen, 303, 314

Dreyfuss, Robert, 139
Drogin, Bob, 239
"dual use" goods, 229
Duarte, Jose Napoleon, 185
Dubois, Pierre, 20
Dudley, Thomas, 97
Dulles, Allen, 17, 97, 101
Dulles, John Foster, 81, 85, 94, 97, 100, 119
Dunant, Henry, 22

E

Eagles Against the Sun (Spector), 42, 44–45, 48, 52–53, 54, 57–58, 65, 71
Eaker, Ira C., 76
East Timor, Indonesian invasion of, 35–36
Eisenhower, Dwight D.
    and attack on Guatemala, 94, 97–106, 109–12
    on use of atomic bombs, 76
    and Vietnam, 117, 119
    and violations of OAS Charter, 111
    and violations of UN Charter, 111
Eisenhower, Milton, 99, 108
Ekéus, Rolf, 234–35, 239
El Pais, 288–89
ElBaradei, Mohamed, 284
Ellsberg, Daniel, 133
Endgame (Ritter), 238–39
Erlich, Mike, 223–24
Estrada, Juan, 169
European Common Market, 178

F

Fahd, King, 210, 212
Faisal II, King, 200
Falk, Richard A., 161–62, 163
FBI
    in Guatemala, 94
    and Iraqi-Al Qaeda link, 289
Feis, Herbert, 68
Fighting for Peace (Rose), 255
Figueres, José, 95
Finnish Inquiry Commission, 157
Fire This Time, The (Clark), 202, 205–206, 207, 210, 221, 224, 225, 245
First Indochina War, The (Moïse), 121–22
Fisk, Robert, 14
FMLN, 183
Ford, Gerald, 17

Ford, Ronnie E., 113, 131, 133
Foreign Operations Appropriations Act (1991), 251
Franck, Peter, 286
Frank, Justin, 304, 309, 312
Franklin, Loren, 306, 310
Franks, Tommy, 231–32
Frontier Justice (Ritter), 238–39, 285–86, 295
Frum, David, 312
FSLN. *See* Sandinista National Liberation Front
Fudge, Judith A., 273
Fuentes, Miguel Ydigoras, 105
Full Spectrum Dominance (Mahajan), 225–26, 228, 235, 295, 297
Fuller, Craig, 216

G

Gaffney, Frank, 191
Gallagher, Bill, 305, 314
Garcia, Lucas, 105–106
Garrido, Guillermo Toriello, 85
Gates, Robert, 212
Gelbard, Robert, 260–61
Gellman, Adeeb, 26–27
Gemma, Gavrielle, 26–27
Genda, Commander, 46
Geneva Convention, 8, 22–24
    NATO violations of, 275–76
    U.S. violations of, 24–28, 138, 162, 243, 300
    and use of atomic bombs, 78
    on Vietnam, 118–19, 129
genocide
    and European colonization, 37–38
    Nazi, 36
Genocide by Sanctions (International Action Centre), 239
Gerger, Haluk, 242
Gerohus of Regensburg, 20
Gifford, Tony, 241
Gingrich, Newt, 295
Glasbeek, H.J., 273
Glaspie, April, 208–209, 241
Globe and Mail, 290
Gonzalez, Alvaro Ramirez, 273
Goodman, Amy, 227
Gordon, Bill, 63–64
Graham, Bob, 291, 297
Graham, David, 36

Grant, Ulysses S., 164
Grew, Joseph C., 62, 65
Guardian International, 286–87
Guatemala
    agrarian reform in, 91–93
    communist party in, 94–95
    economic condition of, 87–88
    history of, 85–86
    and Mayans, 86
    political reforms in, 89
    political unrest in, 88
    repression and human rights abuses in, 105–106
    and threat to U.S. interests, 93–96
    and United Fruit Company, 84
    U.S. attack on, 38, 96–106
Gulf of Tonkin, 113, 130–33, 136–37
Gulf of Tonkin Resolution, 131–32

H

Hague Conventions, 21
Haig, Alexander M., 10, 148–49, 152, 154, 186–87
Halliday, Denis, 226, 292
Halsey, William, 75
Hammarskjöld, Dag, 103
Hanson, Reuben A., 273
Harding, Luke, 289
Hare, Robert D., 302, 304, 307, 317
Harken Energy, 311
Harriman, W. Averill, 75–76
Harvard International Study Group, 226
Hasenfus, Eugene, 189
Havel, Vaclav, 289
Hayden, Robert, 272
Henry of Navarre, 20
Herman, Edward S., 9, 83, 113, 121, 124, 128, 129, 132–33, 135, 156–57, 159, 184–86, 193
Herrick, John J., 130–31, 137
Hersh, Michael, 303, 311, 313
Hersh, Seymour M., 147, 151–55, 158–59, 306–307
Hewitt, Gavin, 302
Hill & Knowlton, 216–17
Hillings, Patrick J., 101
Hiroshima, 73
Hiroshima: Was It Necessary? (Long), 71–72
Ho Chi Minh, 113–16, 119–20

Holbrooke, Richard, 256, 262
Holocaust Ring, The (Graham), 36
Honduras, U.S. attack on, 7
Houston Chronicle, 309
How the U.S. Purchased the 1990 Nicaraguan Elections (Wilson), 192–93
Huck, Jim, 94, 109
Hull, Cordell, 46
Human Rights Caucus, 216–17
Human Rights Watch, 25, 258–60, 262
Hunt, Al, 312
Hussein, King, 210, 212
Hussein, Saddam, 198, 201, 233, 240
    and al Qaeda, 289
    and comparisons to Hitler, 13, 216
    and Iran-Iraq War, 202
    and Iraq War (1991), 207, 208, 213–16, 244
    and Qassem, 200
    and WMD, 287–91
Hutcheson, Ron, 313, 314

I

ibn Hussain, Emir Faisal, 199
ibn Hussain, Ghazi, 199–200
Immerman, Richard H., 80–81, 85, 86, 90–92, 100–104, 106, 108
Impact of the War on Iraq Society (Gellman and Gemma), 26–27
In Retrospect (McNamara), 131
Inter-American Development Bank (IDB), 178
International Action Center (New York), 293
International Atomic Energy Agency (IAEA), 232, 235, 239, 283–84, 287, 300
International Committee for the Relief of the Wounded, 22
International Court of Justice at The Hague. *See* World Court
International Criminal Court at The Hague, 31, 276
International Development Fund, 181
International Herald Tribune, 10
international law
    and courts, 29
    history of, 18–21
    and International Red Cross, 22–24
    U.S. violations of, 298–300
International Monetary Fund (IMF), 7, 178, 181, 194, 249, 250
International Red Cross, 22

International War Crimes Tribunal, 241–45
Iran-Contra, 188–91
Iran-Iraq War, 202–205
Iraq
    colonization of, 199–201
    economic warfare against, 207–208
    oil-for-food program in, 227, 230–31
    sanctions against, 224–32, 239–40, 282
    as U.S. ally, 201–205
    use of chemical weapons by, 204
    and WMD, 232–36, 283–85
Iraq Body Count, 34–35, 293
Iraq Petroleum Company, 201
Iraq War (1991), 8–9
    civilian targets in, 220–24
    and incubator story, 217–18
Iraq War (2003), 9
    bombing of infrastructure in, 281–82
    civilian targets in, 293–94
    and "Coalition of the Willing," 291
    and "preemptive defense," 292
    use of "shock and awe" in, 292
    as violation of UN Charter, 34–35
Iraqi Liberation Act (1998), 296

J

Jackson, Deborah, 242
Jackson, Henry M., 182
Jacobs, David, 276
Japan
    and attack on Pearl Harbor, 46–47
    as an empire, 41–46
    and war with U.S., 40, 46–58
John Wayne Goes to Managua (Telford), 178, 181
Johnson, Clay, 304
Johnson, Lyndon, 8, 127, 129, 131–32, 136–39

K

Kamel, Hussein, 234
Kant, Immanuel, 21
Kantaro, Suzuki, 61, 72, 74
Kapeliouk, Amnon, 139
Karnow, Stanley, 127–28
Kase, Shunichi, 66
Keith, Minor C., 86–87
Keith, Rollie, 262–63
Kemp, Jack, 182
Kennan, George, 108

Kennedy, John F.
  and attack on Vietnam, 123–28
  support of dictators by, 16–17
Kenney, George, 253, 270
Kerry, John F., 189
Khafaji, Fahima, 217
Khan, Kubla, 114
Khan, Sadruddin Aga, 228
Khmer Krom, 145
Khmer Rouge, 141, 157–59
Khmer Serei, 145
Khomeini, Ruhollah, 201
Khrushchev, Nikita, 249
Kiernan, Ben, 302
Killing Hope (Blum), 10, 82–84, 91, 94, 97, 104,
  108, 132, 138, 145, 170, 171, 174–75, 176,
  178, 180, 183, 184, 191, 218, 239–40
Kirkpatrick Jeanne, 182, 295
Kissinger Commission, 182–83, 186
Kissinger, Henry, 10, 140–41, 148–56, 159–60,
  163, 182, 186, 201
Klare, Michael, 297
Knight, Hal, 150
Koichi, Kido, 61
Koiso Government, 61
Kolko, Gabriel, 81, 82–83, 90, 93, 98–99, 174–
  75
Konjevic, Slobodan, 255
Konoye, Fumimaro, 45
Koppel, Ted, 13
Korean War, 116
Kosovo
  NATO war crimes in, 273–77
  and secession from Serbia, 257–73
*Kosovo "Freedom Fighters" Financed by
  Organized Crime* (Chossudovsky), 260
Kosovo Liberation Army (KLA), 259–63, 277
Kosovo Verification Mission, 271
Kristol, William, 295
Krock, Arthur, 72
Kusaka, Admiral, 46
Kuwait, Emir of, 202

L

La Prensa, 172, 174, 185, 192
Laird, Melvin R., 149–50, 153
Landsdale, Edward, 120
Lantos, Tom, 216
Larry King Show, 302, 309

Lasswell, Harold, 9
Latin America Studies Association (LASA),
  184, 186
Laurent, Eric, 213
Le Cao Dai, 139
Le Figaro, 263
Le Monde, 100–101, 263
League of Nations, 29
Leay, William D., 70
LeMay, Curtis E., 58, 70
Libby, Lewis, 295
Liebman, James S., 307
Light, Paul C., 313
Lissner, Will, 96
Lodge, Henry Cabot, 103, 126–27
Lon Nol, 147–48, 154, 156, 160
Long, Doug, 71–72
Lord, Carnes, 270
Los Angeles Times, 254
Lukic, Ksenija, 252
Lumumba, Patrice, 16–17
Lyons, Michael J., 41, 45, 50, 55, 74–75

M

MacArthur, Douglas, 40, 49, 76
Macarthur, John R., 202, 216–18
MacMichael, David, 183
MacMillan, Margaret, 80
Magazine of Wall Street, 84
Mahairas, Evangelos, 251–52
Mahajan, Rahul, 225–26, 228, 235, 295, 297
Maher, Bill, 14
Mandate for Change (Eisenhower), 100, 103–
  104
Mandel, Michael, 270, 273, 276
Mandela, Nelson, 301
Manhattan Project, 61
Manufacturing Consent (Herman and Chomsky),
  121, 124, 128, 132–33, 135, 156–57, 159,
  184–86
Markovic, Ante, 251
Martin, David, 292
Martin, John, 217
Martinez, Tomás, 168, 177
Matar, Mohammed, 217
Mazza, Jerry, 311
McCarthy, Joseph, 81
McClintock, John, 98
McFarlane, Robert, 178, 189, 190

McLoy, John J., 97
McNamara, Robert, 119, 126, 131, 133, 136, 138
Media Beat, 137
Meese III, Edwin, 189
Meet the Press, 305
Memory of Solferino, A (Dunant), 22
Mena, Luís, 169
Mercado, Sergio Ramí, 175
Mikulic, Branko, 250
Militant, The, 256
Miller, Edward, 95
Miller, Mark Crispin, 311
Miller, Roger, 310
Milosevic, Slobodan, 31, 257–58, 262, 277
Ming, General, 126–27
Mintz, Bob, 305
Mitchell, Andrea, 297
Moïse, Edwin, 121–22
Monroe Doctrine, 164
Montenegro, Cesar Mendez, 105
Montt, Efráin Rios, 106
Morales, Moisés Hassan, 175
Mother Jones, 139
Mubarak, Hosni, 212
Myers, Richard, 305

N

Nagasaki, 74
Nambiar, Satish, 265–66, 270
National Agricultural Bank (Guatemala), 93
National Endowment for Democracy (NED), 192–93, 251
National Free Kuwait Day, 216
National Liberation Front (NLF), 122
National Opposition Union (UNO), 192–94
National Patriotic Front (FPN), 175
National Security Agency (NSA), 130
NATO, 38
    atrocities against Serbs by, 252
    bombing of Serbian targets by, 256, 266
    and civilian targets in Serbia, 267–69, 278
    in Kosovo, 263
    and violations of own treaty, 275
Nazi Holocaust, 36
Necessary Illusions (Chomsky), 9, 139
Neill & Co., 216
New Military Humanism, The (Chomsky), 246, 251, 259, 262, 265–67, 270–72

New York Times, 68, 72, 96, 127, 206, 207, 233, 254, 257–58, 303, 314, 315
New Yorker, 306–307
Newsday, 224
Newsweek, 278
Ngo Dinh Diem, 119–27
Ngo Quyen, 114
Nguyen Ai Quoc. *See* Ho Chi Minh
Nguyen Khanh, 128
Nguyen Van Thieu, 128–29
Nicaragua
    and Agrarian Reform Law, 176
    as a "banana republic," 167
    and Fundamental Statute of the Republic of Nicaragua, 177
    history of, 165–73
    1984 elections in, 184–87
    reform in, 176–77
    U.S. attack on, 30, 38
Nicaraguan Democratic Force (FDN). *See* Contras
Nicolas II, Tsar, 79
Nimitz, Chester W., 76
1954: Covert War in Guatemala (Huck), 94, 109
Nixon, Richard M., 9, 140–41, 147, 148–56, 159–63
Noreiga, Manuel, 11
Norodom, King, 142
North, Oliver, 10, 180, 190
NSC-68, 80
Nuremberg Trials, 18–20
Nyerere, Aisha, 242

O

OAS Charter
    Eisenhower's violations of, 111
    Reagan's violations of, 195–96
Office of War Information (OWI), 72
Onishi, Admiral, 55
Operation Desert Fox, 237
Operation Menu, 152, 158
Operation Plan 34A, 130–31
Organization of American States (OAS), 100, 164, 175
Organization of Petroleum states (OPEC), 200
Ortega, Daniel José, 173
Owen, David, 254

P

Pacific Alliance, The (Borden), 84
Pact of Espino Negro, 171
Paltrow, Scott J., 305
Panama Canal Zone, 16
Parenti, Michael, 6, 246, 252, 254–55, 256–57, 260–64, 266, 269–72
Paris 1919 (MacMillan), 80
Paris Peace Agreements (1973), 157
Paris Peace Conference (1919), 29
Parry, Robert, 314, 317
Pasic, Nicola, 248
PBSUCCESS, 99–104
Peled, Matti, 221
Pellecer, Carlos Manuel, 94–95
Pelletreau, Robert, 228
Penn, William, 20–21
Pentagon Papers, 117, 119–23, 127, 136–37
People's Liberation Armed Forces (PLAF), 123
Perle, Richard, 295
Permanent Court of International Justice, 29. *See also* World Court
Perry, Commodore, 41
Perspectives on Power (Chomsky), 83–84
Peurifoy, John E., 99, 102–104, 110–11
Phoenix Program, 136, 138
Pilger, John, 266
Pinochet, Augusto, 7
Plame, Valerie, 315
Plesch, Dan, 286–87
Poindexter, John, 180, 190
Pol Pot, 159, 302
Ponchaud, François, 158
Ponte, Carla Del, 276
Popular Social Christian Party (PPSC), 175
Porter, John, 216
Portillo, Alfonso, 106
Poti, P.S., 242
Potsdam Conference, 62, 65
Potsdam Declaration, 71–73
Powell, Colin, 133, 211–12, 242, 285–87, 289–90, 301
Price of Power, The (Hersh), 147, 151–55, 158–59
Project for the New American Century (PNAC), 294–96
Psychological Operations in Guerilla Warfare (CIA), 180
Psychological Strategy Board, 96

Puntarena Pact, 175

Q

Qassem, Abdul Karim, 200–201
Qichen, Qian, 219

R

Racak massacre, 263
Raddatz, Martha, 267
Radford, Arthur W., 117–18
Rambouillet Peace Agreement, 264–67, 275–76
Ramos, Vanessa, 273
Rampton, Sheldon, 291, 294, 295
Rangwala, Glen, 290
Ratner, Michael, 242
Reagan, Ronald
    and attack on Nicaragua, 9–10, 30, 82, 178–84, 191–97
    on El Salvador elections, 185
    and Iran-Contra, 188–91
    on Nicaraguan elections, 186–87
Reflections on Hiroshima (Gordon), 63–64
Rendon Group, 216
Repo, Marjaleena, 256
Ressler, Robert, 302
Reynolds, Mercer, 310
Richardson, Elliot L., 153
Ritter, Scott, 235–36, 238–39, 285–86, 295
Robertson, Pat, 303
Rogers, William, 149, 153, 182
Rolling Thunder, 134–35
Rolling Thunder (Wilson), 134–35
Roosevelt, Franklin D., 40, 44, 164, 171
Roosevelt, Theodore, 164
Rose, Michael, 254–55
Rove, Karl, 14
Ruder Finn, 256
Rugova, Ibrahim, 258–59
Rumsfeld, Donald, 295, 297
Rusk, Dean, 138
Russell, Richard, 75
Russert, Tim, 305
Russia, 79
Russo-Japanese War, 42
Ryan, John, 152–53

S

Sacasa, Ramiro, 173
Sacasa, Roberto, 168
Sadat, Anwar, 202

Salinger, Pierre, 207, 213
Salisbury, Lord, 21
Sanctions Committee of the Security Council, 225, 230–31
Sandinista National Liberation Front (FSLN), 173–79, 179–85, 191–94
Sandino, Augusto Cesar, 170–71
Sangkum Reastr Niyum, 143
Schlesinger, Arthur, 123
School of the Americas, 104
Schwarzkopf, Norman, 206, 212
Scowcroft, Brent, 214, 301
Seamans, Robert, 152
Seattle Post-Intelligencer, 294
Second Front (Macarthur), 202, 216–18
Secret Dossier (Salinger and Laurent), 213
Seko, Mobutu Sese, 17
Serbia
    civilian bombing targets in, 267–69
    NATO bombing of, 9, 31, 246–47
    U.S. attack of, 265–73
    See also Yugoslavia
Shah of Iran, 7, 201
Shaw, Mary, 313
Shawcross, William, 144, 149–51, 153, 155–56, 158, 160
Shedding New Light on the Gulf of Tonkin Incident (Ford), 113, 131, 133
Shelton, Hugh, 278
Shigenori, Togo, 61, 73
Shultz, George, 179, 187
Sideshow (Shawcross), 144, 149–51, 153, 155–56, 158, 160
Sidqi, Bakr, 199–200
Sihanouk, Prince, 142–48, 152
Sisowath Monivong, 142
Sitton, Ray B., 149–51
60 Minutes, 226–27
Sklar, Holly, 178
Slater, Wayne, 302
Slovenia, 251–53
Smith, Walter Bedell, 98
Sneider, Richard L., 149
Socialist Federated Republic of Yugoslavia (SFRY). *See* Yugoslavia
Socrates, 20
Sofaer, Abraham, 188
Solomon, Norman, 137
Solórzano, Carlos, 170
Somoza, Anastasio Debayle, 94, 98, 172, 173–

76
Somoza, Anastasio García, 171–73
Somoza, Luis, 172
Son Ngoc Thanh, 142–43
Southeast Asia Collective Defense Treaty, 8
Southeast Asia Treaty Organization (SEATO), 144
Soviet Union
    and declaration of war on Japan, 74
    in World War II, 80
    and role in use of atomic bombs, 61–78
    See also Russia
Sowards, Steven W., 255
Spector, Ronald H., 42, 44–45, 48, 52–53, 54, 57–58, 65, 71
Spectrum 7, 310–11
Squier, Ephraim George, 167
St. Petersburg Times, 212
Stahl, Lesley, 226–27
Stalin, Joseph, 62
Standard Fruit Company, 181
State Department (U.S.)
    and Contras, 180
    in Guatemala, 99, 101
    in Nicaragua, 186
Stauber, John, 291, 294, 295
Stephen, Andrew, 311
Stimson, Henry L., 43, 45, 60, 63–64, 68, 76–77, 170–71
Strategic Hamlet Program, 124
Straw, Jack, 291
Strom, Carl, 144
Suharto, General, 7
Sullivan & Cromwell, 97
Sultan, Bandar bin, 211
Sulzberger, Arthur Hays, 96
Sunday Times (London), 270
Symington, Stuart, 83
Szilard, Leo, 63
Szmukler, Beinusz, 273

T

Taylor, Ambassador, 133–34
Taylor, Maxwell, 124, 126
Taylor, Telford, 138
Teitelbaum, Alejandro, 273
Telford, Ryan, 178, 181
Tenet, George, 297
Thanh Ky, 128–29
Thayer, Carlyle, 157

Thorton, Samuel R., 147
Throckmorton, Terry, 312
Time, 278
Tito, Josip Broz, 249–50, 257
To Kill A Nation (Parenti), 246, 252, 254–55, 256–57, 260–64, 266, 269–72
Tojo Government, 61
Tojo, Hideki, 45
Tokugawa, 41
Toward the Present (Penn), 20
Tower Board, 190
Treaty of Berlin (1878), 247
Truman, Harry S.
    and attack on Guatemala, 94, 96, 98
    and attack on Vietnam, 116–17
    and use of atomic bombs, 40, 59–60, 62, 64–78
Tucker, Karla Faye, 301, 309

U

Ubico, Jorge, 87–88
Udel. *See* Democratic Liberation Union
UK Times, 293
Ullman, Harlan K., 292
Understanding Power (Chomsky), 82, 113, 183
UNICEF, 226
United Fruit Company, 16, 84–86, 92–95, 97–99, 109
United Kingdom Atomic Energy Authority, 28
United Nations
    creation of, 32
    Resolution 598, 205
    Resolution 678, 212, 218, 220
    Resolution 706, 227
    Resolution 1441, 283, 299
United Nations Charter
    NATO violations of, 274–75
    purpose of, 32–33
    U.S. violations of, 35–36, 111, 137–38, 161–62, 243–44, 299–300
United Nations Convention on the Prevention and Punishment of the Crime of Genocide
    purpose of, 36–37
    U.S. violations of, 162–63, 244
United Nations Food and Agriculture Organization (FAO), 226
United Nations High Commissioner for Refugees (UNHCFR), 271
United Nations International Law Commission, 19–20

United Nations Security Council, 33
    Resolution 660, 218–19
    Resolution 661, 213, 216, 220, 224
    Resolution 665, 225
    Resolution 687, 232, 236–37, 298
    Resolution 688, 231
    Resolution 1160, 261
United Nations War Crimes Commission, 18
    London Agreement, 19
    Moscow Declaration, 18–19
United States (U.S.)
    attack on Cambodia, 144–46
    dropping of atomic bombs by, 58–78
    expansion of empire, 81–85
    attack on Guatemala, 96–112
    attack on Iraq, 205–206, 207, 220–24
    attack on Nicaragua, 179–84, 187–97
    attack on North Vietnam, 130–33
    attack on South Vietnam, 120–23
    attack on Vietnam, 116–18, 132–36
    support of KLA, 261
    and surrender of Japan, 58–73
    use of communism as tool by, 80–85
    war crimes in Vietnam, 137–38
    war with Japan, 44–58
United States and World War II, The (Buchanan), 42–43, 55
United States Charter, U.S. violations of, 196
United States Information Agency, 97
UNMOVIC, 283–84, 288, 300
UNSCOM, 232–36, 237
U.S.-British Combined Intelligence Committee (CIC), 65
U.S. Complicity (Wilson), 125, 127
U.S. Conspiracy to Initiate the War Against Iraq (Becker), 205–206

V

Vaides, Federico Ponce, 88
Vance, Cyrus, 253
Vanderbilt, Cornelius, 167–68
Vanity Fair, 296
Vickery, Michael, 157
Vietnam, history of, 114–18
Vietnam (Karnow), 127–28
Vietnam War
    lead up to, 113–18
    mass media coverage of, 113
    pacification program in, 124
    U.S. war crimes in, 137–38

and Viet Minh, 115–18, 121
Village Voice, 208
Viorst, Milton, 206
Vo Nguyen Giap, 131

W

Waging Unconventional Warfare, 84
Walker, William, 168, 263
Wall Street Journal, 305, 310, 312
Walsh, Lawrence, 189
War on Terrorism, 27
War Powers Act (1973), 180, 220
Washington Post, 13, 185, 287, 293, 295, 306
Washington's War on Nicaragua (Sklar), 178
Weapons of Mass Deception (Rampton and Stauber), 291, 294, 295
Weisbrot, Mark, 193–94
Weisgerber, Anna, 303
Wells, Milton K., 95
Western Hemisphere Institute for Security Cooperation, 104
Westmoreland, William C., 130, 138
What Everyone Should Know About Nicaragua (Weisbrot), 193–94
What Uncle Sam Really Wants (Chomsky), 84, 95
Wheeler, Earle G., 148, 150–51
Whitman, Ann, 98
Williams, Maurice, 256
Wilson, Joseph, 287, 315, 316
Wilson, S. Brian, 192–93
Wilson, William, 125, 127, 134–35
Wilson, Woodrow, 29
Witness For Peace, 179
Wolfowitz, Paul, 212, 295, 296
Womble, David, 178, 179
Woodward, Bob, 303, 314
World Bank, 7, 178, 181, 194, 249
World Court
    and Nicaragua, 30, 187–88, 196–97
    purpose of, 29–30
World War II (Lyons), 41, 45, 50, 55, 74–75

Y

Yamamoto, Isoroku, 51
Year 501 (Chomsky), 127
Youseff, Fayeza, 217
Yugoslavia
    break-up of republics, 251–52
    economic changes in, 249–50

economic crisis in, 250–51
history of, 247–50

Z

Zacharias, Ellis, 72
Zelaya, Santos, 168–69
ZNET, 297

About the Author

David Model is a professor of political science and economics at Seneca College just north of Toronto. He has previously published *People Before Profits: Reversing the corporate agenda* and *Corporate Rule: Understanding and challenging the new world order*. In addition to his books, he wrote a newspaper column for four years titled *The Global Perspective* and has delivered a number of papers at academic conferences. He has been a social and political activist for over 25 years including president of a constituency association and campaign manager for his constituency. He was on the executive of the Canadian Peace Alliance which had 3 million members and served on the executive of an Amnesty International chapter. He has traveled extensively in a number of countries discussed in this book.